OVID AND THE CULTURAL POLITICS OF TRANSLATION IN EARLY MODERN ENGLAND

Ovid and the Cultural Politics
of Translation in
Early Modern England

Liz Oakley-Brown

Studies in European Cultural Transition

Volume Thirty Four

General Editors: Martin Stannard and Greg Walker

ASHGATE

Published by
Ashgate Publishing Limited
Gower House
Croft Road
Aldershot
Hampshire GU11 3HR
England

Ashgate Publishing Company
Suite 420
101 Cherry Street
Burlington, VT 05401-4405
USA

Ashgate website: http://www.ashgate.com

British Library Cataloguing in Publication Data
Oakley-Brown, Liz
Ovid and the cultural politics of translation in early modern England. – (Studies in European cultural transition)
1.Ovid, 43 B.C.-17 or 18 A.D. Metamorphoses 2.Ovid, 43 B.C.-17 or 18 A.D – Translations into English – History and criticism 3.Ovid, 43 B.C.-17 or 18 A.D – Adaptations – History and criticism 4.Ovid, 43 B.C.-17 or 18 A.D – Appreciation – England 5.Translating and interpreting – Political aspects – England 6.Latin language Translating into English – History 7.English literature – Roman influences 8.Translating and interpreting – England – History 9.Metamorphosis in literature
I.Title
873'.01

Library of Congress Cataloging-in-Publication Data
Oakley-Brown, Liz.
Ovid and the cultural politics of translation in early modern England / Liz Oakley-Brown.
    p. cm. — (Studies in European cultural transition)
Includes bibliographical references and index.
ISBN 0-7546-5155-X (alk. paper)
    1. Ovid, 43 B.C.-17 or 18 A.D. Metamorphoses. 2. Ovid, 43 B.C.-17 or 18 A.D.—Translations into English—History and criticism. 3. Ovid, 43 B.C.-17 or 18 A.D.—Adaptations—History and criticism. 4. Translating and interpreting—Political aspects--England. 5. Ovid, 43 B.C.-17 or 18 A.D.—Appreciation—England. 6. Latin language—Translating into English—History. 7. Translating and interpreting—England—History. 8. English literature—Roman influences. 9. Metamorphosis in literature.
I. Title. II. Series.
PA6519.M9O926 2006
873'.01—dc22

2005026462

ISBN-10: 075465155X

Printed and bound in Great Britain by MPG Books Ltd, Bodmin, Cornwall

Contents

General Editors' Preface

The European dimension of research in the humanities has come into sharp focus over recent years, producing scholarship which ranges across disciplines and national boundaries. Until now there has been no major channel for such work. This series aims to provide one, and to unite the fields of cultural studies and traditional scholarship. It will publish the most exciting new writing in areas such as European history and literature, art history, archaeology, language and translation studies, political, cultural and gay studies, music, psychology, sociology and philosophy. The emphasis will be explicitly European and interdisciplinary, concentrating attention on the relativity of cultural perspectives, with a particular interest in issues of cultural transition.

Martin Stannard
Greg Walker
University of Leicester

List of Illustrations

Acknowledgements

This monograph grew out of my doctoral thesis supervised by Roger Ellis at Cardiff University. I am immensely grateful for his extraordinary combination of intellect, wit and patience. It is impossible for me to name everyone with whom I have discussed ideas and problems related to early modern translation. Nevertheless, special mention must be made of Martin Coyle, Richard Chamberlain, Greg Walker and Ashgate's anonymous reader. I would also like to thank Claire Jowitt for her encouragement, sustained interest in my work and greatly valued friendship.

In researching this book I have worked in various libraries and I have benefited from a wealth of professional knowledge. I would like to thank the librarians at the British Library, Cardiff University, Magdalene College, Cambridge, and the University of Wales, Aberystwyth. I would also like to express my gratitude to the Harrowby Manuscript Trust for allowing me to consult Mary Wortley Montagu's juvenila and the archivists and stewards at Hardwick Hall. May I also take the opportunity to thank the organizers and delegates of the *Translatio* conference held at the University of Aberdeen (2001); I am most appreciative of the helpful comments I received at that colloquium. I am also pleased to acknowledge *Literature Compass* for permission to reproduce part of an article on women as translators of the *Metamorphoses* in Chapter 5; and *Renaissance Studies* for allowing me to reproduce my article on *Titus Andronicus* in Chapter 1.

Much of this book was prepared whilst I was Lecturer in Renaissance Writing English at the University of Wales, Aberystwyth. The financial award from the Senate Research Fund at Aberystwyth enabled me to complete important archival research. I would also like to give credit to members of the English Department at Aberystwyth for their expert comments on various chapters and their fellowship, in particular Tiffany Atkinson, Peter Barry, Matt Jarvis, Sarah Prescott, David Shuttleton and Diane Watt. I am also indebted to colleagues at the English Department, Canterbury Christ Church University for their forbearance as the book reached completion.

The kindness and good humour shown by Rob Douglas, Dennis and Steg throughout this project (and beyond) are cherished. I would like to dedicate this book to my parents, Michael and Dorothy Brown, and to my aunt, Patricia Oakley, for their steadfast support.

Introduction

Translation and Transformation: Ovid's *Metamorphoses* and the Fashioning of Identity in Early Modern England

[...] translation practices the difference between signified and signifier. But if this difference is never pure, no more so is translation, and for the notion of translation we would have to substitute a notion of *transformation*: a regulated transformation of one language by another, of one text by another. We will never have, and in fact have never had, to do with some 'transport' of pure signifieds from one language to another, or within one and the same language, that the signifying instrument would leave virgin and untouched.[1]

The Terms of Translation

Ovid and the Cultural Politics of Translation in Early Modern England argues that English versions of Ovid's *Metamorphoses* are important sites of cultural and textual difference from the fifteenth to the early eighteenth centuries. In particular, the book considers the significance of vernacular renditions of the poem for the fashioning of early modern English identities. Notably, the *Metamorphoses* is a poem which emphasizes the issues of transformation and translation from the outset. As the opening lines of George Sandys's *Ovids Metamorphosis Englished* (1632) announce:

> Of bodies chang'd to other shapes I sing.
> Assist, you Gods (from you these changes spring)
> And, from the Worlds first fabrick to these times,
> Deduce my never-discontinued Rymes. (1. 1-4)[2]

At the beginning of the highly influential *Shakespeare and Ovid*, Jonathan Bate states that 'recent criticism has been much concerned with the "flexibility of the self" in Renaissance literature. Such criticism has not always recognized that the flexible self has a prime classical exemplar in Ovid.'[3] With Bate's comments in mind, the starting point for my own study is that whilst much recent criticism has been concerned with transformation and the 'flexible self', the topic of translation and its relationship to the profusion of English versions of the *Metamorphoses* produced in the early modern period has been relatively ignored.

Given that the processes and practices of translation are explored in Stephen Greenblatt's *Renaissance Self-Fashioning: From More to Shakespeare*, one of the most thoroughly discussed books about the sixteenth century, this neglect is rather perplexing. Here Greenblatt has famously claimed that 'self-fashioning is always, but not exclusively, in language',[4] and, at the centre of the book, he observes that

> there is no translation that is not the same time an interpretation. This conviction [was] stamped indelibly in the mind by the fact that men went to the stake in the early sixteenth century over the rendering of certain Greek and Latin words into English [...].[5]

In this allusion to the execution of men such as William Tyndale, 'the first biblical translator of the Reformation to die – arrested and strangled [in 1536] in his Low Countries exile by the Holy Roman Emperor's officials with the connivance of the Bishop of London and Henry VIII' for so-called heretical versions of the Old and New Testaments,[6] Greenblatt demonstrates the political impact of translation; an impact evinced by his examples of the physical violence perpetrated against translators of religious texts. Yet translators of secular texts were also culturally significant. When Greenblatt says that by analysing Thomas Wyatt's texts 'we glimpse [...] the central place of translation',[7] the ideological worth of this textual, secular mode of production is realised in less terrifying ways.

The importance of vernacular translation is discussed at length in Charles Tomlinson's essay 'The Presence of Translation: A View of English Poetry' in which 'the preferences displayed in editing the *Oxford Book of Verse in English Translation*' are particularly scrutinised.[8] As Tomlinson argues that 'the story of English poetry cannot be truly told without seeing translation as an unavoidable part of that story',[9] he observes how the inclusion of translated texts into the history of English literature makes a difference to the institution of English literature itself. By considering Alexander Pope's translation of Homer's *Iliad* (1715), as well as translations by Geoffrey Chaucer, John Dryden and John Oldham, and by remembering his own Cambridge education where the course on Renaissance poetry took 'a broad look at [Thomas] Wyatt and [Henry] Surrey, both translators, though the fact was never dwelt upon',[10] Tomlinson revises the history of English literature and, implicitly, reforms notions of Englishness. Since Tomlinson's article was published in 1989 there have been considerable developments in the area of translation theory and it may now be argued with impunity that translators as 'inventive mediators' have played,[11] and continue to play, an important role in the construction of subjectivities, foreign and domestic; other and self.[12] However, Lawrence Venuti suggests that 'although the growth of the discipline called "translation studies" has been described as "a success story of the 1980s", the study of the history and theory of translation remains a backwater in the academy'.[13] In its endeavour to make translated texts visible in the midst of institutional imperatives which may continue to efface their influence, Tomlinson's essay continues to offer key critical insights for the exploration of translation's agency.

Indeed, the title of Tomlinson's article ('The Presence of Translation') raises questions about the term 'translation' itself. The most familiar, and most narrow, use of the word is 'to turn something from one language into another'.[14] In the eighteenth and nineteenth centuries, the post-Romantic period which sought to celebrate the status of the original author,[15] translation was largely viewed as a secondary practice. The preface to Richard Blackmore's *A paraphrase on the book of Job as likewise on the songs of Moses, Deborah, David, on four select psalms, some chapters of Isaiah, and the third chapter of Habakkuk* (1700), for example, heralds the prevailing hierarchical binarism of original/translation:

> The *Moderns* have wholly *form'd* themselves on the *Models* of the Ancients, and that we have scarce any thing but the *Greek* and *Latin Poetry* in the World. We have no *Originals*, but all *Copiers* and *Transcribers* of *Homer, Pindar*, and *Theocritus, Virgil, Horace*, and *Ovid*. Their *Design*, their *Phrase*, their *Manner*, and even their *Heathen Theology*, appear in all the *Poems* that have since their *Time* been published to the World, especially in the *Learned Languages*. 'Tis therefore to be wish'd that some *good Genius, qualify'd* for such an *Undertaking*, would break the *Ice*, assert the *Liberty* of *Poetry*, and set up for an *Original* in *Writing* in a way accommodated to the *Religion, Manners*, and other *Circumstances* we are now under.[16]

In early modern England, alongside texts such as Virgil's *Eclogues*, Cicero's letters, selections from Sallust and Caesar and Erasmus's *Colloquies* and *Parabola*, Ovid's poem was an integral part of the humanist programme of education.[17] Certainly, the pedagogical location of translation rendered it a more visible act and some translators enjoyed high status socially. Portraits of both the Greek writer and the English translator, for instance, are shown on the title page of *The crowne of all Homers workes Batrachomyomachia or the battaile of frogs and mise. His hymn's and epigrams translated according to ye. originall by George Chapman* (1624).[18] But since the sixteenth century translation has been gradually isolated from other textual practices which have been deemed primary and original, and various attempts have been made to categorise and limit the term itself: 'this is the series *translatio, paraphrasis, imitatio, allusio*, which tries to draw boundary lines as the version of the original becomes increasingly free'.[19] An early modern example of such pronouncements, based on Cicero's *De oratore*, can be found in Roger Ascham's *The Schoolmaster* (1570):

> Paraphrasis is, to take some eloquent Oration, and some notable common place in Latin, and expresse it with other wordes: Metaphrasis is, to take some notable place out of a good Poete, and turn the same sense into meter, or in other wordes in Prose [...]. But to our purpose, all language, bothe learned and mother tonges, be gotten, and gotten onelie by Imitation.[20]

Arguably, the desire to construct an organizing method for translation gains momentum throughout the early modern period until, in the late seventeenth century, John Dryden's 'Preface Concerning Ovid's Epistles' (1680) sought to divide translation processes into three, as illustrated by the 'three heads' of translation –'metaphrase', 'paraphrase' and 'imitation'. Still later, in the twentieth century, Roman Jakobson defined translation as another tripartite textual and cultural enterprise: interlingual, intralingual and intersemiotic.[21] There are much wider implications, however, to translation than organization and method.

In the words of Terry Eagleton, 'what we are coming to understand, not least through the notion of *intertextuality*, is that every text is, in some sense, a translation'.[22] Further, José Lambert has argued that 'the borderlines between [translation] and related concepts such as adaptation and rewriting are not necessarily clear or uniformly drawn. [...] not only entire texts but also text fragments and discursive patterns may be imported into the target literature'.[23] The English versions of Ovid's *Metamorphoses* which are explored in this book may be defined in terms which move from *translatio* to *allusio*. To be sure, a variety of terms could be used to define the texts discussed here, such as 'adaptation' or 'rewriting'. However, these and their related terms often function as a taxonomy which undermines the cultural politics of translation. As Susan Bassnett concludes:

> It is probably more helpful to think of translation not so much as a category in its own right, but rather as a set of textual practices with which the writer and the reader collude. This suggests that literary studies [...] need to look again at translation, for the investigation of translation as a set of textual practices has not received much attention [...]. It is time to free ourselves from the constraints that the term 'translation' has placed upon us and recognise that we have immense problems pinning down a term that continues to elude us. For whether we know it or not, we have been colluding with alternative notions of translation all our lives.[24]

Thus, with Bassnett's cogent observations in mind, I use the word 'translation' as a means of recalling the ideological facets embedded in the term itself.

Jeanette Beer comments that 'translation never was, and should not now be, envisaged as a genre';[25] a genre implies stasis, whereas translation, as the etymology of the word suggests, is a dynamic process.[26] Nonetheless, as Catherine Belsey explains, translation practices attempt to transport meaning from the place of the other and secure it within the new system and to fix stability in signification:

> When Ferdinand de Saussure drew attention to the problem of translation, he enabled his readers to recognise the inevitability of cultural difference and the impossibility of legislating for its resolution. Words, Saussure pointed out, do not necessarily have exact equivalents from one language to another. As any practising translator knows, not only nuances but pronouns, genders, tenses, and distinctions can be untranslatable. It follows that meanings are not held in place by objects in the world or by concepts independent of language. The signified (meaning) resides in language or, more broadly, in signifying systems (including visual images, for instance) and it is to be found nowhere else. Signification is differential, but the differences are not guaranteed by the world or by ideas. The world may be

encountered as resistance, but it cannot be known outside the systems of differences which define it [...]. [Ideas] are, moreover, deferred by the signifier which produces them. Differed and deferred, supplanted, relegated by the signifier, the signified has no autonomy, no substance.[27]

In Belsey's description of Derridean *différance*,[28] what becomes visible in translation, as Edwin Gentzler has stated, 'is language referring not to things, but to language itself'.[29] Viewed in this way, translation becomes a thoroughly disturbing process at the level of the signifier: a disturbing process that a variety of textual strategies has tried to repress. Most obviously these repressive strategies are inscribed in notions of equivalence – a phrase first popularized by Eugene Nida[30] – where critical approaches to translated texts tend to concentrate on whether the translator has produced a version of the original in terms of a 'word for word' or a 'sense for sense' translation. However, in the words of the epigraph above, 'we will never have, and never have had, to do with some "transport" of pure signifieds from one language to another, or within one and the same language, that the signifying instrument would leave virgin and untouched'.[31] In the processes of translation boundaries and borders are disrupted and frames of signification are ruptured. For Tomlinson, exposing translation's presence fragments conventional notions of English Literature; for the purpose of my book, acknowledging the processes and practices of translation provides further arenas for the exploration of early modern identities.

The foregoing remarks provide the analytical context for the argument that follows. I do not propose to read the vernacular translations of the *Metamorphoses* through a specific theoretical frame, of which there are a large, and increasing, number and which, as Terence Cave has observed, would 'reduce the texts to the status of local illustrations of a modern theory'.[32] Nevertheless, my critical position has undoubtedly been informed by post-Saussurean perspectives on signifying systems and translation. It is this type of thinking about translation which has influenced Tejaswini Niranjana's *Siting Translation: History, Post-Structuralism and the Colonial Context*. In Niranjana's argument, translation 'becomes a significant site for raising questions of representation, power and historicity'.[33] In her discussion of the asymmetrical relationship between England and India from the eighteenth century to the present,[34] translation functions as interpellation, a term derived from Louis Althusser describing 'the "constitution" of subjects in language by ideology'.[35] By theorizing translation in this way, Niranjana posits an important, post-colonial agenda which is pertinent for my own views on translation. The notion of 'translation as interpellation' is not only relevant in the context of translation between languages; the political dimension of 'translation as interpellation' can also be applied to intralingual translations.

For many post-Saussureans the construction of identity is perceived as being 'produced from within language' and depending 'upon both difference (between the self and the other) and accession to the position of a [provisional] "I" within discourse'.[36] In this theoretical context, the translator and the translated text, thoroughly absorbed in issues of signifying systems and difference, are pivotal in constructing and deconstructing the subject.[37] Certainly, there have been arguments which have employed Ovid's *Metamorphoses* as a significant text in the construction of the Petrarchan subject. For example, Lynn Enterline is concerned with the shaping of Petrarch's voice, via Ovid, in the *Canzoniere*:

> Petrarch's complex encounter with Ovid's *Metamorphoses*, as Renaissance literary critics know well, left an indelible mark on the history of European representations of the poet – particularly as that poet represented himself, or herself, as the subject of language and of desire.[38]

Somewhat differently, the overarching project of *Ovid and the Cultural Politics of Translation in Early Modern England* is to examine the 'complex encounters' between the *Metamorphoses* and its English translators in order to consider ways in which the *translator* 'represented himself, or herself, as the subject of language and of desire'.

Figuring Translation

Bate suggests that Ovidian myths allow us to make sense of the world. In the introduction to *Shakespeare and Ovid* he argues that his

> aim has been to present the material in the terms of Ovid and his Renaissance readers, not to translate it into those of some later theorist. There may be a book to be written on Shakespeare and the *Metamorphoses* in relation to Claude Lévi-Strauss's theory that myths encode the deep binary structures of all cultures, but this is not it. Jacques Derrida's essay on Lévi-Strauss, 'Structure Sign and Play in the Discourse of the Human Sciences', is one of the foundation texts of deconstruction, but my aim is to reconstruct, not deconstruct, Renaissance mythography [...]. In order to understand the work that myth does for Shakespeare – and to try out for ourselves whether it can do any work for us – we have to suspend our disbelief in the possibility of words and stories referring to a reality beyond themselves. [...] we do have to believe in the reality of the human conditions and aspirations that are stored in myth [...].[39]

Belsey reminds us, however, that 'language is not transparent, not merely the *medium* in which autonomous individuals transmit messages to each other about an independently constituted world of things'.[40] Meaning in language, 'differed and deferred', is held in place by the ideological concerns of the historical context in which it is employed. Thus the 'human conditions and aspirations' which Bate claims are 'stored in myth' are specific to the culture in which they are produced; identity itself is deconstructed *and* reconstructed in and through texts. Indeed, Ovid's *Metamorphoses* and the English translations of the poem are emblematic representations of the desire for presence in language and are arenas in which the problematic transformation of the subject, through and in history, can be rehearsed.

In the early part of the sixteenth century the vernacular was perceived as a site of lack. According to Thomas M. Greene:

> The focus of England's sense of disjuncture lay most visibly in its embarrassment over its rude vernacular. Translators of the earlier Tudor period ritually deplored 'our own corrupt and base, as al men affyrme it: most barbarous Language,' and comparable expressions are found in so many other contexts as well that the attitude has to be taken seriously. The embarrassment of the English with their language should be read, I think, synecdochically, as an oblique lament over a broader cultural poverty. Not only the language was inadequate; the nation as a whole was seen as suffering from a kind of privation which translations from antiquity or even from the continental vernaculars could only underscore.[41]

As the compulsion to produce texts in the vernacular increased, writers such as George Puttenham in the *Arte of English Poesie* (1589) acknowledged the importance of translations as they simultaneously denounced them:

> It appeareth by sundry records of bookes both printed and written, that many of our countreymen have painfully travelled in this part: of whose works some appeare to be but bare translations, other some matters of their owne invention and very commendable, whereof some recitall shall be made in this place, to th'intent chiefly that their names should not be defrauded of such honour as seemeth due to them for having by their thankefull studies so much beautified our English tong [...].[42]

Puttenham's use of the adjective 'bare' in describing contemporaneous translation practices is telling since it suggests that the translated text is a site of lack compared with other texts which are the products of 'invention'. But behind such emphatic assertions resides a certain lack of confidence in language which, arguably, might be tested by translation. Thus the transmission of culture from either past or present sources is undertaken in order to enrich the status of the English language and, in turn, the nation state. This translative agenda was undertaken so forcefully that, in 1688, John Wilkins could assert that that:

> Since learning began to flourish in our Nation, there have been more than ordinary Changes introduced in our Language: partly by new artificial compositions; partly by enfranchising strange forein words, for their elegance and significancy, which now makes one third part of our language; and partly by refining and mollifying old words, for the more easie and graceful sound: by which means this last Century may be conjectured to have made a greater change in our Tongue, than any of the former, as to the addition of new words.[43]

These 'more than ordinary changes', as Paula Blank has argued, meant that linguistic differences within the English language in terms of dialect ('competing Englishes' in fact) were also manifest.[44]

From Plato's *Cratylus* onwards, history has been troubled by 'the scandal of mutability, the ungrounded contingency of language'.[45] There have been numerous allegorical and emblematic representations about these concerns in the early modern period, figured, for example, as Proteus, Mercury or the dismemberment of Orpheus.[46] Ovid's *Metamorphoses*, a narrative featuring these classical emblems of linguistic mutability, is a text which thoroughly explores the difficulties inherent in making meaning not only in language but in all forms of communication. The epigraph from Jacques Derrida at the head of this chapter has a particular relevance for this discussion as it plays with notions of translation and transformation; issues which are central to English versions of Ovid's poem. In this quotation Derrida seeks to shift concepts of translation (the carrying across of signs from one system of signification into another) towards notions of transformation – a term which suggests a more intertextual relationship between systems of signification. The *Metamorphoses* is a text which provides a variety of etiologies for a single object as well as for the world at large and thus contributes to an ongoing debate about the relationship between the language and representation:

> Without our cultural and personal derivation, our etiology, the sound of the word has no meaning. Given the etiology, the word acquires a kind of ballast and tendency in its drift.[47]

Although words are given stability through the construction of these histories, the very emphasis of that history serves to undermine meaning and much of Ovid's text points to the arbitrariness of language and the gap between the sign and the signified. Indeed, it is a poem thoroughly concerned with the processes, products and politics of signification, and the ways in which humankind is made subject through and in language.

Part of the political project of the *Metamorphoses* is to recount the construction of Rome. But Ovid's version of Roman history offers an important counterpoint to the conventions of a more typical epic such as Virgil's *Aeneid*.[48] As Ovid tells the history of the nation state, from its beginnings in the primeval chaos to the reign of Augustus Caesar, the narrative undermines the teleological structure of the earlier epic.[49] Moreover, it is a text which draws attention to the intertextuality of its own construction. Amongst the several hundred or so myths enclosed within its narrative frame, Ovid's *Metamorphoses* employs translation in its rewriting of other narratives which derive mostly from Greek.[50] Karl Galinsky notes that Ovid's poem can be likened in form to the collective poems of Hesiod and Homeric epic; in terms of content, it has some similarities with the *Ornithogonia* of the Greek poet Boios which deals with the transformations of men into birds and which was translated into Latin by a contemporary of Ovid, Aemilius Macer. Apart from the three attested *Metamorphoses* by later Greek poets, including Parthenius, perhaps the best-known Greek precedent for Ovid's narrative is Nikander of Colophon's *Heteroeumena*.[51] Particularly from the first century BC through to the beginning of the second century AD, as Rita Copeland has shown, the Greeks acknowledged their language as 'the more illustrious language [such that] translation from Greek into Latin can be described as a vertical movement from greater to lesser prestige'.[52] However, this hierarchical model is reversed by the time that Ovid's

Metamorphoses is produced, and the cultural and textual supremacy of Rome is affirmed by Horace in the *Ars poetica*:

> Our own poets have left no style untried, nor has least honour been earned when they have dared to leave the footsteps of the Greeks and sing of deeds at home, whether they have put native tragedies or native comedies upon the stage.[53]

The appropriation of Greek texts remains unacknowledged by Ovid. If these interlingual translations are silently revised, then so too are the intralingual reworkings of Virgil's *Aeneid* and of Ovid's own *Amores* and *Heroides*.

A useful contrast may be made between the beginning of Ovid's text and the opening of Apuleius's *Metamorphoses*. Apuleius begins:

> Who am I? I will tell you briefly. Attic Hymettos and Ephyrean Isthmos and Spartan Taenaros, fruitful lands preserved for ever in even more fruitful books, form my ancient stock. There I served my stint with the Attic tongue in the first campaigns of childhood. Soon afterwards, in the city of the Latins, as a newcomer to Roman studies I attacked and cultivated their native speech with laborious difficulty and no teacher to guide me. So, please, I beg your pardon in advance if as a raw speaker of this foreign tongue of the Forum I commit any blunders. Now in fact this very changing of language corresponds to the type of writing we have undertaken, which is like the skill of a rider jumping from one horse to another. We are about to begin a Greekish story. Pay attention reader and you will find delight.[54]

Although produced in a different historical context, Apuleius's *Metamorphoses* rehearses some familiar problematics of translation. Employing the topos of the humble translator, the formula of humility which will become a common feature of many translations produced in the early modern period, Lucius, the narrator of Apuleius's text, uses the metaphor of a circus rider leaping from one horse to another in order to describe the linguistic move from Greek to Latin. This figure, which undermines any modern notion of equivalence in translation, clearly illustrates the inherent semiotic instability of translation. Apuleius's text was translated by William Adlington in the sixteenth century as *The.xv.Bookes of the Golden Asse, Conteining the Metamorphosie of Lucius Apuleius* (1566) and its employment in Shakespeare's *A Midsummer Night's Dream* (c. 1595) confirms its popularity.[55] But the later classical text does not possess the complex translative genealogy of Ovid's *Metamorphoses* and, intriguingly, Adlington's prose translation remained the only complete English translation in circulation throughout the early modern period. By simply avoiding its intertextual debts, Ovid's *Metamorphoses* immediately authorises its own status; this is a poem which seeks to 'bring down [its] song in unbroken strains from the world's very beginning even unto the present time' (1. 2–4).[56]

Described by Quintilian as a text which 'welds together subjects of the most diverse nature so as to form a continuous whole',[57] Ovid's *Metamorphoses* is framed by a linear, translative impetus that will take the reader from the creation of the world out of chaos to the formation of Rome as a nation state. In the beginning:

Golden was that first age, which, with no one to compel, without a law, of its own will, kept faith and did the right. There was no fear of punishment, no threatening words were to be read on brazen tablets; no suppliant throng gazed fearfully upon its judge's face; but without defenders lived secure. Not yet had the pine-tree, felled on its native mountains, descended thence into the watery plain to visit other lands; men knew no shores except their own. (1. 89-96)

Linguistic difference is not explicitly discussed. From the moment that Lycaon's contempt for the gods is shown in book 1 and the reader is offered the first tale of human transformation into beast,[58] however, myths appear which are concerned with issues of signification and translation. Mercury and Iris, the messengers of Jupiter and Juno respectively, are shown to mediate between the gods and mortals;[59] a number of seers and augers show the necessity for the interpretation of signs as either good or bad omens.[60] As Leonard Barkan has described:

Many of the great figures of Ovid's poem define themselves by their struggle to invent new languages. That is clearest in the case of metamorphic victims like Actaeon or Io, who must labour to use human language fitting their consciousness once their shape has turned beastly.[61]

Whilst Barkan is typically astute in his observation, these two examples are not completely parallel. For Actaeon, transformed into a deer by Diana for spying on her as she bathed, 'words fail his desire' and he is torn to pieces by his own hounds (3. 230 ff.). Io is in a different plight. First ravished by Jupiter, changed by the god into a white heifer and then given as a gift to the jealous Juno (who confers her to Argus to guard), Io's initial attempts to communicate are thwarted:

When she strove to stretch out suppliant arms to Argus she had no arms to stretch; and when she attempted to voice her complaints, she only mooed [...] if only she could speak, she would tell her name and sad misfortune, and beg for aid. But instead of words, she did tell the sad story of her changed form with letters which she traced in the dust with her hoof. (1. 635–50)

Eventually, Io is more successful in her efforts to convey events to her father, Inachus. Either through speech, symbolic gesture, or written text, transformed figures such as Actaeon and Io, and others (for example, Callisto and Ocyrhoë),[62] express the desire to translate. In this context of translation one of the most interesting moments of the *Metamorphoses* occurs in book 6 when the poem describes its own revision. In her contest with Minerva, Arachne, the low-born Maeonian weaver who denied the goddess as her teacher, produces a text full of the 'heavenly crimes' (6. 132) of the gods. Several of these incidents – Jove's abduction of Europa and his violation of Danaë, Pluto's rape of Proserpine and Neptune's rape of Medusa – appear as part of the main narrative frame of the *Metamorphoses* itself.[63] This narrative *mise-en-abîme* is an effective means for exploring the endless play of signification inscribing and circumscribing Ovid's text. The contest between Minerva and Arachne, however, also emphasizes the way in which meaning is held in place by ideological forces as Minerva destroys Arachne's text depicting the nefarious aspects of the gods, and transforms the girl into a spider.

The Latin word *lingua* can be translated as 'tongue' and as 'language'.[64] Significantly, the violent cultural and political implications of translation are taken further in the Ovidian tales which deal with images of the tongue, the border between the body and language, which appears in the central books of the *Metamorphoses*.[65] After scorning Diana's beauty, Chione's tongue is pierced by the goddess's arrow (11. 301). In book 5, Emathion, an old man 'who loved justice and revered gods [...]. [and] since his years forbade warfare, fought with the tongue' (5. 99 ff.) is decapitated by Chromis. The final moment of Emathion's life is thrown into relief as the narrative focuses on the head which 'fell straight on the altar, and there the still half-conscious tongue kept up its execrations' (5. 105). There is a similar image of the autonomous tongue in the episode of the death of Orpheus. Dismembered by the scorned Ciconian women, his head and lyre floated in the stream while 'mournfully the lifeless tongue murmured' (11. 52). One of the most grotesque and brutal episodes of the poem is found in book 6 when Tereus attempts to conceal his rape of his sister-in-law Philomela by cutting out her tongue (6. 549-62). Comparison with the deaths of Emathion and Orpheus clearly shows the explicit nature of the violent act upon the woman. Though the men suffer undeniably cruel deaths, the tragic tenor of this Ovidian narrative is intensified because Philomela does not die. The severity of Tereus's violation is conveyed through the personification of Philomela's tongue which, metonymically, displaces her body. Denied the capacity of speech, Philomela has to translate her mutilation and rape through the woven image delivered to her sister.

These myths, many of which will be discussed in the subsequent chapters of this book, justify Richard Lanham's observation that the *Metamorphoses* is a terrifying world with anger and violence everywhere.[66] As Ovid depicts Rome's inauguration, the narrative is interspersed with violent episodes which focus on the individual, identity and language. However, the narrative voice of the *Metamorphoses*, a 'diffuse authorial self',[67] does not offer these episodes as didactic political propaganda; 'the point is not to hierarchise – there are no hierarchies here, and no perspectives either'.[68] Rather, the reader is confronted with a series of situations which encourage interpretations regarding the construction of identity in terms of nation and gender. Importantly, the type of hermeneutic that Ovid's narrative invites is one placed within the context of translation and transformation: a context taken up and developed by translators in the early modern period.

Translation and Nation

The building of the Tower of Babel in Genesis 11, a bid by the sons of Shem to match God's transcendence, was punished by the multiplication of languages. Before its construction there was only one tongue; following the divine prohibition of God there were many. In England during the late fifteenth and early sixteenth centuries, the ruptured dominance of Latinate Church culture, the re–establishment of Greek and Hebrew and the influx of texts from other contemporary vernacular languages gave rise to what might be termed as a Babel-ling epoch:

> 'Babel' [...]. Telling at least of the inadequation of one tongue to another [...] of language to itself and to meaning, and so forth, it also tells us of the need for figuration, for myths, for tropes, for twists and turns, for translation inadequate to compensate for that which multiplicity denies us.[69]

As Derrida suggests, the Christian narrative of Babel delineates translation's semantic limits. The political and cultural dimensions of translation practices in the early modern period are clearly evident, of course, in the texts of the period which are concerned with religious debate.[70] The English Reformation, as Greenblatt's *Renaissance Self-Fashioning* expertly shows, is largely constructed as well as contested around translations of the Bible in the vernacular. The continual re-citation of Ovid's secular myth of creation, a less dangerous task than the translation of sacred texts, also 'tells us of the need for figuration, for myths, for tropes, for twists and turns, for translation inadequate to compensate for that which multiplicity denies us'. One of the most influential translations of Ovid's poem, Arthur Golding's *Metamorphosis* (first four books published in 1565; completed 1567),[71] domesticates the text 'in language and in cultural context'[72] and is underpinned by 'Calvinist policy and polity'.[73] During this period of political and cultural upheaval, a time when the English language itself is transforming rapidly, it seems to be no coincidence that this historical moment is punctuated by English translations of the *Metamorphoses*.

Scholars of English Literature have long regarded the *Metamorphoses* as important source material for many medieval and early modern texts;[74] many have employed topoi from Ovid's poem in order to stimulate new readings of works by canonical English writers such as Geoffrey Chaucer, John Gower, William Shakespeare, Edmund Spenser and John Milton.[75] A rather different attitude to Ovid's texts begins with Lee T. Pearcy's *The Mediated Muse: English Translations of Ovid, 1560–1700*.[76] As the title of the book indicates, the focus of Pearcy's discussion is on the relationship between the vernacular versions of the *Metamorphoses*; a critical approach which has recently been advanced by way of a range of theoretical perspectives. In terms of reception studies, Sarah Annes Brown's *The Metamorphosis of Ovid: From Chaucer to Ted Hughes* has made an important contribution to the understanding of English Ovidianism.[77] Though Brown includes a discussion of Samuel Garth's collaborative translation of the *Metamorphoses* (1717) in her impressive survey, the cultural politics of translation are not the overt concern of her work. My book shares some common ground with Raphael Lyne's *Ovid's Changing Worlds: English Metamorphoses 1567–1632*; a critical exploration of Ovid's poem which has more obvious connections to recent developments in translation studies. In a careful consideration of the English translations by Golding, Edmund Spenser, Michael Drayton and George Sandys, Lyne begins to discuss the *Metamorphoses* in a way that I develop further.

Primarily concentrating on the 'four works that are [...] the four most substantial meditations on Ovid's greatest work in the period [...]', Lyne's analysis does not set out to 'tackle numerous offshoots of the *Metamorphoses* tradition that have a vibrant but different life in English'.[78] Whereas *Ovid's Changing Worlds* focuses on texts that are united by 'their relationship as a whole' to Ovid's epic poem,[79] *Ovid and the Cultural Politics of Translation in Early Modern England* explores a range of translations produced in the early modern period which engage with the *Metamorphoses* both in its entirety and as textual fragments.

If the term 'translation' is problematic, then trying to define early modern Ovidian translations is equally difficult. Recalling the enigma of Ovid's exile, Fausto Ghisalberti observes that the *Metamorphoses* belongs to the period both of the author's greatest fame and of his greatest disgrace – in AD 8 Augustus banished Ovid from Rome for an unknown offence, and the poet spent the final years of his life in exile on Tomis – which makes it a text eminently suitable for adaptation to Christian purposes.[80] Inheriting much of its didacticism from the medieval *accessus* to the *Metamorphoses*,[81] the early modern moralized tradition of Ovidian translation is obviously represented by the anonymous *Fable of Ovid Treting of Narcissus translated into Englysh mytre, with a moral there unto* (1560) and, in part, by Golding's translation. Ovid's myths were also transposed into playful and erotic epyllia, effectively illustrated by Shakespeare's *Venus and Adonis* (c. 1593) or the numerous versions of the Salmacis and Hermaphroditus narrative that were produced throughout the sixteenth and seventeenth centuries.[82] To be sure, the influence of the *Metamorphoses* upon English literature is so great that any number of texts could have been examined in this study, for example Thomas Hedley's broadside ballad *The Judgement of Midas* (1552), the first known Ovidian myth to be printed in England; John Lyly's *Gallathea* (c. 1592) or Charles Cotton's *Chaucer's Ghoast, or, a Piece of Antiquity. Containing twelve pleasant Fables of Ovid penn'd after the ancient manner of writing in England* (c. 1672).[83] Charles Martindale's anthology of essays, *Ovid Renewed: Ovidian Influences on Literature and Art from the Middle Ages to the Twentieth Century*, is witness to the wide and varied dissemination of Ovid's poem.[84] Mindful that my project can only present a partial scene of Ovidian translation, my choice of texts has been determined by those versions of Ovid's poem which engage with the construction of early modern English identities in specific ways, some of which are eccentric to the usual canon.

My book begins, however, with a play which is often invoked whenever the subject of Ovid and early modern England is discussed and in which a translation of the *Metamorphoses* takes a central role: Shakespeare's *Titus Andronicus* (c. 1594). Adam McKeown has observed that 'not enough critical work has explored the tension surrounding the strange cameo of "Ovid's *Metamorphosis*" in Act 4'.[85] Thus, in Chapter 1, I consider McKeown's perceptive comment in detail by suggesting that the material invocation of the *Metamorphoses* in *Titus Andronicus* initiates an interrogation of the cultural politics of translation and the construction of Elizabethan notions of 'self' and 'other'. Entitled '*Titus Andronicus* and the Sexual Politics of Translation', the critical focus of this section is on the relationship between Lavinia and Ovid's book and the ways in which the processes and products of translation construct the gendered subject; a critical thread which underpins much of the ensuing argument.

Accordingly, in Chapter 2, 'The Heterotopic Place of Translation: *The Third Part of the Countesse of Pembrokes Yvychurch. Entituled, Amintas Dale*', I continue the discussion of the sexual politics of translation which began with Shakespeare's Lavinia. The first known appearance of the *Metamorphoses* in English is the myth of Ceyx and Alcyone in Chaucer's *Book of the Duchess* (c. 1368–72), a narrative focusing on Alcyone's grief following the death of her husband.[86] This gendered notion of loss extends to other English translations of Ovid's *Metamorphoses*, notably Abraham Fraunce's poem. In sum, I suggest that the use of Ovidian myths in this complex pastoral poem, produced for Fraunce's patron Mary Sidney, not only questions the fashioning of the woman translator; Fraunce's text also disrupts the male translator's subject position.

The second chapter, *inter alia*, raises questions about translation and patronage. In Chapter 3, which explores a translation of Ovid's poem produced *cum privilegio*, 'Violence in Translation: George Sandys's *Metamorphosis Englished*, I consider the difficulties faced by a translator who appropriates Ovid as a means of disseminating the policies of Charles I. One of the interesting points about this translation is that Sandys worked on the text whilst he was Treasurer of the Jamestown colony. Lyne has suggested that the cultural politics of this 'Virginian Ovid' can be read as an 'interplay between a classical text and the New World'.[87] Rather differently, I argue that Sandys's translation unwittingly discloses anxieties about English Royalist identity and the fragile nature of the domestic body politic.

The importance of Sandys's translation is demonstrated in the large number of editions through which it passed and in the way later translators worked in his shadow. Chapter 4, 'From *Sandys's Ghost* to Samuel Garth', looks at ways in which Garth's collaborative translation of 1717, the text which heralds the end of this current *aetas Ovidiana*, is haunted by the earlier translation. By contrast with Sandys's Ovid produced *cum privilegio*, this new translation is motivated by changes in commercial publishing and is distinctive for its use of the editorial process as part of its translative strategy. By alluding to contemporaneous scientific discourses in his Preface, Garth attempts to take his reader out of the frame of early modern Christian humanism and into one which is concerned with the kind of empirical enquiry appropriate for its Enlightenment context. Featuring translations by well-known writers of the late seventeenth and early eighteenth centuries, for example John Dryden, Joseph Addison, William Congreve, Alexander Pope and John Gay, Garth's composite translation attempts to fashion a unified edition out of a clearly dialogic and fragmented text.

From the opening chapters of this book it is clear that the relationship between women and Ovid's poem is rather different to that of men. Chapter 5, 'In Arachne's Trace: Women as Translators of the *Metamorphoses*', as the title suggests, considers the ways in which early modern women treat Ovid's myths; a hitherto neglected area of research. As Valerie Traub notes in her Afterword to *Ovid and the Renaissance Body*, with the exception of Louis Labé, markedly a *French* writer, 'the volume is silent about women's engagement with Ovid, either as readers or writers'.[88] In the light of Traub's comments, this penultimate chapter examines Elizabeth Talbot's tapestries depicting the myths of Phaeton, Europa and Actaeon (c. 1601), Elizabeth Singer Rowe's 'The Fable of Phaeton' (1696), Mary, Lady Chudleigh's 'Icarus' (1703) and Mary Wortley Montagu's juvenile translations of Ovidian myths (c. 1704).

Throughout the book, I largely explore Ovidian translation by way of the variable relationships between translator, patron, publisher, readership and critical reception in order to 'critique the violence of my own language'.[89] My aim, then, is not to conduct prescriptive comparative analyses between source and target languages. According to Michael Cronin:

> this prescriptive approach [...] has tended to conceal as much as it reveals. Prescriptive commentary practised by scholars who are proficient in both source and target language tends to be retrospective, i.e. primarily concerned with faithful translation of the source language. This ignores the fact that most people who read a translation do so because they do not speak the source language and therefore that questions of reception and target-language acceptability are central to the translator's practice.[90]

A prescriptive approach also assumes a fixed, textual origin for a translation. The attempt to secure an originary source text for the early modern English translations of the *Metamorphoses*, however, is continually thwarted. The number of manuscripts and printed editions in circulation throughout the early modern period make a convincing philological comparative project almost impossible.[91] Hence, modern scholarship has yet to secure a single source text for Golding's translation.[92] Deborah Rubin's thesis on Sandys's *Metamorphosis Englished* cannot locate a specific Latin text from which it is translated.[93] Yet modes of prescriptive comparative analyses are really tested by the text which is the focus of Chapter 6; William Caxton's prose manuscript version of the *Metamorphoses* (c. 1480). To some, it may seem anomalous to end with a discussion of the earliest complete English translation of Ovid's poem. In many ways, however, this text provides a fitting point of departure for this study. Though produced by a well-known male translator, this rendition of the classical poem (critically overlooked by many recent studies of Ovid in English) inhabits the margins of early modern England. As the concluding chapter contends, however, Caxton's Ovid engages with the cultural politics of translation in fifteenth-century England – and beyond.

Notes

1   Jacques Derrida, *Positions*, trans. by Alan Bass (London: Athlone, 1987), p. 20.

2   George Sandys, *Ovids Metamorphosis Englished, mythologiz'd, and represented in figures. An essay to the translation of Virgil's AEneis. By G.S.* (Oxford: 1632).

3   Jonathan Bate, *Shakespeare and Ovid* (Oxford: Clarendon Press, 1993), pp. 3–4. Bate cites the title of Thomas M. Greene, 'The Flexibility of the Self', in *The Disciplines of*

Criticism: Essays in Literary Theory, Interpretation, and History, ed. by Peter Demetz, Thomas Greene and Lowry Nelson, Jr. (New Haven: Yale University Press, 1968), pp. 241–64.

[4] Stephen Greenblatt, *Renaissance Self-Fashioning: From More to Shakespeare* (Chicago: University of Chicago Press, 1980), p. 9.

[5] Greenblatt, *Renaissance Self-Fashioning*, p. 115.

[6] Diarmaid MacCulloch, *Reformation: Europe's House Divided 1490–1700* (London: Penguin, 2004), p. 203. See also Susan Bassnett, *Translation Studies*, rev. edn. (London: Routledge, 1991), p. 14. Greenblatt discusses Tyndale at length in the second chapter of *Renaissance Self-Fashioning*.

[7] Greenblatt, *Renaissance Self-Fashioning*, p. 145.

[8] Charles Tomlinson, 'The Presence of Translation: A View of English Poetry', in *The Art of Translation: Voices from the Field*, ed. by Rosanna Warren (Boston: Northeastern University Press, 1989), pp. 258–76, p. 258.

[9] Tomlinson, 'The Presence of Translation', p. 272. Tomlinson seemingly responds to Itamar Even-Zohar's argument: 'As a rule, histories of literature mention translations when there is no way to avoid them, when dealing with the Middle Ages or the Renaissance, for instance [...]. As a consequence, one hardly gets any idea of the function of translated literature for a literature as a whole or of its position within that literature. Moreover, there is no awareness of the possible existence of translated literature as a particular literary system'. Itamar Even-Zohar, 'The Position of Translated Literature Within the Literary Polysystem', *Poetics Today*, 11 (1990), 45–51, 45.

[10] Tomlinson, 'The Presence of Translation', p. 261.

[11] Michael Cronin, *Translating Ireland: Translation, Languages, Cultures* (Cork: Cork University Press, 1996).

[12] As Lawrence Venuti explains: 'Translation wields enormous power in constructing representations of foreign cultures, while it simultaneously constructs domestic subjects'. Lawrence Venuti, 'Translation and the Formation of Cultural Identities', in *The Cultural Functions of Translation*, ed. by Christina Schäffner and Helen Kelly-Holmes (Clevedon: Multilingual Matters, 1995), pp. 9–25, p. 9.

[13] Lawrence Venuti, *The Scandals of Translation* (London: Routledge, 1998), p. 8.

[14] Tejaswini Niranjana, *Siting Translation: History, Post-Structuralism and the Colonial Context* (Berkeley: University of California Press, 1992), p. 47.

[15] For a detailed discussion of the status of translator relative to author in terms of copyright law, see Lawrence Venuti, *The Translator's Invisibility* (London: Routledge, 1995), p. 8 ff. and *The Scandals of Translation*, pp. 47–66.

[16] Richard Blackmore, *A paraphrase on the book of Job as likewise on the songs of Moses, Deborah, David, on four select psalms, some chapters of Isaiah, and the third chapter of Habakkuk* (London: 1700), p.1.

[17] According to Mary Thomas Crane, Ovid's *Metamorphoses* was part of the canon from the fourth to sixth forms. Mary Thomas Crane, *Framing Authorities: Sayings, Self and Society in Sixteenth-Century England* (Princeton: Princeton University Press, 1993), p. 87.

[18] The top of the title page depicts Homer seated, alongside Apollo, Mercury and Athene; below, the battle of the frogs and a portrait of Chapman. See Alfred Forbes Johnson, *A Catalogue of Engraved and Etched Title Pages* (Oxford: The Bibliographical Society, 1934), p. 52 and Warren Boutcher, 'The Renaissance', in *The Oxford Guide to*

Literature in English Translation, ed. by Peter France (Oxford: Oxford University Press, 2000), pp. 45–54, p. 50.

[19] Thomas M. Greene, *The Light in Troy: Imitation and Discovery in Renaissance Poetry* (New Haven: Yale University Press, 1982), p. 51.

[20] Roger Ascham, 'The Scholemaster' in *English Works,* ed. by William Aldis Wright (Cambridge: Cambridge University Press, 1904), pp. 243–64.

[21] Roman Jakobson distinguished 'three ways of interpreting a verbal sign: it may be translated into other signs of the same language [intralingual], into another language [interlingual], or into another, nonverbal system of symbols [intersemiotic]'. Roman Jakobson, *Language in Literature* (Massachusetts: Harvard University Press, 1987),
p. 429. However, as Theo Hermans observes, Jacques Derrida has complicated the apparent coherence of Jakobson's tripartite division, 'pointing out that if for Jakobson intralingual translation is a form of translation, then in the essay itself the term "rewording" is a translation of the term "intralingual translation"'. See further Theo Hermans, 'Translation's Other' (London: University College London, 1996), p. 23.

[22] Terry Eagleton, 'Translation and Transformation', *Stand*, 19 (1977), 72–7, 72. Gayatri Chakravorty Spivak makes a similar comment: 'Any act of reading is besieged and delivered by the precarious-ness of intertextuality. And translation is, after all, one version of intertextuality.' Gayatri Chakravorty Spivak, Translator's Preface, in Jacques Derrida, *Of Grammatology*, trans. by Gayatri Chakravorty Spivak (Balitmore: John Hopkins, 1979), pp. ix–xxxviii, p. lxxxvi.

[23] José Lambert, 'Literary Translation', in *The Routledge Encyclopedia of Translation Studies*, ed. by Mona Baker and Kirsten Malmkjæ (London: Routledge, 1998), pp. 130–3, pp. 130–1.

[24] Bassnett, Susan, 'When is a Translation Not a Translation?', in *Constructing Cultures: Essays on Literary Translation*, ed. by Susan Bassnett and André Lefevere (Clevedon: Multilingual Matters, 1998), pp. 25–40, p. 39.

[25] Jeanette Beer, Introduction, in *Translation and the Transmission of Culture Between 1300 and 1600*, ed. by Jeanette Beer and Kenneth Lloyd-Jones (Michigan: Medieval Institute Publications, 1995), pp. vii–xii, p. vii.

[26] The *Oxford English Dictionary*, 'translation', sense I. 1. a and II. 2. a.

[27] Catherine Belsey, 'Postmodern Love: Questioning the Metaphysics of Desire', *New Literary History,* 25 (1994), 683–705, 683–4.

[28] See further Jacques Derrida, 'Différance', in *Margins of Philosophy*, trans. by Alan Bass (Hertfordshire: Harvester Wheatsheaf, 1982), pp. 1–28.

[29] Edwin Gentzler, *Contemporary Translation Theories* (London: Routledge, 1993), p. 147.

[30] Eugene Nida, *Toward a Science of Translating* (Leiden: Brill, 1964), p. 159.

[31] With reference to Derrida's notion of translation and transformation, Ruth Evans inserts an important caveat: '[His] position is however very different from the idea that "pure translatability" is an impossible ideal, but nevertheless an ideal; it is precisely this desire for presence that Derrida critiques'. Ruth Evans, 'Translating Past Cultures?', in *The Medieval Translator 4*, ed. by Roger Ellis and Ruth Evans (Exeter: University of Exeter Press, 1994), pp. 20–45, p. 32.

[32] Terence Cave, *The Cornucopian Text: Problems of Writing in the French Renaissance* (Oxford: Clarendon Press, 1979), p. xvi.

[33] Niranjana, *Siting Translation*, p. 1.

[34] Niranjana, *Siting Translation*, p. 1.

35   Niranjana, *Siting Translation*, p. 11, n. 16.
36   Antony Easthope and Kate McGowan (eds.), *A Critical and Cultural Theory Reader* (Buckingham: Open University Press, 1992), p. 68.
37   Lawrence Venuti argues for a 'translation hermeneutic' which 'assumes a notion of agency that allows for the full complexity of the translator's work [...]. [treating] the translating subject as discursively constructed in self-presentations, theoretical statements, legal codes, the very process of developing a translation strategy, of selecting and arranging signifiers'. Lawrence Venuti, Introduction, in *Rethinking Translation*, ed. by Lawrence Venuti (London: Routledge, 1992), pp. 1–17, p. 11.
38   Lynn Enterline, 'Embodied Voices: Petrarch Reading (Himself Reading) Ovid', in *Desire in the Renaissance: Psychoanalysis and Literature*, ed. by Valeria Finucci and Regina Schwartz (Princeton: Princeton University Press, 1994), pp. 120–45, p. 120. See further Lynn Enterline, *The Rhetoric of the Body: From Ovid to Shakespeare* (Cambridge: Cambridge University Press, 2000), p. 91.
39   Bate, *Shakespeare and Ovid*, p. 19–20. Since I began my own thoughts on Bate's critical practice, Charles Martindale has contested the textual relationship that Bate sets up between Shakespeare and Ovid. See further Charles Martindale, 'Shakespeare's Ovid, Ovid's Shakespeare: A Methodological Postscript', in *Shakespeare's Ovid: The Metamorphoses in the Plays and the Poems*, ed. by A. B. Taylor (Cambridge: Cambridge University Press, 2000), pp. 198–215.
40   Catherine Belsey, *Critical Practice*, 2nd edn (London: Routledge, 2002), p. 4.
41   Greene, *The Light in Troy*, p. 33. Greene's quotation is from the dedication which accompanies Alexander Neville's translation of Seneca's *Oedipus* (1563).
42   George Puttenham, *The Arte of English Poetry*, ed. by Gladys Doidge Willcock and Alice Walker (Cambridge: Cambridge University Press, 1936), p. 59. Although Puttenham concentrates on the achievements of texts which are of the poets' own invention, it is significant that one translation which is commended is Arthur Golding's *Metamorphoses* (1567), p. 61.
43   Cited in Richard Foster Jones, *The Triumph of the English Language: A Survey of Opinions Concerning the Vernacular from the Introduction of Printing to the Restoration* (Stanford: Stanford University Press, 1953), p. 268, n. 72.
44   Paula Blank, *Broken English: Dialects and the Politics of Language in Renaissance Writings* (London: Routledge, 1996), p. 1.
45   Greene, *The Light in Troy*, p. 5.
46   Cave, *The Cornucopian Text*, p. 157.
47   Greene, *The Light in Troy*, p. 16.
48   Karl Galinsky has stated that 'the *Metamorphoses* cannot be properly understood without the realisation that they were meant to be Ovid's answer to V[i]rgil's *Aeneid*'. Karl Galinsky, *Ovid's 'Metamorphoses': An Introduction to the Basic Aspects* (Berkeley: University of California Press, 1975), p. 15. See further the excellent analysis by Stephen Hinds in his chapter entitled 'Repetition and Change' which takes careful account of the shifting relationship between the *Aeneid* and the *Metamorphoses*. Writers have often viewed Ovid as the subordinate term in this classical binarism; within a poststructuralist context, however, Hinds states that his 'mid-90's spin on this [relation] would be that Ovid is engaged in a tendentious poetic appropriation of his predecessor [...]. Rather than construct himself as an epigonal reader of the *Aeneid*, Ovid is constructing Virgil as a hesitant precursor of the *Metamorphoses*'. Stephen Hinds,

Allusion and Intertext: Dynamics of Appropriation in Roman Poetry (Cambridge: Cambridge University Press, 1998), p. 106.

[49] The last six books of the *Metamorphoses* clearly support this view of the whole work. As Leonard Barkan explains, 'the apotheosis of Hercules in book 9 prefigures a sequence of similar events in books 14 and 15, the apotheosis of Aeneas, Romulus and Julius Caesar, who were often identified with Hercules. The culminating figure is Augustus, whose apotheosis (15. 869–70) is inevitable but outside the poem's time span'. Leonard Barkan, *The Gods Made Flesh: Metamorphosis and the Pursuit of Paganism* (New Haven: Yale University Press, 1986), p. 83.

[50] Galinsky, *An Introduction*, p. 4.

[51] Galinsky, *An Introduction*, p. 4.

[52] Rita Copeland, *Rhetoric, Hermeneutics and Translation in the Middle Ages* (Cambridge: Cambridge University Press, 1991), p. 11.

[53] Horace, *Satires, Epistles, and Ars poetica*, ed. and trans. by H. Rushton Fairclough (Cambridge, Mass.: Harvard University Press, 1926), lines 285–8 cited in Copeland, *Rhetoric, Hermeneutics and Translation*, p. 29.

[54] Apuleius, *Metamorphoses*, trans. by J. Arthur Hanson (Cambridge: Harvard University Press, 1989), pp. 2–3. It is noteworthy that Adlington's translation removes the metaphor for translation that I discuss here.

[55] Sarah Annes Brown observes that '*The Golden Ass* would seem to be behind Bottom's metamorphosis in *A Midsummer Night's Dream*'. Sarah Annes Brown, '"There Is No End But Addition": The Latest Reception of Shakespeare's Classicism', in *Shakespeare and the Classics*, ed. by Charles Martindale and A. B. Taylor (Cambridge: Cambridge University Press, 2004), pp. 277–93, p. 288–9.

[56] Quotations from the Latin text are from *Ovid: The Metamorphoses*, trans. by Frank Justus Miller, rev. by G. P. Goold, 2 vols (London: Heinemann, 1984). All subsequent references to the *Metamorphoses* in the introduction refer to this translation.

[57] Quintilian, *Institutio oratoria*, trans. by H. E. Butler, 4 vols (London: Heinemann, 1920–2), 4.1.77.

[58] Andrew Feldherr, 'Metamorphosis in the *Metamorphoses*', in *The Cambridge Companion to Ovid*, ed. by Philip Hardie (Cambridge: Cambridge University Press, 2002), pp. 163–79, p. 169.

[59] A useful article on this subject is Wendy Olmsted, 'On the Margins of Otherness: Metamorphosis and Identity in Homer, Ovid, Sidney, and Milton', *New Literary History*, 27 (1996), 167–87.

[60] Calchas interpreted the omen of the snakes and birds at Aulis (12. 19 ff.). Mopsus is presented as the figure who killed Hodites, but he is also known as a seer (8. 316 ff.).

[61] Barkan, *The Gods Made Flesh*, p. 247. Alison Elliott also makes the point that 'Ovid tells many tales of failure of communication' and lists Io, Callisto, Pyramus and Thisbe, Actaeon, Philomena, Arachne and Orpheus as examples. Alison Goddard Elliott, 'Ovid and the Critics: Seneca, Quintilian and "Seriousness"', *Helios*, 12 (1985), 9–20.

[62] Callisto is changed into a bear and 'with constant moanings she shows her grief, stretches up such hands as are left her to the heavens' (2. 484–7; Ocyrhoë is transformed into a horse. As she changes, Ocyrhoë observes that 'the last part of her complaint became scarce understood and her words were all confused' (2. 665–6.).

[63] 2. 833 ff.; 4. 611; 5. 385 ff.; and 4. 798 respectively.

64   The tongue is an important emblem in the early modern period. Apart from Thomas Tomkis's play *Lingua* (1607), the use of the tongue in the representation of Rumour in the induction of Shakespeare's II *Henry IV* is noteworthy, so too is George Wither's emblem featuring 'the tongues unruly motion' (1635). For a stimulating argument focusing on the Erasmian treatise 'On the Use and Abuse of the Tongue' (1525), see Patricia Parker, 'On the Tongue: Cross-Gendering, Effeminacy and the Art of Words', *Style*, 23 (1989), 445–65. See also Carla Mazzio, 'Sins of the Tongue', in *The Body in Parts: Fantasies of Corporeality in Early Modern Europe*, ed. by David Hillman and Carla Mazzio (London: Routledge, 1997), pp. 53–80.

65   I am drawing here on an essay by Louise O. Fradenburg in which she discusses the image of the severed tongue in the twelfth-century *Sefer Zekirah*, *The Book of Remembrance*: 'The eloquent tongue, subjected to pain, now licks the dust, is now cut off; it is at once mutilated and reduced to embodiment, denied those physical movements that make the tongue something to speak with as well as to eat with, that make the tongue itself capable of the symbolic, the fictive, the creative: that make the tongue itself a subtle and shifting borderline between the body and its meanings'. Louise O. Fradenburg, 'Criticism, Anti–Semitism and the *Prioress's Tale'*, *Exemplaria*, 1 (1989), 69–115, 80.

66   Richard Lanham, *The Motives of Eloquence: Literary Rhetoric in the Renaissance* (New Haven: Yale University Press, 1976), p. 59.

67   Lanham, *The Motives of Eloquence*, p. 36.

68   Lanham, *The Motives of Eloquence*, p. 59.

69   Jacques Derrida, 'Des Tours de Babel', in *Difference in Translation*, trans. and ed. by Joseph F. Graham (Ithaca: Cornell University Press, 1985), pp. 165–207, p. 165.

70   See further Bassnett, *Translation Studies*, p. 15.

71   Arthur Golding, *The fyrst fower bookes of P. Ovidius Nasos worke, intitled Metamorphosis, translated into English meter* (London: 1565); *The xv. Bookes of P. Ovidius Naso, entytuled Metamorphosis, translated oute of Latin into English meeter.* (London: 1567).

72   Raphael Lyne, *Ovid's Changing Worlds: English Metamorphosis 1567–1632* (Oxford: Oxford University Press, 2001), p. 78.

73   Liz Oakley-Brown, 'Translating the Subject: Ovid's *Metamorphoses* in England 1560–7', in *Translation and Nation: Towards a Cultural Politics of Englishness*, ed. by Roger Ellis and Liz Oakley-Brown (Clevedon: Multilingual Matters, 2001), pp. 48–84, p. 80.

74   I am indebted to Rita Copeland's following observation: 'The *Ovide moralisé* has usually been read as a source for other texts, as an inert repository of information about the sources of "canonical" vernacular works, or at best as an instantiation of late mythographical interests'. Copeland, *Rhetoric, Hermeneutics and Translation in the Middle Ages*, p. 108.

75   For example, John Fyler, *Chaucer and Ovid* (New Haven: Yale University Press, 1979); Bruce Harbert, 'Lessons from the Great Clerk: Ovid and John Gower', in *Ovid Renewed: Ovidian Influences on Literature and Art from the Middle Ages to the Twentieth Century*, ed. by Charles Martindale (Cambridge: Cambridge University Press, 1988), pp.83–99; A. B. Taylor (ed.), *Shakespeare's Ovid: The 'Metamorphoses' in the Plays and Poems* (Cambridge: Cambridge University Press, 2000); Syrithe Pugh, *Spenser and Ovid* (Ashgate: Aldershot, 2005); Richard DuRocher, *Milton and Ovid* (Ithaca: Cornell University Press, 1979).

[76] Lee T. Pearcy, *The Mediated Muse: English Translations of Ovid 1560–1700* (Connecticut: Archon, 1984).

[77] Sarah Annes Brown, *The Metamorphosis of Ovid: From Chaucer to Ted Hughes* (London: Duckworth, 1999).

[78] Lyne, *Ovid's Changing Worlds*, p. 21.

[79] Lyne, *Ovid's Changing Worlds*, p. 21.

[80] Faust Ghisalberti, 'Medieval Biographies of Ovid', *Journal of the Warburg and Courtauld Institute*, 9 (1946), 10–59, 16.

[81] For a detailed discussion of traditions of medieval commentary on classical texts, see A. J. Minnis, *Medieval Theory of Authorship*, 2nd edn (Aldershot: Wildwood, 1988) and A. J. Minnis, A. B. Scott and D. Wallace (eds.), *Medieval Literary Theory and Criticism: Criticism c. 1100–c. 1375: The Commentary Tradition* (Oxford: Clarendon Press, 1988).

[82] For example, Thomas Peend, *The Pleasant Fable of Hermaphroditus and Salmacis with a Morall in English Verse* (London: 1565); Francis Beaumont, *Salmacis and Hermaphroditus* (London: 1602); Edward Sherburne, *Salmacis* (London: 1651); Joseph Addison, *The Story of Salmacis* (London: 1694). See further William Keach, *Elizabethan Erotic Narratives* (London: Harvester Press, 1977) and Sandra Clark (ed.), *Amorous Rites: Elizabethan Erotic Verse* (London: Dent, 1994).

[83] Thomas Hedley, *The Judgement of Midas* (London: 1552); John Lyly, *Gallathea. As it was playde before the Queenes Majestie at Greene-wiche, on Newyeeres day at Night. By the Chyldren of Paules* (London: 1592) and Charles Cotton, *Chaucer's Ghoast, or, a Piece of Antiquity. Containing twelve pleasant Fables of Ovid penn'd after the ancient manner of writing in England* (London: 1672). Cotton's text actually contains the following *ten* tales from the *Metamorphoses*: the myths of Pygmalion; Diana and Actaeon; Jupiter and Juno; Apollo and Coronis; Polyphemous and Galatea; the battle between Hercules and Achelous for the love of Deianira; Mars and Venus; Jupiter and Io; Leucothea and Pheobus and Calisto and Jupiter. As I was completing *Ovid and the Cultural Politics of Translation in Early Modern England*, Stuart Gillespie and Robert Cummings published an extremely useful catalogue which gives a sense of the range of interest in Ovidian translation. See Stuart Gillespie and Robert Cummings, 'A Bibliography of Ovidian Translations and Imitations in English', *Translation and Literature*, 13.2 (2004), 207–18.

[84] Charles Martindale (ed.), *Ovid Renewed: Ovidian Influences on Literature and Art from the Middle Ages to the Twentieth Century* (Cambridge: Cambridge University Press, 1988).

[85] Adam McKeown, '"Entreat her hear me but a word": Translation and Foreignness in *Titus Andronicus*', in *The Politics of Translation in the Middle Ages and Renaissance*, ed. by R. Blumenfeld-Kosinski, L. Von Flotow and Daniel Russell (Ottawa: University of Ottawa Press, 2001), pp. 203–18, p. 208.

[86] Christopher Martin, *Ovid in English* (London: Penguin, 1998), p. 1.

[87] Lyne, *Ovid's Changing Worlds*, p. 256.

[88] Valerie Traub, Afterword, in *Ovid and the Renaissance Body*, ed. by Goran V. Stanivukovic (Toronto: University of Toronto Press, 2001), pp. 260–8, p. 266.

[89] I am indebted to Eric Cheyfitz's comments regarding his negotiation of the Indian language and Native American culture. See further Eric Cheyfitz, *The Poetics of Imperialism: Translation and Colonialization from 'The Tempest' to 'Tarzan'* (Oxford: Oxford University Press, 1991), p. xv.

[90]   Cronin, *Translating Ireland*, p. 2.

[91]   For comment on this problem see the introductory passage of Franco Munari, *Catalogue of the MSS of Ovid's 'Metamorphoses'* (London: University of London, 1957), p. 1.

[92]   Whilst William MacIntyre's unpublished Ph.D thesis on Golding's version of the *Metamorphoses* states that the Latin source for the translation, the Regius–Micyllus text (1543), has been established, there is no certainty about the exact edition that Golding used. William Myron MacIntyre, 'A Critical Study of Golding's Translation of Ovid's *Metamorphoses*' (unpublished doctoral thesis, University of California, 1965), p. 15. Grundy Steiner asserts that his discussion of the relationship between the Regius-Micyllus text and Golding's Ovid is 'intended [...] only as the initial treatment of a single strain of source material. It is to be followed by a detailed study (now in preparation) of the bibliographic sources employed by Golding, in so far as they can be identified and recovered'. Grundy Steiner, 'Golding's Use of the Regius-Micyllus Commentary Upon Ovid', *The Journal of English and Germanic Philology*, 49 (1950), 317. To my knowledge, no such study has been completed.

[93]   Deborah Rubin states that she has 'compared all Latin passages [...] to those in the three editions Sandys claims to have used: Regius–Micyllus, Sabinus, and Pontanus', but she can only conclude that 'Sandys *probably* used the text of either Regius–Micyllus or Sabinus' [my emphasis]. Deborah Rubin, *Ovid's 'Metamorphoses Englished': George Sandys as Translator and Mythographer* (New York: Garland, 1985), pp. 178–9.

Chapter 1

Titus Andronicus and the
Sexual Politics of Translation

Staging Ovid

The vernacular translations of Ovid's *Metamorphoses* in early modern England are witness to ways in which 'the foreign text is inscribed with linguistic and cultural values that are intelligible to specific domestic constituencies'.[1] It is not only in the texts that these ideological inscriptions occur: 'the process [...] operates at every stage in the production, circulation and reception'.[2] However, in this chapter it is not a translation that I want to consider. Rather, I want to explore William Shakespeare's *The Most Lamentable Roman Tragedie of Titus Andronicus* (c. 1594) as an arena in which the construction and contestation of Elizabethan identities are violently dramatized.

Shakespeare's spectacularly tragic tale of *Titus Andronicus* occupies a significant place in terms of *Ovid and the Cultural Politics of Translation in Early Modern England*. Both temporally and textually, translation processes frame *Titus Andronicus*. Eugene Vance has written that:

> if translation in the Middle Ages and the Renaissance may be said by us to have a history, writers of those periods saw history itself as a process of translation: hence, the twin doctrines of *translatio imperii* and *translatio studii* in medieval and Renaissance culture.[3]

At the outset, the Roman context of *Titus Andronicus* responds to Renaissance concerns with *translatio imperii*. The play begins with 'the good Andronicus| Patron of virtue' (1. 1. 67–8)[4] returning from war against the 'barbarous Goths' (1. 1. 28), bringing their Queen Tamora, her sons, Alarbus, Chiron, Demetrius, together with Aaron, the 'barbarous Moor' (2. 2. 78), as prisoners. Indeed, the adjective used to describe Rome's Others in the opening Acts is a resonant word in both *Titus Andronicus* and for my argument here. Meaning 'a foreigner, one whose language and customs differ from the speaker's', the term 'barbarous' is inscribed with Elizabethan concerns regarding nationhood and linguistic difference.[5] But it is the onstage appearance of a printed copy of Ovid's poem which throws these issues of nation, language and gender into relief. Adam McKeown has stated that 'not enough critical work has explored the tension surrounding the strange cameo of "Ovid's *Metamorphosis*."'[6] I want to develop this astute observation by suggesting that the play's material invocation of a poem so thoroughly concerned with the transformation of identity initiates a particular interrogation of Elizabethan notions of 'self' and 'other'.

In doing so, the following argument engages with a series of debates which are interested in Shakespeare and translation,[7] most obviously McKeown's essay on 'Translation and Foreignness in *Titus Andronicus.*'[8] This article traverses my own analysis of the play, most notably in its acknowledgement that 'translation, both of language and culture, emerges in *Titus* [...] appropriate to an England that was aggressively but anxiously fashioning a global presence and emulating the continental Renaissance'.[9] The first ten years or so of Elizabeth's reign, as William MacIntyre has observed, produced the greatest number of translations of the century.[10] To be sure, particularly in the early years of Elizabethan England, translation functioned in an iconoclastic environment and the textual strategies employed by translators perform a major role in the reformation of Christian frames of signification.[11] In June 1559, eight months after her accession, Elizabeth issued a set of injunctions to the 'loving subjects' of England for the 'suppression of superstition' and 'to plant a true religion':[12]

> to the intent that all superstition and hypocrisy crept into men's hearts may vanish away, they shall not set faith or extol any images, relics or miracles, for any superstition or lucre, nor allure the people by any enticements, to the pilgrimage of any saint or image, but reproving the same, they shall teach that all goodness, health and grace ought to be asked and looked for only [of] God, as the very author and giver of the same, and none other.[13]

As a result, Elizabethan translators rewrote source texts according to the ideological perspectives of the target audience,[14] and the overwhelming project of translation as it was presented in the printed texts of this time was one which sought to confront particular systems of signification so as to take newly Protestant England out of alignment with Catholic Rome.

According to Warren Boutcher, in the sixteenth century 'translation [was] the exercise at the core of a wide programme of applied learning in a variety of adjacent subjects. This programme is usually referred to as humanism, and its teachers as humanists.'[15] The 'programme' that Boutcher identifies, however, goes beyond the pedagogical confines of the Elizabethan classroom. For a nation that was intent on making its presence visible to the rest of the world, the forging of national identity through and in translation had far-reaching, and markedly violent, implications. As Patricia Palmer has discussed at length in her study of early modern Ireland, England's first colony, 'the relationship between linguistic sentiment and Elizabethan nationalism is complex. Insecurity jostled with linguistic ambition in shaping the Elizabethans' edgy assertiveness.'[16] The quotation from George Puttenham's *Arte of English Poesie* (1589) examined in the Introduction which sets up 'bare translation' against 'invention', for example, arguably expresses the very type of 'edginess' that Palmer mentions. But, as she insightfully explains:

The tentative stirrings of both linguistic and colonial ambitions worked together to build mutually enforcing chauvinisms. Writer-colonialists are not anomalous but exemplary figures: military and linguistic muscle flexed as one to a remarkable degree.[17]

These 'linguistic and colonial ambitions' are clearly evident in texts such as George Sandys's *Metamorphosis Englished* (1632), the translation which is the focus of Chapter 3. Yet Palmer's palpable descriptions of language and ideology are also inscribed in Shakespeare's plays. As the later historical plays such as I and II *Henry IV* and *Henry V* consider more openly, Shakespearean drama often shows translation to be a necessary part of the subjection into English.[18] These same ideological impulses are apparent in *Titus Andronicus*, but in less obvious ways.

Engendering Ovid

It is apparent from its opening declaration, 'of shapes transformde to bodyes strange,| I purpose to entreate' that the *Metamorphoses* is concerned with transgression.[19] Through some 220 myths,[20] framed in an overarching narrative which tells the history of Rome from its beginnings in primeval chaos to the apotheosis of Augustus,[21] the concatenations of the poem move through a breathtaking consideration of ways in which a multiplicity of boundaries – national, gendered, generic – are formed and dismantled. The importance of the relationship between the Elizabethans and Ovid is witnessed some thirty years before the first recorded performance of *Titus Andronicus*, in 1594,[22] with the first Ovidian myth to be published in Elizabethan England, the anonymous *The Fable of Ovid Treting of Narcissus, translated into Englysh mytre, with a moral there unto* (1560). From the perspective of a twenty-first-century, post-Lacanian, reader, Narcissus is always already associated with the dissembling effects of desire upon the subject. As I have argued elsewhere,[23] the initial translation and publication of the *Metamorphoses* in English just two years after the accession of Elizabeth I negotiates the construction of the subject in a way that anticipates certain theoretical positions of modern subjectivity – think of Freud's 'On Narcissism'; think of Lacan's construction of subjectivity by way of the famous episode of the 'mirror stage' where the subject enters the realm of language, the symbolic – and that also signals a clear break from the past.[24] Thus, in its translation of this archetypal myth of the fragmented self, the *Fable of Narcissus* articulates the cultural anxieties of the newly reformed Elizabethan. The complex syntax and often awkward metre of the *Fable of Narcissus* delineates the translator's efforts to render Ovid's Latin poem into the burgeoning English language with the coherence that Arthur Golding would achieve just five years later in *The fyrst fower bookes of P. Ovidius Nasos worke, intitled Metamorphosis, translated into English meter* (1565).[25] Gordon Braden has argued that the 1560 text is 'almost literally unreadable';[26] it is this linguistic labour which aligns the anonymous translator with characters from Ovid's poem.

'Many of the great figures of Ovid's poem', as Leonard Barkan has discussed at length, 'define themselves by their struggle to invent new languages'.[27] As we saw in the Introduction, the Latin word *lingua* can be rendered both as 'tongue' and as 'language'.[28] One of the most cruel incidents in the *Metamorphoses* takes place in book 6 as Tereus attempts to conceal the rape of his sister-in-law by cutting out her tongue. The severity of Tereus's violation is exacerbated through the personification of Philomela's tongue which, metonymically, displaces her body:

> [...] the cruell Tyrant came,
> And with a payre of pinsons fast did catch hir by the tung,
> And with his sword did cut it off. The stumpe whereon it hung
> Did patter still. The tip fell downe, and quivering on the ground
> As though that it had murmured it made a certaine sound.
> And as an Adders tayle cut off doth skip a while: even so
> The tip of *Philomelaas* tongue did wriggle to and fro,
> And nearer to hir mistressward in dying still did go.[29]

With its vivid, yet intimate, depiction of a brutal glossectomy, Bate suggests that this Ovidian episode offers a 'literalisation of the separation of character and language'.[30] Famously, it is this myth that is an important intertext in *Titus Andronicus*.[31] Philomela's tongue, so graphically rendered in the *Metamorphoses*, however, is a silent but significant trace in Shakespeare's play.[32] Barkan explains that:

> The Tereus story attracts Shakespeare because it is centrally concerned with communication. Ovid's Philomela engages in a lengthy tirade after she has been assaulted. Tereus mutilates her to shut her up. She must then convey her message in a tapestry. At the end of her life she is transformed into a nightingale, the very exemplar of beautiful, sad music. So it is not only a myth about communication: it is also a myth about the competition amongst media of communication as Philomela becomes a walking representative of them.[33]

As these comments make clear, the myth extends its interest in textuality beyond language. Ultimately, Philomela is a site for the violent interplay of various systems of signification and it is these aspects of the myth which are explored and dramatized on the Renaissance stage.

In their rape and further mutilation of Lavinia, Demetrius and Chiron seem implicitly aware of Ovid's tale. However, it is Marcus who alerts the audience to the importance of this myth. As a response to the severed body of his niece he announces, 'But sure some Tereus hath deflowered thee| And, lest thou shoulds't detect him, cut thy tongue' (2. 3. 26–27). Lavinia's abuse far exceeds that of Ovid's tragic figure for 'A craftier Tereus [...] hath cut those pretty fingers off,| That could have better sewed than Philomel' (2. 3. 41–43). Indeed, the play's representation of Lavinia's brutal rape and its aftermath extends the examination of power, communication and violence found in its classical precedent. From the moment that Marcus witnesses her disfigurement in Act 2, 'her hands cut off, and her tongue cut out, and ravished' (2. 3), he attempts to make sense of, and sense for, the figure that stands before him. He asks:

Who is this [...]?
Shall I speak for thee? Shall I say 'tis so? (2. 3. 11–33)

Raped and dismembered, Lavinia has been violently fashioned into a problematic sign. Now, she functions as an ontological enigma and this becomes a matter of debate for the male characters who surround her. By announcing to Titus that 'This was thy daughter' (3. 1. 63) Marcus shows how Lavinia oscillates between the virtuous subject of daughter and violated object that defies nomenclature. While Titus insists on her position as his daughter ('so she is', 3. 1. 64), Lavinia's problematic subjectivity is further betrayed as other delineations move from sister to martyr (3. 1. 82; 3. 1. 108),[34] before finally resting on descriptions that emphasize her familial relationship to the men; 'wretched sister' (3. 1. 138) and 'dear niece' (3. 1. 139).

Almost as chilling as the physical atrocities dealt out by the Goths is the displacement of Lavinia's suffering. Instead of dwelling upon the dismembered body of the woman, the play's focus turns to Lucius as he states 'this object kills *me*' (3. 1. 65, my emphasis).[35] To be sure, Titus immediately demands that 'Faint-hearted' Lucius 'arise and look upon her' (3. 1. 66) and he later exclaims 'Look, Marcus, ah, son, Lucius, look on her!' (3. 1. 111). Nevertheless, Titus, Lucius and Marcus continually render Lavinia in, and on, their terms. Marcus's initial reaction to her physical abuse, slowly revealed to him in Act 2, is illustrative of the way in which Lavinia's haemorrhaging body mobilizes a rhetorical display:

> Alas, a crimson river of warm blood,
> Like to a bubbling fountain stirred with wind,
> Doth rise and fall between thy rosed lips,
> Coming and going with thy honey breath. (2. 3. 22–5)

For the past thirty years or so, many readings of *Titus Andronicus*, from a range of theoretical positions, have discussed its preoccupation with semiotics.[36] However, by analysing the play specifically within the context of Elizabethan translation, another facet of Shakespearean concerns with the politics of language becomes visible. In order to negotiate the disfigured, 'othered' body of Lavinia, once described as 'Rome's rich ornament' (1. 1. 55), Marcus employs the rhetorical device of *translatio*: 'the figure by means of which, more than any other, language sought to cope with the experience of the new, the unfamiliar, the Other'.[37] As the drama develops, the trope of *translatio* is explored in detail, most notably in the physical appearance of a book that Elizabethan translators used in their attempts to both master and improve the vernacular language. Crucially, Ovid's *Metamorphoses* makes its entrance as Act 4 opens:

> Enter Lucius's son, and Lavinia running after him, and the boy flies from her with his books under his arm. (4. 1)

In one sense, the pursuit dramatized by Lucius's son and Lavinia, an Ovidian trope in itself, is emblematic of the way in which Ovid's Latin poem is textually elusive.[38] William Keach has explained that 'lascivia is the word which Quintilian uses to characterise the art of Ovid',[39] and the various definitions of the Latin word, 'sportiveness', 'playfulness', 'wantonness' and 'lewdness', are suggestive of the rhetorical, poetical and ideological matrix that the *Metamorphoses* presents to both readers and translators.[40] Still, it is Ovid's artful poem, so far un-named, that will assist Lavinia in her strenuous attempts to communicate her rape and mutilation at the hands of Demetrius and Chiron.

The association of Lavinia with the term 'ornament' in the opening act shows how *Titus Andronicus* repeatedly calls into question, often ironically, the relationship between women, oratory and rhetoric:

> [...] Cornelia never with more care
> Read to her sons than she hath read to thee
> Sweet poetry and Tully's *Orator*. (4. 1. 12–14)

As Lavinia struggles to explain the details of her rape, Marcus emphasizes his niece's lack: she cannot speak like Cornelia, the Roman mother celebrated for the educative instruction of her sons.[41] Brutally denied the linguistic and gestural means which enable the humanistic ideal of rhetoric, as J. L. Simmons has suggested, Lavinia 'comes almost to represent a violated Lady Rhetorica'.[42] It is at this point in *Titus Andronicus* that the sexual politics of humanist education are brought sharply into focus. Indeed, it is the explicit configuration of Ovid's poem with Lavinia which proves to be such an arresting image in the play.

In *Shakespeare and Ovid,* Bate argues that

> by virtue of their reading and imitation of Ovid and classical authors, the characters in the play come to resemble students in grammar school and university. The language of the schoolroom suffuses the play – characters keep coming up with remarks like 'Handle not the theme' [Titus: 3. 2. 29], 'I'll teach thee' [Titus: 4. 1. 119], 'I was their tutor to instruct them' [Aaron: 5. 1. 98], and 'well has thou lessoned us' [Tamora: 5. 2. 110]; they also refer to key educational texts such as Tully's *Orator* [Marcus: 4. 1. 14].[43]

These are judicious observations. In moving the play from its Latin context to its Renaissance performance, however, Bate's analysis neglects the sexual politics of translation in the early modern period: grammar schools and universities were gendered spaces. The *Metamorphoses* was frequently employed in the grammar schools in order to teach boys the basic linguistic aspects of Latin,[44] but women were taught Latin in often very different circumstances. When Bate states that 'like a schoolchild, Lavinia reads from her Ovid and then writes her text: '*Stuprum–Chiron–Demetrius* (4. 1. 77)',[45] her actions are more common for a boy than a young girl. Within this specific sexual/ textual political arena, it is telling that it is a boy of grammar school age, Titus's grandson, who identifies Lavinia's text as 'Ovid's *Metamorphosis*;| My mother gave it me' (4. 1. 42).[46] Though Titus informs the audience that Lavinia 'is deeper read and better skilled' (4. 1. 33) than her nephew, in terms of the sexual politics of translation this seemingly chance remark by the youth evokes a less familiar history of the transmission of Ovid's myths in England. Geoffrey Chaucer's 'Maunciples Tale of the Crowe', for instance, features an episode from the *Metamorphoses* (2. 569 ff.) which is taught to the narrator by his mother: 'But as I seyde, I am nought textueel.| But natheless, thus taughte me my dame'.[47] So it is not just the text but the person who *comments* on the text which becomes a matter of great moment in Shakespeare's play.

The explicit association of woman with both the Latin language and Ovid's text in *Titus Andronicus* is in distinct contrast with the history of textual production which emphasizes the male translators of the *Metamorphoses*. As the title of Sarah Annes Brown's book, *The Metamorphosis of Ovid: From Chaucer to Ted Hughes*, suggests, it is men who are publicly acknowledged as translators of the *Metamorphoses*; this is especially the case in early modern England. Gently-born and bourgeois women were classically educated and functioned as translators, but the texts that they produced were most often of a religious nature, not secular.[48] In *A very fruitfull and pleasant booke, called the Instruction of a Christian Woman*, for example, Jean Luis Vives castigates the author that Lavinia employs:

> Plato casteth out of the common wealth of wise men, which he made, Homer and Hesiodus, the Poets: and yet have they none ill thing in comparison unto Ovid's bookes of love which we reade, and carry them in our handes, and learn them by heart; yea and some school masters teach them to their schollars and some make expositions and expound the vices. Augustus banished Ovid himself, and think you then that hee would have kept these expositours in the country [...].[49]

Vives's perspective is apparently inscribed in the first complete published version of Golding's *Metamorphoses* (1567). As exemplified in Golding's general preface, readers may be addressed according to their social position and gender:

> Yit (gentle Reader) I doo trust my travell in this cace
> May purchace favour in thy sight my dooings to embrace:
> Considring what a sea of goodes and Jewelles thou shalt fynd,
> Not more delyghtfull too the ear than frutefull too the mynd.
> For this doo lerned persons deeme, of Ovids present woorke:
> That in no one of all his bookes, the which he wrate, do lurke
> Mo darke and secret misteries, mo counselles wyse and sage,
> Mo good ensamples, mo reprooves of vyce in youth and age,
> Mo fyne inventions too delight, mo matters clerkly knit,
> No nor more straunge varietie to show a lerned wit.
> The high, the lowe: the riche, the poore: the mayster, and the slave:
> The mayd, the wife: the man, the chyld: the simple and the brave:
> The yoong, the old: the good, the bad: the warriour strong and stout:
> The wyse, the foole: the countrie cloyne: the lerned and the lout,
> And every other living wight shall in this mirrour see
> His whole estate, thoughtes, woordes and deedes expresly showed too bee.[50]

As this extract shows, however, women are offered the limited spaces of either 'mayd' or 'wyf', social positions which define them against their relationships to men. Some women are figured positively. In Golding's epistle to his patron, the Earl of Leicester, for example, the chaste 'Daphnee turnd to Bay| A myrror of virginitie' and the 'fayre Polyxena' who 'dooth show a princely mynd| And firme regard of honour rare engraft in woman kind' are invoked.[51] However, the general preface fashions the woman reader in a specific way:

> If any stomacke be so weake as that it cannot brooke,
> The lively setting forth of things described in this booke,
> I give him counsell too absteine untill he bee more strong,
> And for too use *Ulysses* feat ageinst the Meremayds song.[52]

Raphael Lyne believes that this image is a 'comical one: it comes close to saying, if you cannot approach this work properly, than avoid it'.[53] Humorous though it may be, this prefatory material also incites the reader's desire for the ensuing narrative; by aligning the reader with the wise Ulysses, by extension, the poem becomes a Siren-like feminized site of seduction.[54] In this textual scenario, the translator's consent 'to give *him* counsell too absteine untill *he* bee more strong' [my emphasis]' from the fearful episodes ahead seems ample proof that women are not the addressees of this translation. Quite plainly, the implied 'gentle reader' of Golding's Ovid is a man.

With the words of both Vives and Golding in mind, it is worth noting that Lavinia is not left alone with any books in public. In Act 3, Titus escorts his daughter to a specific place in order to read: 'I'll to thy closet and go read with thee| Sad stories chanced in the times of old' (3. 2. 83–4). In his edition of *Titus Andronicus* Bate glosses 'closet' as a 'private room'.[55] However, as Alan Stewart demonstrates, early modern closets are 'constructed as a place of utter privacy, of total withdrawal from the public sphere of the household – but [they] simultaneously function as a very *public* gesture of withdrawal, a very public sign of privacy'.[56] By announcing that he will escort Lavinia to her closet, Titus makes just this type of 'public gesture', significantly, in relation to women and the act of reading. The line is intriguing as it leaves much open to conjecture. Is Titus going to read *to* her or *with* her? What books are they going to read? Nevertheless, the episode dramatizes a common view of woman's humanist education where learning takes place at home with the father, and Titus's address to Lavinia draws further attention to the play's concerns with gender, textual production and censorship.

Orthodox patriarchal attitudes to Ovid notwithstanding, early modern women had access to the *Metamorphoses*. The name of Tamesyn Audeley, written in a seventeenth-century hand, is inscribed in the margins of the only extant manuscript of Caxton's translation of Ovid's poem,[57] and Anne Clifford notes in her diary that she and her 'coz' have been reading from Ovid's text.[58] Louise Schleiner perceives that one of 'Englishwomen's favourite writings and modes of discourse to echo, tease into their texts, or handle revisionistically' was 'Ovid (the *Metamorphoses*, *Heroides* and the *Amores* in translation)'.[59] But the information that Schleiner places in parenthesis is important. Firstly, each different Ovidian text has a distinctive vernacular reception and genealogy. Although not as contentious as the erotic poems of the *Amores*, translations of the *Metamorphoses* are a precarious project for a woman to undertake. Secondly, Schleiner's bracketed comments point to the very relationship between women and Ovid's text that I have been discussing here. Women, she suggests, are readers of translations; they are not translators. Somewhat differently, *Titus Andronicus* offers an important exploration of the construction of the gendered subject through and in translation.

According to Bate, the role of Titus

> is to translate [Lavinia's] gestures into language, to read, interpret, and transform into speech the 'map of woe' that is her body: 'But I of these will wrest an alphabet,| And by still practice learn to know thy meaning' (3. 2. 44–5).[60]

Eventually, Lavinia manages to turn to 'the tragic tale of Philomel' which 'treats of Tereus' treason and his rape' (4. 1. 47–8) and it is a brief moment where her agency is restored. Lavinia's strenuous performance is dramatically marked by Marcus, 'See brother, see: note how she quotes the leaves' (4. 1. 50), and she elicits an inquisitive response from the surrounding colloquy. As she surrounds herself with the books, Marcus and Titus ask respectively 'What means my niece Lavinia by these signs?' (4. 1. 8) and 'How now, Lavinia? Marcus, what means this?' (4. 1. 30). Although she cannot speak for herself, Ovid's poem enables Lavinia to disrupt the assured and authorial rhetoric of her family, literally and figuratively, as she 'tosseth' (4. 1. 41) the book onto the stage. Once mobilized as reader, Lavinia's combative stance is further developed in the play. Indeed, instead of leaving Titus as a kind of 'translator general',[61] I want to argue that *Titus Andronicus* initiates the notion of Lavinia as a translator herself.

In their Roman context it is hardly surprising that Latin is employed by the figures on the stage. On the one hand, this scene reminds the audience of the elevated, educated status of the Andronici. On the other hand, however, there is a rather different cultural interrogation at work in *Titus Andronicus* which is concerned with the sexual politics of translation in sixteenth-century England. Once Lavinia 'quotes' from the *Metamorphoses* and, more like Io than Philomela,[62] 'takes the staff in her mouth, and guides it with her stumps', Titus informs the audience of the Latin denunciation that she writes on the ground:

Stuprum – Chiron – Demetrius (4. 1. 78)

D. J. Palmer is of the opinion that the word *stuprum* 'does not conceal the horrid deed in the decent obscurity of a dead language, but rather, like Caesar's "Et tu Brute" it gives a sudden actuality to the dramatic moment'.[63] Ideologically, however, there is more to Lavinia's use of Latin than theatrical emphasis. Instead of employing 'a dead language', when Lavinia turns to Ovid and then writes *stuprum* she momentarily possesses certain skills of the kind acquired through humanist education programmes of the time. Significantly, Titus responds to Lavinia's display of Latin with his own:

> *Magni dominator poli,*
> *Tam lentus audis scelera, tam lentus vides?* (4. 1. 81–2)

This quotation from Seneca's *Phaedra* places Titus in a brief contest with Lavinia:[64] a contest which began with the interpretation of Lavinia's corporeal signs which has now moved to the scene of writing. Like the classical model which is so resonant in this play, the move from Lavinia's body to Lavinia's text is suggestive of the complex way in which 'Ovid uses stories about bodily violation to dramatize language's vicissitudes'.[65] Titus attempts to regain control by replacing Lavinia's transient writing with a permanent inscription:

> [...] I will go get a leaf of brass,
> And with a gad of steel will write these words,
> And lay it by. The angry northern wind
> Will blow these sands like Sibyl's leaves abroad,
> And where's our lesson then? [...] (4. 1. 102–6)

His position of textual control is restored, but, as the tentative mode introduced by the question at the end of this quotation implies, a fissure remains in his authority.

If further evidence is needed that *Titus Andronicus* is interested in the cultural politics of translation, the figure of Aaron is worth consideration. In 'Making More of the Moor: Aaron, Othello, and Renaissance Refashionings of Race', Emily Bartels convincingly argues that whilst 'Renaissance representations of the Moor were vague, varied, inconsistent, and contradictory [...] he was nonetheless described as Other'.[66] With the figure of Aaron, Bartels continues, Shakespeare's play 'promotes the darkest vision of the stereotype'.[67] Henry Peacham's famed sketch from *Titus Andronicus* (c. 1595) confirms that, by and large, Aaron's initial difference is emphasized through colour; in performance he is described as a 'swart Cimmerian' (2. 2. 72) and a 'raven–coloured love' (2. 2. 83). Related to this staging of blackness are primarily classical and Christian precepts which help to construct Aaron as 'barbarous Moor' (2. 2. 78), but variable Renaissance discourses converge to make the colour black signify the 'mark of damnation', demonization and eroticization.[68] Yet the Moor that Shakespeare offers is even more complex than he first seems.

In the notes to his edition of *Titus Andronicus*, Bate observes that 'an Elizabethan audience would have known that the biblical Aaron had an eloquent, persuasive tongue'.[69] The 'brief table of the interpretation of the proper names which are chiefly found in the Olde Testament' that accompanies the Geneva Bible as an appendix describes Aaron in Exodus 4. 14 as 'a teacher' develops Bate's note in more detail; this is an intertextual link which alludes to the role that Aaron adopts in this play. It is also noteworthy that Aaron's immediate function is to act as a mediator between Moses, 'slow of speech and slow of tongue' (Exodus 4. 10), and the people. As Moses's intermediary, then, the biblical Aaron is far more than merely eloquent and persuasive, and this genealogy has ramifications for understanding Shakespeare's portrayal of Aaron in *Titus Andronicus* as a dissembling figure, aggressively flaunting his textual dexterity.

With much of his performance taking the form of a soliloquy, Aaron is often shown in alienation from both Romans and Goths. His authorial position is depicted most clearly in the scene which immediately follows the invocation of the *Metamorphoses* in 4. 1. At this point of the play, Titus has sent arrows enveloped with Horatian quotations to Chiron and Demetrius:

Demetrius: What's here? A scroll, and written round about?
                Let's see:
                Integer vitae, scelerisque purus,
                Non egat Mauri iaculis, nec arcu.
Chiron: O, 'tis a verse in Horace; I know it well:
                I read it in the grammar long ago. (4. 2. 18–23)

The Latin lines translate as 'the man who is upright in life and free from crime does not need the javelins or bow of the Moor' and was known in the Renaissance from its use in Lily's Latin Grammar.[70] The combination of Horatian Ode and the arrow, as Heather James comments, is 'quite literally, a barbed allusion'.[71] In an accompanying aside to the audience in which he announces that Demetrius and Chiron possess the knowledge of 'an ass' (4. 2. 25), Aaron makes it clear that the ability to merely recognize a verse from Horace is not a mark of a decent education. By contrast with Tamora's sons, Aaron is able to interpret the significance of the sign and render its meaning closely and his greater textual understanding figures in the shape–shifting roles he adopts in the play.[72] Aaron has previously been shown in a hierarchical system of binaries where he is overtly Other. Now, as Aaron greets his child and his violent predilections are displaced by words of tenderness, that system is disrupted:

[...] is black so base a hue?
Sweet blowze, you are a beauteous blossom, sure. (4. 2. 73–4)

Aaron's villainous qualities are confounded in this address to his son; as he describes himself as 'a mountain lioness' (4. 2. 140) a few lines later, Aaron turns fixed demarcations of gender difference. From his name, which serves as a reminder of the biblical mediator, to his textually disruptive function in the *Titus Andronicus*, Aaron extends the trope of translation that is so deeply embedded in *Titus Andronicus*. His ability to undermine meaning in language, however, cannot be allowed free rein, and at the end of the play Aaron is markedly 'fastened in the earth' (5. 3. 182).[73]

Beyond the stage, moreover, a further translative contest is taking place. With Latin quotation a prominent feature of Shakespeare's play, it seems relevant to question the ability of the audience to understand what is being said. As Andrew Gurr has pointed out, it is notoriously difficult to ascertain with any certainty the 'mental range' of the Elizabethan audience:

The mental composition of any playgoer must have varied according to an enormous complex of factors, ranging from the physical condition of the playgoer's feet or stomach, or the hat worn by the playgoer in front, to the hearer's familiarity with

Ovid or Holinshed. Education, taste in reading, the contrasting social and political allegiances of blue apron and flat cap culture against the court gallants and law students, all influenced the kind of play written for the different playhouses and must to some extent therefore reflect at least the poets' and players' expectations of their customers.[74]

The relationship between the action on stage and the audience is further complicated when other issues of the play's stage history are considered. From the work of G. Harold Metz it is known that the play was widely performed, both in amphitheatre playhouses such as the Rose and in private performance, indicating a somewhat varied social background for those who may have seen *Titus Andronicus*.[75] Nevertheless, even without precise knowledge of the playgoers' 'mental composition', in a play that begins with Saturninus and Bassianus quibbling over the meaning of 'rape',[76] when Lavinia writes *stuprum* in the sand it is a pivotal moment for those watching *Titus Andronicus*. The Latin word remains untranslated and the monolingual member of the audience, in particular, relies on an understanding *stuprum* which is problematically mediated via the men that surround Lavinia.

Accordingly, Emily Detmer-Goebel has explored the importance of fully interpreting the Latinate term: 'just as Lavinia's relatives have trouble seeing her as a source of knowledge, editors of the play fail to look closely at Lavinia's words'.[77] Detmer-Goebel continues her discussion by showing how the semantic value for the Latinate word is so much greater than its vernacular counterpart. With acuity, her argument moves to consider how the word '*stuprum*' marks a clear departure from the Ovidian tale of Philomela. 'Stuprum', according to Detmer-Goebel, is 'only used once in the *Metamorphoses*, in book 2, the story of Callisto':

> Callisto, a member of Diana's chaste group of women, was raped by Jove, who had assumed the form of Diana. Callisto does not tell anyone of her rape, but her 'uncleanliness' is revealed by her pregnancy [...]. As the story goes, Juno, the wife of the rapist, becomes enraged by the injury done to her bed, and calls Callisto 'Stupri' as if calling her 'whore'. Early modern dictionaries do indeed define 'stuprum' as 'rape'. Yet [...] Shakespeare's use of 'stuprum' rather than 'raptus' calls the reader's attention to yet another Ovidian rape and allows us to surmise that Lavinia does more than identify the crime.[78]

Certainly, Lavinia achieves more than this. As she becomes a conflation of Io, Callisto and Philomela, all of whom are Ovidian heroines who articulate the 'failure of communication',[79] Lavinia seems to demonstrate a fairly detailed knowledge of the Latin *Metamorphoses*. Some critics, such as Eve Rachele Sanders, propose that 'Lavinia's reading is important because it exposes the fact of her rape'.[80] But as Detmer-Goebel's thesis illustrates, this scene does not show the 'fact' of her rape. Rather than showing that Lavinia is successful at reading, the dramatic episode suggests that she is capable of close textual analysis and, importantly, that she can critically use Latin. Further, as the play points to Lavinia's translative abilities, *Titus Andronicus* simultaneously reveals the men's failure at translation and exegesis of the Ovidian text.

Erasing Ovid

The sexual politics at stake in Shakespeare's play are further emphasized when compared to Edward Ravenscroft's seventeenth-century revision, *Titus Andronicus, or the Rape of Lavinia* (first performed 1678; first published 1687).[81] Ravenscroft's drama, produced in a cultural moment that had a very different regard for the classics, makes significant changes to the play. As Ravenscroft explains in the preface to the reader which accompanies the published text, these alterations are necessary because Shakespeare's *Titus Andronicus*

> seems rather a heap of Rubbish than a Structure.— However as is some great Building had been design'd, in the removal we found many Large and Square Stones both usefull and Ornamental to the Fabrick, as now Modell'd: Compare the Old Play with this, you'l finde that none in all that Authors Works ever receiv'd greater Alterations or Additions, the Language not only refin'd, but many Scenes entirely New: Besides most of the principal Characters heighten'd, and the Plot much encreas'd.[82]

Like Dryden's preface to *All for Love: or, The World Well Lost* (1678), in which he discusses Shakespearean adaptation as excavation (under 'that heap of Rubbish' he managed to find that 'many excellent thoughts lay wholly buried'),[83] Ravenscroft makes much of his restorative work. However, explicit reference to the Latin language and ancient texts in *Titus Andronicus, or the Rape of Lavinia* are erased. As John W. Velz observes 'the direct quotation of *Metamorphoses* 1. 150 at *Titus Andronicus* 4. 3. 4 ("*Terras Astrea reliquit*") is paraphrased in English, and two prominent Philomela allusions [2. 4. 38–43 and 4. 1.1–58 ...] are pruned away'.[84] Given its prominence in Shakespeare's play, it is the absence of the 'strange cameo' of Ovid's book itself that is most conspicuous.

In keeping with contemporaneous political interests of its seventeenth-century audience, the title of Ravenscroft's revision clearly moves audience attention from the tragedy of Titus to the rape of Lavinia: a focus which is sustained in Act 1.[85] By contrast with her Elizabethan counterpart, for example, Lavinia makes her initial entrance apart from her brothers and following A[a]ron's lines which anticipate her plight: 'With like Successful minutes, to requite| These bloody wrongs and Roman Injuries' (1. 2. sig. B 3ʳ). Whilst Lavinia's physical abuse is emphasized, the textual agency of the Restoration Lavinia is greatly diminished throughout the play.

When Saturninus announces his intention to marry the Andronici woman, Shakespeare's audience receive an important dialogue. The Roman Emperor asks 'Lavinia, you are not displeased with this?' (1. 1. 274), to which she responds:

> Not I, my lord, sith true nobility
> Warrants these words princely courtesy. (1. 1. 275– 6)

In the later version, Lavinia is not asked her opinion and she remains silent. Instead, Ravenscroft's Emperor addresses her thus:

> Come *Lavinia*, thou Trophee of the day,
> And utmost height of all our joys, for thee
> Altars shall be perfum'd with richest Gums,
> And Hymens Tapors there shall Blaze;
> Slowly you give your Hand, and Trembling Move,
> Art thou not so fond of Empire or afraid of Love? (1. 3. sig. C 1ʳ)

Lavinia's silence, a conventional sign of chastity, draws attention to her virginal status and ensures that the ensuing rape and mutilation are more violently spectacular. But her silence also serves to legitimize Bassianus's actions as he seizes Lavinia: 'See Friends what Longing Eyes she casts this way,| And with her sad looks upbraids my servile tameness' (1. 3. sig. C 1ʳ). What is most striking about Ravenscroft's adaptation, then, is that even before she has her tongue cut out the men begin to speak for Lavinia. The Emperor reads Lavinia's fear as she trembles; Bassianus her desire and sadness; and, finally, Titus implores them to see that his daughter is not party to Bassianus's treachery: 'My Lord, see you not Lavinia is surpriz'd? ' (1. 3. C 1ʳ). Ravenscroft's refiguring of Lavinia as a chaste and silent woman continues to the point of her rape. Shakespeare, on the other hand, presents a feisty Lavinia who uses a sexualized discourse in response to Tamora:

> 'Tis thought you have a goodly gift in horning,
> And to be doubted that your Moor and you
> Are singled forth to try experiments. (2. 2. 67–9)

By contrast, Ravenscroft transposes the central tenet of these lines to Bassianus ('Why are you singl'd forth from all your Train| And here retir'd to an obscure place —| Accompany'd but with a Barabarous Moor,| Unless to try Experiments?' (3. 1. sig. D 2ᵛ)), thus removing Lavinia's association with carnal knowledge. The result of these revisions is that the binary opposition between Tamora and Lavinia that is somewhat blurred in Shakespeare's play becomes more sharply focused in Ravenscroft's adaptation.

The difference between the two women is most obvious in the ways in which Tamora's garrulity is developed. Throughout the history of Western patriarchy, woman's outspokenness, often associated with a perceived unruly sexuality, is kept in check.[86] On the Restoration stage this censorship is obviously evident in Lavinia's mutilation, but *Titus Andronicus, or the Rape of Lavinia* dramatizes this violent mode of censorship even more readily than its early modern counterpart. Like the Nurse in Shakespeare (4. 2. 147), the Woman in Ravenscroft is murdered; only this time her death is accompanied with the line that this is 'the only sure way to Lay a Womans tongue' (5. 1. sig. G 1ʳ). In opposition to Lavinia's silence, moreover, it is significant that Ravenscroft's Tamora is portrayed as a woman who uses language adroitly. Her rhetorical ability is apparent in her opening speech (1. 2. sig. B 2ʳ) and she continues in this linguistically expressive mode until her final outcry of the opening act:

Tho' here in Chains, yet I am still a Queen,
And have the noble Courage of a *Goth*.
If in my face you signes of sorrow read
The Frontispiece is unworthy of my mind,
And ill befits the greatness of my Soul (1. 3. sig. B 4ᵛ)

Tamora's impassioned speech is a striking moment in Ravenscroft's play. She understands the ways in which women function in this system of signification and the metaphor she uses is simple. Unlike Lavinia, she cannot be easily read; Tamora is not a text for the men to interpret at their will. Her rhetorical prowess, however, leads to further defamation of this already 'barbarous' character. Tamora's influence upon the Emperor, for instance, is treated with outrage by Bassianus, who calls her an 'Abstract of Woman and of Devil' (2. 1. sig. C 3ᵛ). Described in this way, Tamora not only transgresses boundaries of gender difference; she is unrecognisable as a human subject. But if the Queen of the Goth's subject position is interrogated, the problematic identity that Shakespeare's Lavinia presents to her family is never fully questioned in Ravenscroft's adaptation. When Ravenscroft's Marcus first encounters his niece after she has been raped and mutilated, for instance, instead of the tentative enquiry found in the earlier play, he recognizes her immediately: 'Ha! is not that *Lavinia* turns away?' (4. 1. sig. E 2ʳ). His subsequent questions, 'Why shun you me Lavinia where's your Bridegroom?' (4. 1. sig. E 2ʳ), are also telling. Here, the play shifts attention to the male figures even more swiftly than its predecessor. Unlike Shakespeare's Marcus, who enquires 'Shall I speak for thee? Shall I say 'tis so?' (2. 3. 11–3), Ravenscroft's version moves directly from Marcus asking 'Why do'st not speak to me?' (4. 1. sig. E 2ʳ) to the eloquent description of her dreadful mutilations. With its portrayal of a tragic heroine who is even more silent than in the 'Old Play', Ravenscroft's Marcus succinctly assumes that he will speak for her.

Titus Andronicus, or the Rape of Lavinia is not only concerned with keeping women as silent objects: it is also keen to engender knowledge more acutely than its predecessor. The tension surrounding this issue is revealed in Bassianus's further reaction to the Queen of the Goths in the second act. His exclamation 'Kneel, kneel, Learn to dissemble all,| You have a Woman for your Instructor' (2. 1. sig. C 3ᵛ) illustrates that Ravenscroft's play is more keenly anxious than its predecessor about women's relationship to education and pedagogy. In many ways, Bassianus's insulting remarks are in keeping with contemporaneous discourses on the sexual politics of education. At the time of the play's production, restrictions were increasingly placed around women and the learning of classical languages. As Nancy A. Mace has argued, 'a woman who knew Latin or Greek was considered unmanageable, if not mad'.[87] In her *Essay in Defence of the Female Sex* (1696), Judith Drake illustrates these enforced parameters by asking the woman reader to

look into the manner of our Education, and see wherein it falls short of the Mens, and how the defects of it may be, and are generally supply'd [...] the main defect [is] that we are taught only our Mother Tongue, or perhaps *French*, which is now very fashionable, and almost as Familiar amongst Women of Quality as Men; whereas the other Sex by means of a more extensive Education to the knowledge of the

Roman and *Greek* Languages, have a vaster Field for their Imaginations to rove in, and their Capacities thereby enlarg'd.[88]

Drake thus observes that women are enclosed through linguistic censure, and it is against this cultural background that Ravenscroft's Lavinia finds herself deprived of some significant classical material.

As Lavinia and her nephew take the stage the directions read:

> Enter Junius, with an Arrow in's hand, running from Lavinia, and she pursuing him. (4. 1. sig. F 1ᵛ)

Whereas Shakespeare's Lavinia 'quotes the leaves' (4. 1. 50) of Ovid's text and writes the words which will compel the Andronici to take revenge, Ravenscroft's Lavinia only has the words and actions of Titus himself to follow:

> Observe, Observe *Lavinia* what I'm doing,
> Rape is the word that I have written there;
> Without the help of this one's hand that's left
> If that was not one cause for which thou mourn'st,
> Then here put forth thy foot and blot it out:
> That sigh and mournfull Look tells me it was.
> Beneath it write the wicked Authors Names,
> Decypher in the Sand as I have done, (4. 1. sig. F 2ʳ)

In Shakespeare's play it is Marcus who demonstrates the scribal process by taking a staff in his mouth and writing his name in the dust. Taking his cue from Junius, however, Ravenscroft's Titus holds the arrow in his mouth, but instead of merely showing Lavinia the means by which she can communicate, Titus writes 'Rape' on the ground. Once she has 'confirmed' that this is the appropriate term to use, she follows Titus's method of inscription and scrawls '*Chiron — Demetrius*' (4. 1. sig. F 2ʳ) after him. Titus then asks Junius to 'read what is written there' (4. 1. sig. F 2ʳ). As the title of the play suggests, Lavinia is fashioned as object rather than subject. She cannot write the word that describes her own tragedy; denied Ovid's book and the Latin language that her Shakespearean equivalent displays, Lavinia is neither shown as the reader nor translator of the *Metamorphoses*. Whilst the Andronici in Ravenscroft's play are still shown to be erudite semioticians in their reading of Lavinia and text (they speak of her writing as 'Sands like Sibels Leaves' (4. 1. sig. F 3ʳ), the woman is denied access to the Ancients. If Shakespeare's Lavinia bore traces of Io, Callsito and Philomela, this seventeenth-century adaptation is reminiscent of Echo; a figure destined to reiterate the words of the men who surround her.

By contrast with Ravenscroft's censorious attitude to women and the classics in *Titus Andronicus, or the Rape of Lavinia*, the appearance of Ovid's *Metamorphoses* in Act 4 of Shakespeare's play instigates an exploration of translation, identity and gender. The book which Lavinia so energetically pursues provides a way in which she can respond to Marcus's interrogation, 'Who is this?', and thus regain some kind of position as signifying subject in both Latin and the vernacular. With her body brutally fashioned beyond compare, Lavinia struggles to communicate in numerous ways; she uses what is left of her mutilated body in an attempt to gesture; she tries to 'quote' from printed matter. In the end, it is her choice of the word *stuprum* from Ovid's *Metamorphoses*, laboriously scrawled on the ground, which violently exposes the sexual politics of translation in early modern England.

Notes

[1] Lawrence Venuti, 'Translation and the Formation of Cultural Identities', in *Cultural Functions of Translation*, ed. by Christina Schaffner and Helen Kelly-Holmes (Clevedon: Multilingual Matters, 1995), pp. 9–25, p. 9.

[2] Venuti, 'Translation and the Formation of Cultural Identities', p. 9.

[3] Eugene Vance, *Mervelous Signals: Poetics and Sign Theory in the Middle Ages* (Lincoln: University of Nebraska Press, 1986), p. 312.

[4] All quotations are from William Shakespeare, *Titus Andronicus*, ed. by Jonathan Bate (London: Routledge, 1995).

[5] See *Oxford English Dictionary*, 'barbarous', senses 1–5.

[6] Adam McKeown, '"Entreat her hear me but a word": Translation and Foreignness in *Titus Andronicus*' in *The Politics of Translation in the Middle Ages and the Renaissance*, ed. by Renate Blumenfeld-Kosinski, Luise von Flotow and Daniel Russell (Canada: University of Ottawa Press, 2001), pp. 203–18, p. 208.

[7] See, for example, Michael Neill, 'Broken English and Broken Irish: Nation, Language and the Optic of Power in Shakespeare's History Plays', *Shakespeare Quarterly*, 45 (1994), 1–32; and 'The World Beyond: Shakespeare and the Tropes of Translation', in *Elizabethan Theatre Essays in Honour of S. Schoenbaum*, ed. by R. B. Parker and S. P. Zitner (Newark: University of Delaware Press, 1996), pp. 290–308; Patricia Parker, *Shakespeare from the Margins: Language, Culture, Context* (Chicago: University of Chicago Press, 1996) and Margaret Tudeau-Clayton, 'Scenes of Translation in Jonson and Shakespeare: *Poetaster*, *Hamlet* and *A Midsummer Night's Dream*', *Translation and Literature*, 11 (2002), 1–23.

[8] McKeown, '"Entreat her hear me but a word"', pp. 201–18.

[9] McKeown, '"Entreat her hear me but a word"', pp. 204–5.

[10] William MacIntyre has observed that the years 1558–1572 produced the greatest number of translations of the century: 'The thirty-nine separate new translations which appeared in print during the first decade of Elizabeth's reign, exclusive of reprints, exceed by a considerable number all those published in the reign of Henry VIII. In other words, the rate of translation increased nearly fourfold during the early part of Elizabeth's reign, and, following a marked decline during about 1572, continued for the last three decades of the century at approximately two-thirds as great as that attained in the early part of her reign'. William Myron MacIntyre, 'A Critical Study of Golding's Translation of Ovid's *Metamorphoses*' (unpublished doctoral thesis, University of California, 1965), p. 88.

[11] As Susan Bassnett has noted, 'translation came to be used as a weapon in both dogmatic and political conflicts as nation states began to emerge and the centralisation of the church began to weaken'. Susan Bassnett, *Translation Studies*, rev. edn (London: Routledge, 1991), p. 57.

[12] Eamon Duffy, *The Stripping of the Altars: Traditional Religion in England c. 1400–c. 1580* (New Haven: Yale University Press, 1992), p. 565.

[13] Cited in *Documents of the English Reformation*, ed. by Gerald Bray (Cambridge: James

Clark, 1994), p. 335.

14 See André Lefevere, *Translation, Rewriting and the Manipulation of Literary Fame* (London: Routledge, 1992), esp. pp. 12–13.

15 Warren Boutcher, 'The Renaissance', in *The Oxford Guide to Literature in English Translation*, ed. by Peter France (Oxford: Oxford University Press, 2000), pp. 45–54, p. 48.

16 Patricia Palmer, *Language and Conquest in Early Modern Ireland* (Cambridge: Cambridge University Press, 2001), pp. 109–10.

17 Palmer, *Language and Conquest in Early Modern Ireland*, p. 110.

18 See further Neill, 'Broken English and Broken Irish'.

19 Unless otherwise stated, all quotations from Ovid's poem in this chapter are from Arthur Golding, *The xv. Bookes of P. Ovidius Naso, etytuled Metamorphosis, translated oute of Latin into English meeter* (London: 1567).

20 Karl G. Galinsky, *Ovid's Metamorphoses: An Introduction to the Basic Aspects* (Berkeley: University of California Press, 1975), p. 4.

21 15. 981. For a discussion which considers 'the serious and certainly Augustan apotheosis in the realm of history', see Charles Paul Segal, 'Myth and Philosophy in the *Metamorphoses*: Ovid's Augustanism and the Augustan Conclusion of Book 15', *American Journal of Philology*, 90 (1969), 257–92.

22 G. Harold Metz, 'Stage History of *Titus Andronicus*', *Shakespeare Quarterly*, 28 (1977), 154–69, 155.

23 See Liz Oakley-Brown, 'Translating the Subject: Ovid's *Metamorphoses* in England 1560–7', in *Translation and Nation: Towards a Cultural Politics of Englishness*, ed. by Roger Ellis and Liz Oakley-Brown (Clevedon: Multilingual Matters, 2001), pp. 48–84.

24 For a clear discussion of the relevant Lacanian material see Antony Easthope and Kate McGowan (eds.), *A Critical and Cultural Theory Reader* (Buckingham: Open University Press, 1992).

25 Arthur Golding, *The fyrst fower bookes of P. Ovidius Nasos worke, intitled Metamorphosis, translated into English meter* (London: 1565).

26 Gordon Braden, *The Classics and English Renaissance Poetry: Three Case Studies* (New Haven: Yale University Press, 1978), p. 49.

27 Leonard Barkan, *The Gods Made Flesh: Metamorphosis and the Pursuit of Paganism* (New Haven: Yale University Press, 1986), p. 247.

28 Bate, *Shakespeare and Ovid* (Oxford: Clarendon Press, 1993), p. 116. See also Carla Mazzio, 'The Sins of the Tongue' in *The Body in Parts: Fantasies of Corporeality in Early Modern Europe*, ed. by David Hillman and Carla Mazzio (New York: Routledge, 1997), pp. 53–80.

29 6. 708–15.

30 Bate, *Shakespeare and Ovid*, p. 116.

31 Bate, *Shakespeare and Ovid*, p. 102.

32 For a discussion of the significance of Ovid's Philomela myth in early modern England see Mary Ellen Lamb, 'Singing with the (Tongue) of a Nightingale', in *Gender and Authorship in the Sidney Circle* (Wisconsin: University of Wisconsin Press, 1990), pp. 194–230.

33 Barkan, *The Gods Made Flesh*, p. 245.

34 Lucius: 'Speak gentle sister: who hath martyred thee?' (3. 1. 82); Titus: 'Thou hast no hands to wipe away thy tears,| Nor tongue to tell me who martyred thee;' (3. 1. 107–8).

35 For a related discussion of how Lavinia's relatives perceive her '*as* a mirror and *through* a mirror', see Katherine A. Rowe, 'Dismembering and Forgetting in *Titus Andronicus*', *Shakespeare Quarterly*, 45 (1994), 279–303, 295.

36 See, for example, Mary Fawcett, 'Arms/ Words/ Tears: Language and the body in *Titus Andronicus*', *English Literary History*, 50 (1983), 261–77; Douglas E. Green, 'Interpreting "her martyr'd signs": Gender and Tragedy in *Titus Andronicus*', *Shakespeare Quarterly*, 40 (1989), 317–26; Clark Hulse, 'Wresting the Alphabet: Oratory and Action in *Titus Andronicus*, *Criticism*, 21 (1979), 106–18; Gillian Murray Kendall, '"Lend me thy hand": Metaphor and Mayhem in *Titus Andronicus*', *Shakespeare Quarterly*, 40 (1989), 299–316; D. J. Palmer, 'The Unspeakable in Pursuit of the Uneatable: Language and Action in *Titus Andronicus*', *Critical Quarterly*, 14 (1972), 320–39.

37 Michael Neill, 'The World Beyond: Shakespeare and the Tropes of Translation', p. 291. For a psychoanalytic reading, see Lynn Enterline, *The Rhetoric of the Body: From Ovid to Shakespeare* (Cambridge: Cambridge University Press, 2000), p. 99 ff.

38 For example, the pursuit of Hermaphroditus (4. 351 ff.) and Adonis (10. 596 ff.) by Salmacis and Venus respectively.

39 Charles Segal states that 'lascivia is the word which Quintilian uses to characterise the art of Ovid (*Institutio oratoria*, 4. 1. 77, 10. 1. 88, and 10. 1. 93)'. Cited in William Keach, *Elizabethan Erotic Narratives* (London: Harvester Press, 1977), p. 11, p. 235, n. 12.

40 For the relationship between Ovid and rhetoric in classical scholarship, see Alessandro Schiesaro, 'Ovid and the Professional Discourses of Scholarship, Religion, Rhetoric', in *The Cambridge Companion to Ovid*, ed. by Philip Hardie (Cambridge: Cambridge University Press, 2002), pp. 62–78.

41 Bate, *Titus Andronicus*, p. 211.

42 J. L. Simmons, 'The Tongue and Its Office in *The Revenger's Tragedy*', *Proceedings of the Modern Language Association of America*, 92 (1977), 56–68, 57.

43 Bate, *Shakespeare and Ovid*, p. 104.

44 See further Jean R. Brink, 'Literacy and Education', in *A Companion to English Renaissance Literature and Culture*, ed. by Michael Hattaway (Oxford: Blackwell, 2000), pp. 95–105; and R. W. Maslen, 'Myths Exploited: The Metamorphosis of Ovid in Early Elizabethan England', in *Shakespeare's Ovid*, ed. by A. B. Taylor (Cambridge: Cambridge University Press, 2000), pp. 15–30.

45 Bate, *Shakespeare and Ovid*, p. 104.

46 I would like to thank Roger Ellis for this observation.

47 316–7. All quotations are from Geoffrey Chaucer, *The Riverside Chaucer*, ed. by Larry D. Benson (Oxford: Oxford University Press, 1988).

48 See Margaret P. Hannay (ed.), *Silent But for the Word: Tudor Women as Patrons, Translators and Writers of Religious Works* (Kent, Ohio: Kent State University Press, 1985); Tina Krontiris, *Oppositional Voices: Women as Writers and Translators of Literature in the English Renaissance* (London: Routledge, 1992); and Sherry Simon, *Gender in Translation: Cultural Identity and the Politics of Transmission* (London: Routledge, 1996).

49 Jean Luise Vives, *A verie fruitfull and pleasant booke. called the instruction of a Christian woman. Made first in Latin, by the right famous Clearke M. Levves Vives, and translated out of Latin into English, by Richard Hyrde*, 2nd edn (London: 1592), sig. D 2ᵛ–D 3ʳ.

50 sig. a. iiiᵛ

51 sig. a. iiᵛ; sig. a iiiiᵛ˙

52 sig. A iiiiʳ

53 Raphael Lyne, *Ovid's Changing Worlds: English Metamorphoses 1567–1633* (Oxford: Oxford University Press, 2001), p. 45.

[54] Patricia Parker writes that humanists such as Jean Luis Vives and Roger Ascham characterized romances as nothing but bawdry and 'the reader of such texts is cast as an endangered Odysseus whose only moly is a humanist counter training in virtue and in more canonical reading'. Patricia Parker, *Literary Fat Ladies: Rhetoric, Gender, Property* (London: Methuen, 1987), p. 11. Whilst Golding's translation of the *Metamorphoses* cannot be defined as a romance, Parker's depiction of the reader as classical hero seems relevant here.

[55] Bate, *Titus Andronicus*, p. 210, n. 83. Amongst the many books which have been published on early modern reading practises, one of the most useful in terms of women is Sasha Roberts, *Reading Shakespeare's Poems in Early Modern England* (Basingstoke: Palgrave Macmillan, 2003). See p. 199, n. 8 for an excellent bibliography on the subject so far.

[56] Alan Stewart, 'The Early Modern Closet Discovered', *Representations*, 50 (1995), 76–100, 81.

[57] J. A. W. Bennett, Preface, in Kathleen L. Scott, *The Caxton Master and His Patrons* (Cambridge: Cambridge Bibliographical Society, 1976), p. x.

[58] Anne Clifford, *Diaries*, ed. by D. J. H. Clifford (Gloucestershire: Sutton, 1992), p. 76. Ovid's *Metamorphoses* is amongst the young Anne Clifford's books portrayed in the well-known triptych, *The Great Picture* (1646). See further Nigel Wheale, *Writing and Society: Literacy, Print and Politics* in Britain *1590–1660* (London: Routledge, 1999), pp. 116–31.

[59] Louise Schleiner, *Tudor and Stuart Women Writers* (Bloomington: Indiana University Press, 1994), p. 2.

[60] Bate, *Shakespeare and Ovid*, p. 117.

[61] Thomas Fuller gave this term to the translator Philemon Holland (1552–1637). See F. O. Matthiessen, *Translation: An Elizabethan Art* (New York: Octagon, 1965), pp. 169–227.

[62] Robert S. Miola, '*Titus Andronicus* and The Mythos of Shakespeare's Rome', *Shakespeare Studies*, 14 (1981), 85–98, 86.

[63] Palmer, 'The Unspeakable in Pursuit of the Uneatable', p. 335.

[64] This line translates as 'Ruler of the great heavens, are you so slow to hear crimes, so slow to see?' Bate, *Titus Andronicus*, p. 216, n..

[65] Enterline, *The Rhetoric of the Body*, p. 3.

[66] Emily C. Bartels, 'Making More of the Moor: Aaron, Othello, and Renaissance Refashionings of Race', *Shakespeare Quarterly*, 41 (1990), 433–54, 434–5.

[67] Bartels, 'Making More of the Moor', 442.

[68] Daniel Vitkus, *Turning Turk: English Theatre and the Multicultural Mediterranean, 1570–1630* (Basingstoke: Palgrave Macmillan, 2003), pp. 102–3.

[69] Bate, *Titus Andronicus*, p. 125, n..

[70] Bate, *Titus Andronicus*, p. 220, n..

[71] Heather James, 'Cultural disintegration in *Titus Andronicus*: mutilating Titus, Vergil and Rome', *Violence in Drama, Themes in Drama*, 13 (1991), 123–40, 132, cited in Bate, *Titus Andronicus*, p. 219, n.

[72] Sara Eaton states that 'failing to read well (or interpret correctly) has social and political consequences'. Sara Eaton, 'A Woman of Letters: Lavinia in *Titus Andronicus*', in *Shakespearean Tragedy and Gender*, ed. by Shirley Nelson Grammar and Madelon Spregnether (Bloomington: Indiana University Press, 1996), pp. 54–74, p. 57.

[73] Bartels, 'Making More of the Moor', 447.

[74] Andrew Gurr, *Playgoing in Shakespeare's London*, 2nd edn (Cambridge: Cambridge University Press, 1996), p. 82.

[75] Five performances are recorded by Henslowe on 23 and 28 January, 6 February and 5

and 12 June, 1594. The first three of these performances were by the Sussex's Men at the Rose. A private performance took place at Burley-on-the-Hill, Rutland, on 1 January 1596 as part of the Christmas Revels at Sir John Harington's manor. Metz, 'Stage History of *Titus Andronicus*', p. 155.

76 See 1. 1. 408–13.

77 Emily Detmer-Goebel, 'The Need for Lavinia's Voice: *Titus Andronicus* and the Telling of Rape', *Shakespeare Studies*, 29 (2001), 75–92, 85–6. See further Jocelyn Catty, *Writing Rape, Writing Women in Early Modern England* (Basingstoke: Macmillan, 1999).

78 Detmer-Goebel, 'The Need for Lavinia's Voice', 86.

79 Alison Goddard Elliott, 'Ovid and the Critics: Seneca, Quintilian and "Seriousness"', *Helios*, 12 (1985), 9–20, 17.

80 Eve Rachele Sanders, *Gender and Literacy on Stage in Early Modern England* (Cambridge: Cambridge University Press, 1998), p. 63.

81 Metz, 'Stage History of *Titus Andronicus*', 156.

82 sig. A 2^r. All quotations are from Edward Ravenscroft, *Titus Andronicus, or the Rape of Lavinia* (London: 1687).

83 Cited in Paulina Kewes, *Authorship and Appropriation: Writing for the Stage in England, 1660–1710* (Oxford: Clarendon Press, 1998), p. 59.

84 John W. Velz, 'Topoi in Edward Ravenscroft's Indictment of Shakespeare's *Titus Andronicus*', *Modern Philology*, 83 (1985), 45–50, 47.

85 See Julia Rudolph, 'Rape and Resistance: Women and Consent in Seventeenth-Century English Legal and Political Thought', *Journal of British Studies*, 39 (2000), 167–84. In this article, Rudolph discusses the centrality and significance of the tropes of tyranny and rape during the Exclusion crisis.

86 There is a wide and varied tradition on women's loquaciousness. For an excellent survey, see Alcuin Blamires (ed.), *Woman Defamed and Woman Defended* (Oxford: Clarendon Press, 1992).

87 Nancy A. Mace, *Henry Fielding's Novels and the Classical Tradition* (London: Associated University Presses, 1996), p. 28.

88 Cited in Vivien Jones, *Women in the Eighteenth Century: Constructions of Femininity* (London: Routledge, 1990), p. 205.

Chapter 2

The Heterotopic Place of Translation: *The Third Part of The Countesse of Pembrokes Yvychurch. Entituled, Amintas Dale*

> [...] what interests me among all these emplacements are certain ones that have the curious property of being connected to all the other emplacements, but in such a way that they suspend, neutralize, or reverse the set of relations that are designated, reflected, or represented [*réflechis*] by them.[1]

Translation, Patronage and Power

Lavinia's resolute attempts to use the *Metamorphoses* as a means of conveying her dreadful encounter with Demetrius and Chiron to the Andronici illustrate that the relationship between early modern women and Ovid's poem is quite different to that of men. Moving from the sexual politics of translation on the Renaissance stage, this next chapter considers a vernacular version of the *Metamorphoses* in a generically different, but contemporaneous, text: Abraham Fraunce's *The Third Part of The Countesse of Pembrokes Yvychurch. Entituled, Amintas Dale. Wherein are the most conceited tales of the Pagan Gods in English Hexameters together with their auncient descriptions and Philosophicall explications* (1592).[2] Dedicated to Mary Sidney, this complex reworking of the *Metamorphoses* describes a compelling scene of translation which explores further the construction of the gendered subject.

The three sections which form the complete *The Countesse of Pembrokes Yvychurch* tell the pastoral romance of Amyntas and Phillis. The first part is a three-act play which ends with the two protagonists declaring their undying love for each other. However, as the second part of *Yvychurch* begins the reader learns, somewhat abruptly, that Phillis is dead. The next segment of the complete *Yvychurch* narrative tells of the desolate Amyntas's eleven days of mourning which ends with the death of the heart-broken lover and his transformation into an Amaranthus: a metamorphosis which initiates Fraunce's debt to Ovid in *Amintas Dale*. Both texts were published together as *The Countesse of Pembrokes Ivychurch. Conteining the affectionate life, and unfortunate death of Phillis and Amyntas: That in a Pastorall; This in a Funerall: both in English Hexameters*

(1591).[3] In the final section, characters that have already been introduced in the play gather at the Amintas Dale of the title to commemorate 'that solempne feast of murdred *Amyntas*' (sig. A 3ʳ) in the form of a pastoral colloquy. Under the guidance of the Lady Regent, tales from the *Metamorphoses* are told in verse and these are accompanied by prose explications which are offered by one of her companions, the sage Elpinus. As a text which commemorates the death of the fictional Amyntas, it is not altogether surprising that loss is inscribed throughout *Amintas Dale*. However, in its wider social and cultural contexts, the subject matter of Fraunce's *Yvychurch* also defines it as one of the many texts produced in response to the death of Mary Sidney's brother Philip in battle against the Spanish at Zutphen in 1586.[4]

Fraunce's use of Ovidian tropes in a pastoral setting recall Sidney's *Old* and *New Arcadias*, thus *Amintas Dale* immediately functions as a textual homage to his former patron.[5] Moreover, the importance of Ovid's poem in this Sidneian context is suggested by the motto from the *Metamorphoses* which was inscribed on the personal standard carried in his funeral procession.[6] In her discussion of aristocratic funerals in early modern England, Clare Gittings has explained how 'the ruling was that the mourners had to be of the same sex as the deceased'.[7] This meant that women were 'completely marginalized within the social process of mourning'.[8] In view of this engendering of grief, publications such as *The Countesse of Pembrokes Yvychurch* openly acknowledge Mary Sidney's position as bereaved sister. Nonetheless, Fraunce's exploitation of Ovidian episodes in *Amintas Dale* engage with a sexual politics of loss which extend well beyond his current patron's personal bereavement.

In general, the *Metamorphoses* explores tensions between fundamental binary oppositions. Philip Hardie eloquently explains that 'any and every instance of metamorphosis results in a state that is neither life nor death, but something in between. The product of every metamorphosis is an absent presence'.[9] Notably, thirteen out of the sixteen Ovidian narratives featured in *Amintas Dale* each explore this 'absent presence' in a distinctly gendered fashion. Although some of the tales feature goddesses such as Diana and Minerva, who are known for their chaste and intellectual capabilities, the image of a sexualized Venus is counterpoised against one of her as a grief-stricken woman.[10] However, many of the Ovidian myths that Fraunce has chosen (Syrinx and Pan, Io and Jove, Echo and Narcissus, Galathea and Acis, Proserpina and Pluto, Daphne and Apollo, Venus and Mars, Diana and Actaeon, Venus and Adonis, Salmacis and Hermaphroditus, Semele and Jove, Iphis and Anaxarete, and Pomona and Vertumnus) primarily render women as the objects of sexual desire and the subjects of death.[11] Proserpina, raped and taken by Pluto to the underworld, becomes the lost object for her mother, Ceres. Syrinx, Io and Daphne, transformed into a reed, a cow and laurel, respectively, surrender their womanly identities as they flee from the gods' amorous pursuits. Both Echo and Salmacis lose their corporeal form through dissolution. Out of Fraunce's sample of Ovidian women, it is only Semele, one of the many mortal women who are the object of Jove's desires, who suffers a violent death as she 'burnèd in hir Lovers armes'.[12] Bound by the sexual politics which frame the production of the

Metamorphoses in the early modern period, *Amintas Dale* proves to be a significant location for the interrogation of woman's subjectivity.

Fraunce begins *Amintas Dale* with a suitable address to his patron. The name of Mary Sidney's Wilton residence was *Yvychurch* and the Latin dedication moves toward her Minerva-like apotheosis:

> Illustrissimae, atque ornatissimae Heroinae, piae, formosae, eruditae: Dominae
>   Mariae, Comitissae Pembrokiensi.
> NYmpha Charis Chariton, morientis imago Philippi,
> Accipe spirantem post funerarursus Amintam:
> Accipe nobilium dulcissima dogmata vatum,
> Delicias, Musas, mysteria; denique, quicquid
> Graecia docta dedit, vel regia Roma reliquit,
> Quod fructum flori, quod miscuit vtile dulci. (sig. A 2ʳ)[13]

The perspective of translation had progressed to such a degree that 'by the end of Elizabeth's reign the vernacular success of her poets had proved that English was, after all, an "eloquent" tongue, whose geographic and social marginality was coming to an end'.[14] Fraunce's own sense of eloquence is evident at the end of his dedication which contains the familiar aim of 'teaching with delight'.[15] Author of *The Arcadian rhetorike: or The praecepts of rhetorike made plaine by examples Greeke, Latin, English, Italian, French, Spanish, out of Homers Ilias, and Odissea, Virgils Aeglogs, [...] and Aeneis, Sir Philip Sydnieis Arcadia, songs and sonets [...]*(1588), Fraunce was clearly interested in the formal 'art of speaking' (sig. A. 2ʳ), as he describes it on the opening page of his rhetorical treatise.[16] Similarly, in form and content, as we shall see, *Amintas Dale* can be viewed as a means of schooling its readers in rhetorical strategies. Jean Luis Vives's castigation of Ovid in *The Instruction of a Christian Woman* (discussed in the opening chapter of this book) suggests that the *Metamorphoses* is an unsuitable text for a woman: an issue hinted at in the Greek aphorism 'afar, afar, whoever is sinful' which appears on *Amintas Dale's* title page.[17] However, by encasing Ovidian tales within the frame narrative of the pastoral colloquy Fraunce produces a translation of Ovid's poem which may be fit for Mary Sidney.

Translation and Contestation

Storytelling in the *Metamorphoses* often engages with the themes of authority and subversion. Book 4 shows how the daughters of Minyas defy Bacchic ritual by means of textual production. As they spin (an act which shows their rebellion against the god's edicts) they decide to 'serve a better Sainct Minerva', and to each 'recite [...]| some tale that may delight' while they work.[18] Many of their stories, such as those concerned with Pyramus and Thisbe's clandestine meetings, Venus and Mars' adulterous relationship and Salmacis's pursuit of the reluctant Hermaphroditus which results in the biform figure named after the youth, are about cultural and physical transgression. For their own insurgent behaviour, the Minyaides are turned into bats. In the following book, the Pierides challenge the nine Muses to a competition to see who can recite the most effective poetry.[19] Inevitably, the mortal daughters of Pierus lose and become chattering magpies as punishment for their presumption. As the Lady Regent commands her court to recite tales in order to commemorate the death of Amyntas, *Amintas Dale* takes up the themes of narration and contestation which are found in the *Metamorphoses*. Although the pastors and nymphs give no indication that their stories are derived from the classical poem, the narrative process is clearly inscribed with Ovidian concerns.

The Lady Regent's instructions translate Ovid's introduction to the *Metamorphoses*, 'Of shapes transformed to bodies strange I purpose to entreate,| Ye gods, vouchsafe (for you are they that wrought this wondrous feate)'.[20] She 'wills every man to remember':

> Some one God transformd, or that transformed an other:
> And enjoynes each nymph to recount some tale of a Goddesse
> That was changd herself, or wrought some change in an other: (sig. A 3ʳ)

Then sage Elpinus 'as every tale and history drew to an ending| [...] Shuld his mynd disclose, and learned opinion utter' (sig. A 3ʳ). In the figure of Elpinus, Fraunce constructs a discourse which is suggestive of the allegorical commentaries found in the moralized tradition of Ovidian translation,[21] and it is only in the sage's extensive remarks on the individual narratives that the classical source of the tales is explicitly disclosed. His textual authority notwithstanding, the Lady Regent's influence on the proceedings is clearly evident, at this stage at least. She dictates the structure of the frame narrative and she also controls its content; the shepherds are to tell tales about gods and the nymphs are to tell tales about goddesses.[22] However, the nymphs and pastors that make up the *Yvychurch* circle are not only storytellers. They may also be viewed as a group of Ovidian translators variably responding to a range of cultural and intellectual imperatives which are dictated to them by the Lady Regent and Elpinus. Indeed, *Amintas Dale*'s social formation has parallels with the cultural context in which Fraunce's text is produced. As the pastoral colloquy is under authorial control, Fraunce is subject to his patron, Mary Sidney.

The contest begins with Thirsis's tale of the creation of the world out of chaos to the formation of humankind by the stones thrown by Deucalion and Pyrrha.[23] To begin with, Thirsis pays close attention to his Ovidian source and he positions himself in 'humble obeisance| made to the Lady Regent' (sig. A 3ʳ). After Ovid, Thirsis then turns his attention to the topics of language and meaning:

> Hart conceavd noe harme; tong, harts interpreter only,
> Playnly without any glose or dissimulation op'ned
> Harts harmeles conceipts: hands, true and trusty to practyse,
> Did, what his hart contryu'd, or tong had truly delyv'red. (sig. A 4ʳ)

In the Golden Age, meaning in language was transparent; in Saussurean terms there was no gap between the signifier and the signified. With the loss of the Golden Age, as Thirsis's narrative shows, social and cultural politics have become ever more fraught as meaning in language has become increasingly opaque:

> Every man kept home, and where he receav'd a beginning,
> There did he make his grave, and drew his dayes to an ending.
> Noebodie was soe mad by the ragged rocks to be ranging,
> And with clowds, windes, seaes, nay heav'n and hell to be stryvyng
> Only to spy and ly, and feede fooles eares with a wonder,
> How fro *Geneva* to *Gaunt*, from *Gaunt* he repair'd to *Vienna*,
> How fro the Turk to the Pope, fro the Pope to the Souldan of *Aegipt*,
> And at last came back fro the newfound world as an old foole,
> With foure Dutch-french woords, with a strange-cutt beard, or a Cassock.
> (sig. A 4ʳ–A 4ᵛ)

Jonathan Haynes observes that 'to travel was to give oneself up to mutability, and movement and change were highly suspect in the Renaissance: in a world thought to be decaying, change was synonymous with degeneration'.[24] These negative aspects of Elizabethan expansion are evident in Thirsis's tale; however, this Ovidian rendition has been subtly domesticated. Travel is shown to be the origin of deceit and duplicity, but this notion is realized in pointedly volatile religious terms. Hence, Thiris's tale may also be in accordance with Protestant anxieties which maintained that 'the Devil, the Pope, and the Turk all desired to "convert" good Protestant souls to a state of damnation'.[25] Beginning with the famous locus of Calvinism, Geneva, the verse considers Gaunt (Ghent), an important site of Low Country Protestant/Catholic schism, before resting on Vienna, a city which resisted the rise of Protestantism through the Counter–reformation of 1551.

From these geographical locations, Thirsis explicitly focuses on religious kinds: the Islamic Turk, the Catholic Pope and the Islamic 'Souldan of Aegipt'. When the 'traveller' returns, possessed of 'foure Dutch-french woords' and sporting 'a strange-cutt beard, or a Cassock,'[26] the 'newfound world' has clearly transformed him into an 'old foole' of nondescript religious identity. More specifically, Thirsis's tale may contain an implicit criticism of the pervasive religious fractures of the sixteenth century which led to Philip Sidney's death in battle at Zutphen, the underlying impetus of *Amintas Dale*. As part of a frame-narrative which sets out to commemorate the 'murdred Amyntas', the pastor's tale resonates with the violence and lawlessness typical of the iron age where:

> [...] Wife longs for death of her husband,
> Husband loath's his wife [...] (sig. B 1ʳ)

By contrast, Ovid's poem states that 'the husband longed for the death of his wife, she of her husband'.[27] Arthur Golding's translation also equally apportions blame: 'the goodman seekes the goodwives death, and his againe seekes shee'.[28] However,

Thirsis's rendition reduces the murderous intentions of the male figure. In a text produced for a powerful woman patron whose own position seems to have been elevated by the death of her brother, it is rather disquieting to find that Thirsis's translation calls attention to women's violence. As we shall see, the tales are circumscribed by and inscribed with a sexual politics of translation which becomes increasingly pronounced as *Amintas Dale* progresses.

So far, the pastors have been telling tales which follow Saturn's lineage. But after the second and third tales in which Menalcus and Damoetas each recount the Ovidian myths of Pan and Syrinx and Jupiter and Io, the Lady Regent exerts her authority and decides that 'because Juno was by nature and mariage conjoined with Jupiter, they should also be jointly remembered, before any other of Saturns brood were medled withal' (sig. D 4^r). With its focus more firmly on the women's role, *Amintas Dale*'s revised structure gives weight to the first episode recounted in a woman's voice. As evinced in the eight nymphs who recount tales from the *Metamorphoses*, in this other world of *Yvychurch*, a female figure can be given more freedom to take on the role of a translator of Ovid. Whilst the nymphs' tales of Scylla and Galatea, Proserpina and Pluto and Diana and Actaeon collude with the overarching paradigm of loss established in *Amintas Dale*, the stories told by Fulvia, Cassiopaea, Licoris and Dieromena are worth considering in some detail as their versions of Ovid's Echo and Narcissus, Venus and Adonis, Minerva and Vulcan, and Iphis and Anaxarete engage with notions of translation, language and gender.

Having been requested by the Lady Regent to tell a tale which concerns Juno, Fulvia is the first nymph to recite an Ovidian myth. However, she cannot summon up a story in which the goddess is the main focus. Instead, the nymph quite faithfully tells Ovid's myth of Echo, who she says, trying to align her story with the Lady Regent's request, 'was alwaies taken to be Junoes daughter' (sig. D 4^r). After delivering a lively and succinct translation of the well-known narrative of frustrated female desire, 'How many thousand times, poore soule, she desirde a desiring| And intreating speech to the wandring boy to be uttring?' (sig. D 4^v), Fulvia's story ends with Echo's transformation into a 'voyce':

> Voyce, and onely the voyce of forlorne Eccho remaineth:
> Eccho remaineth a voyce, in deserts Eccho remaineth. (sig. E 1^r)

Significantly, Fulvia does not speak of Narcissus's legendary transformation into the flower; the object of Echo's desire just fades away. Though Fulvia calls her 'the prating Dandiprat *Eccho*' (sig. D 4^v), a vilifying epithet more usually applied to a 'small, insignificant, or contemptible' young boy,[29] the nymph's truncation of Ovid's narrative keeps Echo, the subordinate female subject, in view, ultimately exploring the sexual politics of Ovid's myth.

The negation of female agency is most clearly exposed with Echo's repetition of Narcissus's words of rejection: '*Eccho* sayd nothing, but, I ever yeeld to thy pleasure' (sig. E 1^r).[30] In this context, the various, related meanings of the word 'yeeld' are pertinent. Firstly, it can mean repayment. Echo's sexual desire, of course, is famously unrequited; the tale thus uses the term somewhat ironically. Another meaning, which also mocks the nymph's plight, is one of production or issuing forth. Again, as she can only speak the words of others, Fulvia's choice of vocabulary seems cruelly apt. The third and most telling sense of 'yeeld', however, is one which signifies surrender.[31] It is this understanding of the word which is redolent not only of women's subordination to men but also of the gender politics of textual production in the early modern period. Catherine Belsey observes that women in the sixteenth and seventeenth centuries were 'discouraged from any form of speech which was not an act of submission to the authority of their fathers or husbands'.[32] As Echo 'yeelds' to Narcissus, Fulvia's story gives way to the weight of humanist authority represented by Elpinus's extensive gloss on her text. Pointedly, as a clear marker of his own submission to authority, the sage's commentary ignores the figure of Echo, the subject of Fulvia's text, and concentrates on an explication of Juno, the subject initially requested by the Lady Regent.

From his lengthy comments on Fulvia's story, it is evident that Elpinus is governed by many of the orthodox conventions of early modern gender politics. His glosses on the tales told by the men often observe their rhetorical abilities and intellectual grasp of the subject. For example, the sage states that Menalcus's version of Pan and Syrinx is 'short and sweet' (sig. C 4^v) and Alphesibaeus's tale of Apollo and Daphne proves that the shepherd is 'a good scholler of the best master' (sig. I. 2^v). By contrast, Elpinus avoids overt discussion of women's scholarly accomplishments. His only direct observation on a myth recounted by a nymph concerns Cassiopaea's version of Venus and Adonis. Here, Elpinus notes that the speaker 'hath so passionately discoursed of Venus, that I feare me, under these names, she mourneth her own love, and uttreth her owne affection' (sig. M 3^r). In her discussion of *Amintas Dale* and the 'inscriptions of the Countess of Pembroke', Mary Ellen Lamb argues that 'women readers, generally excluded from the educational process that provided erudite classical reading of myths, were surely often imaged as – and perhaps often were – fairly literal readers and receptive to such aesthetic appreciations as were available to readers without university education'.[33] In the nymph's capacity as translator rather than reader, Elpinus scrutinizes Cassiopaea's treatment of Ovid's myth in exactly the way that Lamb describes. In early modern modes of textual production, as other episodes in *Amintas Dale* illustrate, it seems that women have little success in effacing their bodies as 'textual and sexual experience become fatally linked'.[34]

Fraunce's depiction of women as translators of Ovidian tales is unusual, but he goes even further by allowing certain nymphs to deal with some fairly audacious material. One noteworthy example is Dieromena's tale of the tragic romance of Iphis and Anaxarete; the last Ovidian myth to be recounted in *Yvychurch*. As an episode which has already been briefly mentioned in Sylvia's preceding tale of Pomona and Vertumnus, it is apparently a story of some significance. Disguised as an old woman, the smitten Vertumnus tells an indifferent Pomona stories in order to 'bow [her] hardend hart and make it for too yild'. In Sylvia's translation, it is the 'fatall| Fall of Anaxarete' which shows Pomona how she should 'learne thereby to be lovely' (sig. O 3r). It is this line that Dieromena reiterates and explicates in the following story which tells of 'Iphis, a gentle youth [...]|| Poore, yet rich, but rich in pure affection only' becomes enamoured with Anaxarete, a 'noble dame' (sig. O 3ᵛ). Viewed in its *Yvychurch* setting, Dieromena's Ovidian story is outstanding for its graphic and violent depiction of courtly love. Anaxarete, 'Scorneful [...] with a frowning face, with a hard hart' (sig. O 3ᵛ), continually rejects the advances of Iphis. Eventually, he is driven to suicide and his corpse is presented to Anaxarete in spectacular fashion:

> [...] and there hangd woefuly tottring,
> With corde-strangled throate; his sprawling feete by the downefall
> Knockt her dore by chaunce; knockt dore did yeeld a resounding,
> Yeelded a mourneful sound, and made herself to be open,
> Wide open, to behold so strange and woeful an object. (sig. O 4ʳ)

When Iphis's mother views the body of her dead son she 'clipt, kist, embraced her Iphis| Wept, cried out, hould, roard' (sig. O 4ʳ). Anaxarete remains aloof, until, that is, the secreted gods encourage her to look out of her window to view the passing burial procession and she saw 'poore Iphis laid in a coffin' (sig. O 4ᵛ). At the sight of Iphis's dead body Anaxarete is transformed: 'Out of that sightles sight was starck and stiffe on a sudden,| And her purpled blood to paleness speedily changed' (sig. O 4ᵛ). At the end of her narrative, as in Sylvia's tale, Dieromena declares that 'Ladies' should 'learne to be lovely| And make more account of a gentle minde, then a gentry' (sig. O 4ᵛ). Lamb observes that 'the one tale that is explicated by a character other than Elpinus includes an address to "noble dames". Dieromena [...] explicates the tale of Iphis and Anaxarete not in terms of natural allegory, but as an exemplum for ladies to follow in choosing a suitor worthy of their love.'[35] It is the recapitulation of the sentiment from Sylvia's narrative that 'Ladies' should 'learne to be lovely', rather than the general exegesis of the tale, which is significant. It is by way of this reiterated line and the alliterative collocation of 'ladies', 'learning' and 'lovely' that Dieromena draws attention to questions of rhetorical skill, hermeneutic practice and sexual difference which underpin Fraunce's *Ivychurch* project.

One tale which exemplifies the complex sexual/textual politics of *Amintas Dale* is Licoris's account of Vulcan's attempts to seduce Minerva. Told by a nymph who is defined as a 'mery lasse' (sig. L 1ᵛ), this episode makes much of the erotic dynamic:

> *Vulcan* limps on apace, prowd of so lovely a Lady
> And pearles Paragon: When he came at last to the Pallace,
> And there found *Pallas*, th'oulde buzzard gan to be bussing
> Th'inviolate Virgin: th'oulde fumbler gan to be fingering
> The immaculate mayden: who by and with a stately
> Frowne, and austere looke, his rashness boldly rebuked.
> Blacksmith intreateth, prowd Pallas stoutly denieth,
> Gray-beard contendeth, but manly Minerva repelleth. (sig. L 1ᵛ)

Bearing in mind that Fraunce's dedication aligns Mary Sidney with Minerva, it is hardly surprising that the goddess is described here as a 'pearles Paragon', 'inviolate Virgin', 'immaculate mayden' and, most importantly, 'manly'. The representation of Vulcan as an 'oulde buzzard' only heightens the goddess's chaste and 'stately' position. However, Licoris has to work hard in order to maintain that representation. The account of Vulcan's attempted rape of the goddess is more commonly found in classical Greek literature, such as Apollodorus's the *Library*;[36] Ovid's poem merely carries a trace of the earlier mythology.[37] The predominantly Ovidian part of the story appears in the second half of Licoris's tale and is concerned with the birth of Vulcan's son, Erichthonius, a 'faire boy to the middle| But fowle snake downward' (sig. L 2ʳ).[38] In the *Metamorphoses*, Minerva secretly hid the child in a casket and gave it to three sisters, Pandrosos, Herse and Aglaurus, with the instruction that they must not look inside the box. Aglaurus, however, disobeys the powerful goddess and, in the words of Licoris, 'disclosed a boy, with a serpent' (sig. L 2ʳ). The actions of the wilful sister were told to Minerva by a 'chattring Chough' (sig. L 2ʳ). Instead of thanking the bird, however, Minerva abandoned the 'brew-bate crow' (sig. L 2ʳ) and took another for her handmaid. Whilst Licoris does not tell her audience what happened to Aglaurus, readers familiar with Ovid would know that Minerva, enlisting the assistance of Envy, ensured that the disobedient sister eventually met with a dreadful death.[39] Though Minerva is obviously capable of exacting revenge, in Licoris's narrative she is most memorable as an icon of chastity. In a manoeuvre which endorses this positive image, the nymph's initial digression from the Ovidian narrative offers a lasting impression of Vulcan's pursuit of the goddess:

> At last, with striving and strugling stifly, the sharp-set
> Ould fornicator was now so thoroughly resolved,
> Fully resolved now, and now so fowly resolved,
> That the resolved blood contending long for a passage,
> Powr'd it self at length on th'earth, in steed of a Pallas. (sig. L 1ᵛ)

As Venus's cuckold, Vulcan is the customary target for such treatment. However, unusual in *Amintas Dale* for its particular focus on the male body, Licoris's tale also has a valuable perspective on women and language. It is not with words that Minerva manages to admonish Vulcan's advance but 'with a stately| Frowne, and austere looke, his rashness boldly rebuked'. Although endowed with masculine virility, a noteworthy contrast against the elderly, limping god, Minerva's virtuous image is underlined by her silence.

Lamb remarks that:

> The complementary discourses of the third *Ivychurch* reveal competing interpretive systems that strongly imply gender. Without Elpinus's readings, the third *Ivychurch* would be an anthology of love stories told by graceful pastoral characters under the direction of a lady regent, presented for the readers' simple enjoyment of the narratives for their own sake.[40]

Although she accurately observes the text's complex sexual politics, Licoris's tale of attempted sexual abuse, let alone aged erection, masturbation and subsequent ejaculation (not to mention the phallic allusion in the tale of Erichthonius) seems to undermine the notion of 'gracefulness' that Lamb's reading suggests. Rather, the tale has much in common with the kind of Ovidian erotic epyllia that gained popularity in late sixteenth-century England, such as William Shakespeare's *Venus and Adonis* (c. 1593) and Francis Beaumont's *Salmacis and Hermaphroditus* (1602).[41] Early modern women would not have publicly translated such a text. Yet *Amintas Dale* offers a variety of perspectives through which women translate, and are translated by, the figures found in the *Metamorphoses*. From the Lady Regent, to the nymphs and Ovidian material that they present, to Mary Sidney, *Amintas Dale* constructs a number of conflicting spaces for women. These divergent representations, in themselves, keep women's subjectivity in check:

> A discursive instability in the texts about women has the effect of withholding from women readers any single position which they can identify as theirs. And at the same time a corresponding instability is evident in the utterances attributed to women: they speak with equal conviction from incompatible subject-positions, displaying a discontinuity of being, an 'inconstancy' which is seen as characteristically feminine.[42]

This indeterminacy reveals anxieties in *Amintas Dale* about the role of women. In particular, Elpinus's obsequious discourses emphasize the ways in which humanism tries to control women's engagement with intellectual endeavours and textual production.

Translation and Dilation

Fraunce's Elpinus begins his exegesis in a style familiar to readers of the *Metamorphoses* in the early modern period:

> Poets and Painters (men say) may well goe together, sith pen and pencill be both alike free, and doo equally challeng the selfsame prerogative. (sig. B 1ᵛ)

Citing texts which range from Cicero to Pythagoras to Plato to Solomon and others, and using the vernacular as well as Latin and Greek, Elpinus's prose moves through eighteen pages of protracted allegorical exegesis. With reference to earlier conventions, Elpinus's commentary promotes a moralized hermeneutic:

> Poeticall songs are Galeries set forth with varietie of pictures, to hold every mans eyes, Gardens stored with flowers of sundry savours, to delite every mans sence, orchyards furnished with all kindes of fruite, to please every mans mouth. (sig. B 2ʳ)

Moving from familiar tropes of artifice to those of nature, through sight, odour and taste, Elpinus delineates the sensuous appeal of poetry. Whilst corporeal matter may be used to colour the verse, however, readers should aim to transcend the lure of the body of the text. But according to Elpinus those readers

> whose capacitie is such, as that they can reach somewhat further then the external discourse and history, shall finde a morall sence included therein, extolling vertue, condemning vice, every way profitable for the institution of a practicall and common wealth man. The rest, that are better borne and of a more noble spirit, shall meete with hidden mysteries of naturall, astrologicall, or divine and metaphysicall philosophie, to entertaine their heavenly speculation. (sig. B 2ʳ)

Lamb suggests that Elpinus constructs a 'hierarchy of readers'.[43] Here, as discussed in Chapter 1, there are parallels with Golding's depiction of the readers of his translation. Elpinus's 'common wealth man' might aim to read beyond the immoral web of errors, but the 'better borne' could aspire toward a far more sophisticated level of reading. By interlacing the Ovidian narratives with this form of commentary, Elpinus attempts to guide the 'noble' reader toward this more 'hevenly speculation'. This exegesis, however, is not politically innocent. Indeed, social and cultural differences inform the sage's interpretation throughout *Amintas Dale*. In his later interpretation of Amaryllis's tale of Proserpina and Pluto, Elpinus announces that 'the Platonists call the body a Hell, in respect of the minde' (sig. H 2ʳ). Based on this familiar Platonic binary opposition of male/spirit and female/matter, Elpinus's interpretation of the tales in *Amintas Dale* inevitably emphasizes the gender difference established by the Lady Regent's organization of the pastoral colloquy.

One obvious trait in Elpinus's hermeneutic practice is his to attempt to play down any contemporary, political reading of the Ovidian myth. This is seen most clearly in his commentary on Thirsis's Ovidian translation (the opening tale riven with reference to the text's early modern period of production) where he rehearses the familiar humanist discourses inherited from classical antiquity and Christian ideology:

> Now for the transformation of *Thirsis* his *Chaos*, true it is, that *Ovid* much after this manner discourseth of the creation of the world, of the reducing of the confused *Chaos* into distinct formes, of *Prometheus* his framing of man of the very earth it self: which things no doubt, as also the distinction of times into foure severall ages, of gold, silver, brasse, an yron, were taken, (although in part mistaken) out of the sacred monuments of Moyses. (sig. B 2ʳ)

Departing from Thirsis's Ovidian narrative, on which he should be commenting, Elpinus turns his attentions to Pronapides who 'reporteth another history of the same *matter*, albeit not after the same *manner*' [my emphasis] (sig. B 2ʳ).[44] The sage is somewhat disingenuous in claiming that Pronapides differs only in respect of its 'manner' from the Ovidian version. By contrast with Ovid, the version from Pronapides focuses on the corporeality of Chaos. Strikingly, in a text dedicated to a woman, Elpinus explores creation in terms of dreadful childbirth. Ovid moves swiftly past Chaos in order to focus on processes of division and containment. Pronapides, however, takes quite a different turn. As Elpinus declaims:

> Demogorgon, saith [Pronapides], the great and terrible God of heaven and earth, accompanied only with *Aeternitie* [and] *Chaos* perceaved on a time, an outragious uprore and tumult stirred up in the bely and bowels of the forenamed Chaos: therefore, to ease her, he stretched forth his owne hand and opened her wombe, whence presently came forth a filthie and deformed ofspring, called Litigium, Strife: which no sooner apeared, but immediately it bred brabbles [...]. *Chaos* as yet had not ended her child-bearing labor [and] travaile, but was troubled with heavie burdens, fainty sweats, languishing groanes, [and] fierie tormenting agonies. (sig. B 2^r–B 2^v)

Demogorgon's act upon Chaos is presented as a literal dilation of the womb. As Patricia Parker has discussed, the relationship between *dilatio* as a term of rhetoric and the account of a specific action upon the female body can also be traced through Augustine's *Confessions*. One use of dilation, Parker argues

> occurs in the context of propagation or generation, the postponing of death through natural increase, one of the principal arguments against the premature closure of virginity and a meaning crucial to the potential identification of the rhetorical tradition of 'increase and multiply' [...] – the pregnant female body, promising even as it contains and postpones the appearance of an issue. The generational joins the rhetorical and hermeneutic here through the fact that the command to 'increase and multiply' which stands behind this kind of dilation [...] has its rhetorical counterpart in the tradition of the copia of discourse. Augustine in the *Confessions* has a whole chapter devoted to 'increase and multiply' (13. 24) in the sense of the interpreter's opening and fruitful extension of a closed or hermeneutic scriptural text, what the rhetorical tradition would call 'dilating or enlarging of matter by interpretation'.[45]

Parker's cogent analysis of these rhetorical strategies illustrates the way in which gender binarisms not only become inscribed in texts: they also become part of the hermeneutic practice itself.[46]

Elpinus's commentary on Chaos, itself a kind of dilation upon the Ovidian narrative, comes out of the rhetorical tradition that Parker describes. Whilst attempting to make sense of the tales for his audience, Elipinus's text betrays an anxiety regarding the nature of the generated forms coming out of Chaos and her offspring in its own digression from Thirsis's narrative. In his description of Chaos, a figure seemingly related to Errour in Edmund Spenser's *The Faerie Queene* (c. 1590),[47] Elpinus discloses characteristic early modern anxieties about woman's sexuality which is realized in numerous depictions of her 'grotesque body [which] is unfinished, outgrows itself, transgresses its own limits'.[48] Moreover, defined by the *Oxford English Dictionary* as 'a noisy quarrel' and highly evocative of 'babble',[49] Elpinus's use of the word 'brabbles' in his survey of Pronapides makes further links between women and discordant language. Through an interwoven network of metaphorical devices, Elpinus upholds and reiterates the conventional hierarchical binarisms of early modern gender difference which seek to seal the 'grotesque' orifices of women's bodies through the promotion of chaste and silent codes of conduct. In the cultural regulation of vernacular textual production, as *Amintas Dale* illustrates, translation practices are part of these codes.

Hence, textual control is crucial for *Amintas Dale*'s patriarchal sage. Apart from commenting on the tales told by his fellow pastoralists, Elpinus also refers to other Ovidian myths from the *Metamorphoses* which draw attention to the need for order and restraint. One episode discussed at length is that of Phaeton. Prompted by Alphesibaeus's story of Apollo and Daphne, Elpinus provides almost four pages of explication of the myth in which Apollo's son loses control of his father's chariot, unleashing destruction in his wake.[50] A common early modern trope to warn against unbridled desire, the didacticism of Phaeton's allegorical interpretation is further extended to textual production and patronage. Accordingly, Elpinus's discussion of the myth of Arachne and her contest with Minerva seems resonant with the concerns of a sixteenth-century writer:

> The like mischiefe befell *Arachne*, who being endued with excellent qualities, thought scorne of the goddess which was her good Mistresse, and might have been her patroness; and was therefore transformed to a spyder. (sig. D 4ʳ)

In the *Metamorphoses,* as Chapter 5 will explore in detail, Arachne functions like a translator. The picture that she weaves is partially a repetition of metamorphic narratives which have already been encountered in Ovid's text and which tell of 'the lewdnesse of the Gods', as Golding puts it.[51] However, as Ovid's myth expounds, and as Elpinus's commentary clarifies, it is dangerous to ignore hierarchies of power. With a view to his own status, the sage upholds Minerva who 'might have been her patroness', simultaneously distancing himself from Arachne, the outspoken and the ill-fated female Ovidian translator and interpreter. It comes as no surprise, perhaps, to find that in his later commentary on Dieromena's tale of Iphis and Anaxarete, Elpinus concludes with the warning that 'we must temper our tongs' (sig. O 4ᵛ).

Elsewhere, the sage is more ardently concerned with translation practices. After Fulvia's story, a tale from a 'forren Pastor' (sig. E 2ᵛ) (an echo poem in Italian) is recited in full for 'novelties sake' (sig. E 2ᵛ). The poem is accompanied by the explanation that it is repeated so 'that some of our company may another time either worke on the same ground, or lay himselfe a new foundation' (sig. E 2ᵛ). Here, the text is somewhat self-consciousness about modes of translation and the metaphor of construction employed may extend to the frame of *Amintas Dale* itself. As a strategy for translation, Fraunce has taken a text upon which many have worked before in order to fashion something new. However, as Elpinus shows, textual production is dependent on more than the skill of the translator. The translator is also subject to the authority of the social formation in which his translation is produced. At the end of Elpinus's authoritative commentary on the first tale there is a pause in which the Lady Regent decides that since Pan had been 'mentioned in this his discourse' (sig. C 4ʳ), the next tale, to be told by the pastor Menalcus, 'should be spent on that subject' (sig. C 4ʳ). The power of the patron is thereby reasserted above the sage's knowledge. This continual contest between patron, sage and the translators of the tales plays a significant role in representation of the gendered subjects of the text. From the authorial status of Fraunce to the discourses of Elpinus, tensions and anxieties are present in the masculine frame of *Amintas Dale* which is fissured by the presence of women.

Given this distinctly gendered frame, it is telling that at the centre of the contest between the nymphs and pastors is Damon's tale of Mercury and Battus from book 2 of the *Metamorphoses*.[52] This narrative is significant for its depiction of an Ovidian scene largely concerned with men. Instead of focusing on women's loss, Damon's story about gods and mortal figures absence by way of linguistic mutability and theft. For amusement, Mercury hides Apollo's sheep in a nearby wood, but his deed is witnessed by Battus, an elderly countryman. In exchange for his silence, Mercury offers Battus the gift of a cow, to which the old man says that there is more chance of a stone speaking than himself. But Mercury returns, in disguise, to test Battus's promise. This time, the god offers Battus a cow *and* a bull for information regarding Apollo's sheep. Tempted by the double reward, the countryman tells Mercury where he can find the flock. Upon this betrayal, Mercury reveals his identity and changes the old man into the aforementioned stone. Elpinus's subsequent commentary draws attention to many aspects of Mercury, but most significance is given to the god's association with language. Following a description of 'Mercuries picture' the text states that:

> His winged hat and feete shew, that speech and words (whereof Mercury is the best deliverer) once uttred, fly withoute returne [...]. (sig. K 4[r])

Like Thirsis's tale, Mercury's allegorical representation hints at the uncontrollable nature of language. Moreover, Damon's rendition of Ovid's myth includes additional material which highlights the political use of language in fashioning subjects. The tale's concern with social hierarchy is evident from the emphasis given to Apollo's exilic fall from Olympus to a 'pastors| Poore estate' (sig. K 3[r]). Further, the epithet used in the phrase 'bald Battus' (sig. K 3[v]) accentuates the 'unadorned [...] literary style' of the mortal.[53] Whilst the actual theft is played by Mercury upon Apollo, it is Battus who is the subject of linguistic duplicity:

> for no-bodie saw, but an ould churle,
> One ould canckred churle, which there kept *Mares* by the mountaines,
> Called bald *Battus:* whome *Mercury* friendly saluted,
> Tooke him apart by the hand, and best perswasion used,
> Gave him a lambe for a bribe, and prayd him so to be silent,
> Feare not, alas, faire sir, qd *Battus:* it is but a trifle,
> Tis but a trick of youth, some stragling sheepe to be taking:
> Kings may spare, and lend to the poore: And this very senceles
> Stone (and points to a stone) of this fact shalbe reporter
> As soone, as *Battus: Joues Nuntio* gladly retired,
> Yet, for a further proofe, both face and fashion altred,

Refashioning his speech to accommodate a South–west Midland's dialect,[54] the god thoroughly dupes the mortal:

> And, as a countrey clowne, to a countrey lowt he returned.
> Gaffer, I misse vive sgore vatt wedders: zawst any vilching
> Harlot, roague this way of late? canst tell any tydings?
> Ichill geve the an eawe, with a vayre vatt lamb for a guerdon.
> *Battus* perceaving his former bribe to be doobled,
> Turnd his tale with a trice, and theaft to the theefe he revealed.
> Under yonsame hill they were, yeare while, by the thicket,
> And'cham zure th'are there. Iste true, qd *Mercury* smiling,
> Ist tr'ue, thou false knave, and wilt thou needes be betraying
> Mee to myself? and then false *Battus* turnd to a Tutch stone,
> Tutch stone, yet true stone; which each thing truely bewraieth,
> And no-man thenceforth for no bribe falsely betrayeth.
> At last, all brabling and altercation ended,
> *Mercury* and *Phoebus* made friends, gave one to another
> Mutual embracements, and tokens: (sig. K 3ᵛ)[55]

In part, Fraunce's use of dialect in *Amintas Dale* is aligned with Spenser's contemporary poetics of pastoral poetry in *The Shepheardes Calender* (1579).[56] As the only example of this kind of language use in *Amintas Dale*, however, a significant instance related to the cultural politics of intralingual translation arises.[57]

Beyond sixteenth–century poetics, the text's implicit ideological awareness is evident in the way that mortal Battus employs a sliding dialect. Initially, he uses a courtly mode in order to address Mercury ('Feare not, alas, faire sir, qd *Battus:* it is but a trifle| Tis but a trick of youth, some stragling sheepe to be taking'), yet dialect comes into play when the god returns, disguised as a 'country clowne'. Illustrative of the ways in which social hierarchies are bound up with the use of language, Elpinus's commentary accentuates the filial relationship between the gods whilst berating the rustic character accordingly:

> And this was the meaning of the tale, that maketh Mercury steale Apolloes cattell: for, Apollo noteth Kings and potentates, and his flocks are their wealth and riches, and the Mercuriall is the filcher. If, by chance his Legierdumaine be perceived, he can so finely smooth up al by faculty of discourse, that he never is utterly disgraced by the mighty men. This their friendship and exchange noteth that incomparable union of *Jovial* intelligence with *Mercuriall* eloquence, the only flower of Kings court, and felicity of commonwealths. The perjured *Battus* is as worthyly plagued for his double tongue as the blabbing clawback and Brewbate Crowe for his long tongue. (sig. K 4ʳ)

This interpretation shows how cultural difference is held in place. Mortal Battus, socially inferior but linguistically capable of moving upwards into the realms of the gods, is 'plagued for his double tongue', whilst Mercury, the foremost exponent of eloquent language, can expertly and effectively deceive those in power.

As part of a larger text which is wholly engaged with the sexual and textual politics of early modern England, it is of note that a pastor rather than a nymph tells a tale about language and the interpellation of masculine subjectivities. The numerous treatises on language and rhetoric that were published in late sixteenth-century England is witness to the control that men attempted to exercise upon language, of which Fraunce's own *The Arcadian rhetorike* is just one example.[58] Women, on the other hand, as the closing pages of *Amintas Dale* expose, are marginal to debates of this kind. The contest ends with Daphne's prose narrative which appears to be a final narrative about women and rhetoric. At the outset, Daphne takes issue with the sage as she aims to tell a story which is not 'so full of parables, as that Elpinus shall have need to make any explication' (sig. P 1ʳ). However, her prefatory remarks seem somewhat disingenuous as her complicated story about a group of Cambridge scholars who are trying to get to heaven demands clarification. By looking at the subject matter of this tale alongside contemporary debates concerned with prophecy and the Apocalypse, Gerald Snare states that 'at its conclusion, Fraunce's little book contains an extraordinary satire on astrological prognostications which is good enough, it seems to me, to rival most of the other satiric work on the subject during that sometimes vitriolic controversy'.[59] In his proposal that three figures in Daphne's tale could represent Gabriel, Richard and John Harvey,[60] Snare forges relevant connections between Daphne's tale and material which might range from Richard Harvey's *An astrological discourse upon the great and notable conjunction of the tvvo superiour planets, Saturne and Jupiter, which shall happen the 28 day of April, 1583*,[61] to Thomas Nashe's *Pierce Penilesse. His Suplication to the Devil* (1592).[62] However, as Daphne's introductory comments suggest, there can be no sure way to interpret this text. Indeed, the nymph may offer a further tale about the arbitrariness of meaning in language.

Her tale begins:

> I have heard my mother many times in good sobrietie, make a long discourse of certayne schollers of Cambridge, who would needes finde out some way to mount up to heaven, and understand those mysteries which bee above the Moone. (sig. P 1ʳ)

Overtly eschewing the patriarchal literary forms that the rest of the pastoral colloquy and Elpinus have relied upon, 'Daphne claims a female source' for her story.[63] Like *Amintas Dale* itself, Daphne's story is constructed as a frame-narrative which poses a hermeneutic challenge from the outset. Although it seems removed from the Lady Regent's behest and the rest of the stories told by the colloquy, Daphne's tale is implicitly informed by the Ovidian notions of translation and transformation. She begins with her mother's tale of the Cambridge scholars. But Daphne's narrative focus soon shifts to a 'Stranger' whom they stumble upon as they are about to begin their exploration. This 'Stranger' turns out to be a fellow academic from a University called the Garden and it is his story, told in the first person, that comes next:

> All the Academike Gardiners devised and mused much, how it might be brought to passe. Some remembering Lucians ship, thought it best to goe by water: Others, rather by land, through some great forrest, as Dante did: at last, they all agreed, that the surest way was, to make ladders of the poles that bare up their hoppes, and by the meanes thereof, to builde and rayse up a towre that should over-looke the whole worlde. (sig. P 1ᵛ)

He goes on to tell how Hemlock, Parsnip and Thistle, 'the most accomplished scholars in astrology, mathematics, and philosophy', are chosen as the 'gardeners' representatives and they eventually enter the heaven of the gods by climbing ladders.[64] Having given away the fruit that they had planned to present to Jupiter as a gift, Hemlock and Parsnip are thrown to the ground by the angry god and punished: 'with this transformation, that they should both thencefoorth have the forme and nature of that roote, and weede, whereof they bare the names' (sig. P 4ʳ).

After this Ovidian-like etiology, the tale becomes concerned with Thistle, the gardener, who 'threw himself upon the mercy of Intellectus'.[65] As Lamb recounts, 'Intellectus had just taken Thistle to the Place of Time, when the ship carrying the group encountered a terrible storm.'[66] Before Daphne can resolve her tale, however, she is interrupted by the Lady Regent who asks her to continue 'when they might there meete againe, for the like celebration of *Amyntas* death' (sig. Q 1ʳ). Whilst the invocation of the 'Cambridge schollers' may align the text with the intellectual issues that Snare observes, and although her tale 'cannot be interpreted according to any allegorical system',[67] Daphne's narrative about the academics' efforts to 'finde out some way to mount up to heaven' evokes tropes of Babel. Arguably, Thirsis's opening tale of the lost Golden Age, a time when meaning in language was transparent and the need for interpretation and translation redundant, is dramatized by way of Daphne's myth. Beyond its baffling content, the labyrinthine structure of the nymph's story is seemingly alert to the related problems of translation and interpretation as it resists closure.

Ever-conscious of cultural and sexual politics, the penultimate pages of *Amintas Dale* depict two women of different social status attempting to establish narrative resolution. It is no surprise, however, to learn that the lower-born Daphne must yield to the power of the Lady Regent. In its production of a text for a powerful and erudite patron, Fraunce apparently attempts to provide a space for woman to act in the process of Ovidian translation. Nonetheless, his exploration of the sexual politics of textual production in *Amintas Dale* ends in a conventional manner:

> [...] for a conclusion of this dayes exercise (sith it, seemed convenient to end with him, with whome they began) Amarillis and Cassiopaea sang these verses, which Amyntas living had made of the death of Phillis: which ended, they all departed. (sig. Q1ʳ–1ᵛ)

Like Ovid, Amyntas is immortalized through his poetry.[68] However, as Amarillis and Cassiopaea sing 'Amintas Phillidi consecravit, mortuae moriturus', *Amintas Dale* leaves its reader with women as the both the subjects and objects of loss.

Translation and Reputation

In the hierarchical social system of early modern England, 'women are defined by their difference to men'.[69] Accordingly, the cultural construction of 'women' also involves the cultural construction of 'men'. This is certainly the case with *Amintas Dale*. Fraunce begins his text with the assertion of his own authority as translator. To be sure, Fraunce is observably silent on the subject of Golding's Ovid. In its declaration that the following 'conceited tales of the Pagan Gods' are in 'English Hexameters', however, the title-page apparently iterates its metrical difference from Golding's earlier translation.[70] Establishing a direct line from its classical sources by indicating that *Amintas Dale* makes use of 'whatever Learned Greece has given or regal Rome has left', Fraunce's mode of versification connects his text with its classical predecessors more closely than Golding's heptameters.[71] But even as the title page draws attention to its status as the most extensive classical mythography produced in the English language so far,[72] the explicit association between the *Metamorphoses* and *Amintas Dale* is effaced. The cumulative effect of this prefatory material is to place Fraunce in an intellectually dominant position to his source text, Golding's Ovid, and his patron.

In deference to his social standing, however, Fraunce's Latin dedication figures Mary Sidney as a kind of Minerva, a 'most illustrious and most Jewel-like demi-goddess, kind, beautiful [and] learned'; a common allegorization which had already been employed by Thomas Nashe in his preface to an unauthorized edition of Philip Sidney's *Astrophel and Stella*.[73] Yet to see Mary Sidney as Minerva, the goddess of knowledge, is not merely a form of flattery. The classical form of the dedication insinuates that Mary Sidney was an accomplished translator. She was educated with her brothers at Penshurst and learned the French, Italian, Latin, Greek and Hebrew languages and is most commonly known for her translations of Psalms 44–150 (1586–99), Petrarch's *The Triumph of Death* (c. 1600) and Philippe de Mornay's *A Discourse of Life and Death* (1592).[74] It is significant that in the same year that *Amintas Dale* was published, the first edition of her translation of Robert Garnier's *Marc Antoine* was published as the closet drama *The Tragedie of Antonie*.[75] In particular, the subject matter of this last text takes Sidney beyond the domain of the Renaissance woman as the private translator of religious texts.

The focus of *The Tragedie of Antonie* is the excessive and exotic political figure of Cleopatra and it has been described as 'the first secular play translated by a woman'.[76] However, Sidney's play also uses Ovid in a familiar way. In Act 2, the lamenting Cleopatra is aligned with several Ovidian figures of despair who lose their identities as women: Procne, Alcyone, Niobe, Myrrha and Echo.[77] Markedly these mythical depictions of women and grief intersect with those found in *Amintas Dale*. Fraunce overtly presents Mary Sidney as his social superior, but the dedicatory material carefully negotiates tropes of patronage and power. In spite of Mary Sidney's own intellectual capabilities, Fraunce upholds the familiar definition of his patron as 'the image of the dying Philip' rather than a subject in her own right.[78] Moreover, Fraunce apparently places himself in a hierarchical position to his female patron; a particular depiction of social order which hints at the complex ideological matrices which are at work in the narrative of *Amintas Dale* itself. In a discussion of the representation of women in another Ovidian text, the *Heroides*, Elizabeth Harvey writes that:

> Ovid can write from the perspective of the woman precisely because he is not himself a woman; he metaphorizes the figure of woman, associating her with a constellation of attributes that are already traditional and will remain so: erotic passion, abandonment, desire that cannot be satisfied, rhetorical skill, especially expressed as complaint.[79]

The representation of women in *Amintas Dale* largely follows Harvey's model. By offering his reader translations of Ovid in a woman's voice, Fraunce's text moves around varying configurations of woman, from the wise Minerva to the erotic Licoris to Mary Sidney herself. Against Fraunce's problematic depiction of 'woman', however, the subject of Fraunce as translator becomes equally difficult.

According to Patricia Parker, 'accusations of translation as pilfering were [...] frequent in the sixteenth century; and they increased along with the articulation of notions of authorship, authority, and intellectual property'.[80] At the time that *Amintas Dale* was published, through an accusation of textual theft, Fraunce's literary reputation was being called in question. Like *Amintas Dale*, the other texts which form *The Countesse of Pembrokes Yvychurch* engage with translation practices.[81] The first part, *The Countesse of Pembrokes Yvychurch*, is a translation of Torquato Tasso's play *The Aminta* produced by Fraunce in English hexameters; the second part, *The lamentations of Amyntas for the death of Phillis, paraphrastically translated out of Latine into English hexameters by Abraham Fraunce* (London: c. 1587) is a translation of Thomas Watson's Latin poem *Amyntas* (London: 1585) and it is with this text that Fraunce's position as a translator is challenged.

Between 1587 and 1596 Fraunce published four editions of *The lamentations of Amyntas for the death of Phillis*, neglecting to inform his readers that this was actually a translation of Thomas Watson's Latin poem. Watson took objection to this and in the English epistle to his own translation of his Latin *Meliboeus, An Eglogue Upon the death of the Right Honourable Sir Francis Walsingham* (London: 1590), he states:

> And I intepret my self, lest *Meliboeus*, in speaking English by another mans labour, should leese my name in his chaunge, as my *Amyntas* did.[82]

The first part of the Y*vychurch* series published in 1591 contains Fraunce's only published acknowledgement that the text is translated from Watson's Latin. In the epistle addressed to Mary Sidney Fraunce writes that:

I have somewhat altered S. Tassoes Italian, and M. Watsons Latine Amyntas, to make them both one English.[83]

There is obviously a great deal of difference between producing translations of texts by dead poets and those of living authors. These contemporaneous circumstances concerning the translation, appropriation and authorship of *Amyntas* resonate throughout *Amintas Dale*.

In its construction of a group of nymphs and pastors gathered around the figure of the Lady Regent in order to tell tales which commemorate the death of 'murdred Amyntas', *Amintas Dale* represents Mary Sidney's literary circle in some ways. Louise Schleiner argues that

> Fraunce portrays [Sidney's] reading circle in pastoral form [...]. Fraunce's list of nine women suggests that the countess kept a large entourage of women [...]. In a portrayal implying that the countess actually commemorated her brother's death anniversary each year with lamentational 'passtimes', they meet in the park of her small Ivychurch estate near Wilton to tell stories and read out her poems [...]. Fraunce is no doubt presenting himself in 'Elpinus', supplying learned commentary on the ladies' Ovidian tales. The other swains presumably refer to writers who have praised the countess [...]. Thus the countess's waiting women, perhaps a female relative or two, her doctor and chaplain, along with Fraunce, [Nicholas] Breton, [Samuel] Daniel, and [James] Sanford are roughly the circle we should imagine in the Ivychurch.[84]

Schleiner's discussion is concerned with what she terms the 'psychodynamic and group-centred aspects of [Mary Sidney's] development as translator and writer';[85] for this kind of analysis it is necessary for her to closely equate Fraunce's colloquy with Mary Sidney's literary circle. By contrast with Schleiner's seemingly utopian interpretation of the Ivychurch group, fixed in its biographical figuration of social hierarchies, I want to argue that *Amintas Dale* offers its readers a heterotopia: 'a construction of a revised version of the social and political order which still acknowledges its connections with the material and historical circumstances in which it is embedded'.[86] With its elaborate explorations of translation, patronage and power, Fraunce does not produce a mere *reflection* of translation practices typically found in early modern England. Rather, *Amintas Dale* is a discursive text which negotiates the place of Ovidian translation and the translator in an increasingly complex literary culture.

Fraunce's text is witness to this complexity in the way that it is thoroughly inscribed with the ideologies of translation in this period. With the publication of *The lamentations of Amyntas for the death of Phillis*, Fraunce was made to acknowledge the subservient position of the translator in relation to the 'original' author and there are many tensions in *Amintas Dale* regarding the dynamics of power operating around and upon the translator in the late sixteenth century. In the early sixteenth century, as explained in the Introduction, translation was perceived as a means by which to enlarge the vernacular. Comments deploring the inadequacy of the English language in relation to the rhetorical powers and achievements

associated with classical literature were commonly found in the prefaces of many
translations produced at this time. Because of a variable range of the competing and
colluding discourses of Christian humanism, however, the latter half of the century
witnessed an abundance of texts written and, significantly, printed in English. This
meant that the public perception of translation was changing:

> The image of the translator as slave compelled to obey the source text and its author,
> developed in the sixteenth and seventeenth centuries, the age of the great colonialist
> expansion outside Europe. In his dedication to his translation of the *Aeneid* (1697),
> Dryden complained that translators were 'slaves forced to labour on another man's
> plantation'. This hierarchical model of translation contrasts with the way in which
> translation was viewed in earlier centuries, and is linked to changes in both the
> perception and evaluation of cultural products. The invention of printing had given
> the author a new status as owner or proprietor of the book. The idea of a common
> pool of material from which authors could draw, as exemplified in a text such as
> Malory's late fifteenth century *Morte d'Arthur*, which refers throughout to
> unspecified French source texts with no sense of subservience or inhibition, was
> replaced with the concept of the 'original', the text that had a clear point of origin, a
> clear proprietor and a clearly demarcated frontier.[87]

Produced in the period between Malory's *Morte d'Arthur* and Dryden's *Aeneid*,
Fraunce's Ovid is not easily accommodated into a binarism of original and copy.
Accused of being a plagiarist rather than acclaimed as a translator, this
condemnation of Fraunce is illustrative of the dynamics of power involved in
textual production during the late sixteenth century. *Amintas Dale* is thus produced
by a translator caught in a liminal space; between past and present; between the
dead Philip Sidney and the living Countess of Pembroke; between the Old and the
New Ovid;[88] between original and unoriginal; lastly, between male translator and
female patron. In *Gender and Authorship in the Sidney Circle*, Lamb concludes
that the *Yvychurch* narratives 'have everything to do with Fraunce's fashioning
himself as a male author experiencing the power of a woman reader'.[89] However
women had been figured as readers of Ovid's text; they had not been publicly
recognized as translators of the *Metamorphoses*. Fraunce takes the familiar gender
binarisms of the period in order to construct *Amintas Dale* but the text does not
merely reproduce those binarisms. In his text produced for a woman recognized for
her own translations, Fraunce gives a voice to women as translators of Ovid; yet
Amintas Dale is riven with tensions concerning the position of the male translator.

  In his manuscript treatise 'The Fourth and Last Book of the Philosophy of
Imprese' (c. 1586), Abraham Fraunce acknowledges the arbitrariness of linguistic
signification:

> [...] letters are intelligible only to few, presumably only to the learned [...]. And
> then each individual nation has its own letters. Letters just like languages are
> intelligible only to their own people.[90]

Operating in the interstices of language as an 'inventive mediator',[91] the translator may emphasise the interpellation of identity. Whilst overtly responding to the authority of its patron, Mary Sidney, *Amintas Dale* simultaneously seeks to maintain notions of women as loci of displacement and loss, and to coerce them into accepting the intellectual authority of men. But Fraunce's tacit reworking of Ovid's *Metamorphoses* as part of the *Yvychurch* narratives explores the ways in which language is a site of lack for both patron and translator; woman and man.

Notes

[1] Michel Foucault, 'Different Spaces', in *The Essential Works of Michel Foucault: Aesthetics, Method and Epistemology*, trans. by Robert Hurley, ed. by James Faubion (London: Penguin, 2000), pp. 175–86, p. 178.

[2] All quotations are from *The Third Part of the Countesse of Pembrokes Yvychurch. Entituled, Amintas Dale* (London: 1592).

[3] *The Countesse of Pembrokes Yvychurch. Conteining the affectionate life, and unfortunate death of Phillis and Amyntas: That in a Pastorall; This in a Funerall: both in English Hexameters* (London: 1591). The second section had been previously published as *The Lamentations of Amyntas for the death of Phillis, paraphrastically translated out of Latine into English Hexameters* (London: 1587). This text has a complex history. See further note 82 below.

[4] See, for example, Thomas Churchyard, *The epitaph of Sir Phillip Sidney Knight, lately Lord Governour of Floshing* (London: 1586); Angel Day, *Upon the life and death of the most worthy, and thrise renowned knight, Sir Phillip Sidney a commemoration of his worthines, contayning a briefe recapitulation, of his valiant usage and death taken, in her Majesties services of the warres in the Low-countries of Flaunders* (London: 1586); John Phillips, *The life and death of Sir Phillip Sidney, late lord governour of Flushing his funerals solemnized in Paules Churche where he lyeth interred; with the whole order of the mournfull shewe, as they marched thorowe the citie of London, on Thursday the 16 of February. 1587* (London: 1587); George Whetstone, *Sir Phillip Sidney, his honorable life, his valiant death, and true vertues A perfect myrror for the followers both of Mars and Mercury, who (in the right hardie breaking upon the enemie, by a few of the English, being for the most part gentlemen of honor and name) received his deathes wound, nere unto Sutphen the 22. of September last past, dyed at Aruam the 16. of October following: and with much honor and all possible mone, was solemnely buried in Paules the 16. of February 1586.*[...] (London: 1587).

[5] See further Clare Kinney, 'The Masks of Love: Desire and Metamorphoses in Sidney's *New Arcadia*', *Criticism*, 33 (1991), 461–90.

[6] The inscription reads 'For as to race and ancestry and the deeds that others than ourselves have done, I call those in no true sense our own'. John Buxton, *Sir Philip Sidney and the English Renaissance* (London: Macmillan, 1964), p. 49. In Latin the text is 'Nam genus et proavos et quae non fecimus ipsi, vix ea nostra voco'. *Ovid: The Metamorphoses*, trans. by Frank Justus Miller, rev. by G. P. Goold, 2 vols (London: Heinemann, 1984), 13. 140–41. The quotation is part of Ulysses's reply to Ajax in the contest for the arms of Achilles.

[7] Clare Gittings, *Death, Burial and the Individual in Early Modern England* (London: Croom Helm, 1984), p. 175. See also Ann Rosalind Jones and Peter Stallybrass,

Renaissance Clothing and the Materiality of Memory (Cambridge: Cambridge University Press, 2000), p. 250.

8 Jones and Stallybrass, *Renaissance Clothing and the Materiality of Memory,* p. 250.

9 Philip Hardie, *Ovid's Poetics of Illusion* (Cambridge: Cambridge University Press, 2002), p. 82.

10 As the various readings of Shakespeare's poem *Venus and Adonis* (c. 1593) demonstrate, allegorical interpretations of the goddess in early modern England are complex. A useful discussion of the ways in which Venus is variably signified may be found in Sasha Roberts, *Reading Shakespeare's Poems in Early Modern England* (Basingstoke: Palgrave Macmillan, 2003), pp. 20–91.

11 1. 858 ff.; 1. 722 ff.; 3. 443 ff.; 13. 874 ff.; 5. 484 ff.; 1. 544 ff.; 4. 208 ff.; 3. 207 ff.; 10. 614 ff.; 4. 347 ff.; 3. 316 ff.; 14. 802 ff. and 14. 709 ff. Apart from these narratives there is also Thirsis's tale of the creation of the world from chaos (1. 1 ff.); Damon's tale of Mercury and Battus is also from the *Metamorphoses* (2. 853 ff.). Arthur Golding, *The xv. Bookes of P. Ovidius Naso, etytuled Metamorphosis, translated oute of Latin into English meeter* [...] (London: 1567). Licoris's tale of Minerva and Vulcan does not have a wholly Ovidian precedent. The final tale told by Daphne is in prose and is original to *Amintas Dale*.

12 Golding, *The xv. Bookes*, 3. 389.

13   To the most illustrious and most Jewel-like demi-goddess,
        Kind, beautiful, learned: the Lady Mary, Countess of Pembroke.
        Grace of Graces, the image of the dying Philip,
        Hear Amyntas, breathing again after his death:
        Hear the sweet dogmas of noble prophets,
        Delights, Muses, Mysteries; finally, whatever
        Learned Greece has given, or regal Rome has left,
        Which has mixed the fruit with the blossom
        And teaching with delight.

    Translated in Abraham Fraunce, *The Third Part of the Countess of Pembroke's Ivychurch*, ed. by Gerald Snare (California: California State University Press, 1975), p. 151.

14 Juliet Fleming, 'Dictionary English and the Female Tongue', in *Enclosure Acts: Sexuality, Property and Culture in Early Modern England*, ed. by Richard Burt and John Michael Archer (Ithaca: Cornell University Press, 1994), pp. 290–326, p. 297.

15 In sixteenth-century England this concept of poetry most widely circulated in treatises such as Thomas Wilson, *The art of rhetorique for the use of all such as are studious of eloquence, set forth in English [...] 1553.* (London: 1585); William Webbe, *A Discourse of English Poetrie Together, with the authors judgment, touching the reformation of our English verse* (London: 1586); George Puttenham, *The Arte of English Contrived into three bookes: the first of poets and poesie, the second of proportion, the third of ornament.* (London: 1589); and, of course, Philip Sidney, *An Apologie for Poetrie* (London: 1595). See further Joel Elias Springarn, *A History of Literary Criticism in the Renaissance* (London: Macmillan, 1899).

16 Abraham Fraunce, *The Arcadian rhetorike: or The praecepts of rhetorike made plaine by examples Greeke, Latin, English, Italian, French, Spanish, out of Homers Ilias, and Odissea, Virgils Aeglogs, [...] and Aeneis, Sir Philip Sydnieis Arcadia, songs and sonets* (London: 1588). See further Abraham Fraunce, *The Arcadian Rhetoric*, ed. by Ethel Seaton (Oxford: Blackwell, 1950). For an introduction to Fraunce's life and work, see G. C. Moore-Smith, Preface, in *Victoria: A Latin Comedy* (Louvain: A Uystpryst, 1906), pp. ix–xl.

17 Translated in Snare, *The Third Part of the Countess of Pembroke's Ivychurch*, p. 151.
18 Golding, *The xv. Bookes*, 4. 49–50.
19 Golding, *The xv. Bookes*, 5. 383 ff.
20 Golding, *The xv. Bookes*, 1. 1–2.
21 For a discussion of Elpinus's relationship to actual commentators of the *Metamorphoses*, see further Mary Ellen Lamb, *Gender and Authorship in the Sidney Circle* (Wisconsin: University of Wisconsin Press, 1990), pp. 41 ff. I am greatly indebted to Lamb's discussion of *Amintas Dale*. However, Lamb has confined her discussion to some of Elpinus's commentary and the tales told by Dieromena and Daphne. I have furthered her argument by considering the text in the context of translation practices.
22 The Ovidian tales are equally divided between the genders. In order, the participants in the colloquy are: Thirsis, Menalcus, Dameotas, Fulvia, Philouevia, Amaryllis, Alphesibaeus, Damon, Coridon, Licoris, Aresia, Cassiopaea, Ergastus, Meliboeus, Sylvia, Dieromena and Daphne.
23 Golding, *The xv. Bookes*, 1. 1–492.
24 Haynes continues: 'the Tower of Babel shows that *variety* is the mark of sin; the farther Noah's children wandered, the more barbaric they became (the American Indians were most so) [...]. The peoples who could claim never to have moved and never to have changed – the Athenians, the Germans, the Ethiopians – were thought to be best'. Jonathan Haynes, 'George Sandys's Relation of a Journey Begun An Dom. 1610: The Humanist as Traveller' (unpublished doctoral thesis, Urbana: Illinois, 1980), p. 14.
25 Daniel J. Vitkus, 'Turning Turk in *Othello*: The Conversion and Damnation of the Moor', *Shakespeare Quarterly*, 48 (1997), 145–76, 145.
26 For a fascinating discussion about the semiotics of beards, see Will Fisher, 'Masculinity in Early Modern England', *Renaissance Quarterly*, 54 (2001), 155–87. I would like to thank Kate Wright for bringing this article to my attention.
27 *Ovid: The Metamorphoses*, trans. Miller, 1. 146–7.
28 Golding, *The xv. Bookes*, 1. 166.
29 See *Oxford English Dictionary*, 'dandiprat', sense 2b.
30 Golding's translation uses the word 'take': 'And sayth: I first will die ere thou shalt take of me thy pleasure'. Golding, *The xv. Bookes*, 3. 488.
31 See *Oxford English Dictionary*, 'yield', signification I, II, and III.
32 Catherine Belsey, *The Subject of Tragedy: Identity and Difference in Renaissance Drama* (London: Routledge, 1985), p. 149.
33 Lamb, *Gender and Authorship in the Sidney Circle*, p. 42.
34 Roberts, *Reading Shakespeare's Poems in Early Modern England*, p. 21.
35 Lamb, *Gender and Authorship in the Sidney Circle*, p. 41.
36 Appolodorus, the *Library*, trans. by James George Frazer, 2 vols (London: Heinemann, 1921), 3. 14, 4–6.
37 In Golding's translation: 'A childe calde *Ericthonius,* whome never woman bare'. Golding, *The xv. Bookes*, 2. 695.
38 In Golding's translation: 'And there they saw a childe whose partes beneath were like a Snake'. Golding, *The xv. Bookes*, 2. 704.
39 Though Aglauros is turned into stone by Mercury, Minerva engenders Envy in the girl which leads to her demise. Golding, *The xv. Booke,* 2. 935 ff.
40 Lamb, *Gender and Authorship in the Sidney Circle*, p. 41.

41   See further William Keach, *Elizabethan Erotic Narratives* (London: Harvester Press, 1977) and Sandra Clark, *Amorous Rites: Elizabethan Erotic Verse* (London: Dent, 1994).

42   Belsey, *The Subject of Tragedy*, p. 149.

43   Lamb, *Gender and Authorship in the Sidney Circle*, p. 42.

44   The poet appears in a text by Leone Ebreo, *The Philosophy of Love*. See Snare, *The Third Part of the Countess of Pembroke's Ivychurch*, p. 151.

45   Patricia Parker, *Literary Fat Ladies: Rhetoric, Gender, Property* (London: Methuen, 1987), p. 15.

46   In a later essay Parker discusses ways in which gender politics pervade rhetorical treatises in the early modern period. See Patricia Parker, 'Virile Stile', in *Premodern Sexualities*, ed. by Louise Fradenberg and Carla Freccero (London: Routledge, 1996), pp. 199–222.

47   Edmund Spenser, *The Faerie Queene*, 1. i. 21. In his discussion of 'Ovidian Subtexts in *The Faerie Queene*', Raphael Lyne suggests that 'the hideous spontaneous births of Errours children is compared with the generative power of the Nile mud, itself an Ovidian story [1. 416–37]'. Raphael Lyne, *Ovid's Changing Worlds: English Metamorphoses 1567–1633* (Oxford: Oxford University Press, 2001), p. 99. For a discussion of Errour as 'female genetrix or janitrix who emblematizes the disorderly multiplicity of origins' see Philippa Berry, 'Renewing the Concept of Renaissance: The Cultural Influence of Paganism Reconsidered', in *Textures of Renaissance Knowledge*, ed. by Philippa Berry and Margaret Tudeau-Clayton (Manchester: Manchester University Press, 2003), pp. 17–34, p. 27. The seeming relationship between Chaos and Errour may not be a chance one. Fraunce used quotations from book 2 of *The Faerie Queene* in *The Arcadian rhetorike* two years before books 1–3 were published. See Seaton, *The Arcadian Rhetoric*, p. xl.

48   Mikhail Bakhtin, *Rabelais and His World*, trans. by Helene Iswolsky (Cambridge, Mass.: MIT. Press, 1968), p. 26, cited in Peter Stallybrass, 'Patriarchal Territories: The Body Enclosed' in *Rewriting the Renaissance: The Discourses of Sexual Difference in Early Modern Europe*, ed. by Margaret W. Ferguson, Maureen Quilligan and Nancy J. Vickers (Chicago: University of Chicago Press, 1986), pp. 123–44, p. 124.

49   See *Oxford English Dictionary*, 'brabbles', sense 3.

50   *Amintas Dale*, sig. K 1^r–K 2^v. Golding, *The xv. Bookes*, 2. 1 ff.

51   Golding, *The xv. Bookes*, 6. 164.

52   Golding, *The xv. Bookes*, 2. 853 ff. Damon's tale is eighth.

53   See *Oxford English Dictionary*, 'bald', sense 7.

54   Katherine Koller, 'Abraham Fraunce and Edmund Spenser', *English Literary History*, 7 (1940), 108–20, 116.

55   A. B. Taylor points out that Fraunce appears to be copying Golding as the earlier translator also uses the same dialect in the rendering of this tale. A. B. Taylor, 'Abraham Fraunce's Debts to Arthur Golding in *Amintas Dale*', *Notes and Queries*, 33 (1986), 333–6, 333. For a critical analysis of the episode in Golding's translation, see Raphael Lyne, *Ovid's Changing Worlds*, pp. 58–9.

56   Katherine Koller, 'Abraham Fraunce and Edmund Spenser', *English Literary History*, 7 (1940), 108–20, 116. Paula Blank explains that 'one of the "fresh" aspects of Spenser's diction in *The Shepheardes Calender* is no doubt his use of northern English [...]. The significance of Spenser's use of northern English lies not only in relation to his use of archaisms [...]. The presence of northern English in *The Shepheardes Calender* calls

attention, more generally, to the way that the poet selected among the contemporary variety of "Englishes" – the dialects of English – in his construction of a poetic language'. Paula Blank, *Broken English: Dialects and the Politics of Language in Renaissance Writing*, (London: Routledge, 1996), p.104.

57 Koller states that she sees in Fraunce 'a young poet influenced by those ideas which E.K. sets forth in his letter to Harvey. Fraunce supports E. K's admiration for the use of "rusticall" words as appropriate to pastoral'. Koller, 'Abraham Fraunce and Edmund Spenser', p. 115.

58 For a discussion of the influence of women on the English language, see Juliet Fleming, 'Dictionary English and the Female Tongue', pp. 290–326.

59 Snare, *The Third Part of the Countess of Pembroke's Ivychurch*, p. v.

60 Snare, *The Third Part of the Countess of Pembroke's Ivychurch*, p. ii.

61 Richard Harvey, *An astrological discourse upon the great and notable conjunction of the tvvo superiour planets, Saturne and Jupiter, which shall happen the 28 day of April, 1583 With a briefe declaration of the effectes, which the late eclipse of the sunne 1582. is yet heerafter to woorke. Written newly by Richard Harvey: partely, to supplie that is wanting in common prognostications: and partely by praediction of mischiefes ensuing, either to breed some endevour of prvuention by foresight, so farre as lyeth in us: or at leastwise, to arme us with pacience beforehande* (London: 1583).

62 Nashe wrote: 'Gentlemen, I am sure you have hearde of a ridiculous Asse that many yeares since sold lyers by the great, and wrote an absurd *Astrologicall Discourse* of the terrible Conjunction of *Saturne* and *Jupiter* [...]. Thomas Nashe, *Pierce Penilesse. His Supplication to the Divell* (London: 1592), sig. d4^r.

63 Lamb, *Gender and Authorship in the Sidney Circle*, p. 43.

64 Lamb, *Gender and Authorship in the Sidney Circle*, pp. 43–4.

65 Lamb, *Gender and Authorship in the Sidney Circle*, p. 43.

66 Lamb, *Gender and Authorship in the Sidney Circle*, p. 43.

67 Snare, *The Third Part of the Countess of Pembroke's Ivychurch*, p. 44.

68 Golding, *The xv. Bookes*, 15. 990–5.

69 Belsey, *The Subject of Tragedy*, p. 148.

70 See further Taylor, 'Abraham Fraunce's Debts to Arthur Golding'.

71 Ovid constructed the *Metamorphoses* in hexameters.

72 Douglas Bush, *Mythology and the Renaissance Tradition in English Poetry*, rev. edn (Minnesota: University of Minnesota Press, 1960), p. 30.

73 Thomas Nashe addresses Mary Sidney as the 'fayre sister of Phoebus, [and] eloquent secretary to the Muses, most rare Countesse of Pembroke [...] whom Artes doe adore as a second Minerva'. *Syr P.S. His Astrophel and Stella Wherein the excellence of sweete poesie is concluded. To the end of which are added, sundry other rare sonnets of divers noble men and gentlemen.* (London: 1591), sig. A 4r.

74 S. P. Cerasano and M. Wynne-Davis (eds.), *Renaissance Drama by Women: Texts and Documents* (London: Routledge, 1996), pp. 13–15.

75 The quotations are from Mary Sidney, *The Tragedy of Antonie*, in *Renaissance Drama by Women: Texts and Documents*, ed. by S. P. Cerasano and M. Wynne-Davis (London: Routledge, 1996), pp. 13–42. For a stimulating essay on Sidney's play see Danielle Clarke, 'The Politics of Translation and Gender in the Countess of Pembroke's *Antonie*', *Translation and Literature*, 6.2 (1997), 149–66. See also Danielle Clarke, *The Politics of Early Modern Women's Writing* (Harlow: Longman, 2001), pp. 83–95.

76 Sherry Simon, *Gender in Translation: Cultural Identity and the Politics of Transmission* (London: Routledge, 1996), pp. 47–8.

77 Lines 98–144. In the *Metamorphoses*, Procne is changed into a swallow (6. 846 ff.);

Alcyone becomes a Halcyon (11. 844 ff.); Niobe is transformed into a statue (6. 386 ff.); Myrrha is turned into the myrrh–tree (10. 561 ff.); and Echo fades to the voice which can only repeat the last words of others (3. 427 ff.). Golding, *The xv. Bookes.*

[78] This was a common depiction as the title of Margaret Hannay's book suggests. See further Margaret P. Hannay, *Philip's Phoenix: Mary Sidney, Countess of Pembroke* (Oxford: Oxford University Press, 1990).

[79] Elizabeth D. Harvey, *Ventriloquized Voices: Feminist Theory and Renaissance Texts* (London: Routledge, 1992), p. 29.

[80] Parker goes on to say that 'the English were notorious for translation in this sense. Texts such as Puttenham's *Arte of English Poesie* traced the history of English poetry as a history of translation of foreign texts; and the uncertain boundary between imitation, translation and thievery is a running motif of English literary history'. Patricia Parker, *Shakespeare From the Margins: Language, Culture, Context* (Chicago: University of Chicago Press, 1996), p. 137. The term plagiarism, however, was not common in this period. Harold Ogden White has shown that before 1600 only 'two writers anglicized Martial's figurative use of *plagiarus* (man-stealer) for literary thief'. Harold Ogden White, *Plagiarism and Imitation During the English Renaissance* (London: Frank Cass, 1965), p. 120. See also Paulina Kewes (ed.), *Plagiarism in Early Modern England* (Basingstoke: Palgrave Macmillan, 2003).

[81] Lamb states that 'as partial translations, Fraunce's works are, literally, readings of other authors'. Lamb, *Gender and Authorship in the Sidney Circle*, p. 42.

[82] Cited in *Thomas Watson's Latin Amyntas* (1585); *Abraham Fraunce's The Lamentations of Amyntas* (1587); *Abraham Fraunce's Translation The Lamentations of Amyntas* (1587), ed. by Franklin M. Dickey and Walter F. Staton Jr. (Chicago: University of Chicago Press for the Newberry Library, 1967), p. xx. The details of this accusation against Fraunce are from Dickey and Staton's introduction to this edition.

[83] sig. A 2^r cited in Dickey and Staton (eds.), *Thomas Watson's Latin Amyntas*, p. 93.

[84] Louise Schleiner, *Tudor and Stuart Women Writers* (Bloomington: Indiana University Press, 1994), pp. 54–5.

[85] Louise Schleiner, *Tudor and Stuart Women Writers*, p. 54.

[86] I am drawing here on Anne Fogarty's use of Foucault's notion of heterotopia. Fogarty explains that '[Foucault] propounds the theory that societies maintain themselves by incorporating within their structures "other spaces", or oppositional sites, in which the many facets of their ideologies or belief systems may be simultaneously represented, contested, inverted. While these counter-sites may involve an idealizing moment, Foucault ultimately distinguishes them from the non-place of utopia and prefers instead to refer to them as heterotopias, that is the places of Otherness or difference.' Anne Fogarty, 'The Colonisation of Language: Narrative Strategy in *The Faerie Queene* Book VI', in *Edmund Spenser*, ed. by Andrew Hadfield (London: Longman, 1996), pp. 196–210, p. 197. Fogarty suggests that literature, a site omitted by Foucault, can be added to this list.

[87] Susan Bassnett, 'The Meek or the Mighty: Reappraising the Role of the Translator', in *Translation, Power, Subversion*, ed. by Román Álvarez and M. Carmen-África Vidal (Clevedon: Multilingual Matters, 1996), pp. 10–24, p. 16.

[88] Snare, *The Third Part of the Countess of Pembroke's Ivychurch*, p. xi.

[89] Lamb, *Gender and Authorship in the Sidney Circle*, p. 47.

90 Fraunce's text was originally produced in Latin. The quotation is from Abraham Fraunce, *Symbolicae Philosophiae Liber Quartus et Ultimus*, trans. by Estelle Haan (New York: AMS, 1991), p. 9.

91 Michael Cronin, *Translating Ireland* (Cork: Cork University Press, 1996), p. 1.

Chapter 3

Violence in Translation:
George Sandys's *Metamorphosis Englished*

[T]hose of us who live within the privilege of Western patriarchy live in an increasingly narrow psychic and social space. For we cannot afford to enter most of the social spaces of the world; they have become dangerous to us, filled with the violence of the people we oppress, our own violence in alien forms we refuse to recognise [...]. Terrorizing the world with our wealth and power, we live in a world of terror, afraid to venture out, afraid to think openly. Difference and dialogue are impossible here. We talk to ourselves about ourselves, believing in a grand hallucination that we are talking with others [...].[1]

Translating the King

Richard Lanham has observed that the *Metamorphoses* is a terrifying world with anger and violence everywhere.[2] In telling how the nation state of Rome was formed, Ovid intersperses his epic with scenes which focus on the plight of figures such as Actaeon, Philomela and Marsyas who are subjected to terrifying effects of power. In spite of this interest in physical repression, the narrative voice Ovid's poem, a 'diffuse authorial self',[3] does not offer these violent episodes in a didactic mode of address; 'the point is not to hierarchise – there are no hierarchies here, and no perspectives either'.[4] This is not the case in early modern English translations of the text. The translator's voice, most apparent in the paratextual material that often accompanies the work, considerably alters the political agenda of the *Metamorphoses*. In *Renaissance Self-Fashioning: From More to Shakespeare*, as we saw in the Introduction, Stephen Greenblatt refers to the physical violence inherent in early modern translation practices. Lawrence Venuti contends, however, that 'violence resides in its very purpose and activity' and is 'always configured in hierarchies of dominance and marginality'.[5] With these foregoing remarks in mind, this chapter will argue that these violent translation practices are apparent in the 1632 edition of George Sandys's *Metamorphosis Englished*: a text inscribed with an acute awareness of the domestic political and cultural issues at stake for fashioning and sustaining Caroline subjectivity.

Sandys's own personal and textual lineage distinctly frames his translation of the *Metamorphoses*. The son of Archbishop Edwin Sandys, one of the translators of the Bishops' Bible, Sandys is most commonly associated with translation of

Christian texts,[6] and the 1632 edition of Sandys's Ovid, produced within a context of intellectual and religious sobriety, is the epitome of a conservative text. Now complete with commentary and illustration, this revision of the 1626 translation was printed by John Lichfield of Oxford, who is 'generally associated with Protestant theology of a Calvinist or near Calvinist kind'.[7] The inclusion of the *Metamorphoses* in Lichfield's list of pious publications emphasizes the degree to which this version of Ovid's poem is aligned with the moralized Christian tradition of the vernacular Ovid but, markedly, Sandys's text presents an even more tempered translation than many of his predecessors. Although Sandys's contemporaries, such as George Chapman, used a liberal form of prosody for their translations, the syntax of the *Metamorphosis Englished* is additionally restrained.[8] Compared with Arthur Golding's *Metamorphosis* (1567), for example, Sandys's Ovid has been defined as one which is 'urbane, elliptical, in controlled iambic pentameter' against Golding's 'unsophisticated metaphrase, in trundling fourteeners'.[9] However, the most noteworthy aspect of Sandys's translation is that it was published under the patronage of Charles; the title page announces:

> *Cum privilegio ad imprimendam hanc Ovidii*
> *TRANSLATIONEM*[10]

Clearly, Sandys's Ovid sets out to conform to, and confirm, the King's political agenda.

In his discussion of this ideologically mindful translation, Anthony Brian Taylor suggests that Sandys's translation plays down the dramatic tendencies of Golding's *Metamorphosis*.[11] Nevertheless, implicitly drawing on 'Ovid's own theatrical metaphor, "the gods play their roles (1. 245)"',[12] Marie A. Powles considers the dramatic aspects of Sandys's Ovid that lay beyond the poem. She argues that the material provided by 'Sandys the poet, [Francis] Clein the artist, and [Bernard Salomon] Savery the engraver, contrived together to present Sandys's version of the *Metamorphoses* in a unique way, namely, as a play to be staged and interpreted by the gods'.[13] In the light of this observation, Powles confines her exploration of Sandys's Ovid to the first Plate (Illustration 3.1), which she likens to the 'architectural layout' of an elaborate early modern stage.[14] Yet, this dramatic analogy may be developed further. The 1632 edition, with its elaborate frontispiece, prefatory poem, dedication to the King, panegyrics to the King and Queen, address to the reader, two sections on Ovid, illustrations, annotations and commentaries, can stand comparisons with the opulence of a literary genre in favour at the Caroline court: the masque.

With each frame of text sliding back until the reader reaches the centre stage of the poem, the structure of Sandys's Ovid resembles the *scena ductilis* of the masque. In turn, the translation and the commentary are aligned with the iconographic conventions of the 1630s which assist in fashioning and promoting the King's public image. At the outset, as in the court masque, Sandys's *Metamorphosis Englished* upholds the mythic embodiment of Charles and Henrietta Maria. In Aurelian Townshend's masque *Albion's Triumph* (1632), for instance, Charles as the Emperor Albanctus 'was a noble compliment to Henrietta

Maria as Divine Beauty in *Tempe Restored* (1632)'.[15] In the prefatory material of
Sandys's Ovid, Henrietta Maria is similarly lauded as the 'Faire Queene' on whom
'The Graces will rejoyce, [to] sue' (p. 3ᵛ n. p.), whilst Charles is praised as:

> Jove, whose transcendent Acts the Poets sing,
> By Men made more than Man, is found a King:
> Whose Thunder and inevitable Flame,
> His justice and magestick Awe proclaime:
> His chearfull Influence, and refreshing Showers,
> Mercy and Bounty; Marks of heavenly Powers.
> These, free from Joves disorders, blesse thy Raigne;
> And might restore the golden Age againe, (p. 2ᵛ n. p.)

Although the King is likened to the mighty Jove, it would not be felicitous to
proclaim the English monarch as the type of Jove who, we are soon to be reminded
in Ovid's poem, is the aggressive abductor of both women and men.[16] In which
case, it is necessary for Sandys's panegyric to announce that Charles is a monarch
'free from Jove's disorders' (p. 2ᵛ n. p.). Distinctions of this kind are made
throughout these dedicatory verses, hence it is 'Not Cupid's wild-fiers, but thise
Beames which dart| From Venus purer Sphere inflame thy heart' (p. 2ᵛ n. p.) and
Charles is said to be 'Like Bacchus' in his 'fresh Youth and free delights| Not as
disguised in his frantick Rites' (p. 2ᵛ n. p.). The outworks of the *Metamorphosis
Englished* are thus hard-working in their revision of classical mythologies which
comply with the dominant discourses of the period. The ancient gods required
Mercury and Iris to act as mediators between them and the mortals over whom they
exerted power;[17] as translator *cum privilegio*, Sandys significantly functions as a
mediator of the political ideologies of Charles. In sum, Sandys's Ovid embodies a
complex translation of the court by the court, upholding and promoting an ideology
of subjection and rule through notions of harmony and moderation.

The prevailing image of the royal couple in circulation was one of familial and
nuptial unification. 'Never', wrote Lord Goring in 1633, 'was there a private
family more at full peace and tranquillity than in this glorious kingdom'.[18]
Primarily expressed in terms of the Neoplatonic philosophy brought into the court
by the French Queen, the representation of the royal nucleus was a further
indication of a Golden Age restored:[19]

> Charles and Henrietta Maria, one the son of the pacifist James, the other the
> daughter of the warlike Henri IV, have come together in a perfect union that is
> indissoluble; it is the perfect union Plato described in Aristophanes' speech in the
> *Symposium* that the gods feared lest its power should prove greater than their own; it
> is a manifestation of the love that will restore us to our ancient nature and heal us
> and make us blessed and happy. The platonic hermaphrodite has reappeared as the
> controlling spirit of the blessed islands of Great Britain and its name is
> CarloMaria.[20]

This hermaphroditic image is also constructed in the panegyrics which frame the
Metamorphosis Englished. The CarloMaria inhabits Sandys's address to Charles as

Illustration 3.1 **Frontispiece, George Sandys, *Ovids Metamorphosis Englished Mythologized, and Represented in Figures* (Oxford: 1632)**

'Thou our Mercury' (p. 2^v n. p.) and to Henrietta Maria as the 'Queen of Love' (p. 3^v n. p.). In other words, the royal couple become a Neoplatonic Herm[es]‖ Aphrodite, a figure evident in Sandys's 'The Minde of the Frontispeece And Argument of this Worke':

> FIRE, AIRE, EARTH, WATER, all the Opposites
> That strove in *Chaos*, powerfull LOVE unites;
> And from their Discord drew this Harmonie. (p. 1^v n. p.)

Beyond the boundaries of conjugality, physical desire is denounced and 'Powerful Love' is promoted as the means to reach intellectual bliss:

> [...] But, our *Will*,
> *Desire*, and *Powers Irascible*, the skill
> Of PALLAS orders; who the *Mind* attires
> With all *Heroick Vertues*: [...]
> But who forsake that faire *Intelligence*,
> To follow *Passion*, and voluptuous *Sense*;
> That shun the Path and Toyles of HERCULES;
> Such, charm'd by CIRCES'S luxurie and ease,
> Themselves deforme: 'twixt whom, so great an ods;
> That these are held for Beasts, and those for Gods. (p. 1^v n. p.)

In part inherited from the moralized tradition of Ovidian translation, the hermeneutic practice of reading the *Metamorphoses* through a frame of intellectual reason is typical. Ovid's poem is bound by tales in which chariots race out of control, and Arthur Golding, for example, used this Ovidian trope in order to advise his reader to keep charge of their 'feerce affections'.[21] In Sandys's translation, however, the conventional binarisms of mind and body, reason and passion are used for the explication of Caroline Neoplatonic ideology.

Although exploitative of the Royalist predilection for extravagant display, Charles attempted to control the erotic excesses associated with James I. As Thomas N. Corns explains, 'in place of the sometimes outrageous, sometimes profane, sometimes inebriated and always open court of James I came an obsessive decorum, an obvious piety, a scrupulous sexual morality, and a new fascination with court ritual'.[22] An example of this reformed behaviour may be observed in the treatment of Henry Jermyn, a favourite of Henrietta Maria, and Eleanor Villiers, the Queen's maid. When Villiers became pregnant with Jermyn's child, Charles ordered the courtier to marry her or face exile from the court.[23] Sensual control, therefore, is one of the main concerns of the *Metamorphosis Englished* and 'The Argument of this Worke' sets up the manner in which the reader is to approach Ovid's text. The containment of the translation within a labyrinth of marginal and end comments acts as guide marks for the 'meere English Reader' (p. 4^r n. p.), constantly steering them through the potentially dangerous text. If we recall the supposition that Augustus banished Ovid for the publication of the 'risqué *Ars Amatoria*' and the poet's participation in acts of moral indiscretion,[24] it might seem surprising that Charles endorsed a translation of *Metamorphoses*. But through this system of elaborate textual enclosure, Ovid's text becomes an appropriate text for the King's patronage and an English audience. To begin, in a prefatory section entitled 'The Life of Ovid', Sandys describes the Roman author as a man:

> of meane stature, slender of bodie, spare of diet: and, if not too amorous, every way temperate. hee drunk no wine but what was much alayed with water: an Abhorrer of unnaturall Lusts, from which it would seeme that age was not innocent. (p. 6^r n. p.)

In the following section, 'Ovid Defended', Sandys devotes four pages to compliments given to the classical author from writers ranging from Saint Augustine and Quintilian through to Scaliger and Micyllus. The biographical problems of Ovid notwithstanding, moralized versions of the *Metamorphoses* already place Ovid's text within the precepts of the Christian Church and, in terms of its own political agenda, the poem is particularly suitable for praising the Stuart King. Ovid's complex matrix of metamorphic myths reaches narrative closure with the anticipated apotheosis of Augustus Caesar, another figure that Charles employed in his extensive repertoire of classical iconography. Richard Fanshawe's famous *Ode* of 1630 demonstrates this mythologizing as Charles's rule over Britain, 'A world without the world', is compared with the control that Augustus claimed over his empire. The King is

> Th'Augustus of our world to praise
> In equall verse, author of peace
> And Halcyon Dayes.[25]

As Ovid pays homage to Augustus at the end of the *Metamorphoses*, by declaring that Charles will 'Slowly, yet surely, exchange [his] mortal diadem for an immortal' (p. 2^r n. p.), Sandys transforms his King and patron into an exalted emblem of power.

Moderating Ovid

In her detailed discussion of Sandys's use of the heroic couplet, Deborah Rubin argues that the textual differences in his translation are simply due to 'semantic license'.[26] But these 'minor subtractions or alterations' which Rubin identifies are of ideological importance. In his dedicatory epistle, Sandys states:

> to this have I added, as the Mind to the Body, the History and Philosophicall sence of the Fables (with the shadow of either in Picture) which I humbly offer at the same Alter, that they may as the rest of my labours, receive their estimation from so great an Authority. (p. 2^r n. p.)

Significantly, the relationship between the commentary and the translation is figured 'as the Mind to the Body'. Thus the textual apparatus which surrounds the Ovidian narrative, from the illustrations, the explanatory notes in the margin of the translation to the expansive commentaries which follow each book and the numerous prefatory devices, are all part of an elaborate civilizing process which is in keeping with the Neoplatonic ideologies of the court. Even Sandys's use of the heroic couplet tempers the violence encountered in Ovid's poem and effectively upholds the harmonious enterprise favoured by Charles.[27] This is most obvious in Sandys's treatment of Ovidian myths which are notorious for their images of torture and cruelty, and it is particularly marked in his translation of the myth of Philomela. Rubin suggests that 'when Sandys comes to translate Tereus's inner ravings [...] they acquire a matter - of - fact tone, a remote gloss and balance more characteristic of the narrator than the subject'.[28] In comparison to the Latin text, the restrictive prosody of the couplet form assists in reducing the depiction of the violence wrought against Philomela:

> While she reviles, invokes her father, sought
> To vent her spleen; her tongue in pincers caught,
> His sword devideth from the panting root:
> Which, trembling, murmurs curses at her foot.
> And as a serpents taile, dissever'd, Leaps:
> Even so her tongue; and dying sought her steps. (6. 577–82)

However, the extent to which Sandys plays down the violence is most apparent when his translation is considered alongside Golding's version of the myth:

> But as she yirnde and called ay upon hir fathers name,
> And strived to have spoken still, the cruell tyrant came,
> And with a paire of pinsons fast did catch hir by the tung,
> And with his sword did cut it off. the stumpe wheron it hung
> Did patter still. The tip fell downe, and quivering on the ground
> As though that it had murmured it made a certaine sound,
> And as an Adders tayle cut off doth skip a while: even so
> The tip of *Philomelaas* tongue did wriggle to and fro,
> And nearer to hir mistresse-ward in dying still did go. (6. 707–15)[29]

The anthropomorphic transformation of Philomela's tongue, so poignantly rendered in the Latin text and Golding's translation, is contracted in Sandys's Ovid; this is a translation practice which continues throughout much of the *Metamorphosis Englished*. A further example of Sandys's approach to the text is evident in another disturbing Ovidian episode. When Leucothoë's father buries her alive, Sandys's translation is detached from the tale's violent predilection. Wrongly believing that his daughter had dishonoured him by relinquishing her virginity to Apollo, Leucothoë's father, despite her protestations:

> [...] stern and savage, shuts up all remorse,
> From her that su'd, subdued, she said, by force;
> And Sol to witnesse calls. He his dishonour
> Interrs alive, and casts a Mount upon her. (4. 261–4)

Assisted by the use of alliteration and the enjambed line, Sandys's text is focused on Leucothoë as an emblem of her father's dishonour and her enclosure is swift. Golding takes a different approach to Ovid's narrative. In the earlier translation Leucothoë holds 'up hir hands to heaven when tenderly she wept' (4. 289) and her father 'like a savage beast' (4. 291) buried 'hir déepe in delved ground' (4. 292). Whereas Golding emphasizes the physical atrocities explicit here and in the Philomela myth, Sandys's translation seems to deflect his readers' attention from the tales' corporeal content.

As suggested in its transpositions of the myths of Philomela and Leucothoë, Sandys's Ovid is troubled by women's bodies. Physical desire, denigrated in the Neoplatonic philosophy supported by Charles and Sandys's prefatory poems, has conventionally been allegorized as woman.[30] In his discussion of the sexual politics of the Caroline court, Lawrence Venuti observes that

> the idealization of female beauty reduces woman to a passive ornament which serves man's active reason [...] in many masques, Charles's 'triumphs' are allegories of military, political, and religious domination, whereas Henrietta Maria's are usually psychological and moral reformations of her subjects' sexual morality accomplished by the mere sight of her.[31]

These hierarchical gender binarisms are also realized in Sandys's text. Charles is portrayed as a man who:

> If all men, by thy great Example lead
> Would that prepared way to Vertue tread.
> Rare Cures, deepe Prophesies, harmonious Layes,
>
> Inshear'd Apollo; crown'd with Wisdomes Raies. (sig. A ii^V)

By contrast, Henrietta Maria's corporeality is emphasized. Through physical presence alone she produces a transformative effect upon key Ovidian figures themselves:

> Self-lov'd Narcissus in the Myrror
> Of your faire eyes, now sees his error [...]
> Myrrha, who weeps for her offence,
>
> Presents her teares [...] (sig. A iii^V)

Though Henrietta Maria effects a moral change upon Narcissus and Myrrha, mythic embodiments of self–love and incest respectively,[32] arguably, the panegyric harbours an anxiety about the potentially dangerous agency of the 'Queen of Love' which is at odds with the Neoplatonic interests of Sandys's translation. However, as Ann Baynes Coiro suggests, whilst Henrietta Maria upheld the iconographic role in this 'chaste and silent love regime, she was almost constantly gravid or recovering from childbirth'.[33] Thus Sandys's concerns for women's corporeality have much in common with the 'poetry produced during the Caroline years' in which 'the paradigm at the centre of the court – highly sexual, prolific marriage –

pervades and worries its poetry'.[34] Whilst these anxieties are ultimately resolved in Sandys's description of the 'sweete Union [...] Of Nuptial loves; of Peacefull Dayes' (sig. A iv^r), the dedicatory epistle reveals much about the competing discourses which circulate in the Caroline court.

So far, it may seem that Sandys's translation is concerned to moderate the effects of violence upon, and the violent effects of, women's bodies alone. But his translation also offers the physical ordeals of male figures in less terrifying ways than either Ovid or Golding. For instance, Sandys's rendition of Actaeon's fate reduces the hunter's violent demise:

> I am *Actaeon*, servants, know your Lord!
> Thoughts wanted words, High skies the noyse record [...]
> Now is no roome for wounds. Grones speaks his pangs,
> Though not with human voyce, unlike a Hart:
> In whose laments the knowne Rocks beare a part.
> Pitcht on his knees, like one who pitty craves,
> His silent looks, instead of Armes, he waves. (3. 246–7, 254–8)

Golding's text, on the other hand, draws attention to Actaeon's grief:

> No part of him was frée from wound. He could none other do
> But sigh, and in the shape of Hart with voyce as Hartes are woont,
> (For voyce of man was none now left to helpe him at the brunt)
> By braying shew his secret grief among the Mountaynes hie,
> And knéeling sadly on his knées with dréerie teares in eye,
> As one by humbling of himselfe that mercy séemde to craue,
> With piteous looke in stead of handes his head about to wave. (3. 285–91)

In another Ovidian episode which is concerned with the mutilation of Pentheus's body, Sandys's translation severs the body of Ovid's text:

> Himself he blames, and his offence confest.
> Who cry'd, helpe Aunt Autonoe, I bleed;
> O let Actaeon's ghost soft pity breed!
> Not knowing who Actaeon was, she lops
> His right hand off: the other, Ino crops.
> The wretch now to his Mother would have throwne
> His suppliant hands: but, now his hands were gone. (3. 802–8)

Once more, a comparison with Golding's translation shows that the expansive metre of the earlier text, a version which culminates in Pentheus 'shewing [...] his maimed corse, and wounds yet bléeding warme' (3. 911), allows for a more detailed description of dismemberment. Finally, in the flaying of Marsyas, Sandys keeps the anatomical detail to a minimum:

> *Apollo* from his body stript his hide.
> His body was one wound, blood every way
> Streames from all parts: his sinewes naked lay.

His bare veines pant: his heart you might behold;
And all the fibers in his brest have told. (6. 414–18)

Typically, Golding describes the punishment meted out by Apollo with far more relish as 'o'er all his ears quite pullèd was his skin' (6. 493).[35] From thereon, as 'griesly bloud did spin| From every part' (6. 494–5), Golding describes the blazoning of Marsyas's body in resplendent fashion:

The quivering veynes without a skin lay beating nakedly.
The panting bowels in his bulke ye might have numbred well,
And in his brest the shere small strings a man might easly tell.
(6. 496–98).

As Sandys translates the 11,995 lines of the *Metamorphoses* into approximately 13,210 lines of English, on occasion there is obviously an expansion from the Latin text.[36] However, when Sandys renders corporeal violence into English there is a reduction in detail. By translating the *Metamorphoses* into a style more acceptable to seventeenth-century taste, it seems that Sandys's Ovid effectively intellectualizes corporeal violence.

Sandys's effacement of Ovidian violence is especially significant when we recall that this edition of the text was produced in a period in which the King's voice suppressed the dialogism of parliamentary government, and of his country, in favour of a monologism authorized by and centring on himself. Charles had governed Britain autonomously since 1629 and, in his attempt to reign absolutely, vernacularity became an important political weapon. English was the only language officially spoken at court and, as Kevin Sharpe points out, 'the King dismissed the Queen's French attendants and seemed anxious to keep her and his own contacts with the French court to a minimum'.[37] It is this socio-political context of national monologism which governs the production of the *Metamorphosis Englished*. As translator *cum privilegio*, Sandys is placed within the King's project to contain competing discourses and confirmation of Sandys's support of the all-powerful, governing voice of the King may be found in his commentary to book 4:

[...] we may conclude with Plato, that the Monarchicall government is of all the best: the type of God, and defigured in the Fabrick of mans Body: thus preferred by Homers Ulisses:
   All cannot rule; for many Rulers bring
   Confusion; let there be one Lord, one King. (sig. D 3ʳ)

On 24 April 1626 Sandys was granted the sole right to produce the English translation of the *Metamorphoses* for a twenty-one-year period. Significantly, as Sandys made use of legislation to inhibit publications which contested his own, the publication history of the *Metamorphosis Englished* is illustrative of the restrictive practices which are necessary to maintain control and authority.

To begin, Sandys filed a case in the Stationers' Court to prevent the selling of the pirated 1628 edition of the *Metamorphoses* and legal documents extant in the

Public Records Office tell of another court case involving Sandys and William Stansby, the printer of the first edition of the *Metamorphosis Englished*.[38] The authorization of Sandys as the single voice of *Metamorphosis Englished*, maintained by law, clashes with the moralized mode of address that Sandys adopts in his preface to the reader when he announces that 'it should be the principall end in publishing of Bookes, to informe the understanding, direct the will, and temper the affections' (sig. A i[v]). Although Sandys is overtly conscious of his status *cum privilegio*, he freely uses other versions of the *Metamorphoses*. On an empty page between book 1 and the commentary, 'left by the oversight of the Printer', Sandys eventually provides a list of writers 'least it should be objected how I make my owne which I doe but borrow'. He cites various Greek and Latin authors, church fathers and 'moderne writers: Geraldus, Pontanus, Ficinus, Vives, Comes, Scaliger, Sabinus, Pierius and, the crown of the latter, the Vicount of St Albons [Francis Bacon]' (sig. C 1[v]).[39] Nevertheless, Sandys generally obscures specific details about his use of source texts and much of the material that he uses remains unacknowledged,[40] such as his debt to Golding's earlier vernacular rendition.[41] Thus, in its production, circulation and translation practice the *Metamorphosis Englished* is inscribed with the ideologies of absolutism. Ultimately, both Sandys and Charles share the project of authority and authorship and they each uphold the promotion of the other in order to suppress competing discourses.

Significantly, the 1632 edition of the *Metamorphosis Englished* is accompanied by *An Essay on the Aeneid* – placed after Ovid's poem – and a line from the *Eclogues* is woven into the dedication to Charles:

> To the most High and Mightie Prince Charles, King of Greate Britaine, France and Ireland [...]. Sir [...] Your Gracious acceptance of the first fruits of my Travels [...] we had hoped, ere many yeares had turned about, to have presented you with a rich and peopled Kingdome; from whence now, with my selfe, I onely bring this Composure:
> *Inter victrices Hederam tibi sepere Lauros.*[42]
> It needeth more then a single denization, being a double Stranger: Sprung from the Stocke of the ancient Romanes; but bred in the New World, of the rudenesse whereof it cannot but participate; especially having Warres and Tumults to bring it to light instead of the Muses [...]. (sig A ii[r] n. p.)

Sandys began work on the *Metamorphoses* as he travelled to take up the position of Treasurer for the Virginia Company.[43] By describing the translation as one which had 'Warres and Tumults to bring it to light instead of the Muses', Sandys seems to allude to the violence that erupted in Jamestown in 1622 in the last years of James's sovereignty.[44] But the first priority of Charles's personal rule was peace and the enclosure of Ovid's poem within this Virgilian frame helps Sandys to promote Charles as the Augustan monarch, reigning over an idyllic kingdom where violence and sensuality have been erased. As part of a project which is concerned with the domestication of a foreign text, it is noteworthy that the quotation from the *Eclogues* remains in Latin. On the one hand, the Virgilian line establishes an affiliation between Sandys and Charles, translator and erudite patron, which is distinct from the hierarchical relationship between the translator and his 'meere English Reader'. But, on the other hand, Virgil's image of the poet's ivy enmeshed with the victor's laurels is also suggestive of the complex matrices of poetical and political discourses at work in Sandys's Ovid.

As Kevin Sharpe has discussed, the King 'identified disorder with unbridled passions in the body politic'.[45] With these comments in mind, Sandys's explication of Hercules' defeat of Antaeus (one of the twelve labours that Ovid briefly alludes to in book 9) is pertinent. Antaeus was a giant, Sandys states, who was 'the supposed son of the Earth who compelled forreiners to wrestle, and strangled them with his unmatchable strength' (sig. P p1ᵛ). His mother (the Earth) supplied his strength; as long as he remained in contact with her, the giant was invincible. Knowing this, Hercules lifted Antaeus from the ground and strangled him. Sandys explains that Hercules represents the heat of the sun, whilst Antaeus:

> [...] signifies the contrary with his too much fervour: when by the touch of the Earth, being naturally cold, his strength is restored: approving that Axiome in Physik how contraries are to be cured by Contraries; Yet neither too much to exceed, least the one be made more violent by the opposition of the other: which holds as well in a Politick Body. But the morall is more fruitfull: Hercules being the symbol of the Soule, and Antaeus of the Body. Prudence the essence of the one, and sensual Pleasure of the other, between whom there is a perpetuall conflict. (sig. P p1ᵛ)

The 'toyles' of Hercules have already been introduced in 'The Minde of the Frontispeece' as the model for overcoming 'passion, and voluptuous sense'. Once more, delivered by way of *contrarium*, the rhetorical figure of invention,[46] the same Neoplatonic precepts are the organizing principles of Sandys's discussion of this Ovidian episode. Of particular note, however, is Sandys's observation that the balance of the 'Politick Body' may also suitably maintained by means of this binary system where 'one contrary' is held in place by 'the other'. In the 1630s such order is partly preserved in the form of censorship which controlled oppositional voices.[47] For instance, William Prynne's *Histrio-Mastix: The Players Scourge*, published in the same year as this edition of the *Metamorphosis Englished*,[48] offers a different view of the monarchy and its relation to classical Rome than the one offered in Sandys's translation. Prynne's text, a Puritan diatribe against the stage and players, contained the index reference 'women actors, notorious whores' which was said to be a direct attack on Henrietta Maria, a regular performer in the court masques.[49] Moreover, Prynne was accused of aligning the Caroline court with that of the emperor Nero who was murdered in order to 'to vindicate the honour of the Roman Empire which was [...] basely prostituted by his viciousness'.[50] Almost Ovidian in its treatment of the body, the State tried Prynne for sedition and, as punishment, cut off his ears on the pillory. In spite of the State's brutal use of its subjects, as Sandys's muted translations of Ovid's 'violence in a pastoral landscape' illustrate,[51] the *Metamorphosis Englished* supports Charles's promotion of his country as harmonious.

Prynne's fate, meanwhile, shows how Caroline legislation used corporeal violence in order to restrict the play of signification.[52] As a translator operating in this censorious culture, Sandys attempts to contain the inaccuracies which may lurk in his opulent translation and commentary. His words to the reader conclude:

> lastly, since I cannot but doubt that my errors in so various a subject require a favourable connivence, I am to desire that the Printers may not be added to mine. The literall will easily passe without rubs in the reading; the grosse ones correct themselves; but by those betweene both the sence is in greatest danger to suffer. However, I have sifted out all, or the most materiall, and exposed them in the end of the Volume. (sig. B i^r)

Here the gap between 'literall' and the 'grosse' errors creates difficulties, but Sandys's problem is with errors which cannot be easily defined: 'but by those betweene both the sense is in greatest danger to suffer'. The reader, therefore, is carefully guided through the translation and across the labyrinth of borders and boundaries constructed as vital parts of Sandys's domesticating process. But there is always the danger that impolitic errors might break through textual fissures that cannot be enclosed.

Translating Otherness

Segments of Sandys's translation first appeared in his *Relation of a Journey begun Anno.Domini 1610* (1615).[53] In this popular account of his travels through Turkey, Egypt, the Holy Land and southern Italy, Sandys takes the encyclopedic approach which he later adopts in his 1632 edition of the *Metamorphosis Englished*.[54] The intertextual relationship between the *Relation of a Journey* and the *Metamorphosis* assists in defining Sandys as the embodiment of the traveller/translator who sets out to define and, potentially, domesticate the foreign body. But the extent to which the 'Other' can be contained is problematic and it is an issue which pervades Sandys's *Metamorphosis Englished* in many guises. At the beginning of the commentary to book 15, Sandys declares that 'Now are wee in sight of shore: arrived at the last booke of this admirable Poem' (sig. P pp3^r). According to Raphael Lyne, 'the journey through the work is seen as a kind of voyage, giving a thematic structure to the stories visited along the way'.[55] However, Sandys's sea-faring metaphor also recalls the environment in which his translation was initiated. The events in Jamestown show that the English were thwarted in their attempts to domesticate the colony and, with 'warres and Tumults to bring it to light instead of the Muses', Sandys's Ovid is inscribed with a sense of disruption from the outset. The only successful colonization that Sandys explicitly discusses is of the British by the Romans:

> [...] wherein the conquered were the gainers, having got thereby civility and letters, for a hardly won, nor long detained dominion. (sig. R r2^v)

Although he makes light of the Roman's success, Sandys shows how the processes and products of *translation studii* place the British as an erudite and civil nation above others. Throughout the years of Charles's personal rule, the relationship between Britain and the rest of Europe was unsettled. In 1629 Britain was still at war with France and Spain, two of the most powerful nations in Europe. By 1630 treaties had been signed with both countries, but diplomatic efforts were still needed between Britain and the rest of Europe, and these tensions are apparent in the commentary to the *Metamorphosis Englished*.[56]

As Sandys sees it, Britain's current state is an improvement on the past. The reign of Edward II is associated with famine (sig. M m2[r]), whilst that of Edward III is defined by pestilence (sig. G g3[r]). That England had suffered both famine and plague during the personal rule of Charles is explicitly, though not surprisingly, neglected.[57] Other countries, however, are viewed in less favourable terms. In Germany some say that there are witches 'who take and forsake the shapes of wolves at their pleasure, and for which they are daily executed' (sig. D 4[v]). Spain, according to Sandys's commentary, was once governed by Geryon who was 'fained to have had three heads' (sig. P p1[v]). The French are equally constructed in terms of the fantastic: goats are said to suckle the children of 'those poore women who either want milke; or have other imploiments, which they doe with as great affection and sedulity, as if they were their owne Kids' (sig. M mm3[v]); horns grow on the inhabitants' heads (sig. R rr2[r]) and the devil reanimates the corpses of French women:

> yet by a French gentleman I was told a strange accident, which befell a brother of his who saw on Saint German's bridge by the Louvre a Gentlewoman of no meane beauty, sitting on the stones (there laid to finish that worke) and leaning on her elbow with a pensive aspect. According to the French freedome he began to court her; whom shee intreated for that time to forbeare; yet told him if hee would bestow a visit on her at her lodging about eleven of the clock, he should finde entertainment agreeable to his quality. He came, she receaved him and to bed they went; who found her touch too cold for her youth; when the morning discovered unto him a Coarse by his side, forsaken by the soule the evening before: who halfe distracted ran out at the doore and carried with him a cure for his incontinency. Although this story have no place in my belief; yet is it not incredible that the Divell can enter and actuate the dead by his spirits; as sufficiently appeares by that kinde of witchcraft, which gives answers by dead bodies, reported by divers historians. (sig. A aa1[r])

Although Sandys denounces the truth of this necrophilic tale, the specificity of detail and its relation to historical fact provides a counterpoint to the proposed fictional aspects and, in the end, from corporeal body to the body politic, the French nation and its subjects are obviously disparaged.[58] Indeed, throughout his translation and commentary Sandys shows that both the physical body and the body politic are constructed and controlled through an intricate network of discourses. Whether enclosed within a patriarchal system of binary opposition that portrays the subordinate term as deviant other or exiled from the system of privilege for failing to respect that enclosure, the body is defined and marked by the imperial voice. Pointedly, Sandys's translation of the *Metamorphoses*, a classical text inscribed with corporeal desire, violence and exile, is mindful to echo that imperial voice: to rein in, and reign over, the errant body of the text. The encasement of physical bodies, individually and collectively, functions as a means of political control. In terms of the written word, figurative 'bodies' of language, attempts are often made to restrict the problematic play of signification. As Annabel Patterson has argued, William Prynne's punishment demonstrates both the way in which the 'state functioned as a "reader" of texts' and 'the role and status of ambiguity in the reading process'.[59] The choice of the *Metamorphoses* as a text *cum privilegio* is interesting for it harbours a host of subversive elements, from its classical author's biographical details to the content of the poem itself. Sandys makes every effort to overcome the troubling aspects of the text, but the very processes that enclose the *Metamorphosis Englished* make visible the ideological project of containment.

   In book 1 of Ovid's narrative, the tyrannical acts of Lycaon – an early king of Arcadia and the poem's first tale of human transformation into beast – leads to a striking domestication of the god's court in Sandys's translation:

> A Synod call'd, the summoned appears.
> There is a way, well seene when skies be cleare,
> The *Milkie* nam'd: by this, the Gods resort
> Vnto th' Almightie Thunderers high Court.
> With ever-open doors, on either hand,
> Of nobler Deities the Houses stand,
> The Vulgar dwell disperst: the Chiefe and Great
> In front of all, their shining Mansions seat.
> This glorious Roofe I would not doubt to call,
> Had I but boldnesse lent mee, Heaven's White-Hall. (1. 171–80)[60]

The prefatory panegyrics have already argued that Charles is 'Free from Jove's disorders', but this elision between Jove's court and Whitehall makes further, unwelcome, associations between the god and the British King.[61] Jove intends to punish Lycaon (by turning him into a wolf) and to destroy the race of mankind. In terms of seventeenth-century cultural politics, the god's approach to dissent is relevant:

> Thinke you, you Gods, they can in safety rest,
> When me (of lightning, and of you possest,
> Who both at our Imperiall pleasure sway)
> The sterne *Lycaon* practiz'd to betray?
> All bluster, and in rage the wretch demand.
> So, when bold treason sought, with impious hand,
> By *Caesar's* blood t'out-race the Roman name;
> Man-kind, and all the World's affrighted Frame,
> Astonisht at so great a ruine, shooke.
> Nor thine, for Thee, lesse thought, *Augustus*, tooke,
> Then they for *Jove*. He, when he had supprest
> Their murmur, thus proceeded to the rest. (1. 202–13)

As Jove lectures to the assembled deities, the reader learns about the ways in which he punishes treasonable acts and stifles recalcitrant voices. Heather James observes that Sandys's 'target audience includes a king whose father declared to Parliament in 1610 that "it is sedition in Subjects to dispute what a King may do in the height of his power [...] I will not be content that my power be disputed upon.'"[62] In its depiction of Jove's court, as James discusses, Sandys's translation engages with the potentially volatile issue of absolutism, a subject which is considered further in the commentary. By way of Sabinus and Seneca, Sandys attempts to 'flatter the monarch but critique the theory of monarchical absolutism'.[63] Thus, James's argument exposes some crucial fault-lines in Sandys's commentary which, like Ovid, 'permits topical reference only in the first and last of its fifteen books'.[64] Beyond these examples, however, there are other elements of the *Metamorphosis Englished* which disturb the prevailing Caroline ideologies. Sandys explains to the reader that:

> [...] for thy farther delight I have contracted the substance of every Booke into as many Figures (by the hand of a rare Workman, and as rarely performed, if our judgments may be led by theirs, who are Masters among us in that Faculty) since there is betweene Poetry and Picture so great a congruitie; the one called by *Simonides* a speaking Picture, and the other a silent Poesie: [...] as the rarest peeces in Poets are the descriptions of Pictures, so the Painter expresseth the Poet with equall Felicitie; representing not onely the actions of men, but making their Passions and Affections speake in their faces; in so much as he renders the lively Image of their Minds as well as of their Bodies; (sig B ii^v)

When placed against the orthodox configuration of the nation state in the 1630s, Clein's illustrations provide an alternative view of the cultural context in which Sandys's translation is produced. Of particular interest is the engraving which accompanies book 4 (Illustration 3.2). At the centre are the entwined bodies of Salmacis and Hermaphroditus, with the anxious expression of the latter thrown into relief. This depiction of the way in which 'In one Hermaphrodite, two bodies joyne' (sig. O 3^r), as 'The Argument to the Booke' states, is in direct contrast with the other biform, Neoplatonic figure which prefaces Sandys's translation in 'The Minde of the Frontispeece': the CarloMaria. Indeed, the illustration is an apt accompaniment to Sandys's translation:

> Their cleaving bodies mix: both have one face:
> As when wee two divided scions joyne
> And see them grow together in one rine: (4. 418–20)

Sandys's choice of the verb 'cleaving', signifying both division and attachment,[65] succinctly illustrates the double-bind. The prefatory material is witness to Sandys's careful allegorization of Charles as Jove, although this negotiation is complicated from the moment that Sandys renders Jove's palace as Whitehall. Similarly, Sandys's commentary carefully explains the difference between the idealized image of the Platonic androgyne and the Ovidian hermaphrodite:

Illustration 3.2　　Illustration, book 4, George Sandys, *Ovids Metamorphosis Englished, Mythologized, and Represented in Figures* (Oxford: 1632), p. 123 (facing)

Plato recites a fable, how man at the first was created double, and for his arrogance dissected into male and female: the reason of their affected conjunction, as converting to returne to their originall: [...] So Hermaphroditus and Salmacis retaine in one person both sexes: of whom the like are called Hermaphroditus. (sig. R 4^r)

'Among French humanists of the sixteenth century', as Edgar Wind discusses, 'l'androgyne de Platon became so acceptable an image for the universal man that a painter could apply it without impropriety to an allegorical portrait of Francis I'.[66] In the late sixteenth and early seventeenth centuries, however, the hermaphrodite is also associated with a fissured body politic. In Ambroise Paré's fourth chapter 'Of Hermaphrodites or Scrats' from the popular and widely circulated text *Of Monsters and Modern Prodigies*, the caption to the 'effigie' of a hermaphroditic figure in Thomas Johnson's translation (1634) hints at the connection between the biform figure and the divided nation state: 'the same day the *Venetians* and the *Genoeses* entered into league, there was a monster born in *Italy* having foure armes and feet but one head'.[67] By juxtaposing Plato's narrative alongside Ovid's myth, 'the first mythographer to conflate the Platonic with the Ovidian Hermaphrodite',[68] Sandys attempts to establish a difference between the harmonious image of the CarloMaria, the mythic embodiment of a unified body politic, and the fragmented hermaphrodite, but this is an opposition which ultimately collapses.[69]

Charles sought to present a unified image of the monarchy in which the harmonious body politic itself would be depicted. Likewise Sandys's text, produced *cum privilegio*, promotes an Arcadian image of king, court and country as the nation is held aloft as the epitome of a 'golden age restored'. However, as Graham Parry and others have shown, Charles's period of personal rule was riven with the fear of dissolution, chaos and war.[70] Against this backdrop of history, the fearful face of Clein's Hermaphroditus, an allegorical figure of the divided subject, provides an alternative, but equally valid, view of the nation state. By mediating an imperial voice which aspires to command an ascetic, authorial and unified British subject, Sandys's translation emphasizes the ideological, often violent, strategies employed in the construction of the King's government. In Sandys's commentary other times and other countries are respectively seen as diseased and deviant. But with the Platonic biform figure of the CarloMaria placed in such close proximity to Ovid's fragmented Hermaphroditus, from our historical distance to the text it does not seem that, to use Sandys's words, 'Contraries are to be cured by Contraries'. Rather, the image of hermaphrodite in Sandys's *Metamorphosis Englished* reminds us that 'we talk to ourselves about ourselves, believing in a grand hallucination that we are talking with others'.

Notes

[1] Eric Cheyfitz, *The Poetics of Imperialism: Translation and Colonization from 'The Tempest' to 'Tarzan'* (New York: Oxford University Press, 1991), p. xiv.

[2] Richard Lanham, *The Motives of Eloquence: Literary Rhetoric in the Renaissance* (New Haven: Yale University Press, 1976), p. 59.

3   Lanham, *The Motives of Eloquence*, p. 36.
4   Lanham, *The Motives of Eloquence*, p. 59.
5   Lawrence Venuti, 'Translation as Cultural Politics: Regimes of Domestication in English', *Textual Practice*, 7 (1993), 208–23, 209.
6   Deborah Rubin, *Ovid's 'Metamorphosis Englished': George Sandys as Translator and Mythographer* (New York: Garland, 1985), p. 176. Sandys's other translations are: *A Paraphrase upon the Psalmes of David* (London: 1636), *A Paraphrase upon the Divine Poems* (London: 1638), *Christ's Passion* [translated from Grotius] (1640) and *A Paraphrase upon the Song of Solomon* (London: 1641). See further Richard Beale Davis, *George Sandys: Poet-Adventurer* (London: Bodley Head, 1955).
7   Other texts printed by Lichfield in 1632 which testify to the printer's religious and moral intent include Edward Barewood, *A Second Treatise of the Sabbath or an explication of the Fourth Commandment*; Calybute Downing, *A Discourse of the State Ecclesia-sticall of this Kingdome, in Relation to the* Civill; and *A Summe of Morall Philosophy* by William Pemble. See further Falconer Madan, *The Early Oxford Press: A Bibliography of Printing and Publishing at Oxford 1468–1640* (Oxford: Clarendon Press, 1895), p. 163.
8   Rubin, *Ovid's 'Metamorphosis Englished'*, p. 4.
9   Anthony Brian Taylor, 'George Sandys and Arthur Golding', *Notes and Queries*, 33 (1986), 387–91, 387.
10   All quotations are from George Sandys, *Ovids Metamorphosis Englished, mythologiz'd, and represented in figures. An essay to the translation of Virgil's AEneis* (Oxford: 1632).
11   Taylor, 'George Sandys and Arthur Golding', 388–9.
12   See further, Heather James, 'Ovid and the Question of Politics in Early Modern England', *English Literary History*, 70 (2003), 343–73, 351.
13   Marie A. Powles, 'Dramatic Significance of the "Figures" Prefacing Each Book of Sandys's Translation of Ovid's *Metamorphoses*', *University of Dayton Review*, 10 (1974), 39–45, 40.
14   Powles, 'Dramatic Significance of the "Figures" Prefacing Each Book of Sandys's Translation of Ovid's *Metamorphoses*', 40.
15   John Harris, Stephen Orgel and Roy Strong (eds.), *The King's Arcadia: Inigo Jones and The Royal Court* (London: The Arts Council of Great Britain, 1973), p. 165.
16   Io (1. 588 ff.); Callisto (2. 409 ff.); Europa (2. 846 ff.); Danäe (4. 611 ff.); Leda (6. 109 ff.) and Ganymede (10. 155 ff.), for example. Frank Justus Miller, *Ovid: The Metamorphoses*, rev. by G. P. Goold, 2 vols (London: Heinemann, 1984).
17   See Theo Hermans, 'Translation's Other', An Inaugural Lecture delivered at University College, London (London: University of London, 1996), p. 5
18   Coke MS 46, 2 July 1633, cited in Kevin Sharpe, *The Personal Rule of Charles I* (New Haven: Yale University Press, 1992), p. 185.
19   Ann Baynes Coiro, '"A Ball of Strife": Caroline Poetry and Royal Marriage', in *The Royal Image: Representations of Charles I*', ed. by Thomas N. Corns (Cambridge: Cambridge University Press, 1999), pp. 26–46, p. 26
20   Graham Parry, *The Golden Age Restor'd: The Culture of the Stewart Court 1603–44* (Manchester: Manchester University Press, 1981), p. 184.
21   In book 2 Phaeton fails to control the spirited horses of Phoebus's chariot. In order to save the Earth from destruction, Phaeton is eventually destroyed by Jupiter's thunderbolt. In book 15 Hippolytus is thrown from his chariot and is torn apart. I discuss the myth of Phaeton in more detail in Chapter 5.

22 Thomas N. Corns, 'Duke, Prince, King', in *The Royal Image: Representations of Charles I*, ed. by Thomas N. Corns (Cambridge: Cambridge University Press, 1999), pp. 1–25, p. 16.

23 Sharpe, *The Personal Rule of Charles I*, p. 190.

24 Gareth Williams, 'Ovid's Exile Poetry: *Tristia, Epistulae ex Ponto* and *Ibis*', in *The Cambridge Companion to Ovid*, ed. by Philip Hardie (Cambridge: Cambridge University Press, 2002), pp. 233–45, p. 233.

25 Richard Fanshawe, *Shorter Poems and Translations*, ed. by N. W. Bawcutt (Liverpool: Liverpool University Press, 1964), pp. 5–9, 33, 78–80. The significance of this poem was brought to my attention in Graham Parry, 'A Troubled Arcadia', in *Literature and the English Civil War*, ed. by Thomas Healy and Jonathan Sawday (Cambridge: Cambridge University Press, 1990), pp. 38–58.

26 Rubin, *Ovid's 'Metamorphosis Englished'*, p. 18.

27 Rubin, *Ovid's 'Metamorphosis Englished'*, p. 18.

28 Rubin, *Ovid's 'Metamorphosis Englished'*, pp. 45–6.

29 Arthur Golding, *The xv. Bookes of P. Ovidius Naso, entytuled Metamorphosis, translated oute of Latin into English meeter* [...] (London: William Seres, 1567).

30 Deborah Rubin, 'Sandys, Ovid and Female Chastity: The Encyclopedic Moraler as Moralist', in *The Mythographic Art: Classical Fable and the Rise of the Vernacular in Early Modern France and England*, ed. by Jane Chance (Gainesville: University of Florida Press, 1990), pp. 257–80, p. 257.

31 Lawrence Venuti, *Our Halcyon Dayes: English Prerevolutionary Texts and Postmodern Culture* (Wisconsin: University of Wisconsin Press, 1989), p. 226.

32 Narcissus fell in love with his own image (3. 396 ff.); Myrrha desired her father, Cinyras, (10. 431 ff).

33 Coiro, 'A Ball of Strife', p. 26

34 Coiro, 'A Ball of Strife', p. 27.

35 For a discussion of Golding's translation of this myth in relation to the 'culture of dissection' in the early modern period, see Jonathan Sawday, *The Body Emblazoned: Dissection and the Human Body in Renaissance Culture* (London: Routledge, 1995), p. 186.

36 Rubin, *Ovid's 'Metamorphosis Englished'*, p. 14.

37 Kevin Sharpe, *Criticism and Compliment: The Politics of Literature in the England of Charles I* (Cambridge: Cambridge University Press, 1987), p. 18.

38 See Richard Beale Davis, 'George Sandys v William Stansby: The 1632 Edition of Ovid's *Metamorphosis*', *The Library*, 3 (1949), 193–212.

39 For a discussion of the relationship between Sandys's Ovid and Francis Bacon, see Lee T. Pearcy, *The Mediated Muse: English Translations of Ovid 1560–1700* (Connecticut: Archon, 1984), pp. 37–70.

40 Rubin, *Ovid's 'Metamorphosis Englished'*, p. 178.

41 Taylor, 'George Sandys and Arthur Golding', 388.

42 The *Essay* was a translation of the first book of the *Aeneid*. The Latin quotation, however, is from another Virgilian text, *The Eclogues*, which translates as 'grant that about thy brows this ivy may creep among the victor's laurels'. Virgil, *Eclogues*, trans. by H. Rushton Fairclough, rev. edn (London: Heinemann, 1932), 8. 13.

43 See Raphael Lyne, 'Sandys's Virginian Ovid', in *Ovid's Changing Worlds: English Metamorphoses 1567–1632* (Oxford: Oxford University Press, 2001), pp. 198–258.

[44] See further Walter S. Lim, '"Let Us Possess One World": John Donne, Rationalizing Theology, and the Discourse of Virginia', in *The Arts of Empire: The Poetics of Colonialism from Ralegh to Milton* (Newark: University of Delaware Press, 1998), pp. 31–63.

[45] Sharpe, *The Personal Rule of Charles* I, p. 190.

[46] See, for example, Quintilian, *Institutio oratoria*, trans. by H. E. Butler, 4 vols (London: Heinemann, 1920–22), 9. 1. 34; 9. 3. 90.

[47] Sharpe, *The Personal Rule of Charles I*, p. 645.

[48] Sharpe, *The Personal Rule of Charles I*, p. 648.

[49] Sharpe, *The Personal Rule of Charles I*, p. 648.

[50] Cited in Kevin Sharpe, *The Personal Rule of Charles I*, p. 648.

[51] This phrase is taken from the title of Hugh Parry's essay, 'Ovid's *Metamorphoses*: Violence in a Pastoral Landscape', *Transactions and Proceedings of the American Philological Association*, 95 (1964), 268–82.

[52] Annabel Patterson, *Censorship and Interpretation: The Conditions of Writing and Reading in Early Modern England* (Wisconsin: University of Wisconsin Press, 1984), p. 10.

[53] An edition of *A Relation* was also published in 1632. See Jonathan Haynes, 'George Sandys's Relation of a Journey Begun An Dom. 1610: The Humanist as Traveller' (unpublished doctoral thesis, Urbana, Illinois, 1980), p. 37.

[54] Haynes comments that 'the interplay between what Sandys has seen and what he has read gives a distinctive character to both *A Relation* and his translation of the *Metamorphoses*'. Haynes, 'George Sandys's Relation of a Journey Begun An Dom. 1610', p. 11.

[55] Lyne points out that 'this is also an Ovidian idea: in the *Ars Amatoria* the division between Books 1 and 2 is described in these terms'. Lyne, *Ovid's Changing Worlds*, p. 247.

[56] Sharpe, *The Personal Rule of Charles I*, p. 65 ff.

[57] Sharpe, *The Personal Rule of Charles I*, p. 620 ff. (the plague) and p. 608 ff. (agricultural and economic problems of the 1620s and 1630s).

[58] I would like to thank Claire Jowitt for her comments on this quotation.

[59] Patterson, *Censorship and Interpretation*, p. 10.

[60] See further Judith Sloman, *Dryden: The Poetics of Transmission* (Toronto: University of Toronto Press, 1985), p. 117.

[61] For a sustained and detailed discussion of Sandys's view of Caroline rule, see James Ellison, *George Sandys: Travel, Colonialism and Tolerance in the Seventeenth Century* (Cambridge: Brewer, 2002). On Sandys's translation of this episode, Ellison also observes that 'Sandys's commentary [...] shows that compliment is directed at the English mixed constitution, not absolutism'. Ellison, *George Sandys*, p. 168.

[62] Heather James, 'Ovid and the Question of Politics in Early Modern England, *English Literary History* 70 (2003), 343-73, 354.

[63] James, 'Ovid and the Question of Politics in Early Modern England', p. 353.

[64] James, 'Ovid and the Question of Politics in Early Modern England', p. 350.

[65] *Oxford English Dictionary*, 'cleave', v^1, sense 1; 'cleave', v^2, sense 6.

[66] Edgar Wind, *Pagan Mysteries in the Renaissance* (London: Faber, 1968), p. 213.

[67] Cited in Ann Rosalind Jones and Peter Stallybrass, 'Fetishizing Gender: Constructing the Hermaphrodite in Renaissance Europe', in *Body Guards: The Cultural Politics of Gender Ambiguity*, ed. by Julia Epstein and Kristina Straub (London: Routledge, 1991), pp. 80–111, p. 83. See *The workes of that famous chirurgion Ambrose Parey translated*

out of Latine and compared with the French. by Th[omas] Johnson (London: 1634), sig. N nnn1ᵛ.

⁶⁸ Lauren Silberman, 'Mythographic Transformations of Ovid's Hermaphrodite', *Sixteenth Century Journal*, 19 (1988), 643–52, 643, n. 2.

⁶⁷ For a discussion of the hermaphroditic image in royalist poetry, see Jonathan Sawday, 'Mysteriously Divided': Civil War, Madness and the Divided Self', in *Literature and the English Civil War*, ed. by Thomas Healy and Jonathan Sawday (Cambridge: Cambridge University Press, 1990), pp. 127–46.

⁷⁰ See, for example, Graham Parry, 'A Troubled Arcadia', pp. 38–58. See further the essays collected in *The Royal Image: Representations of Charles I*, ed. by Thomas N. Corns.

Chapter 4

From *Sandys's Ghost* to Samuel Garth: Ovid's *Metamorphoses* in Early Eighteenth-Century England

A masterpiece always moves, by definition, in the manner of a ghost.[1]

Methods of Translation

The prefatory material which accompanies Arthur Golding and George Sandys's translations of the *Metamorphoses* delineates their respective efforts to control the text. By way of an implicit comparison with Phaeton's unsuccessful effort to rein in Apollo's chariot, Golding's epistle to his patron, the Earl of Leicester, in his *Metamorphosis, translated oute of Latin into English meeter* (1567) begins 'at length my chariot wheele about the mark hath found the way,| And at their weery races end, my breathlesse horses stay' (sig. A ii^r). A further perspective on the toil of Ovidian translation is offered in Sandys's preface to the general reader of the *Metamorphosis Englished* (1632). Here Sandys emphasizes the difficult task of producing a version of the poem suitable for 'the meere English Reader, since divers places in our Author are otherwise impossible to be understood but by those who are well versed in the ancient that the ordinary Reader need not reject it as too difficult, nor the learned as too obvious' (p. 4^r n. p.). After placing his reader in a subordinate position, Sandys returns to describe his own translation practice in more detail: 'to the Translation I have given what perfection my Pen could bestow; by polishing, altering, or restoring, the harsh, improper, or mistaken, with a nicer exactnesse then perhaps is required in so long a labour' (p. 4^r n. p.).[2]

Both Golding and Sandys are concerned with the intricate nature of translating Ovid's poem into English. Yet in the period following the Interregnum Ovid's translators appear to ignore the disruptive dialogism of the complete *Metamorphoses* in favour of monologic forms. According to Rachel Trickett, the dominant Ovidian text in the late seventeenth and early eighteenth centuries is the *Heroides* and she discusses the relative dismissal of the *Metamorphoses* in the following way:

> Ovid's influence on English poetry, from the allegorisations of his stories in the Middle Ages to the profusion of material – style, subject-matter, theme – from the *Metamorphoses* which occurred during the Renaissance, had contracted formally [...] to this particular model of the epistolary monologue [...]. A general decay of

belief in the vital symbolism of myth in this period accounts for the comparative neglect of the *Metamorphoses*.[3]

Trickett's explanation suggests that the falling interest in Ovid's poem accompanied the general demise of the exegesis of myth and the growth of certain precepts which called for the subjugation of the imagination to the authority of reason.[4] A useful eighteenth-century gloss to Trickett's opinion may be found in one of Joseph Addison's 'Essays on the Pleasures of the Imagination' originally published in the *Spectator* (417) in 1712:

> [...] when we are in the *Metamorphosis*, we are walking on enchanted Ground, and see nothing but Scenes of Magick lying round us.[5]

Though a favourable observation, as one might expect from a translator of several episodes from the poem,[6] Addison's comments illustrate how 'other' Ovid's poem appears to be in this professedly rational cultural context. The previous chapter examined the ways in which the textual excesses of Sandys's 1632 edition of the *Metamorphosis Englished* unwittingly troubled the ideological position of the Royalist subject and the Caroline body politic. The ensuing discussion considers the strategies employed by Samuel Garth, the contributing editor of the 1717 translation of the *Metamorphoses*, in order to frame a vernacular translation for a period which has an evidently uneasy relationship with Ovid's epic poem.[7]

The early eighteenth century is interesting for its promotion of translations undertaken by various hands; other notable examples are *Ovid's Epistles, Translated by Several Hands* (1680), *Plutarch's Lives, Translated from the Greek by Several Hands* (1683–6) and *Ovid's Art of Love, Translated into English Verse by Several Eminent Hands* (1709).[8] The main reason for the proliferation of collaborative translations at this time is that it was a process which helped to meet commercial requirements. As Susan Bassnett explains, 'the expansion of mass publishing aimed at the emergent middle classes in the late seventeenth century led to a demand for material to supply the needs of its customers'.[9] Significantly, translations are increasingly part of a commercial enterprise and the rise of the general English reader.[10] According to Harold Love:

> Such readers will have rarely been able to read the classics in the original languages, but will have been drawn to them not only by their prestige and intrinsic interest but by a well-founded suspicion that they provided a kind of literary code for keeping ideological debate beyond the understanding of the uneducated.[11]

Attributes such as 'wit', 'taste' and 'decorum', terms which commonly define literary culture at this time, could be easily purchased by way of a classical text in translation. But Love's quotation also exposes a particular discourse, 'a kind of literary code', which places translators of classical texts in a hierarchical position to those who seek erudition. It is out of this eighteenth-century cultural climate of commerce, intellect and aspiration that the 1717 translation develops.

Pieced together from translations produced over a period of three decades by eighteen translators (Joseph Addison, Alexander Catcott, William Congreve, Samuel Croxall, John Dryden, Laurence Eusden, John Gay, Samuel Garth, Stephen Harvey, Arthur Maynwaring, John Ozell, Alexander Pope, Nicholas Rowe, Temple Stanyan, William Stonestreet, Nahum Tate, Thomas Vernon and Leonard Wested), the 1717 translation of the *Metamorphoses* is fragmented from its inception.[12] The piecemeal effect of Garth's Ovid apparently undermines an aesthetic or detailed textual appreciation of the 1717 translation.[13] The problematic nature of Garth's editorial mission is suggested by the later critical reception of his preface.[14] Joseph Warton's *Essay on the Genius and Writings of Pope* (1756), for example, comments that the prefatory material was written in a lively style but contained some 'strange opinions'.[15] Rather more disparagingly, Samuel Johnson's *Lives of the English Poets* (c. 1781) declares that Garth's introduction was 'written with more ostentation than ability: his notions are half-formed, and his materials immethodically confused'.[16] Even modern commentators on Garth's Ovid seem perplexed by the translation. Warren Francis Dwyer wonders whether the text can be called a translation at all,[17] and he emphasizes its pluralistic nature by stating that there are 'at least four Ovids here',[18] and other writers have sought some kind of textual cohesion by focusing on its main contributor (and possible instigator) John Dryden.[19] The translation as has also been viewed as '[representing] a triumph of book-selling over genuine literary impulse',[20] and one of the central tenets of David Hopkins's fascinating discussion of Garth's translation is that the publisher, Jacob Tonson, already had a large proportion of Dryden's translations of the *Metamorphoses* to hand and advertised for translators to fill the spaces.[21] Whilst the importance of changes in the commercial aspects of translation at this time cannot be overestimated, viewing the 1717 *Metamorphoses* as simply an economic exercise effaces the distinctive tenor of Garth's editorial project and his general contributions to the cultural politics of Ovidian translation in eighteenth-century England. Important though these earlier discussions are, they have rather neglected Garth's engagement with Ovid and with his efforts to forge an integrated translation of the *Metamorphoses* out of these 'scenes of magick' and disparate voices which appeals to a general eighteenth-century reader.

At the outset, Garth is keenly aware of the need to make a case for his new edition of Ovid's poem; in the preface he maintains that the classical author is 'too much run down at the present by the critical Spirit of the Nation' (p. xv). The empirical climate of eighteenth-century England altered the relationship between the text and the world, inevitably shaping the study of language and translation practices.[22] As the edicts of the Royal Society suggest, the period possesses an intellectual compulsion to establish a language of pure reason in which the word would be the exact equivalent of the thing and in which the imagination would play little or no part.[23] The increasing pressure to regulate and systematize the English language which, according to Edmund Waller, was 'a daily changing tongue', illustrates further the prevailing cultural desire for order and coherence.[24] In this endeavour for a stable and transparently deployed vernacular language, the project of translation becomes overtly committed to a theorized approach. Though translation practice had been a common theme of many translators' prefaces, such as those which accompany George Chapman's *Iliad* (1589-1611) and John Denham's *The Destruction of Troy* (1656*)*, and in treatises such as the Earl of

Roscommon's *Essay on Translated Verse* (1684), quite possibly the most systematic writing on the subject in the early modern period is Dryden's preface to Ovid's *Epistles* (1680) in which he outlines the 'three heads' of translation:[25]

> First, that of Metaphrase, or turning an Authour word by word, and Line by Line, from one Language to another [...]. The second way is that of Paraphrase, or Translation with Latitude, where the Authour is kept in view by the Translator, so as never to be lost, but his words are not so strictly follow'd as his sense; and that too is admitted to be amplyfied but not alter'd [...]. The third way is that of Imitation, where the Translator (if now he has not lost that Name) assumes the liberty not only to vary from the words and sence, but to forsake them both as he sees occasion: and taking only some general hints from the Original, to run division on the ground-work as he pleases.[26]

Dryden's preface replaces the former amateur practice of translation with a methodological approach in keeping with the orthodox, and increasingly professional, cultural perspectives of the late seventeenth and early eighteenth centuries. It is just this kind of critical mode which informs Garth's introduction to Ovid's poem.

There are to be three distinct sections to Garth's prefatory material; each part aims to consider the primary text, contemporary translation practices and the subsequent English version of Ovid's text. Garth begins:

> The Method I propose in writing this preface, is to take Notice of some of the Beauties of the *Metamorphoses*, and also of the Faults, and particular Affectations. After which I shall proceed to hint at some Rules for Translation in general; and shall give short account of the following Version. (p. i)

In terms of the poem's domestication, the first quotation from the *Metamorphoses* which Garth considers is telling:

> *Nec circumfuso pendebat in aere tellus*
> *Ponderibus librata suis* — (p. ii)

Taken from the opening passage of Ovid's poem, these lines are concerned with the formation of the Earth. In Dryden's translation which opens Garth's edition, the lines are rendered thus: 'Nor yet was Earth suspended in the sky;| Nor pois'd, did on her own Foundations lye' (p. 1). Typically, Garth does not provide a translation of the Latin text or explore the Ovidian principle 'of bodies changed to various forms'. Rather, directing his material to a particular kind of informed reader, Garth analyses the *Metamorphoses* against material which seems to recall the first two books of Isaac Newton's *Philosophie Naturalis Principia Mathematica* (1687), 'Of the Motion of Bodies':

> Thus was the State of Nature before the Creation: And here it is obvious, that *Ovid* had a discerning Notion of the *Gravitation of Bodies*. 'Tis now demonstrated, that

every Part of Matter tends to every Part of Matter with a Force, which is always in a direct simple Proportion of the Quantity of the Matter, and an inverse duplicate of the Proportion of the Distance, which Tendency, or Gravitating is constant, and

universal [...]. There can be no [...] arbitrary Principle, in meer Matter; its Parts cannot move, unless they be mov'd; and cannot do otherwise, when press'd on by other Parts in Motion; and therefore 'tis evident from the following Lines, that *Ovid* strictly adher'd to the Opinion of the most discerning Philosophers, who taught that all things were form'd by a wise and intelligent Mind. (pp. i–ii)

Garth does not invoke Newton by name; nonetheless his editorial strategy takes this translation of Ovid's poem out of the conventional Christian moral frame into the discourses of Newtonian moral empiricism.[27] A page or so later Garth continues with this model:

His super imposuit, liquidem [et] gravitate carentem
Æthera —
Here the Author spreads a thin Veil of *Æther* over his Infant Creation; and tho' his asserting the upper Region to be void of Gravitation, may not, in a Mathematical Rigour, be true; yet 'tis found from the Natural Enquiries made since, and especially from the learned Dr. *Halley's* Discourse on the *Barometer*, that if, on the Surface of the earth, an inch of Quicksilver in the Tube be equal to a Cylinder of Air of 300 Foot, it will be at a Mile's height equal to a Cylinder of Air of 2700000: and therefore the Air at so great a Distance from the Earth, must be rarify'd to so great a Degree that the Space it fills must bear a very small proportion to that which is entirely void of Matter. (p. iii)

Garth apparently attempts to revive critical interest in the *Metamorphoses* by appealing to contemporaneous scientific discourses. Moving from Newtonian principles to Edmund Halley,[28] the new Ovidian translation is immediately defined as something very different from the earlier translation; Sandys's *Metamorphosis Englished*. To strengthen his case further, Garth emphasizes the fragmented, unfinished quality of Ovid's *Metamorphoses* by reminding his informed readers of Ovid's comments about the poem in the *Tristia*:

Orba parente suo quicunque Volumina tangis,
His saltem vestra detur in urbe locus.
Quoque magis faveas, non sunt haec edita ab Ipsi,
Sed quasi de domini funere rapta sui.
Quicquid in his igitur vitii rude carmen habebit,
Emendaturus, si licuisset, erat. (p. i)[29]

In the end, Garth excuses the classical author by saying 'that what appeared an Absurdity in *Ovid,* is not so much his own Fault, as that of the Times before him' (p. xv). As we shall see, it is eighteenth-century England's concern for 'times before' which troubles Garth's editorial and translative project.

Translation and Transmigration

Having begun by considering the *Metamorphoses* in relation to popular methodological and scientific discourses, Garth eventually addresses the older exegetical conventions of Ovidian translation. In keeping with early eighteenth-century cultural sensibilities, the editor stresses that 'Allegories should be obvious, and not like Meteors in the Air, which represent a different Figure to every Eye' (p. xvi). He thus proceeds to offer pithy interpretations of twenty-two Ovidian episodes which offer a distinctive route through Ovid's poem. Starting with the Fable of Deucalion and Pyrrha from book 1 (which tells of the second inception of the human race), Garth ends his catalogue of these 'excellent lessons of morality' with the fifteenth book's tale of Aesculapius's voyage to Rome.[30] Given Garth's profession as a doctor of medicine, his view of Apollo's son who brought back the dead Hippolytus to life and restored health to plague-ridden Rome is significant:

> The legend of *Aesculapius's* voyage to Rome in the form of a snake seems to express the necessary sagacity requir'd in professors that art, for the readier sight into distempers. [...] The venerable Epidaurian assum'd the figure of an animal without hands to take fees: and therefore, grateful posterity honour'd him with a temple. In this manner should wealthy physicians, upon proper occasion practise; and thus their surviving patients reward. (p. xviii)

Described as a 'conscientious member of the Royal College of Physicians', Garth's delivery of the annual Harveian oration in 1696 supported the college's recent proposal that 'for a member's subscription of £10 to establish a dispensary for free medical advice and discounted medicines for the sick poor, the first in England'.[31] In terms of his literary endeavours, Garth is best-known for *The Dispensary, a Poem*, said to be the 'first full-scale mock-epic poem in the English language',[32] which celebrates the successful opening of the college dispensary in the winter of 1697–8. Some twenty years later, Garth's comments on Ovid's myth of *Aesculapius* seem motivated by related cultural concerns about physicians, monetary reward and societal need.

Whilst Garth Tissol rightly observes that Garth's preface offers 'only a few pages of perfunctory moralising',[33] I want to suggest that the general exegetical mode of the earlier translations of the *Metamorphoses* is effaced in preference for contemporaneous readings of Ovidian myths which, on occasion, seem of personal significance to the editor. Partly because he translated this section of Ovid's poem himself, Garth's analysis of the Fable of Cippus from book 15 is also noteworthy:

> In *Cippus* we find a noble Magnanimity, and heavenly Self-denial; he preferr'd the Good of the Republick to his own private Grandeur; and chose, with exemplary Generosity, rather to live a private Free-Man out of Rome, than to command Numbers of Slaves in it. (p. xvii)

In Garth's scrutiny of the eminent Roman praetor, the eighteenth-century reader may observe a contemporary criticism of absolutism in favour of democracy. Indeed, as Sarah Annes Brown's discussion of Garth's comments on Proteus as 'a statesman' who 'can put on any shape' (p. xviii) discerns, the prefatory material 'draws parallels with contemporary politics'.[34] Markedly, though differentiated by their respective cultural and historical milieu, both Sandys's 1632 translation and Garth's edition orbit around royal patrons and readers. Sandys's text produced *cum privilegio* obviously attempts to honour its royal patron Charles I; Garth, a member of the Kit-Cat Club and portrayed by Johnson as an 'active and zealous Whig',[35] was an ardent supporter of the first Hanoverian king, George I. During the latter years of Queen Anne's reign, Garth issued a Latin prose epistle (1711), concerned with a proposed Latin edition of the works of Lucretius, which was dedicated to the future George I;[36] in 1714, following the sudden death of Queen Anne, Garth was knighted and became physician to the new King.[37] With Garth's loyalties already well established, it might be assumed that his edition of the *Metamorphoses* would be dedicated to the current monarch. Rather than paying homage to George I, however, Garth's Ovid demonstrates its royal allegiance through a dedicatory epistle to the Princess of Wales, Caroline of Ansbach, George I's daughter-in-law.

Godfrey Kneller's portrait of Caroline faces Garth's epistle and each of the fifteen books is dedicated to a woman with Whiggish connections.[38] By 1717, Caroline's home, Leicester House, had become something of an intellectual locus. Her academic mentor, 'the learned and Reverend Dr [Samuel] Clarke' (p. xiv), is invoked in the preface as an expert on Homeric linguistics and some of the literary figures featured in Garth's edition were frequent visitors to the royal household.[39] Much of Garth's opening discussion about Ovid's relationship to the natural sciences, astronomy, style, politics, love, rhetoric and allegory, as well as the invocation of erudite figures known to inhabit the Princess's circle, appears to have been written with Caroline's scholarly interests in mind. Yet there may have been other reasons for dedicating the translation to the Princess.

In the same year that Garth's Ovid was initially published, George I banished Caroline and her husband George Augustus from St. James's Palace, due to a 'combination of personal and political reasons',[40] demanding that they leave their children behind.[41] In what would be his final publication, Garth's dedication to the new Ovidian translation demonstrates his affiliation to the wife of the future monarch rather than the present King:

> Madam,
> Since I am allow'd the honour, and Privilege of so easy Access to Your Royal Highness, I dare say, I shall not be the worse receiv'd for bringing Ovid along with me. He comes from Banishment to the Fautress of Liberty; from the Barbarous to the Polite; and has this to recommend him, which never fails with a Clemency, like Yours; He is Unfortunate. Your Royal Highness, who feels for everyone, has lately been the mournful Occasion of a like Sensibility in many Others. Scarce an Eye, that did not tell the Danger You were in: Even Parties, tho' different in Principles, united at that time in their grief, and affectionate concern, for an event of so much consequence to the Interest of Humanity, and Virtue; whilst Your Self was the only Person, Then, unmoved. (sig. A 1[r]–A 1[v] n. p.)

By emphasizing Ovid's exilian context, a particular aspect of the Roman poet's biography which may also allude to Caroline's circumstances, Garth carefully avoids explicit contemporaneous detail and he mindfully includes the statement that 'even Parties, tho' different in Principles [are] united [...] in their grief'. Notably, Garth does not directly appeal to the Princess's intellect or her political status; instead, Caroline is upheld throughout the epistle as an exemplar of womanly behaviour against the 'cruel Tryal' that Garth so enigmatically describes.

If the epistle refers indirectly to some pressing royal matters, however, the preface unmistakably shows that this is a translation which primarily pays homage to a circle of literary kinship rather than to the royal court and kingship. In editing the 1717 *Metamorphoses* Garth attempts to construct an arena in which a group of the literary English elite are gathered together under one name: Dryden. The preface ends with a tribute to the former poet laureate and it is to his memory that Garth's translation is explicitly devoted. Employing a monarchical metaphor which signals Garth's import, Richard Cook writes that 'many saw Garth as the logical heir apparent to the poetical throne left vacant by the elder poet's death'.[42] Although precise details are vague there appears to have been a close friendship between Garth and Dryden. But whatever the nature of their personal association may have been, there is an intertextual relationship between the two writers. Henry Playford and Abel Roper, the editors of *Luctus Britannici: or the Tears of the British Muses: for the Death of John Dryden, esq* (1700), for instance, proclaim Garth the surviving embodiment of Dryden:

> Permit us then, our dutius zeal to prove,
> And make a tender of our tears and love,
> As we with sighs unfeign'd the task pursue,
> And weep him dead, who still must live in you.[43]

Using the conventional trope of poetic transmigration, Playford and Abel's verse illustrates the expectations of Garth's future literary career. Furthermore, the depiction of Garth as Dryden's successor has implications for this collaborative edition of the *Metamorphoses*. To be sure, one way in which this seemingly disjointed translation might be unified is by way of this transmigratory process between Ovid, Dryden and Garth. By comparison with Dryden, Garth published few translations and contributed little to the 'theories' of translation. Yet after Dryden's death, his reputation as a translator was such that his version of the 'Life of Otho' (1702) replaced Thomas Beaumont's version in *Plutarch's Lives* (originally published in five volumes between 1683 and 1686).[44] In the same year as his translation of Plutarch, Garth published a translation from Greek, 'The Second Philippick' in *Several Orations of Demosthenes [...] English'd [...] by Several Hands*.

Though aligned with Dryden and translation, it may seem that apart from the 1717 translation Garth's relationship with the *Metamorphoses* is somewhat arbitrary. His interests in Ovidian translation are clearly evident, however, in *Claremont* (1715), the topographical poem which was published just two years before the collaborative edition. Undoubtedly the *Metamorphoses*, a text concerned with 'the origins of things and accounts in the process for their present character',[45] provides Garth with an apt model for *Claremont*, which presents an etiology of the Earl of Clare's estate. The first 85 lines of *Claremont* distance poet and reader from the common practice of lesser poets flattering ignorant patrons: 'No Bard for bribes shou'd prostitute his Vein;| Nor dare to Flatter where he shou'd Arraign' (39–40).[46] Lord Clare, however, deserves all praise; his estate is so idyllic 'That Swains shall leave their Lawns, and Nymphs their Bow'rs| And quit *Arcadia* for a seat like yours' (73–4). The rest of the poem sets out

> […] to tell how antient Fame
> Records from whence the *Villa* took its name.
> In Times of old, when *British* Nymphs were known
> To love no foreign Fashions like their own;
> When Dress was monstrous, and Fig-leaves the Mode,
> And Quality put on no Paint but Woade.
> Of *Spanish* Red unheard was then the Name;
> For Cheeks were only taught to blush by Shame.
> No beauty, to encrease her Crowd of Slaves,
> Rose out of Wash, as *Venus* out of Waves.
> Not yet Lead Comb was on the Toilett plac'd;
> Not yet broad Eye-brows were reduc'd by Paste: (86–97)

Once *Claremont* moves beyond the familiar eighteenth-century diatribe against women's use of cosmetics,[47] the poem follows the narrative structure of the *Metamorphoses* and offers a history of Britain based on book 1's account of the Golden Age:

> No Shape-smith set up Shop, and drove a Trade
> To mend the Work wise Providence had made.
> Tyres were unheard of, and unknown the Loom,
> And thrifty Silkworms spun for Times to come.
> Bare Limbs were then the Marks of Modesty;
> All like *Diana* were below the Knee.
> The Men appear'd a rough undaunted Race,
> Surly in Show, unfashion'd in Address.
> Upright in Actions, and in Thought sincere;
> And strictly were the same they would appear.
>
> […] Their Taste was, like their Temper, unrefin'd;
> For looks were then the Language of the Mind. (98–117)

The next section of Garth's poem introduces the ancient druids who live in the woods of the estate (126). As James Sambrook notes, 'in the eighteenth century druids were generally idealised as the original patriots, the poet-priests who stand up for liberty in the face of Roman or other oppression'.[48] Already associated with Britain's foundation myths, and described in *Claremont* as a 'Sect' who 'in sacred Veneration held| Opinions, by the Samian Sage reveal'd' (170–1), Garth's druids are shown to be followers of Pythagoras.[49] In book 15 of the *Metamorphoses* Ovid uses Pythagorian disquisition to explore the transmigratory nature of souls as a means of theorizing the narrative's 'unbroken strains from the worlds very beginning even unto the present time'.[50] The druids predict that 'Great Numa, in a Brunswick Prince, [shall] ordain| Good Laws; and Halcyon years shall hush the world again' (195–6), thus the structure of Garth's poem moves from Rome's second king and lawgiver to eighteenth-century England.[51]

By using the *Metamorphoses* as *Claremont*'s overarching model, Garth produces a version of British history which justifies Hanoverian succession. A hundred lines or so after the inaugural invocation of the House of Brunswick, the poem reiterates the point: 'E're twice ten Centuries shall fleet away,| A *Brunswick* Prince shall *Britain's* Scepter sway' (299–300). Just before the text's dedicatee is finally hailed, the closing lines of *Claremont* turn their attention to George Augustus and Caroline, and the continued success of the Hanoverian line:

> Like him, shall his *Augustus* shine in Arms,
> Tho' Captive to his *Carolina's* Charms.
> Ages with future Heroes She shall bless;
> And *Venus* once more found an *Alban* Race. (310–13)

Claremont's debt to Ovidian modes of transformation also fashion Garth as a kind of Ovid. Indeed, Garth's relationship to his classical predecessor is obliquely considered in *Claremont*'s preface:

> after reading the story in the third book of the *Metamorphoses*, 'tis obvious to object (as an ingenious friend has already done) that the renewing the charms of a nymph, of which Ovid had dispossessed her,
> —*vox tantum atque Ossa supersunt*
> is too great a Violation of Poetical Authority. (sig. A 2 ᵛ).

The *Metamorphoses*, as we saw in the Introduction, renews 'the charms' of many earlier myths without such anxiety. But rather than showing indebtedness to his poetical precedent, Garth is concerned to honour the current political climate. As discussed in Chapter 1, the anonymous *Fable of Ovid Treting of Narcissus* (1560) in the opening decade of Elizabeth I's reign is noteworthy for its negotiation of the newly formed English Elizabethan subject. Garth also turns to Ovid's tale of Narcissus and Echo, a myth associated with the construction of identity, as he considers British history in the light of the Hanoverian succession. According to Claremont's prefatory material, the grounds of the Villa recall the *locus amoena* of the Ovidian myth. But instead of Narcissus, the male protagonist of the episode in *Claremont* is 'fair Montano of the Sylvan Race' (205). Beginning with an extensive blazoning of the male body (213-12), the poem unquestionably demonstrates the appropriate use of the epithet. However, whereas the anonymous Elizabethan translator of the *Fable of Ovid Treting of Narcissus* focuses on the youth, as the preface suggests, Garth turns his attention to the figure of Echo.

Following her rejection by Narcissus, Ovid's Echo retreats into caves, where she eventually is reduced to a voice and to bones ['vox tantum atque Ossa supersunt'], then 'only voice; for they say that her bones were turned to stone ['vox manet, ossa ferunt lapidis traxisse figuram]'. [52] Garth takes up the narrative from that point:

> A Grott there was with hoary Moss o'ergrown
> Rough with rude Shells, and arch'd with mouldring Stone;
> Sad Silence reigns within the loansom Wall;
> And weeping Rills but whisper as they fall.
> The clasping Ivys up the Ruin creep;
> And there the Bat, and drowsie Beetle sleep.
> This Cell sad Eccho chose by Love betray'd,
> A fine Retirement for a mourning Maid. (235–42)

As Narcissus was the object of Echo's desire, Echo becomes pursued by Montano:

> Oh whether of a Mortal born! he cries;
> Or some fair Daughter of the distant Skies;
> That, in Compassion leave your Chrystal Sphere,
> To guard some favour'd Charge, and wander here.
> Slight not my Suit, nor too ungentle prove;
> But pity One, a Novice yet in Love.
> If Words avail not; see my suppliant Tears;
> Nor disregard those dumb Petitioners.
> From his Complaint the Tyrant Virgin flies,
> Asserting all the Empire of her Eyes. (251–260)

Brown has argued that 'in a neat reversal of Ovid's story [Echo] is unresponsive to his ardour, and continues to sigh for Narcissus'. [53] The 'neat reversal' to which Brown refers, however, is part of the poem's sexual politics. For *Claremont* presses for a return to a Golden Age in which women are chaste like Diana and anticipates a future in which 'Carolina' becomes a vessel for producing 'Heroes' (313) of the nation state. Thus Montano's loquacious 'Complaint' against Echo's silent response illustrates that in 'renewing the charms of the nymph' Garth has refashioned her into the conventional female object of desire rather than the desiring subject that is witnessed in Ovid. Juno famously punished Echo's garrulity by leaving the nymph with merely the capacity to repeat the words of others. In his revision, Garth completely silences his 'Tyrant Virgin', thus extending the goddess's punishment even further. In book 3 of his poem, Ovid poignantly explores the nymph's compulsion to reveal her passion for Narcissus. As Narcissus emphatically rejects the nymph with the words 'emoriar, quam sit tibi copia nostri' [May I die before I give you power o'er me]', Echo's repetition of 'sit tibi copia nostri' [I give you power o'er me]!' emphasizes her subjection. [54] By contrast, 'Asserting all the Empire of her Eyes' (260), Garth's Echo is presented quite differently; she remains silent in her refutation of Montano's advances. In the end, Montano dies because of the nymph's rejection and Echo is returned to her previous state:

> Sad Eccho now laments her Rigour, more
> Than for Narcissus her loose Flame before.

Her Flesh to Sinew shrinks, her Charms are fled;
All Day in rifted Rocks she hides her Head.
Soon as the Ev'nong shows a Sky serene,
Abroad she strays, but never to be seen.
And ever as the weeping Naiads name
Her Cruelty, the Nymph repeats the same.
With them she joins, her Lover to deplore,
And haunts the lonely Dales, he rang'd before.
Her sex's Privilege she yet retains,
And tho' to Nothing wasted, *Voice* remains. (285–96)

In common with much of the poem's treatment of women, from the condemnation of their use of cosmetics to their role in supplying future champions for 'an Alban Race' (313), it seems as though Garth temporarily resurrects Echo, formerly Ovid's spirited character, only to reiterate her miserable demise. Nonetheless, his use of the myth of Echo in *Claremont* simultaneously reveals a curiosity in disembodied voices and textual echoes which may also be discerned in the 1717 edition of the *Metamorphoses*.

Whilst Garth is keen to encourage certain discourses in the framing of this new edition of the *Metamorphoses*, such as those of Newton and Dryden, he works hard to efface its main rival, George Sandys's *Metamorphosis Englished*. The numerous editions of Sandys's Ovid which were printed in the late seventeenth and early eighteenth centuries are witness to the enduring popularity of the earlier translation. A further seven editions of the 1632 text were produced between 1638 and 1690, though the subsequent printings reduced the extensive introductory material of the initial edition. The 1638 edition, for example, contains only the dedicatory letter to Charles I from the prefatory material; the lengthy allegorical explications of the text have been removed. Nonetheless, later reprints refer the reader back to the 1632 text. Now circulating with traces of the social circumstances which culminated in the execution of Charles I in 1649, it is not altogether unexpected that the translative status of Sandys's text would be in question. To be sure, Sandys's Ovid functions as a reminder of the very form of absolute monarchy that Garth denounces in his interpretation of the myth of Cippus.

In 1692, Peter Motteux, translator and founder of the *Gentleman's Journal; or the Monthly Miscellany* remarked that Sandys

> wrote in an Age when Men were not so nice as they are grown; and tho' none can deny him a great deal of Praise for his Success in so high and laborious a Task, yet they must also grant, that the language and way of writing being much improv'd, his translation cannot please our age so much as it may have pleas'd his.[55]

This quotation illustrates the cultural and textual difference of Sandys's translation. Looking back to the reign of Charles I as a time of instability, the *Gentleman's Journal* looks forward to the future place of translation in the early eighteenth-century social climate. Although it is something of a common-place to discuss the rewriting of texts as part of the project of returning to monarchic rule following the upheaval of the English Civil Wars, it is worth briefly considering the political importance of translation following the Interregnum. It is certainly tempting to view this surge in translation as a result of the political unrest of the Civil War years. As Albert C. Baugh and Thomas Cable comment, 'the age was characterised by a search for stability [...]. We may well believe that permanence and stability would seem like no inconsiderable virtues to a generation that remembered the disorders and changes of the Revolution and Restoration.'[56] Accordingly, Sandys's translation, deemed to have been produced in 'an Age when Men were not so nice as they are grown', is out of joint with contemporary society.

These views on Sandys's translation have a bearing on Garth's edition of the *Metamorphoses*. Having presented the reader with the way in which Ovid bequeathed his unfinished text to future translators, Garth now deals with the subject of Sandys's competing, and culturally ubiquitous, translation. Towards the end of the preface, Sandys's Ovid is invoked as a means of demonstrating Garth's authorial position to an even greater degree:

> Translation is commonly either Verbal, or Paraphrase, or Imitation; of the first is *Mr. Sands's*, which I think the *Metamorphoses* can by no means allow of. It is agreed, the Author left it unfinished; if it had undergone his last Hand, it is more than probable, that many Superfluities had been retrench'd. Where a poem is perfectly finish'd, the Translation, with regard to particular idioms, cannot be too exact; by doing this, the Sense of the Author is more entirely his own, and the Cast of the Periods more faithfully preserv'd: But where a Poem is tedious through Exuberance, or dark through a hasty Brevity, I think the Translator may be excus'd for doing what the Author upon revising, wou'd have done himself. If *Mr. Sands* had been of this Opinion, perhaps other Translations of the *Metamorphoses* had not been attempted. (p. xix)

According to Garth, it was Sandys's reverence for the 'source' which paved the way for this new edition. The literal, or 'verbal', manner in which Sandys translated is deemed inappropriate for a source text, like the *Metamorphoses*, which has been left unfinished. Garth continues to justify the need for the current translation against Sandys's earlier effort:

> A critick has observ'd, that in his Version of this book, he has scrupulously confin'd the Number of his Lines after those of the Original. 'Tis fit I should take the Summ upon Content, and be better bred, than to count after him [...]. The Manner that seems most suited for this present Undertaking, is neither to follow the Author too close out of a Critical Timorousness; nor abandon him too wantonly through a Poetick Boldness. The Original should always be kept in View, without to apparent a Deviation from the Sense. Where it is otherwise; it is not a Version, but an Imitation. The Translator ought to be as intent to keep up the Gracefulness of the Poem, as artful to hide its Imperfections; to copy its Beauties, and to throw a shade over its Blemishes; to be faithful to an Idolatory, where the Author excells, and to take the Licence of a little Paraphrase, where Penury of Fancy, or Dryness of Expression seem to ask for it. (p. xix)

As Hopkins has shown, Dryden's theories of translation are extensively inscribed in Garth's text.[57] Like Dryden, Garth promotes the middle way of paraphrase favoured by the earlier writer. George Steiner explains that 'ideally "paraphrase" will not pre-empt the authority of the original' but will show the target audience what the original would have been like if it had been contemporaneously produced.[58] In other words, the eighteenth-century Ovidian translator needs to keep the Latin text in view but the original text may be domesticated accordingly. Thus, at the end of book 14, a section of Ovid's poem which Garth translated in full, the editorial comments advise the reader that 'where this mark " appears, the Lines of this Book are paraphrased' (p. 507),[59] and he indicates the points at which his translation becomes paraphrase by this very means. Clearly keeping a methodological approach in mind, Garth's insignia attempts to create a distance between Sandys's earlier translation and his own; but his controlling enterprise is disturbed by the obdurate presence of Sandys's text.

The Troubling Ghosts of Translation

The various editions of Sandys's *Metamorphosis Englished* in circulation during the late seventeenth century, then, confirm its popularity with the reading public. The name of 'Mr. Sands' and his Ovidian translation are cited in a diverse range of texts preceding and following Garth, such as Margaret Cavendish's *Philosophical and Physical Opinions* (1655),[60] all the way to Alexander Tytler's *Essay on the Principles of Translation* (1791).[61] Sandys's text is thus constructed as something of a masterpiece; as the Derridean epigraph to this chapter states, 'a masterpiece always moves, by definition, in the manner of a ghost'. Ghosts are disturbing traces from the past and the 'ghostly' manner in which Sandys's 'masterpiece' circulates, a translation 'wrote in an Age when Men were not so nice as they are grown', interrupts Garth's project of translative and editorial control, unsettling the construction of the rational eighteenth-century subject.

At least from the late sixteenth century onwards, most famously with Shakespeare's *Hamlet* perhaps, ghostly images reside in a variety of texts.[62] Spectral images are also familiar tropes within the context of translation, delineating, most often, the transmigration between ancient author and contemporary poet. In George Chapman's poem 'The Tears of Peace' (1609), for instance, Homer's ghost announces to Chapman (who published a complete translation of the *Iliad* in 1611) that

> [...] thou didst inherit
> My true sense, for the time then, in my spirit;
> And I, invisibly, went prompting thee
> To those fair greens where thou didst English me.[63]

In classical literature – particularly in the *Metamorphoses* – there is good precedent for the figure of the ghost to be used in the context of translation. In Ovid's poem the shades of the dead inhabit the underworld in an unproblematic fashion as

witnessed, for example, in the tale of Orpheus. It is when the spirits break through
the boundary between the living and the dead, however, that tensions arise.
Achilles's ghost in book 13, for instance, takes the Greeks to task for their
disregard of him:

> And will ye go? he said. Is then the name
> Of the once great *Achilles* lost to fame?
> Yet stay, ungrateful Greeks; nor let me sue
> In vain for honours to my *Manes* due. (p. 454)[64]

The liminal figure of Achilles, a forerunner of the ghost of Hamlet's father,[65]
emphasizes the function of ghosts as a reminder, and a remainder, of past actions.
Throughout the seventeenth century and into the eighteenth, however, there was an
ongoing and increasing philosophical debate about the textual effects of ghosts. An
example of these discussions can be found in the *Spectator* (419):

> There is a kind of Writing, wherein the Poet quite loses sight of nature, and
> entertains his reader's Imagination with the Characters and Actions of such persons
> as have many of them no Existence, but what he bestows on them. Such are Fairies,
> Witches, Magicians, Demons, and departed Spirits […]. Men of Cold Fancies, and
> philosophical Dispositions, object to this kind of Poetry, that it has not Probability
> enough to affect the Imagination. But to this it may be answered, that we are sure, in
> general, there are many Intellectual Beings in the World besides ourselves, and
> several Species of Spirits, who are subject to different Laws and Oeconomies from
> those of Mankind.[66]

Significantly, ghostly devices are taken up at this time in a particular genre of writing
named by H. F. Brooks as the 'Fictitious Ghost or the Supposed Ghost' which, 'as a
rule [is] satiric, polemic, or admonitory'.[67] The disconcerting effect that Sandys's
Metamorphosis Englished produced in the late seventeenth century is illustrated in a
ballad by Pope entitled *Sandys's Ghost: Or A Proper New Ballad on the New Ovid's
'Metamorphosis'* which, though not included in his list of relevant texts, arguably
belongs to the genre that Brooks has identified. As Pope's poem shows, more like the
troublesome phantom of Achilles than Homer's *revenant* in Chapman's text,
Sandys's ghost returns to disturb the later translations of the *Metamorphoses*.

Indeed, Pope's text functions as a commentary not only on Garth's edition of
the *Metamorphoses* but also on the practice of translation at this time. His impetus
for writing *Sandys's Ghost* comes from the activity surrounding the proposed
translation of Ovid's *Metamorphoses* by Tonson and Garth.[68] Believed to have
been written in the winter of 1716–17, several months before the publication of
Garth's edition, Pope's satirical poem concerns a visitation by the spectral Sandys
to the astronomer and politician Samuel Molyneaux.[69] The opening stanza of
Pope's text suggests that 'Lords and Commons and Men of Wit| And Pleasure
about Town' should 'Read this, e're you translate one bit| Of books of high
renown' (1–4). After warning his readers to 'Beware of Latin Authors all!' (5),
Pope tells of

[...] how a Ghost in dead of Night,
With saucer Eyes of Fire,
In woeful wise did sore affright
A wit and courtly squire. (13–16)

Pope then describes how the trappings of a wealthy gentleman do not make a scholar, and whilst Molyneaux may possess the tools of translation he lacks ability:

[...] Tho' with a golden pen you scrawl,
And scribble in a berlin:
For not the desk with silver nails,
Nor bureau of expence,
Nor standish well japan'd, avails
To writing of good sense. (7–12)[70]

The poet reproaches Molyneaux for his lack of 'good sense' and, as the following lines illustrate, Sandys's ghost is able to inhabit the gaps left by the unskilful translator:

A desk he has of curious work,
With glitt'ring studs about;
Within the same did Sandys lurk,
Tho' Ovid lay without.

Now as he scratch'd to fetch up thought,
Forth popp'd the sprite so thin;
And from the key-hole bolted out,
All upright as a pin,
With whiskers, band, and pantaloon,
And ruff compos'd most duly;
This squire he dropp'd his pen full soon,
While as the light burnt bluely.

Ho! Master Sam, quoth Sandys's sprite,
Write on, nor let me scare ye;
Forsooth, if rhymes fall in not right,
To Budgel seek, or Carey. (25–40)[71]

With the addition of a portrait of Sandys printed opposite the title page, the eighth edition of the *Metamorphosis Englished* (1690) differs from earlier imprints. In Pope's text Sandys's ghost appears as he does in the frontispiece, markedly clothed in garments which are at odds with early eighteenth–century sensibilities. Classical texts such as Suetonius's *Caligula* often suggest that the desire for elaborate clothing underpinned the cultural decline of ancient Rome.[72] Equally, eighteenth-century Neoclassical texts may allude to the relationship between the demise of society and elaborate clothing. Hinting at a similar association, the adornment of Sandys's ghost with whiskers, band, pantaloon and ruff in Pope's satire connects the Cavalier-like translator with the opulence of the dissolute Royal court. In sum,

Pope's representation of Sandys's spectre illustrates the untimely appearance of a translation still circulating in its seventeenth-century weave.

By contrast with the view expressed by Thomas Hobbes in *Leviathan* that 'ghosts [...] signifieth nothing, neither in heaven, nor earth, but the imaginary inhabitants of man's brain',[73] Pope's apparition is not merely an effect of the imagination; *Sandys's Ghost* draws attention to the materiality of the textual invasion by the *Metamorphosis Englished*. Ultimately, Pope's poem suggests that earlier translations may trespass and undermine the current translative projects. Residing in the 'curious' desk with 'glitt'ring studs' (a further reference to the embellished style so harshly criticised in the early eighteenth century), Sandys's ghost seeks to defeat the task of the supposed translator of Ovid. In the course of the ballad, Pope depicts a very particular scene of translation. This is affirmed by the full title of the text in the manuscript, *Sandys's Ghost: A proper new ballad on Tonson's Ovid, to be translated by persons of quality*. Social restrictions are thus placed around those who could take on the translative task and Molyneaux is found to be wanting. Amongst those Pope names as worthy are several translators who went on to contribute to Garth's edition: John Gay, William Congreve, Nicholas Rowe, Temple Stanyan, John Ozell, Joseph Addison, and of course, Pope himself. The fact that Pope depicts the translator of Ovid as Molyneaux, a scientist rather than a grammarian, is seemingly appropriate. Between Sandys's *Metamorphosis Englished* and the 1717 edition, as we have seen, translation had overtly taken on a systemic appearance, of which Pope's poem, inscribed with a scriblerian sensibility, is not altogether approving.[74]

In the preface of the 1632 translation, as discussed in Chapter 3, sustained attempts were made to contain excesses of signification within the labyrinthine structure of the text. If Sandys had a battle to control meaning within the poem, then the appearance of Sandys's ghost in Pope's text makes visible the problems of intralingual translation. Although the Latin source text 'lay without' the desk upon which Molyneaux attempts his translation, 'Within the same did Sandys lurk', a more dangerous place to reside. As Pope describes this contest with a past translator, his poem also emphasizes the constant battle that translators face with regard to rival versions. Line 48, for instance, announces that Tonson 'beats up for Volunteers'. Most obviously, this is a reference to the manner in which Tonson sought the services of translators who were willing to contribute to their enterprise. But in the light of another edition, also published by George Sewell and Edmund Curll in October 1717, the militaristic metaphor can be read as the Garth edition in battle with all opponents. Like Garth's edition of Ovid, the Sewell-Curll edition was a collaborative translation,[75] yet Sewell makes no effort to hide the way in which this version of the *Metamorphoses* is obliged to Sandys's translation. In his dedicatory epistle to Barnham Goodge, Sewell states: 'I am indebted to [Sandys] for some Lines, which I despair'd of translating better'.[76] Garth's preface, somewhat differently, seeks to highlight the temporal difference between Sandys's translation and his own.

Writing on Garth's capabilities as both physician and poet, George Farqher said that his 'prescriptions can restore the living, his pen embalm the dead'.[77] It is fitting, then, that Garth provided the Latin eulogy at Dryden's funeral in 1700,[78] and equally appropriate that the closing paragraphs of Garth's preface to the 1717 edition of the *Metamorphoses* serve as an extended eulogy for Dryden:

> I cannot pass by that Admirable *English* poet, without endeavouring to make his Country sensible of the Obligations they have to his Muse. Whether they consider the flowing Grace of his Versification; the vigorous Sallies of his Fancy; or the peculiar Delicacy of his Periods; they'll discover Excellencies never to be enough admired. If they trace him from the first Productions of his Youth, to the last Performances of his Age, they'll find, that as the Tyranny of Rhyme never impos'd on the Perspicuity of the Sense; so a languid Sense never wanted to be let off by the Harmony or Rhyme [...]. As a Translator he was just; as an Inventer he was rich [...]. The Man, that cou'd make Kings immortal, and raise triumphant Arches to Heroes, now wants a poor square Foot of Stone, to show where the Ashes of the greatest Poets, that ever was upon Earth, are deposited. (p. xx)

One 'detour' through the *Metamorphoses* has been depicted as a 'landscape of tombs and monuments' before the reader reaches the 'Epilogue to the *Metamorphoses* [which] is also the poet's tombstone'.[79] From its title page depicting Ovid's cenotaph (Illustration 4.1)[80] to the topical subject of Dryden's memorial,[81] Garth's edition is suffuse with references to corporeal and textual remains that are already inherent in the classical poem.[82] In book 15, Dryden's translation of the Pythagorean episode states that death should be thought of

> [...] as but an idle Thing.
> Why thus affrighted at an empty Name,
> A Dream of Darkness, and Fictitious Flame?
> Vain themes of Wit, which but in Poems pass,
> And Fables of a World, that never was!
> What feels the Body, when the Soul expires,
> By Time corrupted, or consum'd by Fires?
> Nor dies the Spirit, but new Life repeats
> In other Forms, and only changes Seats. (p. 516)

Whilst it implicitly depicts the relationship between Ovid, Dryden and itself as one of transmigration,[83] Garth's preface is unforthcoming on the subject of Pythagorean metempsychosis. Conspicuously ignoring Garth's associations with Ovid, Blandford Parker defines Garth's general literary enterprise as one of 'urban satire, scientific apology, de-idealised landscape [which] are all part of a unified and empirical imaginative movement and the scientific characteristics [which] combine to replace the remaining traces of Christian iconic lore'.[84] In a period which sought to reconcile religious views on the nature of the soul with post-Cartesian edicts on matter and the origin of the world,[85] and with Parker's comments in mind, perhaps Garth's silence about transmigration is not altogether surprising.[86] Following Dryden again, Garth's only comments on this fundamental aspect of the *Metamorphoses* is that 'where he endeavours to disswade Mankind from indulging carnivorous Appetites in his *Pythagorean* Philosophy, how emphatical is his Reasoning!' (p. x) and, on a similar theme, that 'from the

Pythagorean Philosophy, it may be observed, that Man is the only Animal who kills his Fellow Creature without being angry' (p. xvii).[87] Instead of broaching the somewhat controversial subject of the place of the soul after death,[88] Garth apparently prefers to consider a violent cause of death itself.

Accordingly, in this sepulchral preface, Garth guides the reader to other brutal episodes:

> [Ovid] seems to have taken the most Pains in the First, and Second Book of the *Metamorphoses*, though the Thirteenth abounds with Sentiments most moving, and with calamitous Incidents, introduced with great Art. The Poet here had in view the tragedy of *Hecuba* in Euripides; and tis a wonder, it has never been attempted in our own Tongue. The House of Priam is destroyed, his Royal Daughter a sacrifice to the *Manes* of his that occasion'd it. She is forc'd from the Arms of her unhappy Friends, and hurry'd to the Altar, where she behaves her self with a Decency becoming her Sex, and a Magnanimity equal to her Blood, and so very affecting, that even the Priest wept [...]. (p. xi)

As Hopkins explains in the aptly named 'Dryden and Ovid's "Wit Out of Season"', this Ovidian passage prompted the first recorded instance of such criticism in the elder Seneca's *Controversiae*.[89] In some ways, Garth's invocation might be seen as a means of challenging 'the persistent [...] charge that Ovid trivializes depiction of pain and suffering by the inappropriate display of wit'.[90] However, by referring to Euripides' play *Hecuba*, a text which he states 'has never been attempted in our own Tongue', Garth is able to display erudition, textual mastery and, importantly, the merits of the current translation. By recalling 'the most influential of all ghost plays',[91] Garth's preface sends the reader to book 13 of the *Metamorphoses* which 'abounds with Sentiments most moving, and with calamitous Incidents'. Rather appropriately, this book features Temple Stanyan's translation of Ovid's version of the story of Polyxena and Hecuba and, of course, the ghostly return of Achilles:

> Here the wide op'ning Earth to sudden View,
> Disclos'd *Achilles*, Great as when he drew
> The vital Air, but fierce with proud Disdain,
> As when he sought Briseïs to regain; (p. 454)

Here, the heroic figure is typically arresting. Within the context of the closely defined method of translation that Garth suggests will epitomize his edition, however, it is equally striking that Stanyan's rendition goes beyond the *Metamorphoses*.[92] Briseïs is not a figure invoked in Ovid's epic poem; rather, she is one of the lamenting women who appear in the apparently more popular Ovidian text at this time, the *Heroides*.[93] With this modest, but modish, intertextual example, in a section of the translation that is thoroughly concerned with the spectral image, the ghostly, textual traces of other Ovidian narratives invade Garth's edition of the *Metamorphoses*. But the *Heroides* is not the only intertext lingering in the 1717 translation.

Illustration 4.1   **Title page, Samuel Garth (ed.),** *Ovid's Metamorphoses, by the most Eminent Hands* **(London: 1717)**

As well as the story of Cippus from book 15, Garth translated the penultimate book of the *Metamorphoses* in its entirety. In one of the few discussions of the literary merits of the 1717 Ovid, Brown's overarching view of the editor's contributions is that they 'sometimes read like the work of someone desperately finishing off the bits no one else wanted to do – he is always very happy to truncate'.[94] In many ways, however, Garth exceeds this mechanistic role. Rather than merely filling in the narrative gaps, Garth translates some apt material. What better subject could 'Sir Samuel Garth, M.D.', as he is described in the table of contents, render into English than that part of the *Metamorphoses* which deals with Circe and her 'art in impious pharmacy'? Book 14, however, engages with the overriding concerns of Garth's editorial preface in other notable ways. As Ovid's poem tells of Aeneas's descent into Hell to meet with his father's ghost, the Sibyl's words in Sandys's translation read:

> Yet feare not, Trojan, thy desires enjoy:
> *T'Elysian Fields, Th'infernal Monarchie,*
> And Fathers shade, I will thy person guide. (p. 458)[95]

Similarly, Garth's Sibyl says:

> Tho' great be thy Request, yet shalt thou see
> *Th'Elysian Fields*, *Th'infernal Monarchy*;
> Thy Parent's Shade: This Arm thy Steps shall guide; (p. 484)

Despite Garth's attempts in the preface to undermine Sandys's influence ('Tis fit', he states, that 'I should take the Summ upon Content, and be better bred, than to count after him' (p. xix)), there are 'small, but significant borrowings' from the earlier translation woven throughout the whole of the 1717 edition.[96] Garth wants to present an eighteenth-century Ovid which is clearly distinct from Sandys's translation. Paradoxically, as Dwyer has convincingly shown, Garth follows Sandys's Ovid more closely than any of the other translators.[97]

Several years before the publication of the 1717 translation, Eustace Budgell used a quotation from Ovid's Pythagorean disquisition as the motto for an essay which appeared in the *Spectator* (578):

> — *Eque feris humana in corpora transit,*
> *Inque feras Noster [...]*

Dryden translates the passage as follows:

> Th'unbodied spirit flies–
> And lodges where it lights in man or beast. (p. 517)[98]

The Ovidian quotation frames Budgell's musings on recent debates about the self. At the beginning of the essay he states that 'there has been very great Reason, on several Accounts, for the learned World to endeavour at settling what it was that might be said to compose personal Identity', and he cites 'Mr. Lock's' notion 'that the Word Person properly signifies a thinking intelligent Being that has Reason and Reflection, and can consider it self as it self'.[99] Budgell's use of the *Metamorphoses* exemplifies just how enmeshed the poem is in early eighteenth-century England. Indeed, its pervasiveness in this period, as at other times, 'tells us of the need for figuration, for myths, for tropes'.[100] As Charles Tomlinson rightly observes, moreover, that Ovid's poem 'should have appeared in the middle of what used to be called "our age of prose and reason", dispels somewhat that misconception of Matthew Arnold's on which many of us were brought up, and also powerfully illustrates how the idea of metamorphosis laid hold on the Augustan imagination.'[101] The notable phrase in Tomlinson's quotation, however, is 'dispels somewhat'. Eighteenth-century English translators domesticate Ovid according to contemporaneous ideological concerns. Garth, like Budgell, thus frames Ovid's poem within the context of recent epistemological, political and cultural developments in order to support a translation of the *Metamorphoses* which suits the general eighteenth–century reader and which, importantly, attempts to negate the significance of the earlier translation. Paul Hammond argues that

> all translation entails the management of loss. The original text is no longer present on the page, but lurks behind the translation, temporarily displaced by it, teasingly inaccessible to those who do not have access to the original language, haunting the page like a ghostly presence for those who do.[102]

It is not the Latin source that haunts Garth's Ovid, however, but its intralingual competitor. In this period of emerging empiricism, when the emphasis was on 'what is, not what merely seems',[103] ghostly tropes, figures which oscillate between presence and absence, past and the present, both fascinate and disturb Garth's Ovid. In the end, however, the preface encases a translation which is as unsuccessful as Pope's translator in *Sandys's Ghost* in erasing uninvited voices from the past. Indeed, the spectral traces of Sandys's apparently obsolete *Metamorphosis Englished* continue to 'lurk' in Garth's edition.

Notes

[1] Jacques Derrida, *Specters of Marx*, trans. by Peggy Kamuf (London: Routledge, 1994), p. 18. The quotation used as the epigraph to this chapter refers to *Hamlet* and French translations of the line 'the time is out of joint.' In a passage which suggests ways in which both the processes and products of translation are thoroughly disruptive, Derrida (mediated, of course, through his own translator) goes on to say the following: 'In their plurality, the words of a translation organise themselves, they are not dispersed at random. They disorganise themselves as well through the very effect of the specter, because of the Cause that is called the original and that, like all ghosts, address same-ly disparate demands, which are more than contradictory.'

[2] George Sandys, *Ovid's Metamorphosis Englished, Mythologized, and Represented in Figures* (Oxford: 1632).

[3] Rachel Trickett, 'The *Heroides* and the English Augustans', in *Ovid Renewed: Ovidian Influences on Literature and Art from the Middle Ages to the Twentieth Century*, ed. by

Charles Martindale (Cambridge: Cambridge University Press, 1988), pp. 191–204, p. 191.

4 Richard F. Hardin, 'Ovid in Seventeenth-Century England', *Comparative Literature*, 24 (1972), 44–62, 61.

5 28 June, 1712. All quotations are from *The Spectator*, ed. by Donald F. Bond, 5 vols (Oxford: Clarendon Press, 1965).

6 Addison originally published 'The Story of Salmacis' which appeared in Garth's Ovid in Tonson's *Annual Miscellany* (London: 1694). He subsequently provided translations of books 2 and 3 for the 1717 edition.

7 All quotations are from *Ovid's Metamorphoses, by the most Eminent Hands*, ed. by Samuel Garth (London: 1717).

8 Garth's publisher, Jacob Tonson, published each of these translations. For further discussion of collaborative writing and literary communities in the early eighteenth century, see Moyra Haslett, *Pope to Burney, 1714–1779: Scriblerians to Bluestockings* (Basingstoke: Palgrave Macmillan, 2003).

9 Susan Bassnett, 'The Meek or the Mighty: Reappraising the Role of the Translator', in *Translation, Power, Subversion*, ed. by Román Álvarez and M. Carmen-África Vidal (Clevedon: Multilingual Matters, 1996), pp. 10–24, p. 19.

10 See further Barbara M. Benedict, *Making the Modern Reader: Cultural Mediation in Early Modern Literary Anthologies* (Princeton, N. J.: Princeton University Press, 1996).

11 Harold Love, 'Some Restoration Treatments of Ovid', in *Poetry and Drama 1570–1700: Essays in Honour of Harold F. Brooks*, ed. by Antony Coleman and Antony Hammond (London: Methuen, 1981), pp. 136–55, p. 136.

12 See further Warren Francis Dwyer, 'Profit, Poetry and Politics in Augustan Translation: A Study of the Garth-Tonson *Metamorphoses* of 1717' (unpublished doctoral thesis, Urbana, Illinois, 1969).

13 One notable exception is Charles Tomlinson, who considers this translation 'to be the most splendid *Metamorphoses* we have'. Charles Tomlinson, 'Why Dryden's Translations Matter', *Translation and Literature*, 10 (2001), 3–20, 18.

14 For comment on the significance of the 'editor-function' in the early eighteenth century, see Richard Iliffe, 'Author-Mongering: the "Editor" Between Producer and Consumer', in *The Consumption of Culture 1600–1800: Image, Object, Text*, ed. by Ann Bermingham and John Brewer (London: Routledge, 1995) pp.166–92.

15 Joseph Warton, *An Essay on the Genius and Writings of Pope*, 5th edn, 2 vols (London: W. J. and J. Richardson, 1806), volume 2, p. 25, n. Warton takes issue with Garth's positive views on Ovid by citing Quintilian on the 'pedantic and childish affectation in vogue in the schools marking a transition by some epigram and seeking to win applause by this feat of legerdemain. Ovid is given to this form of affection [...].' Quintilian, *Institutio Oratoria*, trans. by H. E. Butler, 4 vols (London: Heinemann, 1920–22), 4.1.77.

16 Samuel Johnson, *Lives of the Poets*, ed. by Peter Cunningham, 3 vols (London: John Murray, 1854), p. 100. Both Warton and Johnson's comments are noted in Richard Cook, *Sir Samuel Garth* (Boston: Twayne, 1980), p. 157, n. 54.

17 Dwyer, 'Profit, Poetry and Politics in Augustan Translation', p. 46.

18 Dwyer, 'Profit, Poetry and Politics in Augustan Translation', p. 117.

19 See David Hopkins, 'Dryden and the Garth-Tonson *Metamorphoses*', *Review of English Studies*, 39 (1988), 64–74; David Hopkins, 'Dryden and Ovid's "Wit Out of Season"' in *Ovid Renewed: Ovidian Influences on Literature and Art from the Middle Ages to the Twentieth Century*, ed. by Charles Martindale (Cambridge: Cambridge University Press, 1988), pp. 167–90; Sarah Annes Brown, *The Metamorphosis of Ovid:From Chaucer to*

Ted Hughes (London: Duckworth: 1999), pp. 123–40 and Garth Tissol, Introduction, in *Ovid: 'Metamorphoses', Translated by John Dryden and Others, Edited by Sir Samuel Garth* (Hertfordshire: Wordsworth, 1998), pp. xi–xxiv. Brown's discussion is particularly noteworthy for her consideration of the contributions by Arthur Maynwaring, Joseph Addison, Laurence Eusden and William Stonestreet.

20   Dwyer, 'Profit, Poetry and Politics in Augustan Translation', p. 2.

21   Hopkins, 'Dryden and the Garth-Tonson *Metamorphoses*', p. 74.

22   Drawing attention to the cultural politics of translation in the period, Susan Bassnett states that 'by the mid-seventeenth century the effects of the Counter-Reformation, the conflict between absolute monarchy and the developing Parliamentary system, and the widening of the gap between traditional Christian Humanism and science had all led to radical changes in the theory of literature and hence to the role of translation. Descartes' (1596–1650) attempts to formulate a method of inductive reasoning were mirrored in the preoccupation of literary critics to formulate rules of aesthetic reproduction.' Susan Bassnett, *Translation Studies*, rev. edn (London: Routledge, 1991), p. 58.

23   See Albert C. Baugh and Thomas Cable, *A History of the English Language*, 4th edn (London: Routledge, 1993), pp. 249 ff.

24   Edmund Waller, 'Of English Verse', cited in Baugh and Cable, *A History of the English Language*, p. 256.

25   For an extensive study of writing on translation practice in this period, see T. R. Steiner, *English Translation Theory 1650–1800* (Amsterdam: Van Gorum, 1975).

26   John Dryden, *The Works of John Dryden: Poems 1649–1680*, ed. by Edward Niles Hooker and H. T. Swedenberg, Jr. (Berkeley: University of California Press, 1961), p. 119.

27   Newton's text was not published in English until Andrew Motte's translation in 1729, but extracts of the *Principia* circulated in the vernacular. In 1715, John Maxwell produced *A discourse concerning God; wherein the meaning of His name, His Providence, the nature and measure of His Dominion are consider'd, etc. To which is subjoined a translation of Sir Isaac Newton's general scholium [...] concerning the Cartesian Vortices, and concerning God; as also a short account of the Cape of Good Hope* (London: 1715). A year later William Whiston published *Sir Isaac Newton's Mathematick Philosophy more easily demonstrated; with Dr. Halley's Account of Comets illustrated. Being forty lectures read [...] at Cambridge [...] In this English edition, the whole is corrected and improved by the author* (London: 1716).

28   Edmund Halley, 'A Discourse of the Rule of the Decrease of the Height of the Mercury in the Barometer, According as Places are Elevated Above the Surface of the Earth, with an Attempt to Discover the True Reason of the Rising and Falling of the Mercury, upon Change of Weather', *Philosophical Transactions of the Royal Society*, 16 (1686–92), 104–16. For Halley's review of Newton's text, see Edmund Halley, '*Philosophia Naturalis Principia Mathematica Philosophica*', *Transactions of the Royal Society of London*, 15, (1685–6), 291–7. Halley encouraged and financed the publication of Newton's *Principia*.

29   The lines are rendered in translation thus: 'All you who touch these rolls bereft of their father, to them at least let a place be granted in your city! And your indulgence will be all the greater because these were not published by their master, but were rescued from what might be called his funeral. And so whatever defect this rough poem may have I would have corrected, had it been permitted me.' Ovid, *Tristia ex Ponto*, trans. by Arthur Leslie Wheeler, 2nd edn, rev. by G. P. Goold (London: Heinemann, 1924), 7. 35–40.

30   In order, Garth discusses the myths of Deucalion and Pyrrha; Phaeton; Baucis and Philemon; Lycaon; Pentheus; Minos and Scylla; Cippus; Hercules; Romulus; Ariadne;

Althea; Polyphemus and Galatea; Cephalus and Procris; Hippomenes and Atalanta; Medea; Myrrha; Caenis; Tereus; Midas; Pythagoras; Proteus; and Aesculapius.

31   Robert L. Martensen, 'Garth, Sir Samuel (1660/61–1719) *Oxford Dictionary of National Biography*, online edn (Oxford University Press, 2004) <http: //www.oxforddnb.com/ view/article/10414>accessed 4 June 2005.

32   Cook, *Sir Samuel Garth*, p. 59.

33   Tissol, Introduction, p. xx.

34   Brown, *The Metamorphosis of Ovid*, p. 131.

35   Johnson, *Lives of the Poets*, p. 99.

36   The full title of the text is *The dedication for the Latin edition of Lucretius His Highness the Elector of Hanover, now King of Great Britain [..] .Made English by Mr. Oldmixon* (London: 1714).

37   Cook, *Sir Samuel Garth*, p. 25.

38   Book 1 is dedicated to the Duchess of Kingston; book 2 to the Duchess of Roxburgh; book 3 to the Duchess of Newcastle; book 4 to the Countess of Hartford; book 5 to the Countess of Warwick; book 6 to Princess Anne, elder daughter of the Prince and Princess of Wales; book 7 to Lady Cowper; book 8 to the Duchess of Rutland; book 9 to the Countess of Lincoln; book 10 to the Vicountess of Scudamore; book 11 to the Viscountess Townshend; book 12 to Mrs. Walpole; book 13 to Mrs. Margaret Pelham; book 14 to the Countess of Burlington and Lady Juliana Boyle; and book 15 to the Duchess of St. Albans. For a brief discussion of these dedicatees, see Dwyer, 'Profit, Poetry and Politics in Augustan Translation', p. 260. See also Hopkins, 'Dryden and the Garth-Tonson *Metamorphoses*', p. 64.

39   See further R. L. Arkell, *Caroline of Ansbach: George the Second's Queen* (London: Oxford University Press, 1939). Both Clarke and Caroline occupy a significant place in the famous Newton–Leibniz disputes. Caroline had been Leibniz's pupil at the court of Berlin. When she came to London in 1714, she first made contact with Clarke when she tried to find a translator for Lebniz's *Théodicée* (1710). During 1715 and 1716, largely initiated by Caroline, Leibniz exchanged a series of five letters with Clarke. See further Steven Shapin, 'Of Gods and Kings: Natural Philosophy and Politics in the Leibniz–Clarke disputes', *Isis*, 72 (1981), 187–215.

40   Ragnhild Hatton, *George I: Elector and King* (London: Thames and Hudson, 1978), p. 13.

41   See further Peter Quennell, *Caroline of England: An Augustan Portrait* (London: Collins, 1939), p. 1 ff.

42   Cook, *Sir Samuel Garth*, p. 19.

43   Cook, *Sir Samuel Garth*, p. 19. For an interesting discussion on the relationship between Garth's *The Dispensary* and Dryden's translation of Ovid, see David Hopkins, 'Dryden's Cave of Sleep and Garth's *Dispensary*', *Notes and Queries*, 23 (1976), 243–5.

44   Cook, *Sir Samuel Garth*, p. 120. This was the third edition which included other revisions.

45   Belsey, 'Love as Trompe–L'Oeil', p. 259

46   All quotations are from Samuel Garth, *Claremont* (London: 1715).

47   See further Tassie Gwilliam, 'Cosmetic Poetics: Coloring Faces in the Eighteenth Century' in *Body and Text in the Eighteenth Century*, ed. by Veronica Kelly and Dorothea Von Mücke (Stanford: Stanford University Press, 1994), pp. 144–62.

48   James Sambrook, *The Eighteenth Century: The Intellectual and Cultural Context of English Literature, 1700–1789* (London: Longman, 1986), p. 212.

49   Cook interprets the Samian Sage in *Claremont* as Epicurus. *Sir Samuel Garth*, p. 104.

Whilst Epicurean principles were becoming increasingly popular in the late seventeenth and early eighteenth centuries, it seems far more likely to me that the reference alludes to the discourse of Pythagoras from the *Metamorphoses* where he is introduced as a man who was 'a Samian by birth' (13. 60). Epicurus was also known by this epithet but his refusal to believe in life after death is at odds with the druidic tradition that Garth is writing about. See further Paul R. Lonigan, *The Druids: Priests of the Ancient Celts* (Westport, Connecticut: Greenwood Press, 1996).

[50]   Ovid, *The Metamorphoses*, trans. by Frank Justus Miller, rev. by G. P. Goold, 2 vols (London: Heinemann, 1984), 1. 2–4.

[51]   Lonigan, *The Druids*, pp. 37–9.

[52]   'Only her voice and her bones remain.' Ovid, *The Metamorphoses*, trans. Miller, 3. 398.

[53]   Brown, *The Metamorphosis of Ovid*, p. 128.

[54]   Ovid, *The Metamorphoses*, trans. Miller, 3. 391–2. It is noteworthy that Addison's translation considerably truncates Echo's pursuit of Narcissus. For a provocative discussion of the sexual politics of Echo in Sandys's translation, see Gina Bloom, 'Localizing Disembodied Voice in Sandys's Englished "Narcissus and Echo"', in *Ovid and the Renaissance Body*, ed. by Goran V. Stanivukovic (Toronto: University of Toronto Press, 2001), pp. 129–54.

[55]   Cited in Hopkins, 'Dryden and the Garth-Tonson *Metamorphoses*', p. 67.

[56]   See Baugh and Cable, *A History of the English Language*, pp. 250–1.

[57]   See further Tissol, Introduction, pp. xxv.

[58]   George Steiner, *After Babel: Aspects of Language and Translation*, 2nd edn (Oxford: Oxford University Press, 1992), p. 269.

[59]   Out of the 902 lines that Garth translates, he marks 51 lines throughout book 14 in this way. For a statistical analysis, see Dwyer, 'Profit, Poetry and Politics in Augustan Translation', p. 39. The mark " also appears in books 2, 3, 4 and 13.

[60]   In the epistle to the reader, Margaret Cavendish writes that 'if I had been so learned I would have put my boke into Latine, which is a general language through all Europe, and not have writ it in my native language, which goeth no further than the kingdom of England, [...] yet I had rather my book should die in oblivion, then to be divulged to disadvantage, and instead of cloathing it in a new garment, they will dismember the body of sense, as to put out the natural eyes, and put in glasse eyes in the place, or to cut off the legs and then set the body upon wooden stumps, but unless the translator hath a genius suitable to the author of the original, the original will be disfigured with mistakes; yet it is easier to translate prose then verse, for rimes, number, and sense, are hard to match in several languages, it is double labour, and requires double capacitie; for although Ovid and Dubartas were so happy to meet a Sylvester and a Sands, yet very few or no other had the good fortune in our language' (Sig A 2ʳ). I cite this passage at length as Cavendish's text offers an important intervention by a woman into the debates about translation. I would like to thank Paula Goodman for bringing this quotation to my attention. See further Paula Goodman, 'Places, Pictures and Prefaces: Reading Women's Prose Fiction, 1621–1696' (unpublished Ph.D thesis, University of Wales, Cardiff, 1997).

[61]   According to Tytler 'from the time of Sandys who published his translation of the *Metamorphoses* of Ovid in 1626, there does not appear to have been much improvement in the art of translating poetry until Dryden'. Alexander Fraser Tytler, *Essay on the Principles of Translation* (London: Dent, 1907), p. 43.

[62]   For a stimulating discussion on this subject, see the chapter 'Of Ghosts and Garments: the Materiality of Memory on the Renaissance stage', in Ann Rosalind Jones and Peter

Stallybrass, *Renaissance Clothing and the Materiality of Memory* (Cambridge: Cambridge University Press, 2000), pp. 245–68.

63 This famous example is cited in Steiner, *English Translation Theory 1650–1800*, p. 10 and Tejaswini Niranjana, *Siting Translation: History, Post-Structuralism and the Colonial Context* (Berkeley: University of California Press, 1992), p. 53.

64 Other episodes featuring *manes* are found throughout Ovid's text. See *Ovid: The Metamorphoses*, trans. Miller, 1.586; 2.303; 4.437; 5.73; 5.116; 6.569; 6.669; 7.206; 8.488; 9.406; 13.465; 14.105; 15.154.

65 Jones and Stallybrass make this connection throughout their chapter 'Of Ghosts and Garments'.

66 Joseph Addison, 1 July, 1712.

67 H. F. Brook, 'The Fictitious Ghost: A Poetic Genre', *Notes and Queries*, 29 (1982), 51–5, 52.

68 Hopkins, 'Dryden and the Garth-Tonson *Metamorphoses*', p. 77.

69 All quotations are from *The Twickenham Edition of the Poems of Alexander Pope: Minor Poems*, ed. by Norman Ault and John Butt (London: Methuen, 1954), pp. 170–6. The editorial note to *Sandys's Ghost* identifies Molyneaux.

70 According to William Powell Jones 'the only real hostility to science in literature appears in the ridicule of the *virtuoso* by the neo-classical wits'. William Powell Jones, *The Rhetoric of Science: A Study of Scientific Ideas and Imagery in Eighteenth-Century English Poetry* (London: Routledge and Kegan Paul, 1966), p. 65.

71 Pope, *Minor Poems*, p. 172.

72 Suetonius, *Caligula* 35.1. See further Caroline Vout, 'The Myth of the Toga: Understanding the History of Roman Dress', *Greece and Rome*, 43 (1996), 204–220, 215.

73 Part III, Ch. 34, cited in John Redwood, *Reason, Ridicule and Religion:The Age of Enlightenment England 1660–1750*, 2nd edn (London: Thames and Hudson, 1995), p. 133.

74 Dryden admits that translation was not a practice that could be clearly defined by stringent regulation. At the end of the Preface to Ovid's *Epistles*, for instance, he states that he is ready to 'acknowledge that [he has] transgressed the rules which [he has] given'. John Dryden, *The Works of John Dryden: Poems 1649–1680*, ed. by Edward Niles Hooker and H. T. Swedenberg, Jr. (Berkeley: University of California Press, 1961), p. 119. Later, in the Preface to the *Sylvae* (1685), Dryden discusses the way in which translation is not an exact science: 'It was my Lord Roscommon's Essay on translated Verse, which made me uneasie till I try'd whether or no I was capable of following his Rules, and of reducing the speculation into practice. For many a fair Precept in Poetry, is like a seeming Demonstration in the Mathematicks; very specious in the Diagram, but failing in the Mechanic Operation'. *The Works of John Dryden: Poems 1685–1692*, ed. by Earl Miner (Berkeley: University of California Press, 1969), pp. 3–18, p. 3.

75 The Sewell edition was sold at six shillings against the two guineas of the Garth *Metamorphoses* and in its preface it makes it clear that it had set out to rival Garth's edition. See Hopkins, 'Dryden and the Garth-Tonson *Metamorphoses*', p. 65. Dwyer provides the following information regarding the contributors. The Sewell–Curll edition was in two volumes which were translated as follows:

The first volume

Book 1	Sewell and Co.
Book 2	J. Phillips and Co.
Books 3–6	Sewell

Book 7   Sewell and Gay
Book 8   Sewell, Chute and Dart.
The second volume
Books 9–13   Theobold
Book 14   Pope and Theobold
Book 15   Capt. Morrice.

The translation was dedicated to Barnham Goode. See further Dwyer, 'Profit, Poetry and Politics in Augustan Translation', pp. 10–28.

[76] George Sewell, *Ovid's Metamorphoses. In Fifteen Books made English by several hands. Adorn'd with cuts*, 2nd edn (London: 1724).

[77] Cited in Cook, *Sir Samuel Garth*, p. 18.

[78] No copy of the eulogy survives. Cook, *Sir Samuel Garth*, p. 17.

[79] Philip Hardie, *Ovid's Poetics of Illusion* (Cambridge: Cambridge University Press, 2002), p. 81.

[80] As Hopkins notes, the engravings in Garth's edition were by Louis du Guernier, Michael Van der Gucht, Elisha Kirkall, and R. Smith. Hopkins, 'Dryden and the Garth-Tonson *Metamorphoses*', p. 64, n. 3.

[81] Samuel Johnson writes that Dryden 'was buried among the poets in Westminster Abbey, where, though the duke of Newcastle had, in a general dedication prefixed by Congreve to his dramatick works, accepted thanks for his intention of erecting him a monument, he lay long without distinction, till the duke of Buckinghamshire gave him a tablet, inscribed only with the name of DRYDEN.' Johnson, *Lives of the Poets*, p. 324.

[82] It is useful to recall that the earliest definition of 'translation' is concerned with the transportation of the corporeal remains of saints. See the *Oxford English Dictionary*, 'translation', sense I. 1.a.

[83] Perhaps the most celebrated example of this kind of poetic transmigration is between Ovid and Shakespeare. Famously, Francis Meres claimed that 'the sweete wittie soule of Ovid lives in mellifluous and hony-tongued Shakespeare'. See 'A Comparative Discourse of our English Poets with the Greek, Latine, and Italian Poets' in *Palladis Tamia: Wits Treasury* (London: 1598) in *Elizabethan Critical Essays*, ed by G. Gregory Smith, 2 vols (Oxford: Oxford University Press, 1904), pp. 317–18. Another text which should be noted in this context, as it presents a complex poetic transmigration between Ovid, Chaucer and the early modern writer, is Charles Cotton, *Chaucer's Ghoast, or, a Piece of Antiquity. Containing twelve pleasant Fables of Ovid penn'd after the ancient manner of writing in England* (London: 1672).

[84] Parker states that 'it is important to note that Garth also wrote a long landscape poem *Claremont* [...] medical treatises, and Latin translation (including a partial Lucretius)'. Blandford Parker, *The Triumph of Augustan Poetics: English Literary Culture from Butler to Johnson* (Cambridge: Cambridge University Press, 1998), p. 140.

[85] Redwood, *Reason, Ridicule and* Religion, pp. 93–132.

[86] See further Richard Kroll, *The Material Word: Literate Culture in the Restoration and Early Eighteenth Century* (Baltimore: John Hopkins University Press, 1991).

[87] In a discussion of Pythagoras as 'practical moralist', Judith Sloman states that 'Dryden's Pythagoras is important for his attack on cannibalism.' Judith Sloman, *Dryden: The Poetics of Translation* (Toronto: University of Toronto Press, 1985), p. 184.

[88] Sloman observes that 'as late as 1699 that Anglican Bishop of Worcester felt that he had to attack the association of Pythagoras with natural religion and reject his "impudent Diabolical Fictions". The bishop was disgusted with the readiness to confuse Pythagoras's theory of transmigration with the Christian belief in immortality.' Sloman, *Dryden*, p. 183.

89 Hopkins, 'Dryden and Ovid's "Wit Out of Season"', p. 167.
90 Hopkins, 'Dryden and Ovid's "Wit Out of Season"', p. 167.
91 Jones and Stallybrass, *Renaissance Clothing and the Materiality of Memory*, p. 255.
92 Stanyan had previously published books 1 and 2 of his *The Grecian History [...] Adorn'd with Cuts* (London: 1707).
93 Ovid, *Heroides*, trans. by Grant Showerman (London: Heinemann, 1914), book 3. Briseïs is also featured in Homer's *Iliad*. See Eric Smith, *A Dictionary of Classical Reference in English Poetry* (Cambridge: Brewer, 1984), p. 43.
94 Brown, *The Metamorphosis of Ovid*, p. 128.
95 Ovid's *Metamorphoses*, trans. Miller, 14. 110–1.
96 Dwyer says that 'the most significant tribute to Sandys is the way in which virtually all of the Garth translators from Dryden down borrowed rhymes from him freely and often phrases and even lines occasionally'. See Dwyer, 'Profit, Poetry and Politics in Augustan Translation', p. 111.
97 See Dwyer, 'Profit, Poetry and Politics in Augustan Translation', p. 239.
98 August 9, 1714. Bond's notes give Dryden's translation and he points out that Addison also uses the same motto in the *Spectator* 342. Donald F. Bond (ed.), *The Spectator*, vol. 4, p. 575, n. 2.
99 The *Spectator*, 9 August, 1714.
100 Jacques Derrida, 'Des Tours de Babel', in *Difference in Translation*, trans. and ed. by Joseph F. Graham (Ithaca: Cornell University Press, 1985), pp. 165–207, p.165.
101 Charles Tomlinson, 'Why Dryden's Translation's Matter', 18.
102 Paul Hammond, *Dryden and the Traces of Classical Rome* (Oxford: Oxford University Press, 1999), p. 147.
103 Barbara Maria Stafford, *Body Criticism: Imaging the Unseen in Enlightenment Art and Medicine* (London: M.I.T. Press, 1991), p. 17.

Chapter 5

In Arachne's Trace:
Women as Translators of the
Metamorphoses

> In returning to ancient myths and opening them from within to the woman's
> body, the woman's mind, and the woman's voice, contemporary women
> have felt like thieves of language staging a raid on the treasured icons of a
> tradition that has required woman's silence for centuries.[1]

Weaving, Sewing and Writing

With Princess Caroline and the accompanying assembly of aristocratic women as
dedicatees, the 1717 edition of the *Metamorphoses* upholds the conventional
gender binarism that defines the translation and reception of Ovid's poem in early
modern England. From the first known complete translation by William Caxton
through to Samuel Garth's collaborative enterprise, men publicly govern the task of
rendering the *Metamorphoses* into English. Women, however, are constructed as
Ovidian readers rather than as translators, as perceived in Tamesyn Audeley's
autograph on Caxton's manuscript, the respective memoirs of Anne Clifford and
Dorothy Osborne, and Samuel Pepys's account of reading Ovid with his wife,
Elizabeth. The reasoning behind such patriarchal superiority might be found in
classical textual criticism. Quintilian's use of the term *lascivia*, as observed in
Chapter 1, manifestly betrays the poem's complex textuality whilst simultaneously
hinting at its sexually subversive content.[2]

Like *Titus Andronicus*, Shakespeare's *Cymbeline* (c. 1609) dramatizes some of
the cultural anxieties surrounding Ovid's poem at this time. Crucially, the nature of
Iachimo's threat to Imogen is suggested by her bedtime reading: 'She hath been
reading late,| The tale of Tereus, here the leaf's turned down| where Philomel gave
up'.[3] The editor of the Arden Shakespeare notes that the 'ironic relevance [of the
Metamorphoses] to the immediate situation is too obvious to require further
comment'.[4] Given the gendered paradigm of Ovidian translation, however, there is
more to say about the appearance of Ovid's text in Imogen's bedchamber. Much of
Iachimo's onstage menace in this scene is achieved through the interplay of epic
poem and dramatic narrative. In Shakespeare's Jacobean play, as Jonathan Bate
explains, 'the rape is metaphorical. The text that is opened out in *Titus* is folded
back in *Cymbeline*.'[5] Whilst the violence of the Roman tragedy remains implicit in

the later drama, both plays present comparative, though equally problematic, social arenas for women readers of the *Metamorphoses*; neither Lavinia nor Imogen are viewed alone with the book. Iachimo's comment on Philomela's rape in terms of surrender not only effaces Ovidian concerns for the sexual politics of violence which are so brutally realized in Shakespeare's Lavinia; the Italian's insidious presence in Imogen's bedchamber combined with his critical treatment of Ovid's text also suggests that the woman's reading matter is a subject for men to openly discuss, analyse and, of course, translate.

Though general humanist tenets seem to signal a liberal attitude toward women and classical education,[6] as we saw in the opening chapter, from the late sixteenth century onward women's reading becomes increasingly censured.[7] For example, Thomas Salter's *A Mirrhour mete for all Mothers, Matrones, and Maidens, intituled the Mirrhour of Modes* (1579) states that:

> Some perhaps will alledge that a Maiden beyng well learned, and able to searche
> and reade sonderie aucthors, maie become chaste and godlie, by readyng the godlie
> and chaste lives of diverse: but I aunswere who can deny, that, seyng of her self she
> is able to reade and understande the Christian Poetes, too wete, *Prudentio,
> Prospero, Juvenco, Pawlino, Nazianzeno,* and suche like, that shee will not also
> reade the Lascivious bookes, of *Ovide, Catullus, Propercius, Tibullus,* and in Virgill
> of *Eneas,* and Dido, and amonge the Greeke Poettes of the filthie love (if I maie
> terme it love) of the Goddes themselves, and of their wicked addulteries and
> abhominable Fornications, as in Homer and suche like [...].[8]

In its use of the term 'lascivious', applied here to a catalogue of classical poets, Salter's *Mirrhour* seems alert to Quintilian's description of Ovid. These cultural pressures are evident in Abraham Fraunce's *Amintas Dale*, the text which is the focus of the discussion in Chapter 2. Produced for Mary Sidney, an influential and erudite woman, Fraunce's text ultimately exposes the gendered frame of vernacular textual production; a mode of Ovidian translation which culminates with the 1760 publication of *Ovid's Metamorphosis Epitomized in an English Poetical Style, for the Use and Entertainment of the Ladies of Great Britain.*[9] Publicly prohibited from reading certain books, early modern English women are equally restricted in their translation practices.

Translation may be thought of as offering intellectual textual spaces for women writers of the period to inhabit.[10] Through the appropriation of various Christian tracts and select forms of secular material, women might contribute to various ideological debates at large in the late sixteenth and early seventeenth centuries. Nevertheless, translation is a mode of textual production which is bound by the gender politics of early modern England. Margaret Tyler's rendition of a Spanish romance, *A Mirrour of Princely Deeds and Knighthood* (1578) by Diego Ortuñez de Calahorra, for instance, remains outstanding in the period for both its subject matter (a Spanish romance) and 'vigorous preface'.[11] The disappearance of the *Metamorphoses* in Ravenscroft's *Titus*, a revision of Shakespeare's play which literally removes the book from the woman's grasp, is thus emblematic of the tensions surrounding women and

Ovid's poem. If the *Metamorphoses* is one of 'Englishwomen's favourite writings and modes of discourse to echo [...] or handle revisionistically',[12] where is the history of these particular forms of Ovidian translation?

A useful place to begin answering this question is with Ovid's own tale of Arachne. Renowned throughout Lydia for her skill in the art of weaving, the low-born Arachne's refusal to acknowledge Minerva's superior talent paves the way for a contest between the woman and the goddess. Working in separate locations, Arachne and Minerva set up looms upon which they will each 'put in portraiture [...] things done long afore'.[13] Minerva's picture depicts the greatness of the gods. On either side of Jove she figures six gods 'with count'nance grave and full of majesty'.[14] To reinforce her own hierarchical status, Minerva's tapestry shows how she successfully defeated Neptune for the possession of Athens. Presenting a further warning to Arachne about the dangers of human presumption, the goddess places a tale of mortal metamorphosis in each corner:

> The Thracians H[em]e and Rodope the formost corner had,
> Who, being sometime mortall folke, usurpt to them the name
> Of Jove and Juno and were turned to mountaines for the same.
> Pigmie womans piteous chance the second corner shewed
> Whom Juno turned to a crane (bicause she was so lewd
> As for to stand at strife with hir for beauty) charging hir
> Against hir native countryfolk continual war to [s]tir.
> The thirde had proud Antigone, who durst of pride contende
> In beauty with the wife of Jove: by whom she in the ende
> Was turned to Storke, no whit availed hir the town
> Of Troy, or that Laomedon, her father ware a crowne,
> But that she clad in feathers white hir lazie wings must [fl]ap
> And with a bobbed Bill bewayle the cause of her missehap.
> The last had chyldelesse Cinyras: who being turned to stone,
> Was picturde prostate on the ground and weeping all alone
> And culling fast betwéen his armes a Temples grée[c]es fine,
> To which his daughters bodies were transformde by wrath divine.[15]

Triumphantly, the goddess completes her picture with an olive tree: her own emblem, somewhat ironically, of peace.[16] As Arthur Golding's translation states, 'with victorie she finisht up that plat'.[17] By contrast, Arachne produces twenty-one scenes which show how Jove, Neptune, Phoebus, Bacchus and Saturn variously disguise themselves in order to violate women: 'Of all these things she missed not their proper shapes, nor yit| The full and just resemblance of their places for to [h]it'.[18] The Lydian girl finishes her work with a border of flowers and ivy, the latter image the symbol of poets. Arachne's textile is so accomplished that the envious Minerva rips it apart and beats the girl with a boxwood shuttle. Of this attack, the poem states that 'The Maide, impacient in her heart did stomacke this so sore| That by and by she hung hirself'.[19] Apparently full of pity, Minerva prevents Arachne from taking her own life. Instead, using the juice of 'Hecats flowre', the goddess transforms the girl into a spider who ever 'practiseth [...]| The Spinners and the Websters crafts of which she erst had s[kil]l'.[20] In the end, Minerva successfully, and eternally, displaces Arachne's capabilities as a signifying subject. In this liminal position, as Nancy K. Miller remarks, Arachne 'is [still] to hang and yet to live'.[21]

Detecting parallels between Ovid and Arachne's poetic enterprise, Sarah Annes Brown, and Ann Rosalind Jones and Peter Stallybrass discuss the self-reflexive aspects of this myth in terms of their related figures and tropes.[22] Observing further correlations between Ovid and Arachne, A. S. Byatt declares that 'Arachne's tapestry is Ovid's poem, a rush of beings, a rush of animal, vegetable and mineral constantly coming into shape and constantly undone and re-forming'.[23] However, there are other important points of comparison and contrast between the classical author and his own literary creation. As Ovid appropriates Greek narratives into his Latin poem, the opening tale of book 6 is significant for its presentation of Arachne as an Ovidian translator. Several of the scenes in her tapestry – the respective abductions and rapes of Europa, Danaë, Proserpine and Medusa – appear in the wider narrative frame of the *Metamorphoses* itself.[24] Whilst Ovid writes, however, Arachne weaves; whilst Ovid speaks of his poem as one which neither '*Joves* féerce wrath,| Nor swoord, nor fyre, nor freating age with all the force it hath| Are able too abolish quyght',[25] Arachne's weft is destroyed. As this chapter will show, these typical binarisms of writing/weaving and survival/destruction are primarily rooted in sustained constructions of gender difference. But Ovid's tale also raises related questions about hierarchies of class and social status as 'against the classically theocentric balance of [Minerva's] tapestry, Arachne constructs a feminocentric protest'.[26] In its portrayal of the goddess's destruction of the mortal girl's work and subsequent physical abuse, the Ovidian episode emphasizes the ways in which meaning is held in place by ideological forces which either conspire with or censure textual production.

As detailed in Chapter 3 of this book, the overt sexual politics of George Sandys's *Metamorphosis Englished* (1632) owes much to the Neoplatonic discourses of Caroline court culture. A distinctly misogynistic idiom, however, is brought to the fore in the English translator's ultimate 'fear and derision' of Arachne's textual prowess.[27] Defining her as 'wickedly resolute' and 'profane',[28] Sandys's ultimate interpretation of Arachne as a 'subverter of class hierarchies' suggests that she is 'dangerous as an unruly woman and as a political agitator'.[29] In his desire to keep Arachne firmly in her place, thus aligning himself with the goddess rather than with the mortal, Sandys's translation and commentary upholds the very ideological principles which the Ovidian myth exposes. In the words of Josette Wiseman:

> The myth of Arachne the artist defying authority has recently been used to show how the works of female artists and critics have been 'discredited, detached from the cultural record, and finally ignored,' by men who, like gods, tear the texts-tissues to silence the women who wove them.[30]

If Sandys appears more like Minerva, women translators of Ovid in early modern England are in Arachne's trace: their contributions to the history of the

Metamorphoses in English have been effaced. Accordingly, the following discussion of the Ovidian myths produced by Elizabeth Talbot, Elizabeth Singer Rowe, Mary Chudleigh and Mary Wortley Montagu is a nascent attempt to make women's participation in *Ovid and the Cultural Politics of Translation in Early Modern England* visible. Significantly, this genealogy of Ovidian translation begins with an account of textile production.

Elizabeth Talbot: Phaeton, Europa and Actaeon

Challenging the humanist treatises which declared that a girl should 'handle wolle and flaxe' in order to help her to 'holde her tonge demurely',[31] sixteenth century women 'used needlework to explore alternative narratives of the feminine as political, authoritative, active, and expressive, although invariably chaste and productive'.[32] In this specific textual context which allowed women to 'simultaneously [obey] and [defy] the injunction to passive silence',[33] Lisa M. Klein explains how an 'analysis of needlework done by or for Queen Elizabeth shows how [early modern] women fashioned themselves as subjects, promoted their interests, and fostered social relations by exchanging hand-wrought works'.[34] One of the women whom she discusses in this context is Elizabeth Talbot, the Countess of Shrewsbury. More commonly known as Bess of Hardwick, Talbot has earned a reputation for her 'advantageous marriages to four prosperous but short-lived husbands' and 'shrewd business acumen' which led, amongst other things, to the construction of two impressive houses at Chatsworth and Hardwick.[35] In February 1569, her fourth husband (George Talbot, Sixth Earl of Shrewsbury) was appointed Mary Stuart's warden; five years later Talbot took the opportunity to arrange a marriage between her daughter, Elizabeth Cavendish, and Charles Stuart, the son of Margaret, Countess of Lennox (Mary Stuart's mother-in-law). Talbot incurred the Queen's wrath for several reasons. Firstly, contact between Mary and Margaret had been forbidden; secondly, the marriage between Elizabeth and Charles in November 1574 took place without Elizabeth's knowledge or consent. For Talbot, the match meant that her daughter became the monarch's kin and her grandchildren (notably Arbella Stuart) were heirs to the thrones of England and Scotland.[36] Klein records that 'shortly thereafter, some of her husband's servants were arrested on suspicion of carrying messages for Mary, and the Queen began to suspect [Talbot's] loyalty'.[37] It seems that the resourceful Talbot reinstated her position as loyal subject by way of a specially commissioned embroidered cloak which was presented to the Queen as a New Year's gift in 1575.[38] The gift thus 'reaffirmed the mutual but hierarchical relationship of the Queen and her loyal subjects, the Shrewsburys, while it gently coerced the Queen into continued reciprocity'.[39] This biographical episode is important for its demonstration of Talbot's self-fashioning through sewing rather than writing; the form of textual production with which she enters the history of Ovidian translation in early modern England.

In their exploration of the relationship between 'the needle and the pen' in the sixteenth and early seventeenth centuries, Jones and Stallybrass briefly discuss two anonymous textiles featuring episodes from Ovid's poem: a silkwork picture depicting Diana and Actaeon (c. 1650) and a series of elaborate bed valances showing the Philomela myth (c. 1600).[40] Whilst they examine Talbot's textual relationship with Mary Stuart and a general cultural politics of needlework, Jones and Stallybrass ignore her association with the *Metamorphoses*. Among the range of biblical and classical subjects used to decorate Hardwick Hall are three small textiles featuring the Ovidian episodes of Phaeton, Europa and Actaeon (Illustrations 5.1, 5.2 and cover) embellished with the initials 'ES' (c. 1601).[41] Both Marcus in Shakespeare's *Titus Andronicus* and Daphne in *Amintas Dale* (as we saw in Chapters 1 and 2 respectively) emphasize women's role in the oral transmission of narrative. In an episode which specifically dramatizes women's part in the dissemination of the classical poem, Lavinia's nephew identifies the book that his aunt so desperately pursues as 'Ovid's *Metamorphoses*;| My mother gave it me'.[42] Talbot's embroideries form a rather different interventive mode in the predominantly patriarchal history of English Ovids.[43] According to Maureen Quilligan 'nothing expresses the claims for female agency possible to make for embroidery and sewing more clearly than the cloth-draped interior of Hardwick Hall'.[44] Indeed, Talbot's choice of myths and their subsequent domestication adds a further dimension to discussions of gender and the cultural politics of translation in sixteenth-century England.

Ovid's account of Phaeton's doomed aspirations may seem a curious choice for a woman who 'pursued her own dynastic ambitions'.[45] Markedly, the *Metamorphoses* is framed by tales in which chariots race out of control. In the opening two books, Phaeton learns that he is Phoebus's son and may ask his father to grant any favour. Ignoring the paternal advice that he should not ask to take the reigns of the sun god's chariot, Phaeton fails to control the spirited horses and, in order to save the Earth from destruction, he is destroyed by Jove's thunderbolt. In book 15, Hippolytus, thrown from his uncontrollable chariot, is torn apart. In the moralized tradition of Ovidian translation these tales become allegories which warn against of pride, ambition and uncontrollable desire. From Caxton's translation and beyond, Phaeton's demise was commonly allegorized by many early–modern English writers and illustrators.[46] Talbot's scene is partially aligned with two woodcuts from the 1591 edition of Johann Spreng's *Metamorphoses Illustratae*, illustrated by Virgil Solis,[47] which shows how 'Phaeton kindles the world top to bottom' and 'The fall of Phaeton' in which the racing chariot with its fated rider takes centre stage. By showing the path that Phoebus tells Phaeton to take, and by making the horses 'flaming breath' visible, Talbot's image offers a faithful rendition of the Ovidian episode.[48] Though Phaeton's blazing body is the main focus of the pictorial narrative, the most interesting aspects of Talbot's embroidery are the scenes woven beneath the chariot.

Illustration 5.1   Panel, Elizabeth Talbot, Phaeton

Illustration 5.2   Panel, Elizabeth Talbot, Europa

On the far left is Clymene, Phaeton's mother, bent over in sorrow for the death of her son, who 'searched through the universal world from east to west'.[49] Next to Clymene are her daughters, the Heliades, in various stages of the transformation engendered by their grief.[50] In the centre is Earth 'casting up her handl between her forehead and the sun' complete with her 'singed hair'.[51] To the right of this image are a group of women, hands aloft as if to catch the descending youth. The women's gestures, combined with their position in the narrative sequence of the panel, are suggestive of the Naiads; the waternymphs who took care of Phaeton's burning body once it had fallen to the ground. Tucked away in the bottom right-hand corner of the picture, in the doorway of the burning castle, are three rather indiscriminate figures that seem to represent the burning of the world.[52] By contrast with the woodcuts, then, Talbot's translation represents the women who frame Phaeton's story. At first glance, as in Fraunce's *Amintas Dale*, it seems that Talbot uses the myth in order to show women as the subjects of loss. Described by Golding as 'half beside herself with woe, with torn and scratched breast' at the death of her son, Clymene's grief, for instance, is exacerbated. Though the death of her son is at the heart of the narrative, she also helplessly watches her daughters, the Heliades, turn into trees. Her plight is expressed in Ovid's poem: 'What could the mother dol but run, now here, now there'.[53] There are other figures in this tapestry, however, with which Talbot may be more closely identified.

Each of the women worked into the embroidery is shown in early modern dress, but of particular note is the central Naiad-like figure, who is clothed in the kind of aristocratic dress that wealthy women such as Talbot wore. Arguably, this Naiad may even be Talbot. As Mary S. Lovell has argued, the Hardwick tapestries depicting Zenobia, the warrior queen of ancient, and the classical heroine Penelope show a 'distinct resemblance [...] to a portrait of [Talbot] made soon after she became Countess of Shrewsbury'.[54] By contrast with Clymene or the Heliades, moreover, the Naiads have a different role in Phaeton's story. Golding's translation renders the episode as follows:

> The waternymphs of Italy did take his carcass dead
> And buried it, yet smoking still with Jove's three-forked flame,
> And wrate this epitaph in the stone that lay upon the same:
> Here lies the lusty Phaëton, which took in hand to guide
> His father's chariot; from which although he chanced to slide,
> Yet that he gave proud attempt it cannot be denied.[55]

Philip Hardie persuasively argues that Phaeton's body is textualized through 'his mother's search for his remains' and that 'her search ends with the discovery of a process already completed, the transition from lifeless body to name on tomb'.[56] With Hardie's comments in mind, the aristocratic figure in Talbot's picture is perhaps identified with the Ovidian characters who 'wrate' Phaeton's epitaph and who suggest 'the possibility of understanding memorialisation of the dead through funerary inscription'.[57] Instead of simply depicting women in a subordinate position, Talbot's Ovidian translation implicitly promotes their textual agency.

A related trope of textual production is recalled in Talbot's embroidery of Europa; the myth with which the mortal Arachne begins her contest against the gods.[58] Based on the 1582 edition of *Metamorphoses Illustratae*, the women in this embroidery are once again domesticated by way of their Elizabethan dress. A cursory reading of this woven account of Jove's abduction of Europa may interpret Talbot's picture as an allegorization of the subordinate role of women in early modern culture. However, as Leonard Barkan has discussed, the semiotics of this myth are more complex than they initially seem:

> The bull is a god [...] an ancient symbol of male power [...]. The girl is a victim, but her image speaks as much of mastery over the bull as of victimization. Europa sits above the animal, often side-saddle or even defying gravity, while the bull underneath takes flight, taking her through the heavens.[59]

Whilst Ovid's tale is overtly concerned with the god's violation of Europa, the episode may also be viewed as an exploration of female desire. The disguised Jove tricks Europa, 'his wished prey', and carries her off.[60] Before her abduction, however, it is Ovid's description of Europa's 'marvel' (as Golding puts it) at the beautiful white bull, and the subsequent flirtation between beast and girl, which takes prominence:

> But yet to touch him at the furst too bold she durst not be.
> Anon she reaches to his mouth her hand with herbs and flowers;
> The loving beast was glad thereof and neither frowns nor lowers,
> [...]
> He licks her hands and scarce, ah, scarce, the residue forbear.
> Sometimes he frisks and skips about and shows her sport at hand;
> [...]
> At last Europa, knowing not (for so the maid was called)
> On whom she ventured for to ride, was ne're a whit appalled
> To set herself upon his back.[61]

Through sight and touch, Europa is eventually captivated by the animal. Though Talbot's embroidery primarily follows the woodcut in much of its detail, the woven textile can render the sensuous nature of the myth for its audience in ways which the written text and woodcut cannot achieve. The use of shimmering thread in the swathe of fabric which billows over an untroubled Europa as she is carried across the water furthers the impression of movement. It is somewhat disconcerting that the glint of the gold thread also makes this view of female abduction an aesthetic image. In rendering the episode so visually appealing, arguably the spectator of Talbot's embroidery is enticed into Europa's scene of desire.

It is significant, however, that Talbot expands the marginal details of 'the ladies of the court' who accompany Europa.[62] Afforded more textual space than Europa and the bull, Talbot shows the four women left at the water's edge in various degrees of distress surrounded by clusters of flowers, significantly unpicked. This very obvious symbol of female virginity, and popular *locus amoena* in the

Metamorphoses for the gods' numerous abductions and rape of women, adds to the sexual tension already engendered by the Ovidian myth. Talbot's concern to show the pleasing image of Europa astride the disguised god as well as the perturbed group of women in the wake of Europa's abduction, contrasting aspects of wonder and fear, offers an intricate perspective of women's sexuality which resists definition.

If the myth of Europa offers a multifarious exposition of the effects of female desire, Talbot's Ovidian outlook takes a further turn with her version of the Actaeon myth; the mortal torn apart by his own hounds for peering on the naked goddess Diana as she bathed.[63] Wendy Wall notes that the myth was often interpreted in early modern England as 'a struggle between reason and passion'.[64] Rather more pointedly, the sage Elpinus in Fraunce's *Amintas Dale* tells us that Ovid's tale teaches us 'not to be over curious and inquisitive in spying and prying into those matter which be above our reache, lest we be rewarded, as Actaeon was'.[65] Diana was part of the repertoire of classical virginal goddesses identified with Elizabeth I,[66] and with regard to the Queen's apparent misgivings about George Talbot's loyalty and her displeasure at his wife's dynastic ambitions, Elpinus's explication may inform Talbot's tapestry. Sarah Annes Brown has observed how 'the story of Acteon – with its emphasis on the goddess' majesty, virginity and sharp temper – would have been a particularly resonant episode for a readership of Elizabethan courtiers'.[67] Given her biographical background, Talbot's weave may offer a political allegory which implicitly criticizes the monarch's absolute rule.

The most arresting aspect of Talbot's Actaeon, however, is not the tearing of his body by the hounds; the tapestry rather obscures the physical violence detailed in Ovid's myth. Instead, the spectator's gaze is drawn to the bold colloquy of naked women on the left-hand side of the panel.[68] Christopher Allen's comment on the various depictions of the Diana and Actaeon myth in Rococo art that 'the mythological subject has become less a narrative than the occasion for a display of female nudes' seems surprisingly fitting for Talbot's early modern translation. Then again, moving from body to text, the naked women effectively frame the inscription 'Actaeon ego sum [I am Actaeon]';[69] the words which the doomed hunter 'strayned oftentymes to speake, and was about to say […]| But use of wordes and speach did want to utter forth his minde'.[70] Drawn to the very sight that led to Actaeon's tragic demise, momentarily the viewer becomes Actaeon; the subject riven with desire. In this respect, Talbot's picture may function as a conventional reminder of the struggle between reason and passion. Yet in its emphasis on the mortal's compulsion to retain his position as speaking subject, Talbot's Actaeon, paradoxically presented through the medium of weaving rather than writing, emphasizes the cultural, and hierarchical, importance of self-fashioning in and through language; a censored mode of communication for early modern women.

A century later, Thomas Parnell's poem 'To a Young Lady, On Her Translation of the Story of Pheobus and Daphne, from Ovid' (c. 1714) comments on women and their translations of myths from the *Metamorphoses*:

> In Phoebus Wit (as Ovid said)
> Enchanting Beauty woo'd);

In Daphne Beauty coily fled,
While vainly Wit pursu'd.

But when you trace what Ovid writ,
A diff'rent Turn we view;
Beauty no longer flies from Wit,
Since both are joyn'd in You.[71]

Barbara Benedict argues that by 'declaring that her poem revises the mystic pursuit of beauty by wit in the original since both virtues meet in her, [Parnell] applauds her reading, her writing, and her posture as a literary consumer'.[72] Nevertheless, as Parnell praises his addressee, the fact that she is anonymous exposes the sexual politics of Ovidian translation with which this chapter is concerned. A decade or so before Parnell's verse, women begin to publish fragments from the *Metamorphoses* in English, notably, Elizabeth Singer Rowe's 'The Fable of Phaeton Paraphrased from Ovid's *Metamorphoses*' in her collection *Poems on Several Occasions. Written By Philomela* (1696) and Mary, Lady Chudleigh's 'Icarus' in her miscellany *Essays upon Several Subjects in Prose and Verse* (1703).[73] From the type of Ovidian episodes that Rowe and Chudleigh translate, that is ones which are readily associated with the moralized tradition, it appears that the relationship of these women to the *Metamorphoses* remains very different to that of the men. In the early eighteenth century, for instance, Charles Hopkins' use of metamorphic myths in his *Epistolary Poems on Several Occasions with several of the Choicest Stories of Ovid's Metamorphoses and Tibullus's Elegies. Translated into English Verse* (1694; dedicated to Antony Hammond, Esq.) and *The History of Love. A Poem in a letter to a lady* (1695; dedicated to the Duchess of Grafton) illustrate both the varied approaches to Ovid's poem that men enjoy and the different framing devices used according to the gender of the dedicatee.[74] The man is addressed in terms of classical erudition; the woman through the emotional concerns. Encasing their Ovidian translations within the type of anthology common to much writing of this period, women do not explicitly name themselves as translators. Like Talbot's tapestries, however, their texts engage with the cultural politics of Ovidian translation.

Elizabeth Singer Rowe: 'Philomela' and 'The Fable of *Phaeton* Paraphrased from Ovid's *Metamorphoses*'

In recent years, Rowe's representation has undergone something of a transformation. As Kathryn R. King observes, 'celebrated in the eighteenth century as the pious Mrs. Rowe', and read by contemporaneous literary luminaries such as Matthew Prior, Anne Finch and Alexander Pope, 'she has emerged in feminist scholarship as a leading example of a woman writer'.[75] Moreover, as a woman viewed by 'the Athenians and Isaac Watts as exemplifying the virtuous piety that was needed in a national poet dedicated to singing the praises of Whig military glory',[76] Sarah Prescott has shown that Rowe made significant contributions to eighteenth-century political discourse, whilst Norma Clarke describes Rowe as an 'Augustan poet celebrating love – including sexual love [...] who earned a reputation for piety'.[77] Although the word 'piety' is synonymous with Rowe, she is now perceived as the author of a diverse cultural and political textual repertoire who developed 'the project for a poetic tradition based on the Bible rather than the pagan epics'.[78] But by examining her translation of Ovid's *Metamorphoses* in her *Poems on Several Occasions* the recent critical impressions of Rowe's literary career may undergo further revision.[79]

At the outset, Rowe's pseudonym of Philomela, the Ovidian figure strongly aligned with Shakespeare's Lavinia, engages with the foregoing remarks on gender and translation. With acuity, Prescott suggests that her mythical designation refers to 'a play on the connections between Rowe's maiden name Singer, the beautiful song of the nightingale, and her occupation as a poet' rather than 'the gruesome elements' of Ovid's poem.[80] Nevertheless, it is difficult to ignore Rowe's intertextual affiliations with the brutal events of the classical narrative and which are so enmeshed with the sexual politics of communication. John Dunton, the editor of the *Athenian Mercury*, the periodical which first published Rowe's poetry, gave her the pen-name,[81] and this denomination of the woman poet by the male editor seems distantly related to the displacement of Philomela's subjectivity in Ovid's tale.[82] Beyond the editor's appellation, however, Rowe's poems 'A Pastoral', 'A Pastoral Elegy' and 'A Pastoral on the Queen' from *Poems on Several Occasions* demonstrates how she used the name Philomela to fashion her own literary persona and how that name betrays an implicit awareness of early eighteenth-century gender politics and textuality. Read in chronological order, these three texts are related to the tropes of loss which, as we have seen, seem to typify women's relationship to the *Metamorphoses*. 'A Pastoral Elegy' and 'A Pastoral on the Queen' sees Philomela mourn the respective deaths of her nymph companion Daphne and Queen Mary (who may be read as one and the same):

> Alass! the Royal Shepherdess is gone;
> And, with her, the Whole Sex's Glory flown.
> Oh! Could not all those Heavenly Virtues Save
> Divine Maria from th'Insatiate Grave?
> Nor her's, and our Dear Hero's Moving Tears?
> Nor all the poor Lamenting Nations Fears?
> No, no; they could not – She resigns Her Breath;
> The Charming Queen a Trophy falls to Death. (36–43)[83]

In these lines from 'A Pastoral on the Queen', an elegy for Queen Mary who had died from smallpox in 1694, there is a hint of the 'Whig poetic agenda' that is inscribed in much of Rowe's poetry produced at this time.[84] However, it is the first poem of the series, 'A Pastoral', which illustrates Rowe's textual commitment to Ovid.

'A Pastoral' is a 38-line dialogue between Daphne and Philomela, two Ovidian characters closely allied with the subjects of patriarchal violence and poetry. In the *Metamorphoses* Daphne is the goddess who escapes the predatory advances of

Apollo through her transformation into the laurel, the crown of poetic achievement.[85] Philomela is an Athenian princess whose terrifying myth of sexual violation at the hands of her brother-in-law concludes with her metamorphosis into a nightingale: a symbol for poetry itself.[86] Rowe's pastoral poems are part of a particular tradition of English women's poetry from the fifteenth century onwards,[87] and Madeleine Forrell Marshall argues that this genre appealed to women poets as 'pastorals offered female parts, the Sylvias and Daphnes of tradition'.[88] Nonetheless, the longevity of this genre of women's writing did not necessarily mean that the poetry was well received. For example, in a striking reminder of the myth of Philomela, the *Spectator* (606) declared that tapestry is

> the most proper way wherin a Lady can shew a fine Genius, and I cannot forbear wishing, that several Writers of that Sex had chosen to apply themselves rather to Tapestry than Rhime. Your Pastoral Poetesses may vent their Fancy in Rural Landskips, and place despairing Shepherds under silken Willows, or drown them in a Stream of Mohair.[89]

This acerbic edict shows (yet again) how the scene of writing is perceived as a masculine domain; women are meant to inhabit another realm of textual production. When Rowe takes up the name of Philomela herself and uses it to write rather than to weave, her poetry contests the longstanding cultural urge to suppress female authorship and agency.

Significantly, Rowe adapts the classical material in order to construct an eclogue which takes women's sexual desire as its theme; hence the poem begins with Daphne's interrogation of the grief-stricken Philomel:

> Why sigh you so, What Grievance can annoy,
> A Nymph like you? Alas, why sighs my Joy?
> My Philomela, why dost bend thy head,
> Hast lost thy Pipe, or is thy Garland dead?
> Thy flocks are fruitful, flowery all the Plain;
> Thy Father's darling, why should'st thou complain? (1–6)

Ann Messenger cogently remarks that 'love is such a frequent topic in pastoral poetry that by the eighteenth century the terms "swain" and "nymph" were standard designations for a lover and his lady',[90] and Rowe's poem exploits this topical model. After admonishing her colleague's opening question, declaring that Daphne is 'Unfriendly thus, when [she] expect[s] relief' (7), Philomela explains that her tears have been caused by 'the bane of Love' (38):

> Curse of his charms, accurst the unlucky day,
> He sought by chance his wandred flocks this way;
> When gay and careless, leaning on my Crook,
> My roving Eyes this fatal Captive took,
> Well I remember yet with what a grace
> The Youthful Conquerer made his first address;

How moving, how resistless were his sighs;
How soft his Tongue, *how very soft his Eyes.*
When spight of all my Natural Disdain,
I fell a Victim to the smiling Swain!
Ah, how much blest, how happy had I been,
Had I his lovely killing Eyes ne're seen! (19–30)

In more general terms, Norma Clarke has written about the 'libidinised energies' of Rowe's poetry,[91] and in this quotation from 'A Pastoral', as Philomela's 'roving Eyes this fatal Captive took', a specific example of the erotic impulse that Clarke identifies may be observed. Darting from 'eyes' to the 'tongue', the female gaze of the poem emblazons and fetishises the anonymous masculine body. Nonetheless, the overt sexual politics of Rowe's poem are grounded in conventional gender stereotypes. The poem suggests that the fundamental error lies with Philomela, who apparently initiates the exchange between herself and the Swain. Instead of busily tending her flock, she is 'gay and careless, leaning on [her] Crook' and it is this aspect of Idleness which makes the nymph, who once 'knew no passion but disdain' (36), sexually vulnerable.[92]

But Rowe's shepherd is not without blame. Using both linguistic and gestural persuasion, he uses the customary rhetorical arsenal involved in the art of female seduction: 'How moving, how resistless were his sighs| How soft his Tongue, *how very soft his Eyes*'. Indeed, from the beginning of the poem when the shepherd is Philomela's object of desire to the end of the poem when she, more typically, defines herself as 'Victim', the text interrogates the shifting dynamics of desire. With Philomela now figured as the Swain's prey under the gaze of his 'killing' eyes, the familiar Ovidian depiction of 'violence in a pastoral landscape' (as observed in Chapter 3's discussion of Sandys's Ovid) becomes increasingly apparent. To be sure, the treatment of Rowe's 'Philomela' is different from that of her namesake in Ovid's tale; all the same there are other relevant connections in her poetry with the classical precedent.

Rowe's Philomela is transformed from a state of 'Ignorance' (17) to possessing a 'soul infus'd' (38); a disturbing transposition from the desired object of her 'Father's Darling' (6) to desiring subject. But 'A Pastoral' goes beyond questions of sexual politics and female desire, important though they are, in order to take account of a different form of subjection:

In these delightsome Pastures long I kept
My harmless flocks, and as much pleasure reapt,
In being all I hop'd to be, as they,
Whose awful Nods subjected Nations sway. (31–34)

Succinctly aligning Philomela's seduction with that of the populace, Rowe's poem moves from exploring the physical body to considering the body politic. Echoing the frame of Ovid's epic poem itself, Rowe's Philomela moves forward from a golden age to one which is not so readily pleasing. In this way, more Ovidian in style than in narrative detail, 'A Pastoral' draws on the ideological issues prevalent in the

Metamorphoses. It is also significant that both Rowe's authorial identity and poetic persona are connected to Ovid's tragic heroine featured in 'a myth about the competition amongst media of communication as Philomela becomes a walking representative of them'.[93] Yet Rowe's interest in Ovid and the cultural politics of translation becomes more pronounced in 'The Fable of *Phaeton* Paraphrased from Ovid's *Metamorphoses*'.

Rowe's Williamite poems, as Prescott examines in detail, 'first brought her to the attention of the male critical establishment'.[94] The Whiggish sensibilities so clearly evident in panegyrics such as 'Upon King William Passing the Boyn', also included in the 1696 collection, are equally evident in her translation of Ovid's myth. Drawn to its aesthetic qualities (and whose translation of the myth was published in Garth's Ovid of 1717) Joseph Addison commented that 'the story of Phaeton is told with a greater air of majesty and grandeur than any other in Ovid'.[95] By contrast, Rowe's version of 'The Fable of *Phaeton* Paraphrased from Ovid's *Metamorphoses*' is noteworthy for her use of an already thoroughly moralized, domesticated and politicized myth in order to engage with contemporary social concerns. Compared with the catalogue of English translators who use the Phaeton episode either as a social allegory concerned with misguided ambition, Rowe uses the myth rather less figuratively. In a brief footnote, Carol Barash observes that 'the poem reworks an Ovidian narrative to condemn the "Gallick Tyrants" who challenge William's rule'.[96] It is not so much the myth but the allegory that Rowe revises as she emphatically concludes her poem with the following lines:

> So strike the Gallick Tyrant, that has hurl'd
> As guilty flames through the complaining World.
> So awful Jove, so Strike him from his Seat,
> And all his Aim, and all his Hopes defeat. (266–9)

What better text could Rowe have chosen for her admonishment of Louis XIV, the so–called Sun King? Compared with an anonymous version of Ovid's narrative produced a few years earlier, *The Unfortunate Phaeton, or the Fall of Ambition, An Heroick Poem. Written by a Person of Quality* (1686), which takes a broad, allegorical approach to its titular subject, 'Philomela' robustly addresses contemporaneous questions of legitimate and illegitimate rule:

> See the wing'd Vengeance now, see where it breaks,
> On the rash cause of those lamented Wrecks;
> And sends the bold Usurper breathless down
> To the scorch't Earth from his *affected* Throne: (262–5)

Stridently written and ardently political, the final lines of Rowe's poem present a harsh criticism of the French monarchy.

Mary, Lady Chudleigh: 'Icarus'

By examining her renditions of Ovid's *Metamorphoses* in English, it is possible to extend the range of Rowe's poetical achievements and her ideological interests in gender and nation. There are some shared concerns in Mary Chudleigh's translation of Icarus which may not be entirely by chance. Rebecca M. Mills observes that Chudleigh was part of several 'epistolary networks', some of which connect her to the poet and editor of the 1717 translation of the *Metamorphoses*, Samuel Garth,[97] and, importantly, to Rowe. As Barbara Olive explains 'it appears no coincidence that that [she] credits her inspiration to write to "Philomela" in the opening poem of her 1703 collection',[98] *Poems on Several Occasions Together with the Song of the Three Children Paraphrased*. Notably, the address to 'Sad Philomela' (51) in the verse 'On the Death of His Highness the Duke of *Glocester*' establishes both a textual and political relationship between the women poets. The sexual politics at stake in Rowe's pastoral poetry are also inscribed in Chudleigh's first published work, *The Ladies Defence* (1701). Whereas Rowe deals with this topic by transforming herself into Philomela, however, Chudleigh approaches questions of gender and culture through an astute awareness of a range of textual practices, including translation. In her preface 'To All Ingenious Ladies' Chudleigh speaks of Ovid as one of the 'great Masters of Wit and Language […] who are now naturaliz'd, and wear an English Dress'.[99] Implicitly, Chudleigh shows how women's knowledge of classical texts is increasingly dependent on vernacular editions. As Margaret Ezell comments, 'the family memoir notes […] that not understanding any Languages besides her own she was forc'd to content herself with reading the best translations'.[100] But even if Chudleigh cannot engage with the Greek and Latin languages, her writing demonstrates an awareness of the cultural politics of translation and a lively critical interest in the *Metamorphoses*.

In her poem 'To Mr. Dryden, on his excellent Translation of Virgil', Chudleigh establishes a canon of English poets, from Geoffrey Chaucer, Edmund Spenser, Edmund Waller, John Milton, Abraham Cowley, which ends, not surprisingly, with John Dryden. Towards the end of the verse, as she remarks that Virgil is now 'the welcome Native of our Isle' (56),[101] Chudleigh makes a telling observation about translation and domestication. 'The Resolution', a longer verse from *Poems on Several Occasions*, provides equally stimulating comments on an impressive array of writers and their books, ancient and modern. After discussing Lucretius, Virgil and Horace, Ovid is the fourth Roman poet that she favours. Her lines on the *Metamorphoses* begin:

> When by soft moving Ovid I am told,
> Of those strange Changes which were wrought of old,
> When Gods in Brutal Shapes did Mortals court,
> And unbecoming Actions made their Sport,
> When helpless Wretches fled from impious Pow'rs,
> And hid themselves in Birds, Beasts, Trees and Flow'rs:
> When none from Outrage cou'd securely dwell,
> But felt the Rage of heav'n, of Earth and Hell:
> Methinks, I see those Passions well exprest,
> Which play the Tyrant in the Mortal Breast:

> They to Ten thousand Miseries expose,
> And are our only, and our deadly Foes: (409–20)

Dryden translated 'The First Book of Ovid's *Metamorphoses*' together with 'The Fable of Iphis and Ianthe' (book 9) and 'The Fable of Acis, Polyphemus, and Galatea' (book 13) in *Examen Poeticum* (1693) and a number of Ovidian myths appeared in *Fables Ancient and Modern* (1700).[102] Considering their social and intellectual acquaintance, it is possible that Chudleigh's poem describes Dryden's Ovid;[103] it is equally possible that she has another translation, such as Sandys's, in view. 'The Resolution', however, is significant for the general gloss on the *Metamorphoses* that it offers. As she comments that mortal 'Passions well exprest [...] are our only, and our deadly Foes', Chudleigh demonstrates the familiar tenets of those moral allegories which warn against desire. In some ways, her opening perspective on the poem is rather like Arachne's: 'When Gods in Brutal Shapes did Mortals court,| And unbecoming Actions made their Sport'. Although Chudleigh's lines on Ovid are undoubtedly proprietous, the myths of power, subjection and, quite often, eroticism to which she allude, solicit her interest.

Predictably, as part of a collection of poetry addressed to Queen Anne and designed primarily for 'Ladies', Chudleigh does not translate and publish Ovidian myths which are concerned with the 'unbecoming actions' of the gods. Instead, she produces a vernacular version of 'Icarus' from book 8 of the *Metamorphoses*.[104] It is worth noting that although other poems in this collection celebrate Ovid's literary achievements, as with Rowe's 'Fable of Phaeton', Chudleigh's debt to the classical remains unacknowledged. In Ovid's poem both Phaeton and Icarus are obviously connected by their relative associations with Pheobus and in the English moralized tradition the myths are often coupled as allegorical admonitions against vaulting ambition and pride.[105] For example, Francis Lenton, *The young gallants whirligigg; or Youths reakes Demonstrating the inordinate affections, absurd actions, and profuse expences, of unbridled and affectated youth* [...] (1629) is a text which seems custom-made for these particular Ovidian figures and, accordingly, both Phaeton and Icarus's fates are used as exemplars.[106] On a more sombre note, and one which leads more directly towards Chudleigh's 'Icarus', is Nicholas Billingsley's 'On Ambition' taken from *The Infancy of the World* (1658):

> Ambitious *Phaeton* his fond desire
> Ruin'd himselfe, and set the world on fire.
> *Icarus* flyes, but *Icarus* his wings
> Are cing'd, and cold, and head-long ruin brings. (24–30)

Rowe's Phaeton is striking for its political stand against the despised French King; by contrast, Chudleigh's 'Icarus' does not move far from the typical moralized paradigm:

> O may thy Fall be useful made,
> May it to humbler Thoughts persuade:
> To Men th'avoidless Danger Show

Of those who fly too high, or low:
Who from the Paths of Virtue stray,
And keep not in the middle Way:
Who singe their Wings with heav'nly Fire;
Amidst their glorious Hopes expire:
Or with a base and grovelling Mind
Are to the Clods of Earth confin'd. (34–43)

In the commentary to his 1632 translation, George Sandys writes that 'this fable applaudes the golden Meane, and flight of virtue betweene the extreames. *Icarus* falls in aspiring. Yet more commendable then those who creepe on the earth like contemptible wormes.'[107] Both in form and content, this moralization of the Ovidian episode is appreciably evident in Chudleigh's poem.

Chudleigh has been viewed as a polemical writer. The contentious aspect of her poetic persona is demonstrated in texts such as 'To the Queen's most Excellent Majesty', in which Chudleigh declares 'Long may You reign, long fill the British Throne,| And make the haughty Gallick Foe our English Valor own' (30–1).[108] However, there is little in 'Icarus' which engages so forcefully with the political situation of early eighteenth-century England. Whereas Rowe uses Ovid's Phaeton to castigate an unpopular French monarch, Chudleigh employs Icarus as a further expression of the moderate attitude which is apparent in much of her writing. Margaret Ezell concludes that:

> her works read as a whole – a long dialogue poem and two collections of poetry and prose – constitute less a coherent autobiographical chronicle of events than a continuous philosophical exploration of human passions and the ways to live a truly harmonious life, at peace with one's passions.[109]

An example of the mode that Ezell identifies may be found in the preface to Chudleigh's *Poems on Several Occasions*, in which she states that 'Tis impossible to be happy without making Reason the Standard of all our Thoughts, Words and Actions'.[110] In this context, Chudleigh's translation of Icarus, a myth which functions as a warning to 'those who fly too high, or low', seems an allegory of her own textual practice and production. Nonetheless, Chudleigh's translation of 'Icarus' is exceptional for its inclusion in Christopher Martin's anthology *Ovid in English* where it is accompanied by an editorial comment which observes that the poem is 'interesting especially for its reflection of an enduring tradition of "moralised" Ovid'.[111] From a poem addressed 'To Mr. Dryden, on his excellent Translation of Virgil' which celebrates the domestication of classical texts by men, Chudleigh's temperate rendition allows her to enter that canon herself.

Mary Wortley Montagu: Latona, Venus and Adonis, and The Golden Age

Amongst the juvenilia of Mary Wortley Montagu are texts which also fracture the apparently imperious masculine frame of the English *Metamorphoses*. In terms of eighteenth–century literature in general, Montagu is described as 'a great letter-writer [...] accomplished poet [...] and essayist'.[112] Daughter of the Fifth Earl of Kingston, Montagu, nee Pierrepont, was part of a literary coterie which included Joseph Addison, William Congreve and Alexander Pope. Although she is not often discussed specifically as a translator, translations punctuate her textual production.[113] These include a translation of the *Encheiridion* of Epictetus from the Latin and a translation of Boileau's *Contre Les Femmes*;[114] as Robert Halsband has discussed, her play *Simplicity* was the first English version of Marivaux's *Le Jeu de L'amour et du Hasard*.[115] Moreover, her *Letters* contain passages concerned with the processes of translation. Between the years 1716 and 1718 Montagu lived in Constantinople with her husband Edward Wortley who had been appointed Ambassador to the Sublime Porte, and this exile from her native language seems to throw her own translation practices into relief.

Following the translation of some Turkish verse into English, first taking an 'abundance of pains to get [the] Verses in a litteral translation' by a native speaker and then turning 'the whole into the stile of English Poetry to see how 'twould look', she wrote to Pope that she did not

> think our English proper to express such violence of passion, which is very seldom felt amongst us; [...] we want those compound words which are frequent and strong in the Turkish language.[116]

Whilst expressing a sense of lack in the target language, Montagu's perspective of the English language is in keeping with dominant eighteenth-century sensibilities. England is deemed a site of control and reason against 'violent passion', which is seen as the province of the exotic East. The comparative analysis which takes place in Montagu's text between the two cultures is particularly enabled by this double strategy of translating Turkish into English, 'literally' and then into an 'English stile'. In the chapter on Sandys's *Metamorphosis Englished* I suggested that the translator's commentary constructs the English nation against other European countries in terms of 'self' and 'other'. In Montagu's letter, the act of translation is operating within certain ideological discourses, accentuating cultural differences between East and West. As she uses the notion of the exotic 'other' against the English nation in her description of the Turkish language, in her translations of Ovid, Montagu defines herself as 'other' within Englishness itself. Significantly, Montagu cites Ovid's text as the basis for part of her translative activity. 'When I was young', she comments, 'I was a vast admirer of Ovid's *Metamorphoses*, and that was one of the chief reasons that set me upon the thoughts of stealing the Latin language'.[117] Accordingly, the Latin language is perceived by Montagu as the voice of others which may be possessed only through an 'unlawful' act: through theft. Pointedly, it is the *Metamorphoses*, a text concerned with the breaking of boundaries, the construction of new identities and defined through patriarchal history as 'subversive', which is given by Montagu as the impetus for 'stealing the Latin language' and escaping the limitations of the mother tongue.[118]

Montagu's most explicitly Ovidian translation in adult life is restricted to the version of 'Apollo and Daphne', although her name is inextricably linked with that of the Roman poet. Montagu's literary reputation was well enough established to have been associated with the Garth edition of the *Metamorphoses* discussed in the previous chapter. In Pope's poem *Sandys's Ghost* she is *almost* named in his rally for women to come forward and offer their translations of Ovid:

> Ye Ladies too draw forth your pen,
> I pray where can the Hurt lie?
> Since you have Brains as well as Men,
> As witness Lady W–l–y. (65–9)[119]

In fashioning Montagu as translator in this elusive manner, Pope's text emphasizes the gender distinction prevalent in translating the *Metamorphoses*. He asks 'where can the Hurt lie?' in a social arena where women are prohibited from producing classical translations for the public sphere. Even if they manage to gain knowledge of classical languages, the 'hurt lie[s]' in the possibility of inciting public derision for breaking eighteenth-century codes of conduct.[120] To be sure, the publication of any text by women was often cause for debate. 'In the stormy career of Lady Mary Wortley Montagu', comments Isobel Grundy,

> the ambition of authorship played a large but mostly secret part. One of the earliest controversies to involve her was Edmund Curll's illicit publication of three more or less scandalous poems which she had been quietly circulating in manuscript among her friends; one of the latest was the feud that developed between her and the British Resident and British Consul in Venice [...]. Each episode brings out the period's feeling that it was not fitting for a well-born woman to publish verses except in circumstances of the most careful decorum and discretion.[121]

Although Grundy is referring here to 'original' poetry, her description of the 'period's feeling' regarding publication and the 'well-born' woman could be as easily applied to the publication of translated texts, particularly to a narrative as subversive as the *Metamorphoses*.

From source text to target language, Ovid's *Metamorphoses* in English is perceived as a text translated, controlled and, generally, published by men and that Ovid and his text were aligned with this patriarchal mode of production is alluded to by Montagu herself. In her poem 'The Lovers: A Ballad', a text concerned with the social negotiations involved when a woman attempts to preserve her reputation against the persuasive actions of the 'lewd rake' and 'dressed fopling' (45), before whom 'the nice virgin flies' (46), the final couplet knowingly observes that

> [...] as Ovid has sweetly in parables told,
> We harden like trees, and like rivers are cold. (47–8)[122]

In 'The Politics of Female Authorship', Grundy argues that in order to escape unwanted 'amorous advances', Montagu's poem ultimately suggests that women are pushed 'into the metaphorical experience of Ovidian metamorphosis'.[123] The oblique references to Ovid's myths of Daphne and Arethusa in the closing lines of Montagu's poem, changed into tree and water respectively in order to escape rape, serve as an articulation of the double bind of the so-called virtuous female.[124] Women may preserve their virginity, a valorized commodity, but they run the risk of being defined as 'hard' and 'cold'. In a similar fashion, Montagu produced the poem 'Apollo and Daphne':

> I am, cry'd Apollo, and run as he spoke
> But the skittish young Damsel ne'er turn'd back to look,
> I am the great God Tenedos Adores
> And Delos does also acknowledge my power.
> Round my Head the Sun beams you may glittering see
> And no man alive can make Ballads like me,
> All Physics I know–she mended her pace
> And his Godhead halfe tir'd was quitting the Chase.
> Had Apollo known Women, as well as I know 'em,
> He would not have talk'd of a potion or poem,
> But he had appear'd in O[xenden']s Shape,
> By my Soul little Daphne had suffer'd the Rape. (fol. 28ʳ)[125]

The *Metamorphoses* tells of Apollo's desire for the virgin Daphne, which is engendered by the golden arrow shot by a wrathful Cupid. To take matters further, Venus's son then shoots Daphne with a leaden arrow to guarantee her repulsion of the god. Famously, Apollo's pursuit of the girl does not end in rape. Daphne appeals to her father, the river god Peneus, for assistance and he transforms her into the laurel tree. Though the transformation means that Apollo cannot physically violate the nymph, the god 'claims the tree as his own, to be a symbol of military and artistic triumph'.[126] After Ovid, Montagu depicts a gasping god of poetry who, nonetheless, finds just enough breath with which to speak of his textual and intellectual dexterity. Displaying her own propensity for wit, Montagu's verse shows how men seek to appropriate language and exploit knowledge in their attempts to subjugate women. But Montagu stops short of the describing Daphne's transformation. In their allusion to the disreputable behaviour of Sir George Oxenden, the closing lines of the poem adopt a more serious tone.[127] In 1737 Lord Hervey observed that 'Sir George Oxenden, a Lord of the Treasury, [...] was a very vicious, good-for-nothing fellow. He passed his whole life, in all manner of debauchery and with low company.'[128] In Montagu's poem, it is not Daphne who is transformed. Changed into Oxenden, Montagu's Apollo achieves the rape that Ovid's narrative denies. By employing familiar Ovidian tropes, Montagu throws the sexual politics of eighteenth-century English society into relief. Yet it is only before Montagu enters that social formation fully herself, when she is Mary *Pierrepont*, that she names herself as a translator of Ovid.

In two manuscripts dated 1704, thus written at about the age of 14, are her versions of the myths of the Golden Age, Latona, and Venus and Adonis, from books 1, 6 and 10 of the *Metamorphoses* respectively.[129] By relying on a particular understanding of translation, Grundy accounts for Montagu's early achievements in the following way:

> the poems remaining in the mutilated volume Harrowby MS 250 include a mention of [Ovid] and an apparent reference to the *Metamorphoses*, besides the narrative poem standing first in the volume, which recounts a *Metamorphoses* incident [...]. This is, however, a retelling not a rendering of Ovid. It could have been suggested by reading the original or a translation, or by a less direct contact with the work [...] all the knowledge of this work that she shows in her earliest poems could have been acquired second-hand [...] from her brother if not from his tutor.[130]

There is no evidence of a specific source text for Montagu's Ovidian translation. But Grundy's discussion of these 're-tellings,' acquired, she concludes, second-hand from more knowledgeable men, in opposition to a 'rendering', replicates the man/woman; active/passive; translator/reader binarisms contemporaneous with Montagu. Here, Grundy treats the term 'translation' in its narrowest sense; she does not consider a 're-telling' to be a translation.[131] Nonetheless, Montagu's versions of Ovidian myths, whether interlingual or intralingual, are translations; they are to be read as texts which participate in an act which goes further than an exercise in linguistic equivalence. For translation, as Trinh Minh-Ha describes, defines 'a politics of constructing meaning':

> Translation, which is interpellated by ideology [...] can never be objective or neutral [...]. Whether you translate one language into another language, whether you narrate in your own words what you have understood from the other person [...] you are dealing with cultural translation.[132]

In terms of nation, Montagu's *Letters* emphasize the construction of cultural difference between England and Turkey which is revealed in translation: the restrained West meets the passionate East. In terms of gender, Montagu's versions of Ovidian myths begin to break open the limits placed around the English woman translator in the early eighteenth century. Her juvenile poems interrupt the patriarchal genealogy of the translation of the *Metamorphoses* into English by presenting Ovid in a woman's 'voice'.

Classical mythology has a history of constructing woman in terms of the foreign 'other'. In *Nations Without Nationalism*, for example, Julia Kristeva argues that 'the first foreigners mentioned in Greek mythology are women – the Danaides, whose adventures Aeschylus pieced together in *The Suppliants*'.[133] It seems fitting that Montagu's first treatment of a metamorphic myth features the exiled figure of Latona; a woman who is in the place of the foreign 'other' exemplified by Aeschylus. In later life, Montagu 'Wrote in Answer to a Letter in Verse' that 'Celestial Dames, as Ovid sings| (Who was you know inspired),| Cannot bear Rivals upon Earth/ And are with Envy fir'd';[134] an observation expertly illustrated by this early poem. Impregnated by Jove, thus incurring Juno's wrath, the goddess is forced to wander the Earth.[135] Primarily, Ovid presents Latona as an instrument of punishment. When first encountered she turns Niobe into a statue for challenging her status as goddess; finally she turns the Lycians into frogs for refusing her water.[136] Between the metamorphic incidents, however, Latona's history is recounted through the voice of a male narrator. In Sandys's translation, the most contemporary vernacular version available to Montagu and one which highlights Latona's configuration as an icon of power, the episode begins 'In fruitfull Lycia once, said he, there dweltl A sort of Pesants, who her vengeance felt'.[137] The following 26 lines, however, negotiate Latona's exile in a telling manner. Whilst Jove's actions against Latona are left unspoken, the reader only has 'fretful' Juno's reactions from which to draw conclusions. In this translation, which is governed by male perspectives, the issue of Latona's exile is depicted as one which is contested between women. Montagu's version views the events rather differently.

Signalling the importance of this myth, the tale of Latona is the first text on the page of her earliest manuscript, Harrowby MS 250, taking the form of a preface to her compilation of texts:

> By all abandon'd poor Latona fled
> With Fear and Werieness half dead,
> In Lycia First she stops and on her knees
> Thus prays to him that now regardless sees.
> Oh Jupiter (with Lift up hands she cries
> With riseing sighs and red swoln streaming eyes)
> Oh Hear mee, oh relentless Jove
> And pity her–that's ruin'd by thy Love.
> Alas, As ruinous it proves to mee
> As to the lost, the wretched Semelé,
> And Thou oh Juno! has not yet
> These miseries, these tears appeas'd thy Hate?
> Can't all my sufferings, all these sighs attone–
> Already I am quite undone,
> But oh I fear–
> Thy hate won't bee appeas'd tho' by my Bloud
> But all that's mine will bee Like mee persue'd.
> The unborn innocent, Oh Jupiter! oh save
> And Let the wretched mother find a grave–
> This said she rais'd her eyes , and saw a Fountain near,
> The... [the text ends here]. (fol. 1ᵛ)

When compared to Sandys's translation the difference is immediate. Montagu's text breaks off at the moment that the narrative reaches the myth concerning the transformation of the Lycians. Most importantly, the reader is presented with a version of Latona's history which is presented through and in a woman's voice. In contrast to Ovid and the published translations of the poem in English which recount Latona's narrative, Montagu enables the goddess to 'voice' her own history.

Notably, Montagu's textual manoeuvre reverses an Ovidian trope. Ovid epitomizes the appropriation of the female voice by men in the early modern period which Elizabeth Harvey defines as 'transvestite ventriloquism'.[138] Montagu's rendition of the Latona myth invites comparison with Ovid's *Heroides*,[139] and this epistolary collection is the text that Harvey discusses in detail to support her thesis. Through an intricate argument which explores the interplay of voice, textuality and gender, Harvey's compelling discussion shows how Ovid disrupts notions of 'the naturalistic dimensions of gender identities'.[140] Whilst Harvey states that epistolary forms highlight 'the problems of communication',[141] the *Metamorphoses* problematizes the cultural construction of gender and voice.[142] As Olga Grlic has discussed, Ovid's epic poem contains many myths which explore gender politics:

> The main examples, in order of appearance, would be Jupiter's assuming the shape of Diana in order to trick Callisto, Tiresias's eight years spent as a woman, Iphys's transformation into a boy on her wedding, Caenis's wish to become a man so that she could not be raped again and Vertumnus's transformation into an old woman in order to approach Pomona [...]. Ovid [therefore] manages to represent the tensions arising from the uneven sexual distribution of power in the patriarchal society of his own time. [143]

Comparable tensions are resonant in Montagu's text. Whereas Ovid's account for Latona's exile is an issue between women, Montagu reminds the reader of her plight at the hands of both Jove and Juno. By invoking Semele from book 3 of the *Metamorphoses*, Montagu's tale exacerbates Jupiter's actions.[144] Like Latona, Semele becomes pregnant by the god; an encounter which engenders his wife's anger. Juno's punishment of Semele, however, goes further than exile. Through artful planning, Juno actually arranges for her adulterous husband to unwittingly kill Semele on their wedding night; as the argument to book 3 in Sandys's translation so graphically states, 'Semele doth friel in wisht embraces'.[145] Woman's body is thus a contentious site in Montagu's verse.

In this respect, as Grundy points out, Montagu 'made Latona flee through Lycia before the birth of her children instead of, like Ovid, afterwards'.[146] One particular effect of this striking transposition is to heighten the emotional intensity of Latona's complaint. Placing emphasis upon the expectant female form, from 'red swoln streaming eyes' to 'blood', Montagu's Latona ends with the focus on her progeny, declaring that 'all that's mine will bee Like mee persue'd'. This line, together with her final plea to Jupiter to save 'the unborn innocent', accentuates Latona's configuration as maternal subject. In comparison to Ovid's narrative, the somatic element of Montagu's translation is most striking as she first constructs Latona as a *mater dolorosa*, seemingly subservient in her actions: 'In Lycia First she stops and on her knees/ Thus prays to him that now regardless sees'. Both Latona's children (Apollo, the god of poetry, and Diana, the goddess of chastity) are gendered objects of desire. As Montagu reminds her readers in her poem 'Apollo and Daphne', the god is typically admired for the masculine qualities of rhetorical display. Diana, like Daphne, on the other hand, is generally remembered for her virginal status.

Montagu's Ovidian fragment thus calls into question the ways in which gender difference is written on and through the body.

Translation can be deemed a discursive practice, marking the body as subject within patriarchal ideology. Latona's petition alludes to the kind of perjorative association between women and the body ascribed by early modern culture and which is apparent in Sandys's *Metamorphosis Englished*. Hence, Deborah Rubin discusses the 'distinctive features of late encyclopaedic mythography [which] are exploited [... in order] to maintain an ideology of gender identity and social relations'.[147] Rubin argues that Sandys's text

> is a late representative of a long tradition of European allegorizing criticism of the Greek and Latin classics. As such, it is riddled with truisms about female vice and virtue, praising the abstraction of chastity and little else about women [...]. The problem is, of course, not unchaste or vicious women, but the sex itself.[148]

Whilst Sandys's commentary does not mention Latona's impregnation by Jupiter, the text does refer to her daughter, Diana. When commenting on book 3's myth of Actaeon and Diana, and in a move which seeks to dignify the male voyeur at the expense of Diana, Sandys writes:

> *Juno* in *Lucian* upbraides *Latona* that her daughter *Diana* converted *Actaeon*, having seen her naked, into a Hart; for feare he should divulge her deformity: and not out of modesty; being so farre from a Virgin, as continually conversant at the labours of women, like a publicke midwife.[149]

After reading Sandys's poem, Latona's declaration that 'all that's mine will be like me pursued' seems strangely apposite; even a chaste woman such as Diana can be named otherwise by the dominant patriarchal discourses of language. By drawing attention to the relationship between women and corporeality, Montagu's Latona implicitly interrogates the construction of 'woman' as the subordinate term.

Montagu's Ovidian poem concentrates on the desperation of a woman 'ruin'd' by man and exiled from the sphere in which she once prominently featured. Through Latona, a figure who 'prays to him that now regardless sees', an appeal is made from beyond the boundaries of the socio-political frame. Ultimately, Montagu's translation practice calls into question both the representation of women by men and the masculine dominance of translating the *Metamorphoses*:

> A woman writer in a patriarchal culture must develop strategies against her own internalization of the oppressive ideologies around her; for when she experiences conflict between her desire and what she has been taught is right and proper, she must try to accommodate both desire and the ideology that denies it. Such strategies – whether consciously or unconsciously used – profoundly determine the shape of women's literary style.[150]

As Latona's voice replaces the male voices of Ovid's text, Montagu inserts her own voice into the male lineage of vernacular versions of Ovid's texts. Montagu's

Latona shows translation to be the site of many differences – textual, gender, cultural – from text(s) to context(s); her verse exposes the translated text as an arena in which cultural meanings and identities are continually constructed and deconstructed. Grundy argues that Montagu's translation is not a literal one. To be sure, as with all of the women's translations explored in this chapter, Montagu's Ovid is not aligned with any prescribed model of contemporaneous translation; her verse is not paraphrase, metaphrase or imitation. In this respect, Montagu's Ovidian verses are removed from the boundaries of so-called normative theory and practice. She thus employs other textual strategies in an attempt to defy the cultural enclosures placed around women and English versions of the *Metamorphoses*.

Apart from myths which directly discuss the mutability of gender positions, the *Metamorphoses* also contains episodes which emphasise homosocial desire, particularly those told in book 10's Song of Orpheus. Following the death of Euridice, in Sandys's translation Orpheus declares:

> From Jove, o Muse, my Mother, draw my verse;
> All bow to Jove: Joves powre we oft rehearse.
> And late of Giants sung, in loftie straines,
> Foil'd by his thunder on Phlegean plaines.
> Now, in a lower tune, to lovely boyes
> Belov'd of Gods, turne we our softer layes:
> And women well deserving punishment, [...][151]

Orpheus's narratives include the episodes of Jove and Ganymede, Apollo and Hyacinthus and, significantly, Venus and Adonis, the next myth which interests the youthful Montagu. Through Latona, Montagu makes subject the conventionally marginalized and objectified woman. In her treatment of Venus and Adonis in Harrowby MS 251, a text which Montagu called 'The Entire Works of Clarinda', she is able to explore women and desire. As with the earlier translation, her poem is not a literal translation or even an imitation of the Latin source. Even so, the title Montagu's text, 'From Ovid's *Metamorphoses*', illustrates her aspiration to be associated with the epic poem:

> From Ovid's *Metamorphoses*
> When young Adonis dy'd the Queen of Love
> With loud complaints ran to the fatal Grove.
> Adonis! charming youth, she weeping cry'd
> And the dear name each babling Nymph reply'd,
> Ran throu' the Briars which unregarded stood
> And dy'd the rose tree with the Goddess' blood.
> From those fine drops then came them Lovely reds
> Which still the charming Leaves o're spreads
> Since then–
> It makes the glory of the gay bouquette
> Where choicest flowers are in Asemblie met,
> When the most beauteous does the Charm Compose
> None is so much regarded as the *Rose*

> For charming Scent and Lovely colour'd Leaves,
> Nor is't ingrate for what the Goddess gave,
> All the return a Flower can make it pays
> And shows its gratitude a thousand ways.
> To Beauty t'is an everlasting Freind,
> Often unforc'd to beauteous hands will bend,
> If *Pastorella* puts them in her hair
> In gratitude the[y] make her seem more fair,
> Adds a fresh Lustre and Vermillion grace
> To all the other beauties of her Face,
> Value'd by beauties t'is to beauty Kind,
> They Friends to it and it to them a Friend. (fol. 11ᵛ)

Grundy has indicated that as both writers begin with the death of Adonis, there are greater similarities between Montagu's text and Thomas Stanley's translation from the Greek of Bion's *Epitaph on Adonis* (1651) than with Ovid's poem.[152] From the outset of Stanley's translation the reader is presented with a text delineating male desire as the narrator's gaze moves across the dead body of the youth:

> Adonis I lament; he's dead! the fair
> Adonis dead is! [...]
> A Boares white tusk hath gor'd his whiter thigh:
> [...]
> Black blood distains
> His snowy Skin, his Eye no life retains:
> The Rose is from his pale Lip fled [...]
> Whilst babling gore, sprung from his thigh oreflow,
> His breast; the whiteness which so late orespred
> His limbs, is now converted into red.[153]

Beginning with the fatal wound, the narrator's perusal of Adonis then skims the surface of the body (the 'whiter thigh', 'snowy skin', 'eye', 'pale lip', 'breast', 'limbs') before glancing back at the thigh which turns from white to red as the 'babling gore oreflows'. Stanley's poem employs tropes which conventionally delineate female beauty, the blazon of white skin and rose-red lips, to eroticize the dying Adonis. However, the *Epitaph on Adonis* is not only significant for throwing homosocial desire into relief; the death of Adonis also marks the death of Venus as an object of desire:

> Her beauty with her beauteous Spouse she lost
> Whilst her Adonis liv'd Venus could boast
> Her form; but that (alas) did with him dy:[154]

In a poem which seeks to erase female desire, it is telling that Venus does not overtly effect Adonis's transformation. In Stanley's translation, somewhat passively, it is Venus's tears which become the anemone, the transient wind-flower, whilst Adonis's blood becomes the rose:

Poor Venus thy Adonis murder'd lies!
For every drop of blood he shed, her eyes
Let fall a tear, which earth in flowers bestows,
Tears rais'd th' Anemony and Blood the Rose.[155]

Stanley's representation contrasts well with Ovid's Venus, the mythic protagonist who retains her position as powerful goddess by transforming Adonis's blood into the wind-flower.[156] In this respect, Montagu's translation is more like Ovid than Bion and Stanley. Through her agency as translator, however, Montagu considerably modifies the classical material.

Catherine Belsey observes that 'Ovid's *Metamorphoses* records the origins of things and accounts in the process for their present character'.[157] In what arguably is the most Ovidian characteristic in the poem, Montagu follows the paradigm which Belsey outlines as she attempts to provide an origin for the present meaning of the red rose. Whereas the *Metamorphoses* sets out to define the wind–flower as a signifier of transient masculine beauty, Montagu strives to make her poem a celebration of Venus and the red rose a signifier of female desire. The opening octet of the poem describes the way in which the rose became red. Following a turn which states 'since then–', the next sixteen lines bring the subject of the poem from the past into the present. Although Montagu concentrates on a seemingly benign aspect of the rose (it is there merely to enhance woman as object of desire), a detailed examination of subjectivity and representation is at work in her text. Montagu's violent etiological account of the red rose becomes a site for the wider interrogation of ideology, meaning and language. In 'Poetry and Grammar', Gertrude Stein explores the figurative nature of poetry through the use of the deliberately elusive phrase 'a rose is a rose is a rose is a rose'.[158] By using a noun which is thoroughly excessive in terms of its semiotic value, Stein's aphorism shows how

> meaning is an effect of relations and differences among signifiers along a potentially endless chain (polysemous, intertextual, subject to infinite linkages), it is always differential and deferred, never present as an original unity.[159]

Although Montagu attempts to fix the meaning of the red rose as a sign of female beauty, the representation of woman itself is problematic. At the outset of the poem the reader is presented with an allegorical figure, Venus, a replacement for the concept of female sexual desire. In turn, Venus's blood metonymically displaces Venus. The blood then transforms the rose into the symbol of the red rose. From then on, Montagu complicates the issue even further by having the red rose, a symbol of Venus, adorn another allegorical figure: Pastorella.

In English literature one of the best-known evocations of the figure of Pastorella is found in book 6 of Edmund Spenser's *The Faerie Queene* (c. 1590).[160] In Spenser's poem, the epithet commonly used to describe the shepherdess is that of 'fair' and Montagu develops this aspect of Pastorella,[161] commenting that the wearing of the red rose makes her seem 'more fair'. Indeed, the very presence of the rose seems to rejuvenate the figure, for it 'adds a fresh Lustre and Vermillion grace| To all the other beauties of her Face'. The inclusion of the figure of Pastorella within Montagu's etiology of the red rose, however, further problematizes issues of meaning and identity. In *The Faerie Queene*, as A. C. Hamilton explains, Pastorella is presented to the reader with 'deliberate mystification'.[162] Introduced in canto 9, the shepherdess is named by other pastoral characters:

> Who admiring her as some heavenly wight,
> Did for their Soveraine goddesse her esteeme,
> And caroling her name both day and night,
> The fairest Pastorella her by name did hight.[163]

However, as her supposed father explains that he 'Found her by fortune, which to him befell| In th'open fields an Infant left alone', the poem suggests that Pastorella's identity is in question.[164] During the next three cantos, as Pastorella is amorously pursued by both Sir Calidore and Coridon and kidnapped by a band of thieves, the troubled romance of Sir Bellamoure and Claribell comes to the fore. It is revealed that Claribell 'a mayden child forth brought' whom she tearfully leaves in an empty field.[165] As Claribell takes one last look at the child:

> Upon the little brest like christall bright
> She mote perceive a little purple mold
> That like a rose her silken leaves did faire unfold.[166]

This is the 'rosie mark' which eventually reunites Pastorella with her real parents.[167] Claribell's matron declares that it is the 'little purple rose [...]| Wherof her name ye then to her did give'.[168] However, 'in accord with pastoral convention',[169] *The Faerie Queene* never reveals what that name is. Similarly, Montagu constructs an open-ended textual labyrinth. As the sign of the rose becomes interrogated, so too is the construction of the female identity. For Montagu's text offers a representation of woman which is grounded more in absence than presence. Through this process of translation, moving from the past to the present, from Venus to Pastorella, Montagu's poem 'From Ovid's *Metamorphoses*' does not merely question the origins of the red rose. Ultimately, her text suggests that, like the symbol of the rose, the meaning of 'woman' is constantly deferred and displaced.

   With Montagu's interest in origins manifest in 'From Ovid's *Metamorphoses*', it seems appropriate that the final Ovidian myth in Montagu's juvenile collection, also in Harrowby MS 251, is 'The Golden Age':

> The Golden Age
> There was (But ah! Long past) a Golden Age
> When men did not deceive nor Tyrants rage,
> Where noe Injustice, nor noe fears did reign
> Exempt from pride, Ambition, and from pain,
> None stood in fear of plots or factious men

And Innocence was all their Armour then.
The Earth unforce't yeilded a Bounteous store,
They neither wanted nor they wish'd for more,
Calmly their hours Past, and no Deceit
Was known in their affairs of Love or State.
There was no giveing Rich, Nor begging poor,
In common all enjoy'd an equall store,
Gold and its Impious use was still unknown
Before mankind was interested grown.
Ettenal Blooming Spring, Look't allways gay,
Perpetuall sun-shine and continue'd May
A Lasting Equinox through out the year
And Men were Strangers unto Vice and Care,
Fruits Bounteous Nature Lavishly Bestow'd,
Rivers of Nectar, springs of milk there flow'd,
Their harmless feasts unsullie'd was by Blood
And Man unawe'd and Natively was Good.
Thus free and Blest with peace Live'd all man kind
Before that Laws enchain'd the Godlike mind. (fols. 24^V–25^r)

In the late seventeenth century, as we have seen, Dryden translated Ovid's myth of the Golden Age, and Aphra Behn also published a poem entitled *The Golden Age: A Paraphrase on a Translation out of the French* (1684), though Behn's poem relies more on the pastoral mode of Tasso's *Aminta* than Ovid.[170] The first twenty-two lines of Montagu's version, however, follow the Ovidian paradigm, and her poem moves through the familiar aspects which characterize the Golden Age: justice, economic equality and material provision.

By placing the subject of law at the end of her poem, however, Montagu conspicuously revises Ovid's narrative. As she writes of 'Laws' which now 'enchain'd the Godlike mind', the reader is arguably encouraged to consider the Ovidian figures that Montagu has employed in the earlier poems of both manuscripts. Both Latona and Venus are powerful goddesses who defy boundaries of normative behaviour prescribed by patriarchal culture. As such, they are palpably different from Daphne and Arethusa, the mythic women who feature in Montagu's published poems. Both the juvenile texts concerned with Latona and Venus explore the construction of gender difference through language, exploring the ways in which women are interpellated through the inscriptions of, and on, their bodies. Yet Montagu cannot fully escape the limitations placed around the woman translator in this period. She acknowledges these cultural boundaries in the form of a repudiation placed above the myth of Latona:

I Question not but here is very manny faults but if any reasonable person considers 3 thing[s] they would forgive them
1. I am a woman
2. Without any advantage of Education
3. All these was writ at the age of 14. (fol. 1^V)

Montagu describes her own scene of writing as one of restriction. Gender, lack of knowledge and age are accepted as significant reasons for the 'faults' presented in this manuscript. All the same, the juvenile poetic persona of Mary Montagu has a confidence which the adult does not appear to possess.

In a letter written to her daughter, Lady Bute, in 1753, some fifty years after she produced her Ovidian translations, Montagu stated the following:

> To say Truth, there is no part of the World where our Sex is treated with so much contempt as in England [...]. I think it the highest injustice to be dabarr'd the Entertainment of my Closet, and that the same Studies which raise the character of a Man should hurt that of a Woman. We are educated in the grossest ignorance, and no art omitted to stifle our natural reason; if some few get above their Nurse's instructions, our knowledge must rest conceal'd and be as useless to the World as Gold in the Mine.[171]

Placed against this complaint, her youthful attempt to produce Latona's narrative in the vernacular, doubly defiant in its use of a woman's voice (the translator's and Latona's) is even more potent than it first seemed. Montagu's rendition of Venus and Adonis interrogates women and representation, whilst her myth of the Golden Age considers a time before the inscription of law and the construction of androcentric codes of conduct which determine the sexual politics of translation.

Notes

[1]   Patricia Klindienst, 'The Voice of the Shuttle is Ours', *The Stanford Literature Review*, 1, (1984), 25–53, 25.

[2]   Charles Segal states that 'lascivia is the word which Quintilian uses to characterise the art of Ovid (*Institutio oratoria*, 4. 1. 77, 10. 1. 88, and 10. 1. 93)' cited in William Keach, *Elizabethan Erotic Narratives* (London: Harvester Press, 1977), p. 11, p. 235, n. 12.

[3]   William Shakespeare, *Cymbeline*, ed. by J. M. Nosworthy (London: Routledge, 1988), 2. 1. 44–5.

[4]   In addition, Nosworthy notes that even though 'Shakespeare doubtless knew the versions of the tale by Chaucer, Gower and Painter, [...] we may reasonably suppose that Imogen's book was Ovid's *Metamorphoses*'. Shakespeare, *Cymbeline*, p. 51, n. 45.

[5]   Jonathan Bate, *Shakespeare and Ovid* (Oxford: Clarendon Press, 1993), p. 216.

[6]   For a consideration of the 'extent and nature of women's knowledge of Latin (and to a lesser extent, Greek) language in the sixteenth and seventeenth centuries', see Jane Stevenson, 'Women Latin Poets in Britain in the Seventeenth and Eighteenth Centuries', *The Seventeenth Century*, 16 (2001), 1–36.

[7]   Pearl Hogrefe, *Tudor Women: Commoners and Queens* (Ames: Iowa State University Press, 1975), p. 115.

[8]   Thomas Salter, *A Mirrhour mete for all Mothers, Matrones, and Maidens, intituled the Mirrhour of Modestie* (London: 1579), sig. B vii[v].

9   Anon, *Ovid's Metamorphosis Epitomized in an English Poetical Style, for the Use and Entertainment of the Ladies of Great Britain* (London: 1760).

10 In an immensely valuable discussion of women and translation, Danielle Clarke writes that 'in seeking to establish women's texts as valid objects of inquiry, criticism has often failed to recognise the extent to which they are indebted to the mainstream assumptions of literary culture more generally in this period. A good example of this tendency is the attitude taken to translations by women. As modern Anglo-American culture becomes ever more monolingual, and dependent upon notions of literary value based on ideas of originality, translation becomes extremely difficult to read. One major form of literary production engaged in by women writers in the Renaissance is translation (in a more or less narrow sense), a fact which has been recognised by critics but inadequately dealt with'. Danielle Clarke, *The Politics of Early Modern Women's Writing* (London: Longman, 2001), p. 13.

11 Margaret Tyler, *The mirrour of princely deedes and knighthood wherein is shewed the worthinesse of the Knight of the Sunne, and his brother Rosicleer, sonnes to the great Emperour Trebetio: with the strange love of the beautifull and excellent princesse Briana, and the valiant actes of other noble princes and knightes. Now newly translated out of Spanish into our vulgar English tongue* [...] (London: 1578). See further Sherry Simon, *Gender in Translation: Cultural Identity and the Politics of Transmission* (London: Routledge, 1996), p. 48; Margaret Tyler, *A Mirrour of Princely Deeds and Knighthood*, ed. by Kathryn Coad (Aldershot and Vermont: Scolar Press, 1996).

12 Louise Schleiner, *Tudor and Stuart Women Writers* (Bloomington: Indiana University Press, 1994), p. 2.

13 Arthur Golding, *The xv. Bookes of P. Ovidius Naso, etytuled Metamorphosis, translated oute of Latin into English meeter* [...] (London: 1567), 6. 84. For comparison, throughout this chapter I am using the most recent contemporaneous, and complete, published versions of the *Metamorphoses* in English which were available to each of these translators.

14 Golding, *The xv. Bookes*, 6. 89.

15 Golding, *The xv. Bookes*, 6. 105–21.

16 Sarah Annes Brown suggests that 'Minerva's tapestry, with its depictions of punishment and suffering, is sufficiently ambiguous to make her final border of 'peaceful' olives seem ironic'. Sarah Annes Brown, *The Metamorphosis of Ovid: From Chaucer to Ted Hughes* (London: Duckworth, 1999), p. 46.

17 Golding, *The xv. Bookes*, 6. 100.

18 Golding, *The xv. Bookes*, 6. 150–1.

19 Golding, *The xv. Bookes*, 6. 167–68.

20 Golding, *The xv. Bookes*, 6. 180–81.

21 Nancy K. Miller, *Subject to Change: Reading Feminist Writing* (New York: Columbia University Press, 1988), p. 82.

22 Brown, *The Metamorphosis of Ovid*, pp. 40, 126 and *Ovid: Myth and Metamorphosis* (London: Duckworth, 2005), pp. 105, 108. Ann Rosalind Jones and Peter Stallybrass, *Renaissance Clothing and the Materials of Memory* (Cambridge: Cambridge University Press, 2000), p. 98.

23 A. S. Byatt, 'Arachne', in *Ovid Metamorphosed*, ed. by Philip Terry (London: Chatto and Windus, 2000), pp. 131–57, p. 141. Leonard Barkan makes a similar observation: 'it requires no great leap of the imagination to see in Arachne's tapestry all the elements of Ovid's poetic form in the *Metamorphoses*, which is, after all, a poem that eschews a

clear narrative structure and rather creates a finely woven fabric of stories related via transformation'. Leonard Barkan, *The Gods Made Flesh: Metamorphosis and the Pursuit of Paganism* (New Haven: Yale University Press, 1986), p. 4.

24   Golding, *The xv. Bookes*, 2. 1044 ff.; 4. 699 ff.; 5. 434 ff. and 4. 971 ff. respectively.

25   Golding, *The xv. Bookes*, 15. 871–2.

26   Miller, *Subject to Change*, p. 81. See also Nona Fienberg, 'Mary Wroth's Poetics of the Self', *Studies in English Literature 1500–1900*, 42 (2002), 121–36.

27   Jones and Stallybrass, *Renaissance Clothing and the Materials of Memory*, p. 99.

28   George Sandys, *Ovids Metamorphosis Englished, Mythologized, and Represented in Figures* (Oxford: 1632), p. 217, p. 220.

29   Jones and Stallybrass, *Renaissance Clothing and the Materials of Memory*, p. 98.

30   Josette A. Wiseman, 'Christine de Pizan and Arachne's *Metamorphoses*', *Fifteenth-Century Studies*, 23 (1997), 138–151, 138. Wiseman cites Nancy K. Miller, *Subject to Change*, p. 78.

31   Jean Luis Vives, *A verie fruitfull and pleasant booke. called the instruction of a Christian woman,* trans. by Richarde Hyrde, 2nd edn (London: 1592), sig. C iii^v cited in Susan Frye, 'Sewing Connections: Elizabeth Tudor, Mary Stuart, Elizabeth Talbot, and Seventeenth Century Anonymous Needleworkers', in *Maids, Mistresses, Cousins and Queens: Women's Alliances in Early Modern England*, ed. by Susan Frye and Karen Robertson (New York: Oxford University Press, 1999), pp. 165–182, p. 180, n. 1.

32   Frye, 'Sewing Connections', p. 166.

33   Frye, 'Sewing Connections', p. 166

34   Lisa M. Klein, 'Your Humble Handmaid: Elizabethan Gifts of Needlework', *Renaissance Quarterly*, 50 (1997), 459–93, 462. See also Susan Frye, 'Sewing Connections: Elizabeth Tudor, Mary Stuart, Elizabeth Talbot, and Seventeenth Century Anonymous Needleworkers', in *Maids, Mistresses, Cousins and Queens: Women's Alliances in Early Modern England*, ed. by Susan Frye and Karen Robertson (New York: Oxford University Press, 1999), pp. 165–82.

35   David N. Durant, *Bess of Hardwick: Portrait of an Elizabethan Dynast*, rev. edn (London: Peter Owen, 1999), book cover blurb.

36   Durant, *Bess of Hardwick,* pp. 469–70. See also Trevor Lummis and Jan Marsh, *The Woman's Domain: Women and the English Country House* (London: Penguin, 1990).

37   Klein, 'Your Humble Handmaid', p. 470.

38   For a detailed description of Talbot's embroidered gifts to the Queen, see Durant, *Bess of Hardwick*, p. 92.

39   Klein, 'Your Humble Handmaid', p. 470.

40   Jones and Stallybrass, *Renaissance Clothing and the Materials of Memory*, p. 95.

41   See Golding, *The xv. Bookes*, 2. 1 ff, 2. 1043 and 3. 180 ff. As Santina M. Levey discusses, there is little information available about the furnishing of the Old Hall and the New Hall. Much of the detail comes from Bess's will of 27 April 1601. Santina M. Levey, *Elizabethan Treasures: The Hardwick Hall Textiles* (London: National Trust, 1998), p. 19. Although Jones and Stallybrass comment that Talbot generally used this cipher to identify herself as the producer of the work, it is difficult to establish with absolute surety whether she embroidered the Ovidian texts herself. Levey observes that each one 'bears a silver and gold monogram ES [...] and although this was likely to indicate the owner rather than the embroiderer, Bess was clearly closely involved in their production, including the choice of subject matter'. Levey, *Elizabethan Treasures*, p. 49. This process of textual production may be analogous with that of the scribes who

worked on the Caxton translation discussed in the next chapter. Evidence of the various 'hands' used throughout the manuscript in which the colophon states that it was 'translated and finished by me William Caxton' have not undermined his role in the work. Similarly, Talbot's agency in the production of these Ovidian episodes seems apparent, thus affording her embroidered translations a significant place in the vernacular genealogy of the *Metamorphoses*.

42 William Shakespeare, *Titus Andronicus*, 4. 1. 42. All quotations are from William Shakespeare, *Titus Andronicus*, ed. by Jonathan Bate (London: Routledge, 1995).

43 Talbot's Ovidian embroideries may also be considered a significant addition to the 'Ovide imagisé', the tradition of Ovidian illustration of which the engravings used in Sandys's *Metamorphosis Englished* are an apt example. For a discussion of the 'Ovide imagisé' see Barkan, *The Gods Made Flesh*, p. 188. See also Nigel Llewellyn, 'Illustrating Ovid', in *Ovid Renewed: Ovidian Influences on Literature and Art from the Middle Ages to the Twentieth century*, ed. by Charles Martindale (Cambridge: Cambridge University Press, 1988), pp. 151–66; Paul Barolsky, 'As in Ovid, So in Renaissance Art', *Renaissance Quarterly*, 51 (1998), 451–74 and Christopher Allen, 'Ovid and Art', in *The Cambridge Companion to Ovid*, ed. by Philip Hardie (Cambridge: Cambridge University Press, 2002), pp. 336–67.

44 Maureen Quilligan, 'Elizabeth's Embroidery', *Shakespeare Studies*, 29 (2001), 208–15, 208.

45 Klein, 'Your Humble Handmaid', p. 470.

46 In 1480, Caxton's Ovid explained that 'Pheton is to understonde a man that by hys pryde and overmoche wenyng wil mounte and enhaunce higher himself than it ne apparteyneth to hym' (fol. 45ᵛ). Later, the tale of Phaeton also proved exceptionally useful for the promotion of Calvinist ideology in early Protestant England. Unlike Luther, Calvin had little to say about freedom and much to say about the servitude of a Christian. According to William Bouwsma, Calvin 'praised religion because it prohibited "wandering freely"; godliness "keeps itself within proper limits." Christianity, Calvin thought, acted to "restrain and bridle" the mind and "make it captive."' William Bouwsma, *John Calvin: A Sixteenth-Century Portrait* (Oxford: Oxford University Press, 1988), p. 86. The epistle addressed to the Earl of Leicester at the start of Golding's Calvinist-inspired *Metamorphoses* shows how the translator obliquely uses the Phaeton episode in order to promote a particular ideological position:

> At length my chariot wheele about the mark hath found the way,
> And at their weery races end, my breathlesse horses stay.
> The woork is brought too end by which the author did account
> (And rightly) with eternall fame above the starres to mount,
> For whatsoever hath bene writ of auncient tyme in greeke
> By sundry men dispersedly, and in the latin eeke,
> Of this same dark Philosophie of turned shapes, the same
> Hath Ovid into one whole masse in this boke brought in frame. (1–8)

Golding emphasizes control and this is a recurring theme throughout the 838 lines of the prefatory material. By drawing attention to both the form and the content of the *Metamorphoses*, Golding depicts Ovid as a writer who has managed to synthesize 'into one whole masse' a variety of Greek and Latin texts by 'sundry men dispersedly'. Thus, Ovid's accomplishments as a translator are acknowledged. But as the successful driver of the textual chariot of this vernacular translation, Golding positions himself as the one who is in ultimate control over the *Metamorphoses* in English. Towards the end of the epistle, Golding uses the trope of the chariot again in order to instruct the reader in the following way:

> The use of this same booke therfore is this: that every man
> (Endeavouring for to know himself as neerly as he can,
> As though he in a chariot sate well ordered), should direct
> His mynd by reason in the way of vertue, and correct
> His feerce affections with the bit of temprance, lest perchaunce
> They taking bridle in the teeth lyke wilful jades doo praunce
> Away, and headlong carie him to every filthy pit
> Of vyce, and drinking of the same defyle his soule with it:
> Or else doo headlong harrie him uppon the rockes of sin,
> And over throwing forcibly the chariot he sits in,
> Doo teare him worse than ever was Hippolytus the sonne
> Of Theseus when he went about his fathers wrath to shun. (569–80)

These lines explain the violent outcome of 'feerce affections'; in the search to know the self, the newly reformed English Protestant subject should steer a course away from sin and vice. Indeed, Golding also uses the myth to warn against political insurrection:

> This fable also dooth advyse all parents and all such
> As bring up youth, too take good heede of cockering them too much.
> It further dooth commende the meane: and willeth too beware
> Of rash and hasty promises which most pernicious are,
> And not too bee performed: and in fine it playnly showes
> What sorrow too the parents and too all the kinred growes
> By disobedience of the chyld: and in the chyld is ment
> The disobedient subject that ageinst his prince is bent. (77–84)

In 1632, after considering Lactantius, Aristotle and Francis Bacon ('the Viscount of Saint Albons'), Sandys's commentary interprets the tale as a rather different political allegory. He works towards an analysis which reads Phaeton as a 'rash and ambitious prince' and the 'Horses of the Sun [...] are the common people [...] who finding the weakness of the Prince, fly out into all exorbitancies to a general confusion'. Sandys, *Ovids Metamorphosis Englished, Mythologized, and Represented in Figures* (Oxford: 1632), sig. H 3ᵛ.

47 Levey states that Talbot's embroideries are based on Virgilio Solis's illustrations. Levey, *Elizabethan Treasures*, p. 51. For a comparison of Talbot's tapestries with the editions of Johann Spreng's *Metamorphoses Illustratae*, illustrated by Virgil Solis, published in 1557, 1563, 1582 and 1591 see *Ovid Illustrated: The Renaissance Reception of Ovid in Image and Text*, featuring *Metamorphoses* illustrations by Virgil Solis *et al.*. Site constructed by Daniel Kinney with Elizabeth Styron <http://etext.virginia.edu/latin/ovid/ovid1563.html5> accessed 25 June 2004.

48 Golding, *The xv. Bookes*, 2. 170 ff. and 2. 204.

49 Golding, *The xv. Bookes*, 2. 421–4.

50 Golding, *The xv. Bookes*, 2. 429 ff.

51 Golding, *The xv. Bookes*, 2. 350 and 2. 359.

52 Golding, *The xv. Bookes*, 2. 71ff.

53 Golding, *The xv. Bookes*, 2. 423 and 2. 448.

54 Mary S. Lovell, *Bess of Hardwick: Countess of Shrewsbury* (London: Little, Brown, 2005), p. 221

55 Golding, *The xv. Bookes*, 2. 410–5.

56 Philip Hardie, *Ovid's Poetics of Illusion* (Cambridge: Cambridge University Press, 2002), p. 83.

57 Hardie, *Ovid's Poetics of Illusion*, p. 83.

58 Golding, *The xv. Bookes*, 2. 1043. For a discussion of the 'complementarity' of Arachne and Europa in Renaissance painting, see Barkan, *The Gods Made Flesh*, p. 8 ff. For a survey of the Europa myth in the Renaissance, see Llewellyn, 'Illustrating Ovid', pp. 162–66.

59 Barkan, *The Gods Made Flesh*, p. 8.

60 Golding, *The xv. Bookes*, 2. 1091.

61 Golding, *The xv. Bookes*, 2. 1076–87.

62 Golding, *The xv. Bookes*, 2. 1055.

63 Golding, *The xv. Bookes*, 3. 180 ff.

64 Wendy Wall, *The Imprint of Gender: Authorship and Publication in the English Renaissance* (Ithaca: Cornell University Press, 1993), p. 225.

65 Abraham Fraunce, *The Third Part of the Countesse of Pembrokes Yvychurch. Entitled Amintas Dale* (London: 1592), M 1ʳ.

66 Other allegorical representations of the Queen include Astrea and Venus-Virgo. See further Susan Doran, *Queen Elizabeth I* (London: The British Library, 2003), p. 117.

67 Brown, *Ovid: Myth and Metamorphosis*, p. 72.

68 Allen, 'Ovid and Art', p. 366.

69 Ovid, *The Metamorphoses*, trans. by Frank Justus Miller, rev. by G. P. Goold, 2 vols (London: Heinemann, 1984), 3. 277.

70 Golding, *The xv. Bookes*, 3. 266–8.

71 Thomas Parnell, *Collected Poems of Thomas Parnell*, ed. by Claude Rawson and F. P. Lock (Newark: University of Delaware Press, 1989), pp. 114, 1–8.

72 Barbara Benedict, *Making the Modern Reader: Cultural Mediation in Early Modern Literary Anthologies* (Princeton. N. J.: Princeton University Press, 1996), p. 121.

73 A few decades later, Elizabeth Tollet published a translation of 'Apollo and Daphne' in her collection *Poem on Several Occasions* (1724). See further Claudia Thomas Kairoff, 'Classical and Biblical Models: The Female Poetic Tradition', in *Women and Poetry, 1660–1750*, ed. by David Shuttleton and Sarah Prescott (Basingstoke: Palgrave, 2003), pp. 183–202, p. 190.

74 Charles Hopkins, *Epistolary Poems on Several Occasions with several of the Choicest Stories of Ovid's Metamorphoses and Tibullus's Elegies. Translated into English Verse* (London: 1694) contains the following myths: Phoebus and Daphne; Jupiter and Europa; Cynras and Myrrha; Ceyx and Halcyone. *The History of Love. A Poem in a letter to a lady* (London: 1695) contains the following myths: Perseus and Andromeda; Pigmalion; Hippomanes and Procris; Cephalus and Procris; Orpheus and Eurydice; Narcissus and Echo; Salmacis and Hermaphroditus and Scylla and Minos.

75 Kathryn R. King, 'Elizabeth Singer Rowe's Tactical Use of Print and Manuscript', in *Women's Writing and the Circulation of Ideas: Manuscript Publication in England, 1550–1800*, ed. by George L. Justice and Nathan Tinker (Cambridge: Cambridge University Press, 2002), pp. 158–181, p. 160.

76 Sarah Prescott, *Women, Authorship and Literary Culture, 1690–1740* (Basingstoke: Palgrave, 2003), p. 165.

77 Norma Clarke, 'Soft Passions and Darling Themes: From Elizabeth Singer Rowe (1674–1737) to Elizabeth Carter (1717–1806)', *Women's Writing*, 7 (2000), 353–71, 368.

[78]　Prescott, *Women, Authorship and Literary Culture*, p. 165.

[79]　The other translations in Rowe's collection are aligned with Prescott's model. They are: 'Paraphrase on John 3. 16'; 'A Paraphrase on the Canticles (Chap. I. Chap. II. Chap. III. Chap. IV. Chap. V. Chap. VI)'; 'Paraphrase on John 21. 17'; 'Paraphrase on Cant. 5,6'; 'Paraphrase on Revel. Chap. 1. from v. 13. to v. 18'; 'Paraphrase on Malachy 3, 14' and 'Paraphrase on Canticles, 7, 11'.

[80]　Prescott, *Women, Authorship and Literary Culture*, p. 142.

[81]　Clarke, 'Soft Passions and Darling Themes', p. 355.

[82]　For a discussion of the textual relationship between Rowe and Dunston, see King, 'Elizabeth Singer Rowe's Tactical Use of Print and Manuscript', pp. 161 ff.

[83]　All quotations are from Elizabeth Singer Rowe, *Poems on Several Occasions. Written by Philomela* (London: 1696).

[84]　Prescott, *Women, Authorship and Literary Culture*, p. 142

[85]　Sandys, *Ovids Metamorphosis Englished*, 1. 471 ff.

[86]　Sandys, *Ovids Metamorphosis Englished*, 6. 606 ff.

[87]　Ann Messenger, *Pastoral Tradition and the Female Talent: Studies in Augustan Poetry* (New York: AMS Press, 2001), p. 3.

[88]　Madeleine Forell Marshall, *The Poetry of Elizabeth Singer Rowe* (Lewiston, Queenston: The Edwin Mellen Press, 1989), p. 14.

[89]　13 October 1714. *The Spectator*, ed. by Donald F. Bond, 5 vols. (Oxford: Clarendon Press, 1965). See Messenger, *Pastoral Tradition and the Female Talent*, p. 6.

[90]　Messenger, *Pastoral Tradition and the Female Talent*, p. 5.

[91]　Clarke, 'Soft Passions and Darling Themes', p. 362.

[92]　See, for example, Guillaume de Lorris, *The Romance of the Rose*, ed. by F. Horgan (Oxford: Oxford University Press, 1994), p. 11.

[93]　Barkan, *The Gods Made Flesh*, p. 245.

[94]　Prescott, *Women, Authorship and Literary Culture*, p. 165

[95]　Joseph Addison, *The Works*, ed. by Henry G. Bohn, 6 vols. (London: Bohn, 1856), pp. 139–40. See Margaret Doody, *The Daring Muse: Augustan Poetry Reconsidered* (Cambridge: Cambridge University Press, 1985), p. 85.

[96]　Carol Barash, *English Women's Poetry, 1649–1714: Politics, Community and Linguistic Authority* (Oxford: Clarendon Press, 1996), p. 105, n. 17.

[97]　Rebecca M. Mills, 'Mary, Lady Chudleigh: Poet, Protofeminist and Patron', in *Women and Poetry 1660–1750*, ed. by Sarah Prescott and David Shuttleton (Basingstoke: Palgrave, 2003), pp. 50–7.

[98]　Barbara Olive, 'A Puritan Subject's Panegyrics to Queen Anne', *Studies in English Literature*, 42 (2002), 475–99, 479. All quotations of Mary Chudleigh's Ovidian texts are from *Poems on Several Occasions Together with the Song of the Three Children Paraphrased* (London: 1703).

[99]　Mary, Lady Chudleigh, 'The Ladies Defence', in *The Poems and Prose of Mary, Lady Chudleigh*, ed. by Margaret J. M. Ezell (Oxford: Oxford University Press, 1993), pp. 1–40, p. 9.

[100]　Ezell, *The Poems and Prose of Mary, Lady Chudleigh*, p. xxvii.

[101]　Dryden's translations were central to Chudleigh's writing in general. See further Ezell, *The Poems and Prose of Mary, Lady Chudleigh*, p. xxviii.

[102]　Dryden also translated the myths of Meleager and Atlanta; Baucis and Philemon; Pygmalion and the Statue; Cinyras and Myrrha; Ceyx and Alcyone; The Twelfth Book of Ovid; The Speeches of Ajax and Ulysses and 'Of the Pythagorean Philosophy'. See

further Judith Sloman, *Dryden:The Poetics of Translation* (Toronto: University of Toronto Press, 1985). See also Paul Hammond, 'Mutability and Metamorphosis', in *Dryden and the Traces of Classical Rome* (Oxford: Oxford University Press, 1999), pp. 143–217.

[103] Olive, 'A Puritan Subject's Panegyrics to Queen Anne', p. 497, n. 44.

[104] Sandys, *Ovids Metamorphosis Englished*, 8.195 ff.

[105] For an excellent survey, see Niall Rudd, 'Daedalus and Icarus: From the Renaissance to the Present Day', in *Ovid Renewed: Ovidian Influences on Literature and Art from the Middle Ages to the Twentieth Century*, ed. by Charles Martindale (Cambridge: Cambridge University Press, 1988), pp. 37–53.

[106] Francis Lenten, *The young gallants whirligigg; or Youths reakes Demonstrating the inordinate affections, absurd actions, and profuse expences, of unbridled and affectated youth* [...] (London: 1629), sig. C 2^r.

[107] Sandys, *Ovids Metamorphosis Englished*, sig. L 1^v.

[108] Olive states that 'we do not often associate female writers with panegyric, especially when it is employed as a form of political commentary, as it frequently was by the end of the seventeenth century'. Olive, 'A Puritan Subject's Panegyrics to Queen Anne', p. 475.

[109] Chudleigh, *The Poems and Prose of Mary, Lady Chudleigh*, p. xxiii.

[110] Chudleigh, *The Poems and Prose of Mary, Lady Chudleigh*, p. 44.

[111] Christopher Martin (ed.), *Ovid in English* (London: Penguin, 1998), p. 237.

[112] Mary Wortley Montagu, *Essays and Poems and Simplicity, A Comedy*, ed. by Robert Halsband and Isobel Grundy (Oxford: Clarendon Press, 1977), p. 3.

[113] Grundy's unpublished doctoral thesis, however, contains a chapter entitled 'Translation, Parody and Imitation'. Isobel Grundy, 'The Verse of Lady Mary Wortley Montagu: A Critical Edition' (Oxford: unpublished DPhil thesis, 1971), pp. 79–95.

[114] Felicity A. Nussbaum, *The Brink of All We Hate: English Satires on Women 1660–1750* (Kentucky: University of Kentucky Press, 1984), p. 3.

[115] Robert Halsband, 'The First Version of Marivaux's *Le Jeu de L'amour et du Hasard*', *Modern Philology*, 79 (1981), 16–23.

[116] Lady Mary Wortley Montagu, *Complete Letters*, ed. by Robert Halsband, 3 vols (Oxford: Clarenden Press, 1965–7), p. 337, cited in Grundy, 1971, 'The Verse of Lady Mary Wortley Montagu: A Critical Edition', p. 81.

[117] Cited in Isobel Grundy, 'Ovid and Eighteenth-Century Divorce: An Unpublished Poem by Lady Mary Wortley Montagu', *Review of English Studies*, 23 (1972), 417–28, 418. However, as Grundy points out in a later publication, Montagu 'told an admiring Spence on the one hand that her "stealing the Latin language" began from her admiring Ovid, on the other hand it began from "somebody's" chance remark'. Isobel Grundy, *Lady Mary Wortley Montagu: Comet of the Enlightenment* (Oxford: Oxford University Press, 1999), p. 15.

[118] Cited in Grundy, 'Ovid and Eighteenth-Century Divorce', p. 420.

[119] Alexander Pope, 'Sandys's Ghost', in *The Twickenham Edition of the Poems of Alexander Pope: Minor Poems*, ed. by Norman Ault and John Butt (London: Methuen, 1954), pp. 170–6, p. 173. Commenting on these lines, Valerie Rumbold writes that 'it is something of a puzzle to know whether the lines on her wit in *Sandys's Ghost* [...] are a playful compliment [...] or an ironic belittlement. Although they seem admiring, their context – Pope is arguing ironically that the field of translation is equally open to the

competent and incompetent – is ambiguous'. Valerie Rumbold, *Women's Place in Pope's World* (Cambridge: Cambridge University Press, 1989), p. 135.

[120] Grundy points to contradictory statements in Montagu's letters about her knowledge of Latin. See Grundy, 'The Verse of Lady Mary Wortley Montagu: A Critical Edition', p. 17 ff. When placed in the cultural context discussed in this chapter, however, these contradictions are easy to understand.

[121] Isobel Grundy, 'The Politics of Female Authorship', *The Book Collector*, 31 (1982), 19–37, 19.

[122] Montagu, *Essays and Poems*, pp. 234–6.

[123] Grundy, 'The Politics of Female Authorship', p. 29.

[124] *Ovid: The Metamorphoses*, trans. Miller, 1. 548ff. and 5. 572ff.

[125] Harrowby MS 255. Halsband and Grundy state that 'this *Metamorphoses* incident was burlesqued by other writers (*The Hive*, 1724, pp. 226–7; Prior, *Works*, I. 413–7; Tickell, *Poems*, 1779, p.146). Lady Mary transcribed the first two with her own version, and probably knew the last.' Montagu, *Essays and Poems*, p. 298. All quotations of Montagu's translations of Ovid are cited from the manuscripts. I would like to thank the Harrowby Manuscript Trust for allowing access to this material.

[126] Sarah Annes Brown, *Ovid: Myth and Metamorphosis*, p. 45.

[127] Halsband and Grundy suppose that the poem was 'written before July 1739, probably on the occasion of one of the scandals concerning Oxenden'. Montagu, *Essays and Poems*, p. 298.

[128] Hervey continues: 'he had, too, committed incest with his sister; that is he had two children by his wife's sister [Arabella], who was married to his most intimate friend Mr. Thompson, from whom, upon Sir George Oxenden's account, she was separated and died in childbed not without Sir George's being suspected of having a greater share in her catastrophe than merely having got the child. Besides this, Sir George Oxenden had debauched the wife of the eldest son of his friend, benefactor and patron, Sir Robert Walpole [...]. Lord Hervey, *Memoirs*, ed. by Romney Sedgewick (Harmondsworth: Penguin, 1984), p. 195.

[129] The other translation in Harrowby MS 250 is entitled 'The Greek of Moschus Paraphras'd'. In Harrowby MS 251, apart from the two Ovidian narratives, there are an English version of Virgil, 'The Tenth Eclogue of Virgil Imitated' and several 'Epistles' in imitation of Ovid. For these translations, Montagu actually employs a term associated with contemporary translation theory: 'paraphrase' or 'imitation'. See Grundy, 'The Verse of Lady Mary Wortley Montagu: A Critical Edition', pp. 244–5, pp. 286–7 and pp. 306–7 for her edited versions of the poems discussed in this chapter. I am, of course, also indebted to Isobel Grundy's work, here and elsewhere, on Montagu.

[130] Grundy, 'The Verse of Lady Mary Wortley Montagu: A Critical Edition', p. 19.

[131] Douglas Robinson's conclusion to 'Theorising Translation in A Woman's Voice' states that: 'A normative definition of theory by definition precludes (and thus blinds many scholars to) reflections, ponderings, remarks, insights that can be enormously productive in rethinking both translation today and its many historical metamorphoses in the past'. Douglas Robinson, 'Theorizing Translation in A Woman's Voice: Subverting the Rhetoric of Patronage, Courtly Love and Morality', *The Translator*, 1(1995), 153–75, 175.

[132] Trinh T. Minh-Ha, *Framer Framed* (London: Routledge, 1992), pp. 127–8.

[133] Julia Kristeva, *Nations Without Nationalism*, trans. by Leon S. Roudiez (New York: Columbia University Press, 1993), p. 17.

[134] Lines 25–8 cited in Montagu, *Essays and Poems*, pp. 238–40.

[135] There are many Greek precedents for the myth, for example Apollodorus's the *Library* (1. 4. 1, 3. 10. 4); the Homeric hymn To Delian Apollo (3); Hesiod's *Theogony* (404–10, 918–20). The myth is also referred to in Homer's the *Iliad* (1. 447–8) and the *Odyssey* (11. 576–81). See Eric Smith, *A Dictionary of Classical Reference in English Poetry* (Cambridge: Brewer, 1984), p. 134. Ovid presents Latona in a more detailed manner than these Greek antecedents.

[136] There is no evidence that Mary Wortley Montagu read this translation, but from her *Letters* it is known that she read Sandys's *A Relation of a Journey Begun An Dom. 1610*. Montagu, *The Complete Letters*, p. 419.

[137] Sandys, *Ovids Metamorphosis Englished*, 6. 341–2.

[138] Elizabeth D. Harvey, *Ventriloquized Voices: Feminist Theory and Renaissance Texts* (London: Routledge, 1992), p. 32.

[139] Isobel Grudy suggests that 'her [juvenile] verse was less responsive to the mythological narrative of [the *Metamorphoses*] than to the psychological self-dramatizations of the *Heroides*'. Isobel Grundy, '"The Entire Works of Clarinda": Unpublished Juvenile Verse by Lady Mary Wortley Montagu', *The Yearbook of English Studies*, 7 (1977), 91–107, 98.

[140] Grundy, '"The Entire Works of Clarinda"', p. 98.

[141] Catherine Belsey, 'The Name of the Rose in *Romeo and Juliet*', *Yearbook of English Studies*, 23, (1993), 127–42, 135.

[142] Whilst Harvey emphasizes the intertextuality of the *Metamorphoses*, and notes the importance of the Echo myth, it is significant that she does not tackle Ovid's 'ventriloquized cross–dressing' in this poem.

[143] Olga Grlic, 'Vernacular and Latin Readings of Ovid's *Metamorphosis* in the Middle Ages' (unpublished doctoral thesis, University of California at Berkeley, 1991), pp. 135–41. Grlic, rather surprisingly, neglects the tale of Salmacis and Hermaphroditus.

[144] Sandys, *Ovids Metamorphosis Englished*, 3. 261. ff.

[145] Sandys, *Ovids Metamorphosis Englished*, sig. K 3^r.

[146] Grundy, '"The Entire Works of Clarinda"', p. 92.

[147] Deborah Rubin, 'Sandys, Ovid and Female Chastity: The Encyclopedic Mythographer as Moralist', in *The Mythographic Art: Classical Fable and the Rise of the Vernacular in Early France and England*, ed. by Jane Chance (Gainesville: University of Florida Press, 1990), pp. 257–80, p. 258.

[148] Rubin, 'Sandys, Ovid and Female Chastity', p. 257.

[149] Sandys, *Ovids Metamorphosis*, sig. M 4^v, cited in Rubin, 'Sandys, Ovid and Female Chastity', p. 262.

[150] Tina Krontiris, *Oppositional Voices: Women as Writers and Translators of Literature in the English Renaissance* (London: Routledge, 1992), pp. 22–3.

[151] Sandys, *Ovids Metamorphosis Englished*, 10. 157–63.

[152] Grundy observes that 'the poetic anecdote which she entitles from 'From Ovid's *Metamorphoses*' has in fact no real parallel there'. Grundy, 'The Verse of Lady Mary Wortley Montagu: A Critical Edition', p. 19.

[153] Thomas Stanley, 'Epitaph on Adonis', in *Poems and Translations*, ed. by Galbraith Miller Crump (Oxford: Clarendon, 1962), pp. 101–5, lines 1–2, 8–11, 25–7.

[154] Stanley, 'Epitaph on Adonis', 29–31.

[155] Stanley, 'Epitaph on Adonis', 63–6.

[156] Catherine Belsey comments that 'the flower – beautiful, fragile, mutable, and all that remains of a youth who became an object of desire for the goddess of love – thus appears in its elusiveness the quintessential signifier of desire itself. Nor is it named: even the identity of the windflower is deferred for the reader, the unspecified answer to a kind of riddle constructed by the text'. Catherine Belsey, 'Love as Trompe–L'Oeil: Taxonomies of Desire in Venus and Adonis', *Shakespeare Quarterly*, 46 (1995), 257– 76, 261.

[157] Belsey, 'Love as Trompe–L'Oeil', p. 259

[158] Gertrude Stein, 'Poetry and Grammar', in *Look At Me Now And Here I Am*, ed. by Patricia Meyerowitz (London: Penguin, 1971), pp. 125–47, p. 138.

[159] This description of Derridean *différance* is from Lawrence Venuti, *The Translator's Invisibility* (London: Routledge, 1995), p. 17.

[160] All quotations are from Edmund Spenser, *The Faerie Queene*, ed. by A. C. Hamilton (London: Longman, 1977).

[161] Book 6's argument, for example, defines her as 'fayrest Pastorell'.

[162] A. C. Hamilton (ed.), *The Spenser Encyclopedia* (London: Routledge, 1990), p. 533.

[163] Spenser, *The Faerie Queene*, 6. 9. 9.

[164] Spenser, *The Faerie Queene*, 6. 9. 14.

[165] Spenser, *The Faerie Queene*, 6. 12. 6.

[166] Spenser, *The Faerie Queene*, 6. 12. 7

[167] Spenser, *The Faerie Queene*, 6. 12. 14.

[168] Spenser, *The Faerie Queene*, 6. 12. 18.

[169] Spenser, *The Faerie Queene*, p. 685, n..

[170] Barash, *English Women's Poetry 1649–1714*, p. 107.

[171] Montagu, *The Complete Letters*, p. 40. See also Nancy A. Mace, *Henry Fielding's Novels and the Classical Tradition* (London: Associated University Presses, 1996), p. 28.

Chapter 6

The Curious Case of Caxton's Ovid

If translation does not start as the original question then it is, at the very least, a start in the questioning of the origin.[1]

Framing Caxton's Ovid

The translations produced by Elizabeth Talbot, Elizabeth Singer Rowe, Mary Chudleigh and Mary Wortley Montagu are examples of the variable approaches that early modern women take to the *Metamorphoses* and the range of discourses – from the moral to the erotic – which are inscribed in their texts. In form and content, their works articulate the intricate ways in which subjectivities are interpellated through and in Ovidian translation. Nevertheless, their contributions to the history of Ovid in English have been largely ignored. Oddly similar is the translation which is the focus of this final chapter: William Caxton's prose manuscript rendition of the *Metamorphoses* (c. 1480). Whilst it may seem unusual to conclude with a discussion of the earliest translation, Caxton's Ovid provides a fitting point of departure for this study. The quotation from Andrew Benjamin which serves as the epigraph to this section suggests that translation may be perceived as a disruptive textual practice. The dialectical interplay between 'origin' and 'copy' that resides in translation interrogates orthodox assumptions about temporality and linearity. Described as a 'false start' in the poem's vernacular genealogy,[2] Caxton's Ovid seems to justify Benjamin's claims that 'if translation does not start as the original question then it is, at the very least, a start in the questioning of the origin'. Indeed, as we shall see, this fifteenth-century *Metamorphoses*, a text which loiters in the margins of the early modern period, engages with the cultural politics of translation in fifteenth-century England and troubles the definition of translation itself.

In the Prologue to his translation Caxton sets out the text's didactic purpose:

> Alle scriptures and wrytyngis ben they good or evyll ben wreton for our prouffyt and doctryne. The good to thende to take ensample by them to doo well. And the evyll to thende that we sholde kepe and absteyne us to do evyll. Hyt is sayd comunely and it is trouth that wysdom or scyence hyd is but lost. and is moche to be desprysed And therfore it ought not to be hyd but to publysshe and shewe it unto them that can not ne knowe it not. For whych cause I wil recyte aftir myn Auctour Ovyde the fables of the olde and anncyent tyme aftir that I understande by my symple and lytyl understandyng. (fols. 16ʳ–16ᵛ)[3]

Employing the conventions of Pauline exegesis, the Prologue declares its aim to 'publysshe' (make publicly known) Ovid's narratives as moral *exempla*.[4] In practice, however, Caxton's rendition of the classical poem has had little impact upon critical sensibilities. Rosemond Tuve's study of the influences of medieval allegory on the literary culture of the sixteenth and seventeenth centuries, for example, declines to discuss Caxton's Ovid 'because it had no currency'.[5] In one sense, of course, Tuve's exclusion of the text from her discussion is apt; Caxton's translation is known only through a single manuscript, and there is no evidence that it was printed. To be sure, Tuve's comments emphasize the limited agency of this single manuscript when compared with other extant versions of Ovid's *Metamorphoses* published in England in the early modern period,[6] and this perspective has remained the dominant one, particularly in English literary studies. In another sense, though, Tuve's explanation avoids the most interesting problems raised by Caxton's Ovid which are concerned with translation and critical practice.

This is a difficult text for modern criticism to come to terms with, partly because

> in analytic terms, we are not skilled in discussing imitative works as imitations. Once we have noted a so-called model or source, we are only beginning to understand the model as a constitutive element of the literary structure, an element whose dynamic presence has to be accounted for [...]. For once the positivist stage of investigation is passed, then the structures of imitative texts confront one with the enigmas of literary history, enigmas that call into question the meaning of periodization, the nature of historical understanding, the precise operations of change, the diachronic nature of language.[7]

Although Thomas Greene is explicitly discussing the related figure of *imitatio* rather than *translatio*, his remarks in this quotation are useful for thinking about the general ways in which translation throws fixed notions of history and the transparency of meaning in language into disarray. In the concluding chapter of *The Translator's Invisibility*, provocatively entitled 'Call to Action', Lawrence Venuti states that 'because translation is a double writing, a rewriting of the foreign text according to domestic cultural values, any translation requires a double reading – as both communication and inscription'.[8] Venuti's concerns with '*double* writing' and '*double* reading' (phrases which recall the humanist practice of '*double* translation'),[9] evoke the inherently excessive nature of translation. Dialogic from the outset, the textual surfeit of translated texts rupture ideological boundaries which seek to encase them; contemporary criticism is one such frame.

The fact that there is little commentary on Caxton's Ovid suggests that it is a text which has perpetually confounded literary critics who lack a vocabulary with which to speak of it. Raphael Lyne's comments hint at this terminological poverty:

> The 'translation' of Ovid that emerges from the cradle of printing is not a humanist triumph of classical learning but William Caxton's verbatim version of a French redacation of the *Ovide moralisé*.[10]

Here Caxton's text is relegated to a subordinate position in relation to Arthur Golding's *Metamorphoses* (1567), the 'humanist triumph of classical learning' to which Lyne refers. These remarks help to demonstrate that when Caxton's Ovid is invoked it is most often in an aside or a footnote which unfavourably compares it with another text, in this case the sixteenth-century translation. Whilst this chapter will show that Lyne's use of the adjective 'verbatim' to describe Caxton's Ovid is somewhat problematic, the most arresting aspect of Lyne's discussion is the term 'translation'. Undoubtedly, Caxton's Ovid has a very different lineage than Golding's text. However, the quotation marks which the frame this key word suggest that the fifteenth-century prose manuscript, apparently rendered word for word from intermediary French sources into the vernacular, is not worthy of such a definition. Yet Caxton's Ovid is thoroughly inscribed with, and marked by, the cultural politics of translation.

Tropes of translation characterize much of Caxton's biographical detail, from the early period of his life as a mercer involved in overseas trade, to the 1460s when he was governor of the English nation in Bruges and, of course, to textual production. Much of Caxton's translative impetus may have been initiated through the years that he 'lived within the territory of the Dukes of Burgundy'.[11] According to Norman Blake, during this time Caxton may have become

> acquainted with the two secular libraries in Burgundy, one belonging to the Dukes themselves and the other to Louis of Bruges, Seigneur de la Gruthuyse, for he had business associations with some of the booksellers who provided books for them. He would almost certainly have accepted these libraries as the ideal to be followed by any collector. He was not alone. When Edward IV fled to the Low Countries in 1470 he stayed with Louis of Bruges and was greatly impressed with his host's library. When Edward returned to England he extended his own library to make it more fashionable by buying foreign manuscripts. [...] In chivalry and courtly behaviour England looked to Burgundy for a lead.[12]

By producing the first complete *Metamorphoses* in English (a text which he may have come across in the ducal libraries), Caxton responds to contemporaneous pressures for vernacular manuscript volumes with a courtly flavour,[13] whilst engaging with fifteenth-century scenes of English translation in notable ways.

Indeed, as the Prohemye to Caxton's Ovid examines the classical poet's appropriation of earlier Greek and Latin texts, the topic of literary translation is raised at the outset. According to Caxton, 'the name Methamorphose' may be interpreted as the

> transmutacion of one fable in to another or interpretacion of theym for he seeng as wel the latyn poetes as the poetes of Grece that hade ben to fore hym and hys tyme hade touched in wrytyng many fables and them passed superfycyelly without expressynge theyre knowlege or entendement. The sayde Ovide hath opend unto the latyns the way as wel in the fables of Grekes as in other And hath them tyssued and woven by so grete subtyltee [...] and solitcytude in suche wyse that one by that other that it myght be sayde very semblably that they depended one of another [...]. (fols. 13^r–13^v)

Quintilian observes that the *Metamorphoses* 'welds together subjects of the most diverse nature so as to form a continuous whole';[14] similarly, Caxton's translation emphasizes Ovid's enterprise. A few folios later, the Prohemye provides detail of the current translation:

> Many have essayed and begonne this werke withoute fynysshyng and accomplysshynge of the same. And how be it that in me is nomore wytte ne understandyng than in them that supposed to have ended it Nevertheles I wyll sette my trust and affyance in almyghty god that hydeth hys werkes frome saige and wyse folk and reveleth and sheweth to humble and smale chyldren. the which gyve and graunte me to translate this werke that all men may take therby ensample to doo well and eschewe evyll And my mater well to begynne and better contynue And best of all to brynge to a ryght good ende. (fol. 16ᵛ)

In keeping with much of the material in Caxton's *Metamorphoses*, the Prohemye is a version of the kind of prologue found in the French vernacular prose and verse translations of Ovid's text. Comparison with a prose manuscript, London British Library Royal 17. E. iv and with Colard Mansion's printed prose translation (1484),[15] 'a French prose version of the *Metamorphoses* with allegorical interpretations derived from Pierre Bersuire's Latin *Ovidius moralizatus* and the *Ovide moralise'*,[16] shows that common ground is shared here and throughout the translation. As in the French moralized tradition, Caxton's Prohemye makes God the prime mover and Ovid the 'moved efficient cause'.[17] Yet the prefatory material which accompanies Caxton's translation is unhelpful about the circumstances of its own production. The translator's modest assertion that he intends 'to translate this sayd book of Methamorphose in to Anglysshe tonge aftir the lytyl connyng that god hath departed to me' (fol. 15ʳ)' obscures the relationship between the source text and the English rendition. Whilst the Prohemye alludes to others who have 'essayed and begonne this werke without fynysshyng', Caxton's textual adversaries remain anonymous.

Caxton's Ovid is an enigmatic text in many ways. Almost from the moment of its completion (and certainly from the end of the sixteenth century), Caxton's translation was not available as a whole, until books 1 to 9 were rediscovered in 1964.[18] The first nine books become separated from the final six at some point, and what happened to that portion of the text until 1964 is likely to remain a mystery. Before the recovery of this material, H. F. Brett-Smith, using the usual model for Caxton's prologues which offer details about production and patronage, discussed what the missing folios might contain:

> there are some things indeed that might reasonably be expected in a prologue to one of Caxton's versions from the French. He would first have paid tribute to the patron who had set him upon the task, and would have acknowledged that the book had been translated out of French into English according to the simple and rude cunning that God had lent him, disclaiming for himself any beauty or good endyting.[19]

If Brett-Smith's conjecture was correct the manuscript may have been produced for either one of his best-known dedicatees: Margaret of York, Duchess of Burgundy and the sister of Edward IV, or Elizabeth Woodville, the King's wife.[20] The four illustrations subsequently found in the first volume suggest that Caxton's Ovid was intended for a wealthy audience.[21] However, the Prologue to Caxton's Ovid defies the common paradigm that Brett-Smith considers. The one clue about its provenance is the colophon on the final folio which states that the *Metamorphoses* was translated and finished by William Caxton at Westminster, 22 April 1480; the site of his printing press, established c. 1477, which was conveniently situated for the British court.[22] The only other information that Caxton provides about the translation's origins is found in his Prologue to the *Golden Legend* (1483), where he comments that 'the xv bookes of Metamorphoseos in whyche ben conteyned the fables of ovyde' are amongst 'dyvers werkys and hystoryes translated out of frensshe in to englysshe at the requeste of certeyn lordes, ladyes and gentylmen'.[23] Retrospectively, Caxton announces that his Ovidian translation is from French sources, a detail that he omits in the Prohemye to the translation itself. With no fixed source text, known patron or clear history of production, Caxton's Ovid becomes an object of historical contestation and appropriation in discourses other than those of textual criticism.

Translation and Currency

The fractional, material history of Caxton's Ovid mirrors the aporias surrounding its sources and literary traditions. The manuscript's marginal signatures give some indication of that history. The name of a well-known sixteenth-century collector of books and Old English manuscripts, Lord John Lumley is inscribed on the opening folio of the volume containing books 10–15, evidence perhaps that the manuscript had become divided by his lifetime.[24] On 12 March 1688 this part of the manuscript reappears in an anonymous auction catalogue. The record shows that Samuel Pepys bought the manuscript; there are no details of the time or manner of purchase and Pepys does not account for its acquisition elsewhere. As a mark of ownership, Pepys printed his portrait in the space left for the illustration to book 10. Arguably, Pepys used the manuscript as an object with which to speak of his own erudition. A letter from John Evelyn to Pepys on 12 August 1689 betrays the ideological impulses which lay behind such book collecting:

> Your library being by this accession made suitable to your generous mind and steady virtue, I know none living master of more happiness, since besides the possession of so many curiosities, you understand to use and improve them likewise, and have declared that you will endeavour to secure what with so much cost and industry you have collected, from the sad dispersions many noble libraries and cabinets have suffered in these late times: one auction, I may call it diminution, of a day or two, having scattered what has been gathering these many years. Hence it is that we are in England so defective of good libraries among the gentlemen, and in our greatest towns: Paris alone, I am persuaded, being able to

show more than all the three nations of Great Britain [...]. This great and august
city of London, abounding with so many wits and lettered persons, has scarce one
library furnished and endowed for the public.[25]

The letter is an overt acclamation of the Pepysian individualist project. In a wider
social and historical context, Evelyn's remarks also bear witness to the
preservation of manuscripts, cabinets and all manner of rare and curious objects as
a means of improving the intellectual status of the nation, particularly in
comparison with the French.[26] The correspondence addresses tensions similar to
those existing some hundred years earlier, when the translation of texts into the
vernacular was called for as part of the Renaissance mission of *copia verborum*.
For these Restoration men of letters, though, there is a rather different sense of the
rivalry between England and France. In late seventeenth-century England, as
Richard Kroll discusses, 'the circulation of artifacts' works to 'restrengthen the
sinews of the body politic';[27] an idea which Evelyn's further remarks support:

> But there is hope his Majesty's [library] at Saint James's may emerge and be in
> some measure restored again [...].There are in it a great many noble manuscripts
> yet remaining, besides the *Tecla*; and more would be did some royal or generous
> hand cause those to be brought back to it, which still are lying in mercenary hands
> for want of two or three hundred pounds to pay for their binding; many of which
> being in Oriental tongues, will soon else find Jews and chapmen that will purchase
> and transport them, from whence we shall never retrieve them again.[28]

Evelyn's censorious and caustic comments are made in the name of the aesthetic
rather than the economic interests which are clearly at work here. Though mostly
relegated to the footnotes and the margins of literary history, it is noteworthy that
the circulation of Caxton's Ovid can be traced most visibly through financial
records. Excluded from vernacular linguistic currency, Caxton's Ovid existed in
the early modern period principally as a curious object within a system of
economic exchange.

When he died in 1709, Pepys left his collection to Magdalene College,
Cambridge. George Hibbert edited a version of Caxton's Ovid from Pepys's
manuscript for the Roxburghe Club in 1819, but when Montague Rhodes James
catalogued the medieval manuscripts in the Pepysian library in 1923, he omitted
any mention of the fifteenth-century manuscript.[29] Once again, the translation is
buried in history, only reappearing in 1964. Books 1 to 9 were found in a pile of
paper in the library of antiquary and bibliophile Thomas Phillipps: in 1966, the
manuscript was sold at an auction of Phillipps's collection at Sotheby's.[30] During
1966–68 the *Times Literary Supplement* ran a series of short articles campaigning
to keep the complete manuscript in the United Kingdom, and these pieces have
formed the most sustained discussion of the complete translation to date. Lawrence
Venuti has described 'the translator's invisibility';[31] the history of the reception of
Caxton's Ovid amongst readers and critics alike is more suggestive of the
translation's invisibility. Though Caxton's role as translator has been well
documented, this particular text has been repeatedly overlooked. Like the return of

the repressed, however, the temporary reappearances of the divided manuscript at different historical moments have left their marks on its surface.

The frontispiece of the so-called 'Pepys's manuscript', displaying Pepys's portrait and Lumley's autograph, is just one example of this temporal inscription; there are also a number of signatures from other periods which chart the manuscript's circulation. The names of Rychard Wastffeld (at the foot of fol. 399ʳ) and Audley Seeley (in a blank space at the bottom of the final folio), both in a sixteenth-century hand, appear in the second volume of the translation.[32] At the foot of fol. 143ʳ of the first volume, and also produced in the sixteenth century, is the maxim 'a fraynde is to hys fraynd a nother to hym self': the name Tamesyn Audeley is written underneath the phrase in seventeenth-century script.[33] Like many medieval manuscripts, Caxton's Ovid invited its early modern readers to mark their identities upon the page.[34] Critics who have attempted to write *about* Caxton's Ovid, rather than *on* it, however, have usually been motivated by different cultural and political desires.

Hence, the attempt to situate Caxton's translation within the vernacular tradition, whilst keeping it firmly in its place as subordinate translation, becomes focused upon the now canonical figure of John Gower. As the title of Christopher Ricks's essay '*Metamorphoses* in Other Words' suggests, Gower's use of metamorphic myths in the *Confessio Amantis* is so extensive that it might even be considered a translation of Ovid's text.[35] However, as Rick's definition of 'Gower's enterprise [as] a meta-metamorphosis of Ovid's *Metamorphoses*'[36] illustrates, the set of textual practices used to produce the *Confessio* are clearly different from those of Caxton's Ovid. Caxton published the *Confessio* in 1483, three years after the manuscript of his English *Metamorphoses* was completed, the publication thus forming a link between Caxton and Gower that would be developed in later criticism. Although Brett-Smith and Stephen Gaselee comment that Caxton had added a 'touch of the unfamiliar' to Ovid's story of Ceyx and Alcyone,[37] J. A. W. Bennett begins to construct a hierarchical relationship between the two writers which undermines Brett-Smith and Gaselee's observation. The later critic argues that

> in 1480 Caxton prepared a version of the *Metamorphoses*, basing it on a French translation [...]. If we compare his version of the story of Ceyx and Alcyone with Gower's, it becomes evident that when he came to this point he consulted, or remembered, Gower's rendering of it in the *Confessio*.[38]

Bennett places Gower's text alongside a Latin version of the *Metamorphoses* in order to demonstrate how Gower, not Caxton as Brett-Smith and Gaselee thought, deviates from an apparent 'source'. Bennett contends that 'Gower has turned Juno's injunction into *oratio obliqua*, Iris's *velamina mille colorum* into a "reyny Cope [...] begon with colours of diverse hewe", and glossed *ebenus* as "that slepi tree"'.[39] His assertion that Caxton's Ovid uses phrases taken directly from the *Confessio* is accentuated in a later article:

That in any case Caxton did not follow his original word by word we know from various passages in the Pepysian part. Thus when he comes to tell – and how well he tells it! – the story of Ceyx and Alcyone he says that Iris 'dyde on hys rayny cope. And descended by the firmament by hys bowe which was bende and dyversly colowred', by the house of the god of sleep a brook 'resouneth for to gyve apetyte to slepe', and the god's couch was made 'of Hebenus that sleepi tree'. None of these phrases are to be found in the French: they come straight out of Gower's memorable version of the story in *Confessio Amantis*.[40]

Thus Caxton's Ovid is an example of intralingual as well as interlingual Ovidian translation. Yet the significant observation that Bennett makes about Caxton's divergence from the supposed source text is obscured by his excitement about the Gowerian involvement in the enterprise.

Against Bennett's exclamation we would do well to set Conrad Mainzer's important caveat:

> In the thirteenth century, there were few manuscripts of the *Metamorphoses* without glosses or commentaries. In connection with the *Metamorphoses* a moralizing interpretation had arisen; this apparently occurred as early as the eleventh century [...]. In attaching named moralizing interpretations to Gower's stories, one must keep in mind that the authors of these works were themselves working against the background of the glossed texts; for instance, the author of the *Ovide moralisé* several times cites the glosses as his authority. Details in common to Gower's stories and the moralizing interpretations could well have been common also to the glosses and commentaries at this time.[41]

In order to demonstrate its textual variants, Bennett compares Gower only with a modern edition of Ovid's Latin text and, in doing so, elides the intermediate steps between the two. But handling the cluster of Ovidian commentaries and glosses in circulation from the eleventh to the fourteenth centuries, as Mainzer indicates, requires careful negotiation. These difficulties are amplified when working with both Latin and vernacular versions of the *Metamorphoses*. In order to construct Gower as 'original' author, Bennett's article greatly simplifies the complex processes of comparative analysis. Until the total manuscript tradition of the *Metamorphoses* is examined – a seemingly impossible task – the link between these writers cannot be explained, simply, as Gower's influence upon Caxton.

J. D. Burnley's discussion of *enditer*, *compilator* and the 'uncertain relationship between translated text and original' in the Middle Ages usefully demonstrates that 'the cult of authorial personality was only just emerging, and the formulation of literary values had not such a grip as they do upon modern scholars'.[42] Burnley's comments not only disrupt the hierarchical relationship between translated text and original, they also highlight the historical and cultural differences between medieval and modern critical sensibilities. Although the name of Gower has featured in the canon of English literature from the late sixteenth century onwards,[43] over the last forty years or so the study of the *Confessio Amantis* has moved from the margins of medieval literature to the central canon of Middle English.[44] 'The concept of the original', as Susan Bassnett has argued, 'is a modern invention, belonging to a materialist age, and carries with it all kinds of commercial implications about translation, originality and textual ownership'.[45] Evidently, this post-Enlightenment, hierarchical thinking about literary texts which constructs Gower as original author against secondary translator is inscribed in the critical treatment of Caxton's Ovid. As Gower's skill as 'creator' has been increasingly revered, Caxton's translation of the *Metamorphoses* has been ignored.[46] Bennett's argument displays a mid-twentieth-century desire to relegate Caxton's translation, along with translated texts in general, to the margins of critical discussion, in order to fashion Gower as an 'original' author. This is not to suggest that the link between Caxton and Gower is illusory. Rather, it is the inherent ideological assumptions of Bennett's critical practices that construct Caxton's Ovid as a secondary text.

Towards a Cultural Politics of Caxton's Ovid

Literary translations, then, unsettle the hierarchical binary opposition of 'original' and 'copy'. Indeed, 'they pose serious challenges to our canons and to critical narratives about those canons'.[47] What becomes most visible in translation, however, 'is language referring not to things, but to language itself'.[48] Viewed in this way, translation becomes a thoroughly disturbing process at the level of the signifier. This disquieting facet of textuality is evoked in Caxton's Ovid.

A decade after the completion of his translation of the *Metamorphoses*, the Prologue to Caxton's English translation of Virgil's *Aeneid*, defined by Eugene Vance as a 'footloose French paraphrase,'[49] describes the dynamism and intralingual complexities of fifteenth-century English:

> certaynly our language now used varyeth ferre from that whiche was used and spoken whan I was borne/ For we englysshe men/ ben borne under the domynacyon of the mone, which is never stedfaste/ but ever wavereth/ wexyng one season/ and waneth and discreaseth another season/ And that comyn englysshe that is spoken in one shyre varieth from another.[50]

Caxton's depiction of vernacular heteroglossia which prefaces his Virgilian rendition, linguistic differences which fragment 'the myth of a language that' in later historical periods 'presumes to be completely unified',[51] are evident in his Ovidian translation. The first folios of Caxton's translation take the form of a detailed 'table of this booke' (ff. 1^r–9^v). In the midst of this opening catalogue, designed to assist the reader's navigation through particular Ovidian episodes and their accompanying allegorical expositions, is the distinctive description which anticipates the story of Pallas and Yranes. The table announces that this tale is

> Of the debate that was betwen Pallas and yranes And how Pallas torned her in to a loppe or spyder [...]. How Yranes henge her self And how Pallas torned her in to an Yrane or a loppe or a spither or a spyncoppe. (fols. 4^r–4^v)

It is striking that Yranes's transformation into a spider is variously defined: as loppe, spyder, yrane, spither and spyncoppe. Drawing on words that have etymological resonances with Old English ('loppe', 'spither' and 'spyder'), Dutch and Flemish ('spyncoppe') and French ('yranes'),[52] this passage promotes the textuality of translation through the figure of the Lydian girl who is known for the weaving of texts and Ovidian adaptation.

This eye-catching description of Yranes emphasizes the complex,[53] figurative association 'between weaving (textiles) and language (texts) [which] becomes so entangled as to be almost impossible to separate'.[54] Notably, Caxton's treatment of the Ovidian myth exposes the ideological discourses which attempt to fix meaning in language. The violent nature of this episode has been discussed at length in the previous chapter, but Caxton's depiction of how the goddess 'brake the cloth and smote with the swerd that she hade many strokes on the heed of Yranes' (fol. 163ᵛ), takes an even more aggressive turn. Instead of beating the girl with a wooden shuttle, the goddess's tormenting instrument in Golding's translation and a punishment already painful enough to encourage Yranes's suicide, Caxton's Pallas 'smote' her with a sword; a verb which marks the girl as defiled subject as it simultaneously describes the action of physical abuse.[55]

As the contest between goddess and a girl who was 'come of lowe kynred' (fol. 160ᵛ) is explained in the 'sens hystoryal to the fable', Caxton's Ovid inflects this myth of textile production, authority and subjection with further social tensions:

> By this ensample of Yranes. late everyman beware and absteyne hym to gayn saye
> and stryve ayenst hys maistre. or agayn hym that is strenger than he is hym self.
> Alway the rych wynneth And the poure man may have no ryghte. (fol. 164ᵛ)

As part of a manuscript which seems likely (though not conclusively) to have been produced for an affluent audience, the allegory may address the concerns of this implied reader. Though Yranes is not constructed as a sympathetic protagonist, the myth's brusque conclusion that 'alway the rych wynneth And the poure man may have no ryghte' throws the economic base at the heart of social and cultural difference into relief. Moreover, if the manuscript was produced for either Margaret of York or Elizabeth Woodville, Caxton's translation would fit easily into the familiar hierarchical paradigm of male translator/woman reader which has been explored throughout this book. The frustrating lack of dedicatory material and other factual details about the translation's production prohibits such a specific analysis. Nonetheless, as with all of the translations explored in this study, Caxton's Ovid is a discursive site for the sexual politics of the period in which the translation is produced. In this respect, Valerie Traub's brief discussion of Caxton's translation of the myth of Iphis and Ianthe from book 9 of the *Metamorphoses* which condemns sex between women is worth considering in more detail.[56]

After Ovid, Caxton's translation tells of how Ligdus, a 'baron noble and ryche' (fol. 268ᵛ), regretfully warns his pregnant wife, Thelecusa, that 'yf ye have a daughter beware that I see it not. but do it anon to be slayn' (f. 268ᵛ). In Ligdus's opinion, 'a woman hath overmoch annoye and gryef. [...] A woman is withoute strength and valour. By women many there be put to gret shame and sorow' (f. 268ᵛ). Accordingly, Thelecusa conceals the subsequent birth of her daughter from her husband by successfully disguising the child, Yphis, as a boy. Ovid's myth thus begins as a depiction of women's subjugation in the hands of men. Once Yphis's father arranges the betrothal between his fair 'son' and the equally beautiful Yente, however, the narrative becomes one of the poem's tales of frustrated sexual appetite and cultural taboos.[57] Clearly attracted to Yente, Yphis 'laments that her desire for another woman is monstrous and unnatural':[58] she cries that the gods 'destroye' her 'by this fowle amerous rage' (fol. 270ᵛ). As her wedding day approaches, the prospect of sexual disappointment lies ahead: 'in the myddes of the water we shal deye for thurst. ffor I may not doo with her as a man ought to do with hys wyf' (fol. 271ʳ). In the end, however, there is a fruitful resolution. At the behest of Thelecusa and her disguised daughter, the gods change Yphis into the boy that she longs to be. Now the youth

> hade lasse white in her vysage than she had before And her heers were shorter and harder And she was more vygorous and stronger than she hade ben tofore ne than woman myght be by nature She had chaunged al her femenyne nature in to masculyne. Thus as ye have herd became Yphis a strong and a fayre yong man. (fol. 272ʳ)

By way of Ligdus's pejorative analysis of women, Ovid exposes the cultural construction of gender roles. As Olga Grlic observes, 'there is no doubt that in the *Metamorphoses* the changes from female to male are perceived as an improvement of status, a reward or compensation, in any case, a step up in the hierarchy of beings, whereas the reverse transformation carries the connotation of debasement and degradation'.[59] However, in the myth's description of gender reconfiguration there is one aspect of Yphis's 'masculyne nature' which is missing from the narrative's catalogue of corporeal change.

Though Ovid's myth delineates desire between women, in order to consummate that desire fifteenth-century women have to emulate heterosexual activity. This stance is plainly expressed in Caxton's exposition of the tale:

> It may wel be that in ancyent tyme was a woman that ware the habyte of a man whych semed a man And they that saw her had supposed well that she so had be [...] And it myght hapen that some fair mayde sawe her fair gente and plaisant in thabyte of a man and byleved that she was a man and desired to have her in maryage And she whyche was folysh [...] espoused her how wel she hade not thynstruments of nature [...] so moche complayned she that the folysshe love tempted her that by tharte and craft of an old and evil bawde achievyd her fowl desyre by a membre apostat and deceyved this wif. whiche by lawe of mariage ought not to have her And whan she apperceyved it she hydd it no but shewd and told it. Wherof she had ever aftir all her lyf shame and vylonye and was sore blamed And that other fledd and absented her fro the contrey. Now ther be none that have to doo with suche werke. ffor it is overmoch vylanous [...]. (fols. 272ʳ–3ᵛ)

Before her transformation Yphis 'hade not thynstruments of nature': the gods have clearly added this crucial body part. In the absence of an Ovidian *deus ex machina*, fifteenth-century women may be assisted by 'on old and evil bawde' in their quest to achieve their 'fowl desyre'. Deuteronomy 22.5 states that women 'shall not wear that which pertaineth unto [men]',[60] thus the classical myth's cross-dressing premise immediately contravenes Christian doctrine. As Yphis wore men's clothes as a means of social integration, Caxton's Christian allegory tells its reader that women use a 'membre apostat' in order to engage sexually with other women; a far more significant transgression: 'the use of "instruments" such as dildos was considered far more serious than simple rubbing or mutual masturbation'.[61] In the words of Hincmor of Reims, women

> do not put flesh to flesh in the sense of the genital organ of one within the body of the other, since nature precludes this, but they do transform the use of the member in question into an unnatural one, in that they are reported to use certain instruments of diabolical operation to execute desire. Thus they sin nonetheless by committing fornication against their own bodies.[62]

Diane Watt states that 'such sex came under the definition of sodomy, [yet] there is little or no surviving evidence in England or Wales of women being examined about sexual misconduct with women'.[63] Given its general accommodation of patriarchal ideologies, Caxton's translation is concerned to dispatch Ovid's sodomitical tale to history, asserting that 'now ther be none that have to doo with suche werke'. Yet even as it seeks to render such acts invisible, like Ovid's Ligdus, Caxton's moral bears traces of an ideological agenda which takes female sexuality seriously when it 'threaten[s] male privilege or the natural hierarchy of genders'.[64]

Sex between women, therefore, is a taboo subject. Anxieties about other communities of women also pervade Caxton's Ovid. A marked example of this tension is found in Caxton's version of the myth of Salmacys and Hermofrodytus, the Ovidian episode which, as we have seen in Chapter 3, became a popular myth in the sixteenth and seventeenth centuries: here, it is told completely for the first time in the vernacular.[65] Found in book 4 of the *Metamorphoses*, Salmacys and Hermofrodytus is the final story told by the daughters of Minyas; the rebellious women who defy the Bacchanalic laws of their country by weaving. As they spin, they tell tales: a further level of transgression. Warren Ginsberg has observed that 'the Minyaides represent the Roman ideal of women, that is they remain inside the house. And yet, by their conscious decision to suppress passion and act rationally they also behave in manly fashion.'[66] Significantly, the narrators' capacity to aggravate the cultural norms of gender construction extends to their own stories. Caxton's Lenchotoe mentions another tale which could be told in place of the one about Salmacys and Hermofrodytus:

> Also I coud tell you how Syton dyversyfyed hym self agaynst nature in suche wyse that on houre he was a man and another he was a woman. This Syton entremeted hym of grete fylthe. ffor he was one tyme Actyf And another tyme passyf. (fol. 111ᵛ)

Even before Caxton's Ovid provides the etiological and allegorical account of the hermaphrodite, a contemptuous attitude toward 'deviant' gender positions is apparent. Lenchotoe states that Salmacys is a 'mayd [...] that alway had be ydle. ffor she had never lerned to do ony werke' (fol. 112^r), a description which aligns the nymph with the stereotypical medieval figure of Idleness.[67] These malignant qualities are developed further as Lenchotoe describes the way that she 'aourned and arrayed her right curyously' (fol. 112^v). Stephen Scrope's translation of Christine's de Pizan's *L'Epître d'Othea a Hector* (c. 1400), constructed as text, gloss and allegory, obliquely draws upon the Ovidian episode in order to demonstrate that 'it is vileine and a fowl thing to refuse or to graunte with greet daunger that the which may not turne to vice ne prejudice, though it may be granted'.[68] Yet the focus of Scrope's translation is not the figure of Salmacys; in this version, the pursuer of 'Hermofrodicus' is merely called 'the fayrie'.[69] By contrast, Caxton's Salmacys is associated with corporeality and physical desire and, in the manner of Echo before her and Venus, who comes after, she transgresses the cultural boundary of female passivity by approaching her object of desire, Hermofrodytus.

The myth's interest in gender and sexuality is developed through the relationship between women, speech and vice: 'As soone as she had seen the yong man she was sore esprysed wyth his love and came anon to Hermofrodytus and began to resone with hym' (fol. 112^r). Following Ovid, Caxton's Salmacys takes on the masculine role of spectator. As she watches the youth, Salmacys mimics the words spoken by Odysseus to Nausicaa in book 6 of the *Odyssey*.[70] Whereas Odysseus's speech is deemed 'subtle', however, the reasoning attributed to Salmacys by Caxton's translation forms part of her defamation. Negative perceptions of the nymph are heightened by Hermofrodytus's response: he 'spake not one worde' (f. 112^v). By inhabiting the conventionally masculine roles of voyeur, hunter and rhetorician, Salmacys is condemned in the moralized tradition.[71] Caxton explains:

> By Salmacys is understonden woman that setteth alle her entente [...] to kymbe. pyk and aourne her wyth gaye and fresshe aray for to abuse the musards and fooles. and wil use alle her lyf in vanytees. lustes and delytes of the flessh They ben fooles and [...] that [...] flee not from suche wymen (fol. 114^r)

This particular notion of women is upheld in the text's treatment of the daughters of Minyas themselves. In the *Ovide moralisé*, these women can be read in opposing ways; either as disobeying the Word of God, or as signifying the three estates of perfection.[72] Caxton's Ovid, however, erases the ambiguity:

> They that despyse bachus are they that drynke not wyne oultrageously And also they that sette not by drynkynge. ffor thise III. susters dranke oultrageously. And what ever they gate with spynnynge.tyssuyinge or cardynge. they despended it in mete and drynke. And for taccomplysshe the same they dispended alle theyre clothes and other thyngs. (fol. 114^v)

The Minyaides are figured as 'material girls' and, as such, they have much in common with Salmacys. Caxton's translation plainly regards their transformation into bats, a biform creature categorized in Leviticus 11.23 and Deuteronomy 14.18 as 'unclean', as a punishment:

> And thus they were naked and bare of all goodes. Wherfore the fable fayneth that
> they wer transformed in to backes that nothyng have But the skynne only and abyde
> in derk places. (fol. 114^v)

For those familiar with typical medieval representations of women, the translation may present few novelties. But Caxton's treatment of this myth, like that of Pallas and Arachne, keenly points out the dangers of transgressive behaviour for its English reader.

One further, and arguably fundamental, example of this ideological underpinning may be found in Caxton's rendition of the Narcissus episode, that archetypal myth of identity and difference. Ovid's Narcissus, aged sixteen and neither man nor boy, shuns love; paradoxically, both men and women love him. In the Middle Ages, the tale of Narcissus was most commonly used as a warning against the sin of pride. However, Alain de Lille employed the myth 'to illustrate the danger of self-love, that is, the danger of love of a body for another of the same kind'.[73] In his description of 'how Narcissus went to the fountayne where he sawe hys umbre or shadowe on which he was enamoured (fol. 87^r), Caxton introduces the tale according to typical medieval conventions: he tells of how 'Narcissus despysed Echo and many other damoyselless. to whom he wolde in no wyse graunte theyre request ne never enjoyed ony of them of his love' (fol. 87^r). As a result of the youth's dismissive behaviour, the women pray to God that he will suffer as much as they do and he is duly punished. With reference to the courtly discourse used in the 1480 translation of the *Metamorphoses*, Douglas Bush announces that Caxton adds 'something rich and strange' to Ovid's poem: 'Hector and Achilles are medieval knights [...] and romance is more romantic, more magical, than in Ovid':[74] an observation which may be usefully developed in terms of Caxton's depiction of Narcissus.

Whilst the allegory states that the youth 'hated both men and women' (fol. 90^r), once Narcissus reaches the fountain Caxton's Ovid situates the classical figure in a courtly romance:

> and anone as he saw hys fayre vysage he thought and wened it had been som lady or
> damoyselle And forthwyth he was so esprysed of hys love as he that never had felte
> what thynge it was to love. [...] And many tymes he kyssed the water. and hym
> semed he kissed her and that she kyssed hym. And after he put in his armes wenynge
> to have take her. Narcissus sette [...] his entente for to beholde his owne ymage
> withyn the fontayne. he coude not leve ne withdrawe his syghte fro it. [...] Thenne
> he adressed hym and stood up on his feet and began to make pyetous bewayllyng
> [...]. Whan I bowe me to kysse her that I see in the water on who I have sette al the
> love of my herte the fontayne taketh [...] and me semeth that I have her but alway I
> faylle. (fols. 87^v–8^r)

Enamoured with what he thinks is a woman, Narcissus's demise is based on his failure to engage in a heterosexual relationship.[75] His dramatic declaration of 'iste ego sum [I am that he]',[76] a phrase encompassing the complex gender politics at stake in Ovid's myth, is eclipsed in Caxton's translation thus: 'I am the requyrant and also that is requyred' (fols. 88ᵛ). By negotiating the homosocial aspects of the tale in this way, Caxton's youth becomes subject to general, rather than gendered, cathexes of desire.

With its interest in the punishment of moral turpitude, Caxton's Ovid maintains the common conventions of its didactic antecedents. This ideological revision of the classical text is clearly shown in the illustration depicting 'How Ovide at the beginning of his booke maketh Invocation for helpe and dyvyne ayde' (fol. 17ʳ). To accompany the image of the supplicant poet, the Prohemye offers its readers the conventional medieval apology for poetry and instructions for the Christian appropriation of pagan mythology:

> How be it ther ben many that bycause of ygnorance blamen or at leste despysen. and despreysen the Arte or Science called and named Poetrye. yet it behoveth not therfore ne for their folysshe Jugement obeye ne ensiewe them. But more ought we to here Seynt Jerome Seynt Augustyn Alactance Boece and many other that by example of the Bee that by fleyng from flour to flour hath transversyd and ronne over the bookes of the paynems now here. now there gadryng to gydre and takyng the juse of good odure and savoure of swetnes ffor what that the utylite and profyte of the Arte of poetrye is. (fol. 10ʳ)[77]

But the responsibility is not wholly upon the reader and Caxton's Prohemye discusses the textual editing of the secular and pagan author in the following way:

> Anon after [Seynt Jerome] they red in Deuteronome the comandement of the mouthe of god that said. That we shold cut of alle the heeris as wel off the heed and off the browes as other And with that also cut of the ungles or nayles of the body of a woman that was bonde or prysonner. and this shold he do that wolde take her in maryage and adjousted hym self [...] I myself wil cutte and take away that which may hurte and not avaylle. And thus thenne have we the forme and the manere how we oughte to take and rede the Poetes [...] (fols. 12ᵛ–3ʳ)

The Prohemye repeats many of the patristic conventions which seek to prohibit textual and corporeal excess. According to Carolyn Dinshaw, Jerome defends his use of pagan literature on 'the basis of its carnal attractiveness, the elegance of its classical style: "is it surprising that I, too, admiring the fairness of her form and the grace of her eloquence, desire to make the secular wisdom which is my captive and handmaiden, a matron of the true Israel"'.[78] After Jerome, Caxton's Ovid actively promotes these exegetical manoeuvres. The text is perceived as a feminized site of seduction that, as shown in Chapter 1, is still apparent in Golding's later description of the reader and Ovid's poem as Ulysses and the Sirens respectively. The problematic materiality of the text is realized further in Jerome's *Letter to Pammachius*, where he observes that 'writing is served [...] by wide diversity of rhetorical figures [...] so that, until one flees the tedium of writing, one weaves webs of errors'.[79] Both the written text and the woman's body are viewed by Caxton's translation as vessels of desire, as 'webs of errors', which entice and trap the unsuspecting reader. This attempt at patriarchal asceticism is a vital aspect of the hermeneutic practice dictated by Caxton's Prohemye and Prologue and one which is in operation throughout the translation.

Image and text in Caxton's Ovid delineate the conversion of the ancient author and his poem. In its catalogue of authorial biblical and patriarchal luminaries, the prefatory material seeks to secure Ovid's text within a Christian frame:

> Ovyde in hys begynnynge called god in plurel nombre [...]. For what somever the paynems belevyd on dyverses goddes we ought fermly to beleve that ther is but one veray god in thre persones of one equalite of one escence and of one eternyte. the fader. the sone and the holygoste. Alle thoo that beleve not that these thre persones be not one god. and that the sone descended not fro hevyn and becam very man to save us that were lost shal be damped. (fol. 17ᵛ)

Patently, those readers who do not follow 'the understandynge of this booke' (fol. 16ᵛ) which offers an overtly Christian structure for the *Metamorphoses*, progressing from the anticipation of the birth of 'Jhesu Cryst' in book 1 (fol. 16ᵛ) to the birth of 'Jhesu Crist' in the 'tyme of Cesar Augustus' (fol. 477ʳ), will be punished. Nonetheless there are other discourses at work in Caxton's translation besides those of orthodox religiosity.

Trade and Translation

I suggested in the opening pages of this chapter that from the late seventeenth century to the mid-twentieth century, Caxton's translation is enmeshed in a fiscal network which valorizes the material object above the written text. Evidently, the translation itself is concerned with pecuniary issues. Commenting upon the 'stern economic' lesson taught by the allegory that accompanies Caxton's myth of Actaeon, Lyne observes that this translation 'prefers drawing lessons for life in the material world to reading through the veil of allegory for Christian truths';[80] a general interpretation which, as we have seen, is upheld by Caxton's treatment of the myths of Salmacys and Arachne. In her discussion of Bersuire's *Ovidius moralizatus*, Ann Moss explains that

> allegorical reading depends on *similitudo*, and the interpretation of a fable or personage will depend on likenesses which the reader can detect between elements in the narrative or description and the traditional components and language (often itself highly metaphorical) of the particular allegorical *sensus* which is being applied. So Acteon may have analogies both with Christ and the worldly rich, depending on the way we choose to look at his story and the allegorical context we choose to give it. [...] Bersuire's use of the process of allegorical interpretation [...] is to make Ovid's poem relevant to Christian theology and to the contemporary social scene.[81]

These comments equally describe Caxton's domestication of Ovid's poem. As with Bersuire's commentary, the translation's 'moral and tropological interpretations [...] often turn into social satire, where the gods and heroes become rich men and poor men, good and bad priests, usurers and temptresses, in short the whole pageant of medieval society, enacting the moral fables appropriate to a particular vice or social class'.[82]

With these societal concerns in mind, it is telling that the final allegory openly offered in Caxton's Ovid complements the tale of Midas: the Phrygian king in book 11 who asked Bacchus to turn all that he touches into gold. The allegory concludes that

> Mydas may [...] sygnefye a man ryche and covetous whyche may never satisfye ne stanch hys herte fro the goodes of the worlde in whyche he brenneth And by veray desyr amasseth alway more and more And the more he hath. the lasse he is satysfyed and fylde ffor whyche he leveth. mete. drynke and reste and forgeteth god and his neyghbour. But whan he apperceyveth the grete harme that is comynge to hym therby he renounceth the world and alle hys delytes and wesshyd hym by confessyon and clenseth hym by gyvynge hys gold and hys rychesses largely to poure peple. (fol. 307ᵛ)

Originally intended as a reward for kindness, the potentially life-threatening power that the god bestows upon Midas is eventually removed by immersion in the river Pactolus. Indeed, Caxton's allegory neatly transposes Ovid's scene of material divestment into one of Christian absolution. As the narrative moves toward 'the right begynnynge of thystorye of Troye' (fol. 309ᵛ ff.), it seems as if this English Ovid 'forgeteth god'. Though subtle forms of allegory remain (Polymestor, for example, is likened to Judas (fol. 404ᵛ)), from this point forward, the absence of *explicit* moral guidance might be seen as providing the reader with another test of faith; the Christian reader may need to be mindful of becoming trapped in the ensuing Hieronymian textual web.

Prefaced by Midas's religious conversion, 'thystorye of Troye' is disturbed by an episode in which the cultural politics of translation are made visible. As Blake describes, 'the first book Caxton issued in England was the *editio princeps* of Chaucer's *The Canterbury Tales* (c. 1478)':[83] in c. 1483 Caxton printed another of Chaucerian text, the *House of Fame*. The future publication is seemingly in view as he translates the Ovidian poem. In the midst of book 12's narrative, the following invocation appears: 'wel wryteth Geffreey Chawcer that noble man of the discripcon of this hows in hys booke named the book of Fame' (fol. 359ᵛ). One book later, the English translator interrupts Ovid's account of Troy with reference to some other noteworthy material:

> I can nomore saye but I shold telle you alle the bataylle. whych ye may wel knowe of the monke of Bury in ballade. and in the recueil of Troye whyche I translated in prose al alonge. There ye may see. how the Cyte was taken. betrayed. solde to the Grekes and alle brente. destroyed and confounded. (fol. 403ʳ)[84]

The early printed book with which Caxton might share a source, Colard Mansion's edition of the *Metamorphoses* (1484), directs its readers to the history of Troy by 'Guy de Colompne'.[85] Caxton, on the other hand, prefers to recall an English author, John Lydgate, 'the monke of Bury', and the 'Troy Book' (c. 1420) which Lydgate had translated in verse from the Latin text by 'Guy de Colompne'.[86] Rather more shrewdly, with a glance towards his prospective market perhaps, Caxton also recommends his own prose translation of Raoul Lefevre's *The Recuyell of the Histories of Troy*, his first English translation published in Bruges c. 1473–4. In these few intrusive lines Caxton describes a fifteenth-century scene of translation in which his own vernacular prose version of the history of Troy is pitched primarily against Lydgate's earlier verse form.[87]

Caxton's suspension of the Ovidian narrative with what is arguably a subtle recommendation of vernacular texts printed by him disrupts the spiritual claims of the prefatory matter. The translator's incursions delineate a shift from the moralized tradition of Ovidian translation towards a mode of textual production underpinned by mercantile obligations. That Caxton publicized the output of his printing houses is not unusual. 'In fact', Paul Voss comments, 'William Caxton [...] printed the first English advertisement' in 1477 when he produced a 'single-sheet fragment, advertising the sale of Sarum Ordinals'.[88] Blake continues:

> we must abandon the idea that, as long as [Caxton] produced suitable literatures, noble clients would simply drop into his shop and buy his book. Books were wares that had to be marketed – and this is precisely the function which he intended for his prologues. Many are the equivalent of the modern publisher's blurb. The inclusion of a prologue in a text is usually a sign that he was putting particular effort into a sale – and this in turn implies that there was no ready sale for it in Caxton's opinion. A demand had to be created [...].[89]

Although the sole extant manuscript of Caxton's Ovid remains detached from the specific cultural exigencies of incunabula, the translator's rather idiosyncratic disruption of the Ovidian narrative shares some cultural concerns with the economic discourses which define the burgeoning age of print.

The intersection of trade and translation is explored in Caxton's rendition of Io's transformation. Daughter of the river god Inachus, Io is one of the many women raped by Jupiter in the opening books of the *Metamorphoses*. As Caxton puts it:

> Jupiter on a day went playenge in the royame of Grece and sawe the mayde Yo upon the Ryvere of paterne on whome anon he was amorous and forthwith requyred her of her love. The mayde that was shamefast wold not consente. but for fer that he shuld not enforce her she fledd over the feldes of Lycye [...] the god Jupyter for to take her made obscurte and derknes for to com by whiche the mayde was trowbled that she myghte not see wheder she myghte flee. Thus thenne Jupiter toke her and dyde hys will and deflowred her. (fol. 33ᵛ)

Juno realizes what Jupiter has done and 'by her puissance and power she made thobscurte and derknes to departe. to thend that she myght surpryse and take her husbond wit the feat and dede' (fols. 33ᵛ–34ʳ). In order to escape Juno's wrath, Jupiter turns Yo into a cow. Unfortunately, the goddess sees through Yo's new identity and asks Jupiter to give the animal to her:

> Whan Jupiter herd this request he was alle abasshed and wist not what to doo. ffor to gyve hys love in to the handes of her ennemye hym semed it was over grevous a thynge to doo. Nevertheles for worse and for more evyll teschewe and also for to take away al suspecion he gaf it to her. (fol. 34ʳ)

Juno remains doubtful and, in an attempt to thwart Jupiter's adulterous behaviour, the goddess places Yo under the watchful gaze of Argus, her cowherd with 'an hundred eyen in his heed' (fol. 34ᵛ). In losing her role as a human speaking subject Yo functions as little more than a disputed commodity in one of the couple's many disagreements. The question of Yo's identity is pursued in more detail as she catches sight of her own transformation:

> It hapend on a day that the cowe went in to the Ryvere Ynachus her fader And beheld her forme in the water And whan she sawe her selfe in lyknes of a cowe she supposed to have spoken. but anone she began to mowe and crye Wherof she was sorowfull of her mutacon and transfourmynge but she coude not amende it. (fol. 34ᵛ)

This episode prefigures Narcissus's tragedy of misrecognition. Whereas Narcissus initially thought his mirror image to be another, however, Yo immediately realizes that this transformed image is she. This typically Ovidian tension between the inner and outer self is efficiently clarified in a later French manuscript in which the illustrator, 'anxious that Io should be identifiable, shows her through a window in the cow's flank'.[90] Despite her loss of speech, however, Yo is able to communicate with Ynachus by making marks in the dust:

> Thenne thoughte Ynachus that the clyft that was in the rounde of the foot sygnefied a .y. and the roundenes signefyed an .o. And of these two lettres is signefyed the name of Yo hys doughter. (fol. 34ᵛ–5ʳ)

Correctly interpreted, these marks restore Ynachus's subject position as father, but Yo continues to be represented in terms of a lost object. Jupiter 'myghte no lenger hys love to be kepte in this fylthe' (fol. 35ʳ) and he seeks the assistance of Mercury to free Yo. Once liberated, however, running 'as a beste cryeng and brayinge', the transformed Yo is 'chaced and hunted throughout alle the world' by the god's relentlessly jealous wife (fol. 36ᵛ). Eventually, coming to rest in Egypt, Yo falls down into the river Nile and appeals to Jupiter for help. In turn, the god appeals to Juno to forgive Yo, promising that he will cease all contact with the mortal woman. Appeased, Juno repents and returns Yo to her former human identity.

In the twenty-first century, this Ovidian myth has been viewed as an 'aetiology of the invention of writing'.[91] More generally, Simon Goldhill suggests that 'the story of Io is [also] a foundational myth of East–West conflict [and] of the origin of cultural and political difference'.[92] Plutarch's *Moralia*, for instance, describes Io as

> the daughter of Inachus, whom all Greeks suppose to have received divine honours at the hands of the barbarians and to have won such fame that many seas and the most famous straits were named after her and to be the source from which the most notable royal families sprung.[93]

In Caxton's Ovid, however, Yo may represent the fusion of economic materiality with religious translation. 'In Grece', Caxton's allegorical exposition advises, 'was somtyme a ryche man that Ovyd callid Ynachus' who had 'a ryght fayr doughter and playsant that was named Yo' (fols. 37ʳ–37ᵛ). The translation continues:

> Jupiter [...] lovyd this mayd paramours And by hys subtyll wytte he withdrewe her fro her fader and deflowred her of her vyrgynyte And after that she becam comyn and habandonned unto all Luxurye. The fader knewe not wher she was become. Wherfor he sought her longe tyme. And atte laste he founde her atte bordell poure and meschant in such wyse that for sorowe he wold gladly have ben dede But notwithstondyng the fader coude not withdrawe ne make her to torne fro her folye ne for prayer ne for promesse ne for ony chastysynge that he coude doo tyll she wexed old And yet in her eage she becam a bawde. Notwythstondynge she understood clergye and was ryght subtyll. And for this cause the peple of Egypte honoured and worshipped her as a goddesse [...]. This was she that translated the Arte of clergye from greek into Egipozen. (fol. 37ᵛ)[94]

By extending the trope of commodification already embedded in Ovid's myth, Caxton's commentary displays a further interest in the business of women and sex. Bearing traces of Arnulf of Orleans's *accessus* (one of Ovid's earliest moral commentators) who claimed that the woman was changed into a cow because she fell into vice,[95] Caxton's text shows how Yo was found in a bordello. Mindful of social and historical difference, Ruth Mazo Karras states that modern culture considers prostitution in economic terms whereas medieval culture's defamation of its practise is located in discourses of promiscuity.[96] Nevertheless, the fourteenth-century preacher's handbook *Fasciculus Morum* decreed that the term 'prostitute [...] must be applied only to those women who give themselves to anyone and will refuse no one, and that for monetary gain',[97] thus the discourses of economics and promiscuity are bound together in Caxton's description of Yo's fall 'unto all Luxurye'. Moreover, despite her father's protestations, being described as a 'bawd', Yo eventually took charge.

Caxton's allegory, however, moves swiftly from the subject of trade to piety, stating that it 'was she that translated the Arte of clergye from greek into Egipozen'. In doing so, Caxton's account also presents Yo as a translator, an 'inventive mediator',[98] who takes not just Hellenism, but also Western Christianity, to the East. The etymology of the word 'translation', signifying the transport of property as well as the transfer of linguistic meaning, becomes pertinent here.[99] For Caxton's Yo embodies the processes of translation itself and the subsequent engendering of 'the metaphorics of translation' that partly inscribes its practice in early modern England,[100] witnessed, for instance, in John Florio's edict from the first edition of his translation of *The essayes or morall, politike and millitarie discourses of Lo: Michaell de Montaigne* (1603) that 'all translations are reputed femalls'.[101] As illustrated in the passage from Deuteronomy that foreshadows the entire translation, Caxton's Ovid shows how both translated texts and women are subordinate objects which are fashioned by men.[102] Examined in the light of the critical reception of Caxton's text in the twentieth and twenty-first centuries, Yo and the translation of Ovid in which she appears share other uncanny similarities. Yo and Caxton's Ovidian translation are treated as items of economic value which mediate the words of others. But Caxton's Yo also dramatizes the cultural politics of translation and the aggressive textual practices that Caxton's Ovid quietly exerts. As Yo takes Greek into Egypt, so Latin (as the Prohemye to Caxton's Ovid demonstrates) will eventually replace Greek: 'The sayd Ovide hath opend unto the latyns the way as wel in the fables of Grekes as in other' (fols. 12^r–13^v). Caxton's Ovid, the first complete translation of the *Metamorphoses* in English, markedly, seeks to supplant both the Latin text *and* its French sources.

In the Preface to Kathleen L. Scott's *The Caxton Master*, Bennett provides a crucial gloss on his earlier comments concerning the relationship between Gower's *Confessio Amantis* and Caxton's Ovid. He argues that in addition to 'simply [substituting] Anglysshe for françoise in his original', Caxton has also 'added a formula of humility that is almost a sign-manual, being a variant of phrases found frequently in the prologues of his own composition. The formula is [...] almost the only personal reference in the whole work.'[103] These glimpses of the translator's visibility align Caxton's Ovid with the paradigm of difference, substitution and appropriation which characterize the cultural politics of translation and which are at work throughout the text. If Ovid's *Metamorphoses* is punctuated with myths which are emblematic of the desire for presence in language, then Caxton's Ovid evinces the desire to express that presence in English.

Notes

1   Andrew Benjamin, 'Translating Origins: Psychoanalysis and Philosophy', in *Rethinking Translation: Discourse, Subjectivity, Ideology*, ed. by Lawrence Venuti (Routledge: London, 1992), pp. 18–41, p. 18.

2   Raphael Lyne, 'Ovid in English Translation', in *The Cambridge Companion to Ovid*, ed. by Philip Hardie (Cambridge: Cambridge University Press, 2002), pp. 249–63, p. 250.

3   All quotations are from the MS held in the Pepysian Library at Magdalene College, Cambridge. I have modernized the letters *i* and *j*, *u* and *v*, the long *s*, and the ampersand. Contracted words have been expanded. The foliations are my own. A complete modern edition of Caxton's Ovid has yet to be produced, though it is Diana Rumrich's intention to publish a modern edition of book 1 in 2006-7. Caxton's translation of the Philomela myth from book 6 has been published in Norman Blake, *Selections From William Caxton* (Oxford: Clarendon Press, 1973) and Christopher Martin, (ed.), *Ovid in*

English (London: Penguin, 1998); the myth of Pylemon and Baucis from book 8 is available in Andrew Johnson (ed.), *Pylemon and Baucis* (Cambridge: The Gabriel Press, 1999).

4 Romans 15:4. See Alistair J. Minnis, *Medieval Theory of Authorship: Scholastic Literary Attitudes in the later Middle Ages* (Aldershot: Wildwood House, 1988), p. 206 and Rita Copeland, *Rhetoric, Hermeneutics and Translation* (Cambridge: Cambridge University Press, 1991), p. 110. According to the *Middle English Dictionary* the most common meaning of the term 'publysshe' in this period is 'to make publicly known'.

5 Rosemond Tuve, *Allegorical Imagery: Some Mediaeval Books and their Posterity* (Princeton: Princeton University Press, 1966), p. 319.

6 See further Sarah Annes Brown, *The Metamorphosis of Ovid: From Chaucer to Ted Hughes* (London: Duckworth, 1999).

7 Thomas Greene, *The Light in Troy: Imitation and Discovery in Renaissance Poetry* (New Haven: Yale University Press, 1982), p. 1.

8 Lawrence Venuti, *The Translator's Invisibility* (London: Routledge, 1995), p. 312.

9 Roger Ascham illustrates the process of double translation in 'The first booke for the youth' of *The Schoolmaster* (1570) when he describes how students translate Latin passages into English and then back into Latin. See Jean R. Brink, 'Literacy and Education', in *A Companion to English Renaissance Literature and Culture*, ed. by Michael Hattaway (Oxford: Blackwell, 2000), pp. 95–106.

10 Raphael Lyne, *Ovid's Changing World: English Metamorphoses 1567–1632* (Oxford: Oxford University Press, 2001), p. 29.

11 Norman Blake, 'Caxton, William (1415–1492), in *Oxford Dictionary of National Biography*, online edn (Oxford University Press, 2004), http:/ /www. oxforddnb.com/ view/ article/4963, accessed 4 April 2005.

12 Blake, *Caxton and His World*, (London: Andre Deutsch, 1969), p. 68.

13 Richard Altick, 'The English Common Reader: From Caxton to the Eighteenth Century', in *The Book History Reader*, ed. by David Finkelstein and Alistair McCleery (London: Routledge, 2002), pp. 340–9, p. 340.

14 Quintilian, *Institutio oratoria*, trans. by H. E. Butler, 4 vols (London: Heinemann, 1921–2), p. 4. 1. 77.

15 R. McKittrick, *Catalogue of the Pepys Library at Magdalene College, Cambridge* (Cambridge: Brewer, 1992), p. 52.

16 For a detailed study of the French tradition, see Ann Moss, *Ovid in Renaissance France: A Survey of the Latin Editions of Ovid and Commentaries Printed in France before 1600* (London: Warburg Institute, 1982), p. 23.

17 A. J. Minnis, A. B. Scott and D. Wallace, eds., *Medieval Literary Theory and Criticism c. 1100–c. 1375: The Commentary Tradition* (Oxford: Clarendon Press, 1988), p. 321.

18 Bennett, J. A. W., Preface, in Kathleen Scott, *The Caxton Master and His Patrons* (Cambridge: Cambridge Bibliographical Society, 1976), pp. ix–xvi, p. ix. Scott's study critically considers the illustrations in detail.

19 H. Brett-Smith, 'Caxton's Ovid', in *Ovyde hys Booke of Metamorphose*, ed. by H. F. B. Brett-Smith and S. Gaselee (Oxford: Blackwell, 1924), p. xxvij.

20 Brett-Smith, 'Caxton's Ovid', p. xxvij.

21 According to Norman Blake, 'manuscripts were luxury goods which could only be sold to the wealthy [...] hand-written copies of Caxton's translations may occasionally have been produced as de luxe presentation volumes, as is possibly the case with

Ovid's *Metamorphoses.*' Norman Blake, *William Caxton and English Literary Culture* (London: Hambledon Press, 1991), p. 34.

22   Jean Delisle and Judith Woodsworth (eds.), *Translators Through History* (Amsterdam: Benjamins, 1995), p 30.

23   Cited in Bennett, Preface, *The Caxton Master*, p. xi.

24   J. A. W. Bennett, *Times Literary Supplement*, 24 November 1966, 1088. Details about the manuscript's ownership are from this article.

25   John Evelyn, *Diary and Correspondence: Volume 3*, ed. by William Bray (London: Routledge, 1906), p. 305. This correspondence is discussed in Richard Kroll, *The Material Word: Literate Culture in the Restoration and Early Eighteenth Century* (Baltimore: Johns Hopkins University Press, 1991), p. 175.

26   For a detailed discussion of the topic of 'curiosities', see Patrick Mauriès, *Cabinets of Curiosities* (London: Thames and Hudson, 2002) and Barbara M. Benedict, *Curiosity: A Cultural History of Early Modern Enquiry* (Chicago: University of Chicago Press, 2001).

27   Kroll, *The Material Word*, p. 175.

28   Evelyn, *Diary and Correspondence: Volume 3*, p. 306.

29   Francis Wormald, 'Caxton's Ovid Re–United', *Times Literary Supplement*, 19 September 1968, 1059.

30   J. A. W. Bennett, Preface, *The Caxton Master*, p. ix. See further Sotheby and Co., *Sale of Bibliotheca Phillippica: The Celebrated Collection of Manuscripts formed by Sir Thomas Phillipps*, new series, 2nd part (London: Sotheby's, 1966), pp. 12–16.

31   Lawrence Venuti, *The Translator's Invisibility* (London: Routledge, 1995).

32   Bennett, Preface, *The Caxton Master*, p. x.

33   Bennett, Preface, *The Caxton Master*, p. x

34   See further H. J. Jackson, *Marginalia: Readers Writing in Books* (New Haven: Yale University Press, 2001).

35   Christopher Ricks, 'Metamorphosis in Other Words', in *Gower's 'Confessio Amantis': Responses and Reassessments*, ed. by A. J. Minnis (Cambridge: Cambridge University Press, 1983), pp. 25–49, p. 31. See also Peter Beidler (ed), *John Gower's Literary Transformations in the 'Confessio Amantis'* (Washington D.C.: University Press of America, 1982); Conrad Mainzer, 'John Gower's Use of the "Medieval Ovid" in the *Confessio Amantis*', *Medium Aevum*, 41 (1972), 215–29; Thomas J. Hatton, 'John Gower's Use of Ovid in Book III of the *Confessio Amantis*', *Medieavalia*, 13 (1987), 257–74.

36   Ricks, 'Metamorphosis in Other Words', p. 31.

37   Wormald, 'Caxton's Ovid Re-United', 1059

38   J. A. W. Bennett, 'Caxton and Gower', *Modern Language Review*, 45 (1950), pp. 215–16, p. 216.

39   Bennett, 'Caxton and Gower', p. 216.

40   Bennett, *Times Literary Supplement*, 1088.

41   Mainzer, 'John Gower's Use of the "Medieval Ovid" in the *Confessio Amantis*', p. 220.

42   J. D. Burnley, 'Late Medieval English Translation: Types and Reflections', in *The Medieval Translator*, ed. by Roger Ellis (Cambridge: Brewer, 1989), pp. 53–68, p. 53.

43   See further Derek Pearsall, 'The Gower Tradition', in *Gower's 'Confessio Amantis': Responses and Reassessments*, pp. 179–97.

[44]   The collection of essays edited by Alistair J. Minnis, *Gower's 'Confessio Amantis':*
       Responses and Reassessments, is an example of the improved critical reception of
       Gower's text.

[45]   Susan Bassnett, 'When is a Translation Not a Translation?', in *Constructing Cultures:*
       Essays on Literary Translation, ed. by Susan Bassnett and André Lefevere (Clevedon:
       Multilingual Matters, 1998), pp. 25–40, p. 38.

[46]   Hatton, 'John Gower's Use of Ovid', p. 257.

[47]   A. E. B. Coldiron, 'Translation's Challenge to Critical Categories: Verses from
       French in the Early English Renaissance', *The Yale Journal of Criticism*, 16 (2003),
       315–44, 315.

[48]   Edwin Gentzler, *Contemporary Translation Theories* (London: Routledge, 1993),
       p. 147.

[49]   Eugene Vance, *Mervelous Signals: Poetics and Sign Theory in the Middle Ages*
       (Lincoln: University of Nebraska Press, 1986), p. 323.

[50]   William Caxton, *Caxton's Eneydos,[1490,] Englisht from the French Livre des Eneydes*,
       1483, ed. by W. T. Cully and F. J. Furnivall, Early English Text Society (London: N.
       Trubner, 1890), p. 2, cited in Eugene Vance, *Mervelous Signals*, p. 323.

[51]   Mikhail Bakhtin, *The Dialogic Imagination*, trans. by Caryl Emerson and Michael
       Holquist, ed. by Michael Holquist (Austin, Texas: University of Texas Press, 1981), p.
       68. I was reminded of this quotation in Diane Watt, *Amoral Gower: Language, Sex and*
       Politics (Minneapolis: University of Minnesota Press, 2003), p. 24.

[52]   For a definition of 'spyncoppe' the *Oxford English Dictionary* cites only Caxton. He
       uses the word in *The Game of Chesse* (1474), II, iii; *The Myrror of Knighthood*
       (1480) II, xv, 101 and *The Golden Legend* (1483), II, 4/1.

[53]   Bennett is also attracted by the word 'spyncoppe' and he says that 'it recalls Caxton's
       years in the Low Countries'. Bennett, Preface, *The Caxton Master*, p. xiv.

[54]   Kathryn Sullivan Kruger, *Weaving the Word: The Metaphorics of Weaving and*
       Female Textual Production (Selinsgrove: Susquehanna University Press, 2001),
       p. 29.

[55]   See 'smite'. From OE. 'to daub, smear'; OHG. 'smîzan to rub, strike'; Latin. 'to spot,
       mark'. Ernest Klein, *A Comprehensive Etymological Dictionary of the English*
       Language, 2 vols (Amsterdam: Elsevier, 1967).

[56]   Valerie Traub, *The Renaissance of Lesbianism in Early Modern England* (Cambridge:
       Cambridge University Press, 2002), p. 283.

[57]   For example, Byblis (9. fol. 262^r ff.) and Myrrha's (10. fol. 301^r ff.) demonstrate
       incestuous desire for their brother and father respectively.

[58]   Watt, *Amoral Gower*, p. 75.

[59]   Olga Grlic, 'Vernacular and Latin Readings of Ovid's *Metamorphosis* in the Middle
       Ages' (unpublished doctoral thesis, University of California at Berkeley, 1991), pp.
       135–41.

[60]   Cited in Vern L. Bullough, 'Cross Dressing and Gender Role Change in the Middle
       Ages', in *Handbook of Medieval Sexuality*, ed. by Vern L. Bullough and James A.
       Brundage (New York: Garland, 1996), pp. 223–42, p. 224

[61]   Jacqueline Murray, 'Twice Marginal and Twice Invisible: Lesbians in the Middle
       Ages', in *Handbook of Medieval Sexuality*, ed. by Vern L. Bullough and James A.
       Brundage (New York: Garland, 1996), pp. 191–222, p. 198.

[62]   Hincmor of Reims, *De divortio Lothari et Tetbergae*, cited in Murray, 'Twice Marginal
       and Twice Invisible: Lesbians in the Middle Ages', p. 204.

63 Watt, *Amoral Gower*, p. 75.

64 Murray, 'Twice Marginal and Twice Invisible: Lesbians in the Middle Ages', p. 199.

65 Neither Chaucer nor Gower uses the myth in the English vernacular, although Gower uses it in *Mirour de L'Omme*, (1021–32). I would like to thank Diane Watt for this information.

66 Warren Ginsberg, 'Ovid and the Problem of Gender', *Mediaevalia*, 13 (1987), 9–28, 20.

67 See, for example, Guillaume de Lorris, *The Romance of the Rose,* ed. by F. Horgan (Oxford: Oxford University Press, 1994), p. 11.

68 Christine de Pizan, *The Epistle of Othea,* trans. by Steven Scrope, ed. by Curt F. Bühler, Early English Text Society (Oxford: Oxford University Press, 1970). Another translation was produced by Anthony Babington and printed by Robert Wyer (c. 1540). See Bühler, *The Epistle of Othea,* pp. xi–xii. For a discussion of ways in which de Pizan's *Othea* 'challenges normative construction of desire', see Marilynn Desmond and Pamela Sheingorn, 'Queering Ovidian Myth: Bestiality and Desire in Christine de Pizan's *Epistre Othea*', in *Queering the Middle Ages,* ed. by Glenn Burger and Steven F. Kruger (Minneapolis: University of Minneapolis Press, 2001), pp. 1–27.

69 de Pizan, *The Epistle of Othea,* p. 82.

70 Charles Martindale, Introduction, in *Ovid Renewed: Ovidian Influences on Literature and Art from the Middle Ages to the Twentieth Century,* ed. by Charles Martindale (Cambridge: Cambridge University Press, 1988), pp. 1–20, p. 12.

71 See further Lauren Silberman, 'Mythographic Transformations of Ovid's Hermaphrodite', *Sixteenth Century Journal,* 19 (1988), 643–52.

72 *Ovide moralisé: Poème du Commencement du Quartorzième Siècle: Tome II,* ed. by C. de Boer (Amsterdam: Johannes Müller, 1920), 2532–40.

73 Mark D. Jordan, *The Invention of Sodomy in Christian Theology* (Chicago: Chicago University Press, 1997), p. 83, cited in Watt, *Amoral Gower,* p. 77.

74 Douglas Bush, *Mythology and the Renaissance Tradition in English Poetry,* rev. edn (Minnesota: University of Minnesota Press, 1960), p. 33. Norman Blake also argues that it is quite typical to find interpolations and additions in Caxton's translations of either the 'religious' or 'chivalric' kind. Blake, *Caxton and His World,* p. 128.

75 Gower's treatment of the myth in *Confessio Amantis* (1. 2315–21) also makes it clear to the reader that Narcissus thinks that his reflection is a woman. See Watt, *Amoral Gower,* pp. 77–8.

76 Frank Justus Miller, *Ovid: The Metamorphoses,* rev. by G. P. Goold, 2 vols (London: Heinemann, 1984), 3. 463.

77 See further Jane Chance, *The Mythographic Art: Classical Fable and the Rise of the Vernacular in Early France and England* (Gainesville: University of Florida Press, 1990), pp. 3–46.

78 Jerome, *Epistle,* letter 70 (to Magnus), cited in Carolyn Dinshaw, *Chaucer's Sexual Poetics* (Wisconsin: University of Wisconsin Press, 1989), p. 23.

79 Cited in Rita Copeland, *Rhetoric, Hermeneutics and Translation in the Middle Ages* (Cambridge: Cambridge University Press, 1991), p. 41.

80 Lyne, 'Ovid in English Translation', p. 251.

81 Moss, *Ovid in Renaissance France,* p. 25.

82 Moss, *Ovid in Renaissance France,* p. 26.

83 Blake, *William Caxton and English Literary Culture,* p. 150.

[84] Brett-Smith and Gaselee, *Ovyde hys Booke of Metamorphose*, p. xxiv and Bennett, Preface, *The Caxton Master*, p. xiii observe the interpolations that I discuss here.

[85] Brett-Smith and Gaselee, *Ovyde hys Booke of Metamorphose*, p. xxiv.

[86] Roger Ellis, 'The Middle Ages', in *The Oxford Guide to Literature in English Translation*, ed. by Peter France (Oxford: Oxford University Press, 2000), pp. 45–39, p. 44–5.

[87] Roger Ellis notes that 'Caxton's first translation and first published work was [...] a prose version of the Troy story offered in spite of the existence of Lydgate's verse version because Lydgate "translated after some other author than this" [...] and because some people might prefer to read the story in prose.' Ellis, 'The Middle Ages', p. 45.

[88] Paul J. Voss, 'Books for Sale: Advertising and Patronage in Late Elizabethan England', *Sixteenth Century Journal*, 29 (1998), 733–56, 736, n. 14.

[89] Blake, *William Caxton and English Literary Culture*, p. 206.

[90] Mercury, Argus and Io, from *Dieux et dresses du paganisme* (sixteenth century) Bibliotheque de L'Arsenal, Paris, Ms. cod. fr. 5066, cited in Marina Warner, *Fantastic Metamorphoses, Other Worlds* (Oxford: Oxford University Press, 2002), p. 16.

[91] Philip Hardie, *Ovid's Poetics of Illusion* (Cambridge: Cambridge University Press, 2002), p. 253.

[92] Simon Goldhill, *Who Needs Greek? Contests in the Cultural History of Hellenism* (Cambridge: Cambridge University Press, 2002), p. 276.

[93] Plutarch, *Moralia*, trans. by L. Pearson and F. H. Sandbach (London: Heinemann, 1927), 854E.

[94] Ovid says that Io is 'worshipped as a goddess by the linen–robed throng' which merely hints at the cultural politics of translation that are inscribed in this myth. *Ovid: The Metamorphoses*, trans. by Frank Justus Miller, rev. by G. P. Goold, 2 vols (London: Harvard University Press, 1984), 1. 747. Following the conventions of the French moralized Ovids, Caxton's translation reads Yo in a more complex and syncretic fashion.

[95] Caroline Walker Bynum, *Metamorphosis and Identity* (New York: Zone Books, 2001), p. 99.

[96] Ruth Mazo Karra, 'Prostitution in Medieval Europe', in *Handbook of Medieval Sexuality*, ed. by Vern L. Bullough and James A. Brundage (New York: Garland, 1996), pp. 243–60, p. 243.

[97] Cited in Karra, 'Prostitution in Medieval Europe', p. 243.

[98] Michael Cronin, *Translating Ireland* (Cork: Cork University Press, 1996), p. 1.

[99] According to the *Oxford English Dictionary*, 'translation' may be defined as: I. 1.a. Transference; removal or conveyance from one person, place, or condition to another. c. Removal from earth to heaven, *orig.* without death, as the translation of Enoch; but in later use also said *fig.* of the death of the righteous. II. 2.a. The action or process of turning from one language into another; also, the product of this; a version in a different language. 3. a. Transformation, alteration, change; changing or adapting to another use; renovation.

[100] This quotation refers to the title of Lori Chamberlain, 'Gender and the Metaphorics of Translation' in *Rethinking Translation: Discourse, Subjectivity, Ideology*, ed. by Lawrence Venuti (London: Routledge, 1992), pp. 57–75.

101 John Florio, *The essayes or morall, politike and millitarie discourses of Lo: Michaell de Montaigne, Knight of the noble Order of St. Michaell, and one of the gentlemen in ordinary of the French king, Henry the third his chamber* (London: 1603), sig. A 1^r n. p.

102 Carolyn Dinshaw states that 'Jerome [...] represents the reading of the pagan text as a captive woman's passage between men, her marriage and her domestication'. See further Dinshaw, *Chaucer's Sexual Poetics*, pp. 22–5.

103 Bennett, Preface, *The Caxton Master*, p. xii.

Epilogue

Translation and Fragmentation

> Translation is the sheer play of difference: it constantly makes allusion to difference, dissimulates difference, but by occasionally revealing and often accentuating it, translation becomes the very life of this difference.[1]

Translation, as the quotation from Maurice Blanchot at the head of this epilogue points out, is the 'life of difference'. Throughout *Ovid and the Cultural Politics of Translation in Early Modern England* this difference has primarily been realized in terms of 'self' and 'other'; national and gendered. According to Theo Hermans:

> Translation presents a privileged index of cultural self-reference, or, if you prefer, self-definition. In reflecting about itself, a culture, or a section of it, tends to define its own identity in terms of 'self' and 'other', i.e. in relation to that which it perceives as different from itself, that which lies outside the boundary of its own sphere of operations, outside its own 'system'. Translation offers a window on cultural self-definition in that it involves not only the selection and importation of cultural goods from the outside world, but at the same time, in the same breath as it were, their transformation into terms which the recipient culture recognises, to some extent, as its own.[2]

Subject positions are thus constructed and contested in all translated texts, but Ovid's *Metamorphoses*, thoroughly inscribed with notions of translation and transformation at the outset, throws the interpellation of identity into relief. Indeed, Leonard Barkan observes that 'the experience of metamorphosis [...] raises essential questions about selfhood, typically for the first time. For identity, as soon as metamorphosis is divorced from corporeal shape, suddenly comes to be isolated as a thing in itself'.[3] From the narrative voice of the *Metamorphoses* which presents the reader with a 'diffuse authorial self'[4] to the individual myths, Ovid's text interrogates the construction of subjectivity in and through language.

What many of the different translations explored in this book have in common, in one way or another, is that they aspire to the unity they thought they saw in Ovid's text, but were unavoidably trapped by the fragmentation which was at the heart of Ovid's narrative method and, moreover, the effects of *différance* in language itself. To use an Ovidian trope, the translator is like Mercury. The gods speak a different language from mortals; the shape-shifting god is a necessary mediator, and interpreter, between the deities and their human subjects.[5] The Ovidian translator moves between different frames of linguistic reference, domesticating the classical material for their audience. Yet this mortal go-between cannot be in absolute control of language:

The *Metamorphoses* presents a peculiar set of interpretive challenges. Ovid, who delights in teasing his readers, claims he will write a '*perpetuum* [...] *carmen*' and then blithely presents the reader with a maddening collection of fables, some linked serially, others embedded in some instances two-levels deep, in other narrative structures [...]. Study of the responses of generations of interpreters to this particular challenge reveals certain other general principles: that as explicators we need, in general, and as readers want, a firmer, more graspable framework;[6]

Translators of the *Metamorphoses* also desire textual stability. Much of this study, therefore, has been concerned with the frames of the various translations of English Ovids, the paratextual material, which has enabled the translators to give contemporary cultural significance to their translations and to rein in the problematic play of language.[7]

At the outset of this book I suggested that the English translations of Ovid have largely been treated as supplements in relation to many canonical texts in English literature; the final chapter on Caxton's translation of Ovid epitomizes this concern. Although the last ten years or so have witnessed a 'cultural turn' in translation studies which have enabled particular translations to enter the critical fray, the reception of Caxton's Ovid (with its ill-defined origin, uncertain history and limited critical reception) shows how certain texts continue to defy the familiar discourses of textual and cultural analysis which seem unable to understand translations as anything other than supplementary in relation to 'original' literary works. In a post-structuralist sense, of course, translations *are* supplements which threaten 'to take the place of' the original or,[8] at the very least, to fragment the problematic binary opposition of 'original' and 'translation'. English translations of the *Metamorphoses* are the 'very life of difference'; indeed, they are sites of *différance* in which the translation and transformation, construction and deconstruction, of English subjectivities may be explored.

Notes

[1]   Maurice Blanchot, 'Translating', trans. by Richard Sieburth, *Sulfur*, 26 (1990), 82–6, 83, cited in Lawrence Venuti, Introduction, in *Rethinking Translation: Discourse, Subjectivity, Ideology*, ed. by Lawrence Venuti (Routledge: London, 1992), pp. 1–13, 13.

[2]   Theo Hermans, 'Translation's Other', An Inaugural Lecture delivered at University College (London: University of London, 1996), p. 15.

[3]   Leonard Barkan, *The Gods Made Flesh: Metamorphosis and the Pursuit of Paganism*, (New Haven: Yale University Press, 1986), pp. 14–15.

[4]   Richard Lanham, *The Motives of Eloquence: Literary Rhetoric in the Renaissance* (New Haven: Yale University Press, 1976), p. 36.

[5]   As Theo Hermans puts it: 'The gods speak a language different from ours, therefore Hermes has to mediate and interpret between them and us'. Hermans, 'Translation's Other', p. 5.

[6]   Ralph Hexter, 'Medieval Articulations of Ovid's *Metamorphoses*: From Lactantian Segmentation to Arnulfian Allegory', *Mediaevalia*, 13 (1987), pp. 63–82, pp. 63–64.

7   For a discussion of Golding's paratexts, see Lyne, *Ovid's Changing World*, p. 32 ff.
8   See Terence Cave, *The Cornucopian Text: Problems of Writing in the French Renaissance* (Oxford: Clarendon Press, 1979), p. xxi: '"Supplement" comes from "suppléer," "to supply," "to fulfil a need," but also "to take the place of," "displace" [...]. Language is a "supplement" in that it is both unavoidable and superfluous.' Cave, is writing on the supplement after Derrida. See Jacques Derrida, '...That Dangerous Supplement...', in *Of Grammatology*, trans. by Gayatri Chakravorty Spivak (Baltimore: Johns Hopkins University Press, 1976), pp. 141-57.

Bibliography

Addison, Joseph, *The Story of Salmacis* in *The Annual miscellany, for the year 1694 being the fourth part of Miscellany poems: containing great variety of new translations and original copies / by the most eminent hands* (London: 1694), pp. 139–47

Addison, Joseph, *The Spectator*, ed. by Donald F. Bond, 5 vols (Oxford: Clarendon Press, 1965)

Alain of Lille, *De Planctu Naturae*, trans. by James J. Sheridan (Toronto: Pontifical Institute of Medieval Studies, 1980)

Alexander, Nigel, *Elizabethan Narrative Verse* (London: Edward Arnold, 1968)

Allen, Christopher, 'Ovid and Art', in *The Cambridge Companion to Ovid*, ed. by Philip Hardie (Cambridge: Cambridge University Press, 2002), pp. 336–67

Allen, Robert, *The Clubs of Augustan London* (Connecticut: Archon, 1967)

Altick, Richard, 'The English Common Reader: From Caxton to the Eighteenth Century', in *The Book History Reader*, ed. by David Finkelstein and Alistair McCleery (London: Routledge, 2002), pp. 340–49

Anon., *Ovid's Metamorphoses Epitomized in an English Poetical Style, for the Use and Entertainment of the Ladies of Great Britain* (London: 1760)

Anon., *The Fable of Ovid treting of Narcissus translated into Englysh mytre, with a moral there unto* (London: 1560)

Apollodorus, *the Library*, trans. by George James Frazer, 2 vols (London: Heinemann, 1921)

Apuleius, *Metamorphoses*, trans. by J. Arthur Hanson (Cambridge: Harvard University Press, 1989)

Arkell, R. L., *Caroline of Ansbach: George the Second's Queen* (London: Oxford University Press, 1939)

Ascham, Roger, *'The Scholemaster'*, in *English Works,* ed. by William Aldis Wright (Cambridge: Cambridge University Press, 1904), pp. 243–64

Aston, Margaret, 'God, Saints and Reformer: Portraiture and Protestant England', in *Albion's Classicism: The Visual Arts in Britain 1550–1660*, ed. by Lucy Gent (New Haven: Yale University Press, 1995), pp. 181–220

Aston, Margaret, *England's Iconoclasts Vol. I: Laws Against Images* (Oxford: Oxford University Press, 1988)

Attridge, Derek, *Well–Weighed Syllables* (Cambridge: Cambridge University Press, 1974)

Augherson, Kate (ed.), *Renaissance Woman: A Sourcebook* (London: Routledge, 1995)

Bakhtin, Mikhail, *The Dialogic Imagination*, trans. by Caryl Emerson and Michael Holquist, ed. by Michael Holquist (Austin, Texas: University of Texas Press, 1981)

Ballaster, Ros, 'Seizing the Means of Seduction: Fiction and Feminine Identity in Aphra Behn and Delarivier Manley', in *Women, Writing, History*, ed. by Isobel Grundy and Susan Wiseman (London: Batsford, 1992), pp. 93–108

Barash, Carol, *English Women's Poetry 1649–1714: Politics, Community and Linguistic Authority* (Oxford: Clarendon Press, 1996)

Barkan, Leonard, *The Gods Made Flesh: Metamorphosis and the Pursuit of Paganism* (New Haven: Yale University Press, 1986)

Barolsky, Paul, 'As in Ovid, So in Renaissance Art', *Renaissance Quarterly*, 51 (1998), 451–74

Bartels, Emily C., 'Making More of the Moor: Aaron, Othello, and Renaissance Refashionings of Race', *Shakespeare Quarterly*, 41 (1990), 433–54

Bassnett, Susan, 'When is a Translation Not a Translation?', in *Constructing Cultures: Essays on Literary Translation*, ed. by Susan Bassnett and André Lefevere (Clevedon: Multilingual Matters, 1998), pp. 25–40

Bassnett, Susan, 'The Meek or the Mighty: Reappraising the Role of the Translator', in *Translation, Power, Subversion*, ed. by Román Álvarez and M. Carmen-África Vidal (Clevedon: Multilingual Matters, 1996), pp. 10–24

Bassnett, Susan, *Comparative Literature: A Critical Introduction* (Oxford: Blackwell, 1993)

Bassnett, Susan, *Translation Studies*, rev. edn (London: Routledge, 1991)

Bassnett, Susan and André Lefevere, General Editors' Preface, in *Translation/History/Culture*, ed. by André Lefevere (London: Routledge, 1992)

Bate, Jonathan, *Shakespeare and Ovid* (Oxford: Clarendon Press, 1993)

Baugh, Albert C. and Thomas Cable, *A History of the English Language*, 4th edn (London: Routledge, 1993)

Beaumont, Francis, *Salmacis and Hermaphroditus* (London: 1602)

Beer, Gillian, '"Our Unnatural No-Voice": The Heroic Epistle, Pope and Women's Gothic', *The Yearbook of English Studies*, 12 (1982), 125–51

Beer, Jeanette, Introduction, in *Translation and the Transmission of Culture Between 1300 and 1600*, ed. by Jeanette Beer and Kenneth Lloyd-Jones (Michigan: Medieval Institute Publications, 1995), pp. vii–xii

Behn, Aphra, 'The Golden Age', in *The Works of Aphra Behn*, ed. by Janet Todd, 4 vols (London: William Pickering, 1993), pp. 101–5

Beidler, Peter (ed.), *John Gower's Literary Transformations in the 'Confessio Amantis'* (Washington D. C.: University Press of America, 1982)

Belsey, Catherine, *Critical Practice*, 2nd edn (London: Routledge, 2002)

Belsey, Catherine, 'Love as Trompe–L'Oeil: Taxonomies of Desire in *Venus and Adonis*', *Shakespeare Quarterly*, 46 (1995), 257–76

Belsey, Catherine, 'Postmodern Love: Questioning the Metaphysics of Desire', *New Literary History*, 25 (1994), 683–705

Belsey, Catherine, 'The Name of the Rose in *Romeo and Juliet*', *Yearbook of English Studies*, 23 (1993), 127–42

Belsey, Catherine, *The Subject of Tragedy: Identity and Difference in Renaissance Drama* (London: Routledge, 1985)

Benedict, Barbara M., *Curiosity: A Cultural History of Early Modern Enquiry* (Chicago: University of Chicago Press, 2001)

Benedict, Barbara M., *Making the Modern Reader: Cultural Mediation in Early Modern Literary Anthologies* (Princeton: Princeton University Press, 1996)

Benjamin, Andrew, 'Translating Origins: Psychoanalysis and Philosophy', in *Rethinking Translation*, ed. by Lawrence Venuti (London: Routledge, 1992), pp. 18–41

Bennett, J. A. W., Preface, in Kathleen Scott, *The Caxton Master and His Patrons* (Cambridge: Cambridge Bibliographical Society, 1976), pp. ix–xvi

Bennett, J. A. W., 'Caxton's Ovid', *Times Literary Supplement*, 24 November 1966, 1108

Bennett, J. A. W., 'Caxton and Gower', *Modern Language Review*, 45 (1950), 215–16

Berry, Philippa, 'Renewing the Concept of Renaissance: The Cultural Influence of Paganism Reconsidered', in *Textures of Renaissance Knowledge*, ed. by Philippa Berry and Margaret Tudeau-Clayton (Manchester: Manchester University Press, 2003), pp. 17–34

Blackmore, Richard, *A paraphrase on the book of Job as likewise on the songs of Moses, Deborah, David, on four select psalms, some chapters of Isaiah, and the third chapter of Habakkuk* (London: 1700)

Blake, Norman, 'Caxton, William (1415–1492)', in *Oxford Dictionary of National Biography*, online edn (Oxford University Press, 2004), <http://www.oxforddnb.com/view/article/4963>, accessed 4 April 2005

Blake, Norman, *William Caxton and the English Literary Culture* (London: Hambledon Press, 1991)

Blake, Norman, *Selections From William Caxton* (Oxford: Clarendon Press, 1973a)

Blake, Norman, *Caxton's Own Prose* (London: Andre Deutsch: 1973b)

Blake, Norman, *Caxton and His World* (London: Andre Deutsch, 1969)

Blamires, Alcuin (ed.), *Woman Defamed and Woman Defended* (Oxford: Clarendon Press, 1992)

Blank, Paula, *Broken English: Dialects and the Politics of Language in Renaissance Writing* (London: Routledge, 1996)

Bloom, Gina, 'Localizing Disembodied Voice in Sandys's Englished "Narcissus and Echo"', in *Ovid and the Renaissance Body*, ed. by Goran V. Stanivukovic (Toronto: University of Toronto Press, 2001), pp. 129–54

Boutcher, Warren, 'The Renaissance', in *The Oxford Guide to Literature in English Translation*, ed. by Peter France (Oxford: Oxford University Press, 2000), pp. 45–54

Bouwsma, William, *John Calvin: A Sixteenth-Century Portrait* (Oxford: Oxford University Press, 1988)

Bowers, Fredson and Richard Beale Davis, 'George Sandys: Bibliographic Catalogue of Printed Editions in England to 1700', *Bulletin of the New York Public Library*, 53 (1950), 159–81

Braden, Gordon, *The Classics and English Renaissance Poetry* (New York: Yale University Press, 1978)

Bray, Gerald (ed.), *Documents of the English Reformation* (Cambridge: James Clarke, 1994)

Brennan, Michael G., 'The Date of the Death of Abraham Fraunce', *The Library*, 5 (1983), 391–2

Brink, Jean R.,'Literacy and Education', in *A Companion to English Renaissance Literature and Culture*, ed. by Michael Hattaway (Oxford: Blackwell, 2000), pp. 95–105

Britnell, Richard, *The Closing of the Middle Ages?: England, 1471–1529* (Oxford: Blackwell, 1997)

Brook, H. F., 'The Fictitious Ghost: A Poetic Genre', *Notes and Queries*, 29 (1982), 51–5

Brown, Sarah Annes, *Ovid: Myth and Metamorphosis* (London: Duckworth, 2005)

Brown, Sarah Annes, '"There Is No End But Addition": The Latest Reception of Shakespeare's Classicism', in *Shakespeare and the Classics*, ed. by Charles Martindale and A. B. Taylor (Cambridge: Cambridge University Press, 2004), pp. 277–93

Brown, Sarah Annes, *The Metamorphosis of Ovid: From Chaucer to Ted Hughes* (London: Duckworth, 1999)

Brown, Sarah Annes, 'Some Aspects of the Critical Reception of Ovid's *Metamorphoses*: Chaucer, Spenser, Shakespeare and Milton' (unpublished Ph.D thesis, University of Bristol, 1994)

Budick, Sanford and Wolfgang Iser (eds.), *The Translatability of Cultures: Figurations of the Space Between* (Stanford: Stanford University Press, 1996)

Bullough, Vern L., 'Cross Dressing and Gender Role Change in the Middle Ages', in *Handbook of Medieval Sexuality*, ed. by. Vern L. Bullough and James A. Brundage (New York: Garland, 1996), pp. 223–42.

Burnley, J. D., 'Late Medieval English Translation: Types and Reflections', in *The Medieval Translator*, ed. by Roger Ellis (Cambridge: Brewer, 1989), pp. 55–68

Bush, Douglas, *Mythology and the Renaissance Tradition in English Poetry*, rev. edn (Minnesota: University of Minnesota Press, 1960)

Buxton, John, *Sir Philip Sidney and the English Renaissance* (London: Macmillan, 1964)

Byatt, A. S., 'Arachne', in *Ovid Metamorphosed*, ed. by Philip Terry (London: Chatto and Windus, 2000), pp. 131–57

Bynum, Caroline Walker, *Metamorphosis and Identity* (New York: Zone Books, 2001)

Calvin, John, *Institutes of the Christian Religion*, trans. by Ford Lewis Battle (Philadelphia: Westminster Press, 1960)

Carroll, William C., *The Metamorphoses of Shakespearean Comedy* (Princeton: Princeton University Press, 1985)

Carter, Harry, *A History of the Oxford University Press* (Oxford: Clarendon Press, 1975)

Cary. M. and others (eds.), *The Oxford Classical Dictionary* (Oxford: Clarendon Press, 1949)

Catty, Joecelyn, *Writing Rape, Writing Women in Early Modern England* (Basingstoke: Macmillan, 1999)

Cave, Terence, *The Cornucopian Text: Problems of Writing in the French Renaissance* (Oxford: Clarendon Press, 1979)

Cavendish, Margaret, *The Philosophical and Physical Opinions* (London: 1655)

Caxton, William, 'Here begynneth the table of this book of Ovyde [...]' (c. 1480), Phillipps MS and Pepys's MS facsimile (New York: George Braziller, 1968)

Caxton, William, *The Prologues and Epilogues*, ed. by W. J. B. Crotch, Early English Text Society (London: Oxford University Press, 1928)

Caxton, William, *Ovyde Hys Booke of Methamorphose Books X–XV*, ed. by. H. F. B. Brett-Smith and Stephen Gaselee (Oxford: Basil Blackwell, 1924)

Caxton, William *Six Bookes of Metamorphoses*, ed. by George Hibbert (London: William Bulmer, 1819)

Cerasano, S. P. and M. Wynne–Davis (eds.), *Renaissance Drama by Women* (London: Routledge, 1996)

Chamberlain, Lori, 'Gender and the Metaphorics of Translation', in *Rethinking Translation: Discourse, Subjectivity, Ideology*, ed. by Lawrence Venuti (London: Routledge, 1992), pp. 57–75

Chance, Jane, 'The Medieval Apology for Poetry', in *The Mythographic Art: Classical Fable and the Rise of the Vernacular in Early France and England*, ed. by Jane Chance (Gainesville: University of Florida Press, 1990), pp. 3–46

Chaucer, Geoffrey, *The Riverside Chaucer*, ed. by Larry D. Benson (Oxford: Oxford University Press, 1987)

Cheyfitz, Eric, *The Poetics of Imperialism: Translation and Colonization from 'The Tempest' to 'Tarzan'* (Oxford: Oxford University Press, 1991)

Chudleigh, Lady Mary, *The Poems and Prose of Mary, Lady Chudleigh*, ed. by Margaret J. M. Ezell (New York: Oxford University Press, 1993)

Chudleigh, Lady Mary, *Essays Upon Several Subjects in Prose and Verse* (London: 1710)

Chudleigh, Lady Mary, *The Ladies Defence: or, the Bride-Woman's Counsellor answered* (London: 1709)

Chudleigh, Lady Mary, *Poems on Several Occasions; together with The Song of the Three Children, paraphrased* (London: 1703)

Clark, Sandra, *Amorous Rites: Elizabethan Erotic Verse* (London: Dent, 1994)

Clarke, Danielle, *The Politics of Early Modern Women's Writing* (Harlow: Longman, 2001)

Clarke, Danielle, 'The Politics of Translation and Gender in the Countess of Pembroke's *Antonie*', *Translation and Literature* 6, (1997), 149–66

Clarke, Norma, 'Soft Passions and Darling Themes: From Elizabeth Singer Rowe (1674–1737) to Elizabeth Carter (1717–1806)', *Women's Writing*, 7 (2000), 353–71

Clifford, Anne, *Diaries*, ed. by D. J. H. Clifford (Gloucestershire: Sutton, 1992)

Coiro, Ann Baynes, '"A Ball of Strife": Caroline Poetry and Royal Marriage', in *The Royal Image: Representations of Charles I*, ed. by Thomas N. Corns (Cambridge: Cambridge University Press, 1999), pp. 26–46

Coldiron, A. E. B., 'Translation's Challenge to Critical Categories: Verses from French in the Early English Renaissance', *The Yale Journal of Criticism*, 16 (2003), 315–44

Collinson, Patrick, 'Protestant Culture and the Cultural Revolution', in *Reformation to Revolution: Politics and Religion in Early Modern England*, ed. by Margot Todd (London: Routledge, 1995), pp. 33–52

Cook, Richard, *Sir Samuel Garth* (Boston: Twayne, 1980)

Cooper, Helen, *Pastoral: Mediaeval into Renaissance* (Ipswich: Brewer, 1977)

Copeland, Rita, *Rhetoric, Hermeneutics and Translation in the Middle Ages* (Cambridge: Cambridge University Press, 1991)

Corns, Thomas N., 'Duke, Prince, King', in *The Royal Image: Representations of Charles I*, ed. by Thomas N. Corns (Cambridge: Cambridge University Press, 1999), pp. 1–25

Cotton, Charles, *Chaucer's Ghoast, or, a Piece of Antiquity. Containing twelve pleasant Fables of Ovid penn'd after the ancient manner of writing in England* (London: 1672)

Coupe, Laurence, *Myth* (London: Routledge, 1997)

Crane, Mary Thomas, *Framing Authorities: Sayings, Self and Society in Sixteenth-Century England* (Princeton: Princeton University Press, 1993)

Crawford, Patricia, *Women and Religion in England 1500–1720* (London: Routledge, 1996)

Cronin, Michael, *Translating Ireland: Translation, Languages, Cultures* (Cork: Cork University Press, 1996)

Davis, Richard Beale, *George Sandys: Poet-Adventurer* (London: Bodley Head, 1955)

Davis, Richard Beale, 'George Sandys v. William Stansby: the 1632 Edition of Ovid's *Metamorphosis*', *The Library*, 3, (1949), 193–212

Davis, Richard Beale, 'Early Editions of George Sandys's "Ovid": The Circumstances of Production', *Papers of the Bibliographical Society of America*, 35 (1941), 1–22

De Grazia, Margreta, 'Shakespeare's View of Language: An Historical Perspective', *Shakespeare Quarterly*, 29 (1978), 375–9

De Lorris, Guillaume, *The Romance of the Rose,* ed. by F. Horgan (Oxford: Oxford University Press, 1994)

De Pizan, Christine, *The Epistle of Othea*, trans. by Steven Scrope, ed. by Curt F. Bühler, Early English Text Society (Oxford: Oxford University Press, 1970)

Deferrari, R. J., Sister M. Inviolata Barry and Martin R. P. McGuire (eds.), *A Concordance of Ovid* (Washington: The Catholic University of America Press, 1939)

Delisle, Jean and Judith Woodsworth (eds.), *Translators Through History* (Amsterdam: Benjamins, 1995)

Denham, John, *The Poetical Works of John Denham*, ed. by Theodore Howard Banks, 2nd edn (Connecticut: Archon, 1969)

Derrida, Jacques, *Specters of Marx*, trans. by Peggy Kamuf (London: Routledge, 1994)

Derrida, Jacques, *Positions*, trans. by Alan Bass (London: Athlone, 1987)

Derrida, Jacques, 'Des Tours de Babel', in *Difference in Translation*, trans. and ed. by Joseph F. Graham (Ithaca: Cornell University Press, 1985), pp. 165–207

Derrida, Jacques, 'Différance', in *Margins of Philosophy*, trans. by Alan Bass (Hertfordshire: Harvester Wheatsheaf, 1982), pp. 1–28

Derrida, Jacques, '...That Dangerous Supplement...', in *Of Grammatology,* trans. by Gayatri Chakravorty Spivak (Baltimore: John Hopkins University Press, 1979), pp. 141–64

Desmond, Marilynn and Pamela Sheingorn, 'Queering Ovidian Myth: Bestiality and Desire in Christine de Pizan's *Epistre Othea*', in *Queering the Middle Ages*, ed. by Glenn Burger and Steven F. Kruger (Minneapolis: University of Minneapolis Press, 2001), pp. 1–27

Detmer-Goebel, Emily, 'The Need for Lavinia's Voice: *Titus Andronicus* and the Telling of Rape', *Shakespeare Studies*, 29 (2001), 75–92

Dinshaw, Carolyn, *Chaucer's Sexual Poetics* (Wisconsin: University of Wisconsin Press, 1989)

Dixon, Peter, *Rhetoric* (London: Methuen, 1971)

Donno, Elizabeth Story, *Elizabethan Minor Epics* (London: Routledge and Kegan Paul, 1963)

Doody, Margaret, *The Daring Muse: Augustan Poetry Reconsidered* (Cambridge: Cambridge University Press, 1985)

Doran, Susan, *Elizabeth I and Religion 1558–1603* (London: Routledge, 1994)

Dowie, J. A., *To Settle the Succession of the State: Literature and Politics, 1678–1750* (Basingstoke: Macmillan, 1994)

Drake, Gertrude, 'Ovid's *Metamorphoses*, the Facsimile of the Caxton MS and Sandys's 1632 version', *Papers on Language and Literature*, 7 (1971), 313–35

Dryden, John, *The Works of John Dryden: Poems 1685–1692*, ed. by Earl Miner (Berkeley: University of California Press, 1969)

Dryden, John, *The Works of John Dryden: Poems 1649–1680*, ed. by Edward Niles Hooker and H. T. Swedenberg, Jr. (Berkeley: University of California Press, 1961)

Due, Otto Steen, *Changing Forms: Studies in the 'Metamorphoses' of Ovid* (Copenhagen: Gyldendal, 1974)

Duffy, Eamon, *The Stripping of the Altars: Traditional Religion in England c. 1400–c. 1580* (New Haven: Yale University Press, 1992)

Duncan Jones, Katherine, *Sir Philip Sidney: Courtier Poet* (New Haven: Yale University Press, 1991)

Durant, David N., *Bess of Hardwick: Portrait of an Elizabethan Dynast*, rev. edn (London: Peter Owen, 1999)

DuRocher, Richard, *Milton and Ovid* (Ithaca: Cornell University Press, 1979)

Dwyer, Warren Francis, 'Profit, Poetry and Politics in Augustan Translation: A Study of the Garth-Tonson *Metamorphoses* of 1717' (unpublished doctoral thesis, Urbana, Illinois, 1969)

Eagleton, Terry, 'Translation and Transformation', *Stand*, 19 (1977), 72–7

Easthope, Antony and Kate McGowan (eds.), *A Critical and Cultural Theory Reader* (Buckingham: Open University Press, 1992)

Eaton, Sara, 'A Woman of Letters: Lavinia in *Titus Andronicus*', in *Shakespearean Tragedy and Gender*, ed. by Shirley Nelson Grammar and Madelon Spregnether (Bloomington: Indiana University Press, 1996), pp. 54–74

Elliott, Alison Goddard, 'Ovid and the Critics: Seneca, Quintilian and "Seriousness"', *Helios*, 12 (1985), 9–20

Elliott, Alison Goddard, '*Accessus* and *Auctores*: Twelfth-Century Introductions to Ovid', *Allegorica*, 5 (1980), 6–48

Ellis, Roger, 'The Middle Ages', in *The Oxford Guide to Literature in English Translation*, ed. by Peter France (Oxford: Oxford University Press, 2000), pp. 45–39, p. 44–5

Ellis, Roger and Liz Oakley–Brown, 'The British Tradition', in *The Routledge Encyclopedia of Translation Studies*, ed. by M. Baker and K. Malmkjæ (London: Routledge, 1998), pp. 333–46

Ellison, James, *George Sandys: Travel, Colonialism and Tolerance in the Seventeenth Century* (Cambridge: Brewer, 2002)

Enterline, Lynn, *The Rhetoric of the Body: From Ovid to Shakespeare* (Cambridge: Cambridge University Press, 2000)

Enterline, Lynn, 'Embodied Voices: Petrarch Reading (Himself Reading) Ovid', in *Desire in the Renaissance: Psychoanalysis and Literature*, ed. by Valeria Finucci and Regina Schwartz (Princeton: Princeton University Press, 1994), pp. 120–45

Evans, Ruth, 'Translating Past Cultures?', in *The Medieval Translator 4*, ed. by Roger Ellis and Ruth Evans (Exeter: University of Exeter Press, 1994), pp. 20–45

Evelyn, John, *Diary and Correspondence*, ed. by William Bray (London: Routledge, 1906)

Even-Zohar, Itamar, 'The Position of Translated Literature Within the Literary Polysystem', *Poetics Today*, 11 (1990), 45–51

Fanshawe, Richard, *Shorter Poems and Translations*, ed. by N. W. Bawcutt (Liverpool: Liverpool University Press, 1964)

Fawcett, Mary, 'Arms/ Words/ Tears: Language and the Body in *Titus Andronicus*', *English Literary History*, 50 (1983), 261–77

Feldherr, Andrew, 'Metamorphosis in the *Metamorphoses*', in *The Cambridge Companion to Ovid*, ed. by Philip Hardie (Cambridge: Cambridge University Press, 2002), pp. 163–79

Ferguson, Moira, *Eighteenth-Century Women Poets: Nation, Class, and Gender* (Albany: State University of New York Press, 1995)

Fienberg, Nona, 'Mary Wroth's Poetics of the Self', *Studies in English Literature 1500–1900*, 42 (2002), 121–36

Fisher, Will, 'Masculinity in Early Modern England', *Renaissance Quarterly*, 54 (2001), 155–87

Fleming, Juliet, 'Dictionary English and the Female Tongue', in *Enclosure Acts: Sexuality, Property, and Culture in Early Modern England*, ed. by Richard Burt and John Michael Archer (Ithaca: Cornell University Press, 1994), pp. 290–326

Florio, John, *The essayes or morall, politike and millitarie discourses of Lo: Michaell de Montaigne, Knight of the noble Order of St. Michaell, and one of the gentlemen in ordinary of the French king, Henry the third his chamber* (London: 1603)

Fogarty, Anne, 'The Colonisation of Language: Narrative Strategy in *The Faerie Queene* Book 6', in *Edmund Spenser*, ed. by Andrew Hadfield (London: Longman, 1996), pp. 196–210

Foucault, Michel, 'Different Spaces', in *The Essential Works of Michel Foucault: Aesthetics, Method and Epistemology,* trans. by Robert Hurley, ed. by James Faubion (London: Penguin, 2000), pp. 175–86

Fox, Alistair, 'Elizabethan Petrarchism and the Protestant Location of the Self', in *The English Renaissance: Identity and Representation in Elizabethan England* (Oxford: Blackwell, 1997), pp. 59–92

Fradenburg, Louise O., 'Criticism, Anti-Semitism and the *Prioress's Tale*', *Exemplaria*, 1 (1989), 69–115

Frantzen, Alan J., *Desire for Origins* (New Brunswick: Rutgers University Press, 1990)

Fraunce, Abraham, *Symbolicae Philosophiae Liber Quartus et Ultimus*, trans. by Estelle Haan (New York: AMS, 1991)

Fraunce, Abraham, *The Third Part of the Countess of Pembroke's Ivychurch* (1592), ed. by Gerald Snare (California: California State University Press, 1975)

Fraunce, Abraham, *The Arcadian Rhetoric* (1588), ed. by Ethel Seaton (Oxford: Blackwell, 1950)

Fraunce, Abraham, *The Third Part of the Countesse of Pembrokes Yvychurch. Entitled Amintas Dale* (London: 1592)

Fraunce, Abraham, *The Countesse of Pembrokes Life, and Unfortunate Death of Phillis and Amyntas: That in a Pastorall; This in a Funerall: both in English Hexameters* (London: 1591)

Fraunce, Abraham, *The Arcadian rhetorike: or The praecepts of rhetorike made plaine by examples Greeke, Latin, English, Italian, French, Spanish, out of Homers Ilias, and Odissea, Virgils Aeglogs,* [...] *and Aeneis, Sir Philip Sydnieis Arcadia, songs and sonets* (London: 1588)

Freccero, John, 'Dante's Ulysses', in *Concepts of the Hero in the Middle Ages and the Renaissance*, ed. by Norman T. Burns and Christopher Reagan (London: Hodder and Stoughton, 1976), pp. 101–19

Frye, Susan, 'Sewing Connections: Elizabeth Tudor, Mary Stuart, Elizabeth Talbot, and Seventeenth Century Anonymous Needleworkers', in *Maids, Mistresses, Cousins and Queens: Women's Alliances in Early Modern England*, ed. by Susan Frye and Karen Robertson (New York: Oxford University Press, 1999), pp. 165–82

Fyler, John, *Chaucer and Ovid* (New Haven: Yale University Press, 1979)

Galinsky, Karl G., *Ovid's 'Metamorphoses': An Introduction to the Basic Aspects* (Berkeley: University of California Press, 1975)

Garth, Samuel, ed., *Ovid's Metamorphoses, by the most Eminent Hands* (London: 1717)

Garth, Samuel, *Claremont* (London: 1715).

Geneva Bible (1560), ed. by Lloyd E. Berry (Milwaukee: University of Wisconsin Press, 1969)

Gentzler, Edwin, *Contemporary Translation Theories* (London: Routledge, 1993)

Geyer-Ryan, Helga, *Fables of Desire* (Cambridge: Polity, 1994)

Ghisalberti, F., 'Medieval Biographies of Ovid', *Journal of the Warburg and Courtauld Institute*, 9 (1946), 10–59

Gillespie, Stuart and Robert Cummings, 'A Bibliography of Ovidian Translations and Imitations in English', *Translation and Literature*, 13.2 (2004), 207–18.

Ginsberg, Warren, 'Ovid and the Problem of Gender', *Mediaevalia*, 13 (1987) 9–28

Gittings, Clare, *Death, Burial and the Individual in Early Modern England* (London: Croom Helm, 1984)

Goldberg, Jonathan, 'The Countess of Pembroke's Literal Translation', in *Subject and Object in Renaissance Culture*, ed. by Margreta de Grazia, Maureen Quilligan, and Peter Stallybrass (Cambridge: Cambridge University Press, 1996), pp. 321–36

Goldhill, Simon, *Who Needs Greek? Contests in the Cultural History of Hellenism* (Cambridge: Cambridge University Press, 2002)

Golding, Arthur, *The xv. Bookes of P. Ovidius Naso, etytuled Metamorphosis, translated oute of Latin into English meeter* [...] (London: 1567)

Golding, Arthur, *The fyrst fower bookes of P. Ovidius Nasos worke, intitled Metamorphosis, translated into English meter* (London: 1565)

Golding, Louis Thorn, *An Elizabethan Puritan: Arthur Golding* (New York: R. R. Smith, 1937)

Goodman, Paula, 'Places, Pictures and Prefaces: Reading Women's Prose Fiction 1621–1696' (unpublished Ph.D thesis, University of Wales, Cardiff, 1997)

Gower, John, *Confessio Amantis*, ed. by Henry Morley (London: Routledge, 1989)

Green, Douglas E., 'Interpreting "her martyr'd signs": Gender and Tragedy in *Titus Andronicus*', *Shakespeare Quarterly*, 40 (1989), 317–26

Greenblatt, Stephen, *Renaissance Self-Fashioning: From More to Shakespeare* (Chicago: University of Chicago Press, 1980)

Greene, Thomas M., *The Light in Troy: Imitation and Discovery in Renaissance Poetry* (New Haven: Yale University Press, 1982)

Greene, Thomas M., 'The Flexibility of the Self in Renaissance Literature', in *The Disciplines of Criticism: Essays in Literary Theory, Interpretation, and History*, ed. by Peter Demetz, Thomas Greene and Lowry Nelson, Jr. (New Haven: Yale University Press, 1968), pp. 241–64

Gregerson, Linda, *The Reformation of the Subject: Spenser, Milton, and the Protestant Epic* (Cambridge: Cambridge University Press, 1995)

Gregerson, Linda, 'Narcissus Interrupted: Specularity and the Subject of the Tudor State', *Criticism*, 35 (1993), 1–40

Grlic, Olga, 'Vernacular and Latin Readings of Ovid's *Metamorphosis* in the Middle Ages', (unpublished doctoral thesis, University of California at Berkeley, 1991)

Grose, Christopher, *Ovid's 'Metamorphoses': An Index to the 1632 Commentary of George Sandys* (Malibu: Undena, 1981)

Grundy, Isobel, *Lady Mary Wortley Montagu: Comet of the Enlightenment* (Oxford: Oxford University Press, 1999)

Grundy, Isobel, 'The Politics of Female Authorship', *The Book Collector*, 31 (1982), 19–37

Grundy, Isobel, '"The Entire Works of Clarinda": Unpublished Juvenile Verse by Lady Mary Wortley Montagu', *The Yearbook of English Studies*, 7 (1977), 91–107

Grundy, Isobel, 'Ovid and Eighteenth-Century Divorce: An Unpublished Poem by Lady Mary Wortley Montagu', *Review of English Studies*, 23 (1972), 417–28

Grundy, Isobel, 'The Verse of Lady Mary Wortley Montagu: A Critical Edition' (unpublished DPhil thesis, Oxford, 1971)

Gurr, Andrew, *Playgoing in Shakespeare's London*, 2nd edn (Cambridge: Cambridge University Press, 1996)

Gwilliam, Tassie, 'Cosmetic Poetics: Coloring Faces in the Eighteenth Century', in *Body and Text in the Eighteenth Century*, ed. by Veronica Kelly and Dorothea Von Mücke (Stanford: Stanford University Press, 1994), pp. 144–62

Hadfield, Andrew, *Shakespeare, Spenser and the Matter of Britain* (Basingstoke: Palgrave Macmillan, 2004)

Hadfield, Andrew, *Literature, Politics and National Identity* (Cambridge: Cambridge University Press, 1994)

Halley, Edmund, 'A Discourse of the Rule of the Decrease of the Height of the Mercury in the Barometer, According as Places are Elevated Above the Surface of the Earth, with an Attempt to Discover the True Reason of the Rising and Falling of the Mercury, upon Change of Weather', *Philosophical Transactions of the Royal Society*, 16 (1686–92), 104–16

Halley, Edmund, '*Philosophia Naturalis Principia Mathematica Philosophical*', *Transactions of the Royal Society of London*, 15 (1685–86), 291–7

Halsband, Robert, 'The First Version of Marivaux's *Le Jeu de L'amour et du Hasard*', *Modern Philology*, 79 (1981), 16–23

Hamilton, A. C. (ed.), *The Spenser Encyclopedia* (London: Routledge, 1990)

Hammond, Paul, *Dryden and the Traces of Classical Rome* (Oxford: Oxford University Press, 1999)

Hannay, Margaret P., *Philip's Phoenix: Mary Sidney, Countess of Pembroke* (Oxford: Oxford University Press, 1990)

Hannay, Margaret P (ed.), *Silent But for the Word: Tudor Women as Patrons, Translators and Writers of Religious Works* (Kent, Ohio: Kent State University Press, 1985)

Harbert, Bruce, 'Lessons from the Great Clerk: Ovid and John Gower', in *Ovid Renewed: Ovidian Influences on Literature and Art from the Middle Ages to the Twentieth Century*, ed. by Charles Martindale (Cambridge: Cambridge University Press, 1988), pp. 83–99

Hardie, Philip, *Ovid's Poetics of Illusion* (Cambridge: Cambridge University Press, 2002)

Hardin, Richard F., 'Ovid in Seventeenth-Century England', *Comparative Literature*, 24 (1972), 44–62

Harris, John, Stephen Orgel and Roy Strong (eds.), *The King's Arcadia: Inigo Jones and the Royal Court* (London: The Arts Council of Great Britain, 1973)

Harvey, Elizabeth D., *Ventriloquized Voices: Feminist Theory and Renaissance Texts* (London: Routledge, 1992)

Haslett, Moyra, *Pope to Burney 1714–1779: Scriblerians to Bluestockings* (Basingstoke: Palgrave Macmillan, 2003)

Hatton, Ragnhild, *George I: Elector and King* (London: Thames and Hudson, 1978)

Hatton, Thomas J., 'John Gower's Use of Ovid in Book III of the *Confessio Amantis*', *Mediaevalia*, 13 (1987), 257–74

Haynes, Jonathan, 'George Sandys's Relation of a Journey Begun An Dom. 1610: The Humanist as Traveller' (unpublished doctoral thesis, Urbana, Illinois, 1980)

Healy, Thomas, 'Gendered Readings', in *New Latitudes: Theory and English Renaissance Literature* (London: Edward Arnold, 1992), pp. 145–78

Hedley, Thomas, *The Judgement of Midas* (London: 1552)

Heinrichs, Katherine, *The Myth of Love: Classical Lovers in Medieval Literature* (London: Pennsylvania University Press, 1990)

Henderson, Mae, *Borders, Boundaries and Frames: Essays in Cultural Criticism and Cultural Studies* (London: Croom Helm, 1985)

Hermans, Theo, 'Norms of Translation', in *The Oxford Guide to Translation*, ed. by Peter France (Oxford and New York: Oxford University Press, 2000), pp. 10–14

Hermans, Theo, 'Translation's Other: An Inaugural Lecture Delivered at University College London on Tuesday 19 March 1996' (London: University College London, 1996)

Hermans, Theo, 'Images of Translation', in *The Manipulation of Literature: Studies in Literary Translation* (London: Croom Helm, 1985), pp. 103–35

Hervey, Lord. *Memoirs*, ed. by Romney Sedgewick (Harmondsworth: Penguin, 1984)

Hexter, Ralph, 'Medieval Articulations of Ovid's *Metamorphoses*: From Lactantian Segmentation to Arnulfian Allegory', *Mediaevalia*, 13 (1987), 63–82

Hinds, Stephen, *Allusion and Intertext: Dynamics of Appropriation in Roman Poetry* (Cambridge: Cambridge University Press, 1998)

Hogrefe, Pearl, *Tudor Women: Commoners and Queens* (Ames: Iowa State University Press, 1975)

Hopkins, Charles, *The History of Love. A Poem in a letter to a lady* (London: 1695)

Hopkins, Charles, *Epistolary Poems on Several Occasions with several of the Choicest Stories of Ovid's Metamorphoses and Tibullus's Elegies. Translated into English Verse* (London: 1694)

Hopkins, David, 'Dryden and the Garth-Tonson *Metamorphoses*', *Review of English Studies*, 39 (1988a), 64–74

Hopkins, David, 'Dryden and Ovid's "Wit Out of Season"' in *Ovid Renewed: Ovidian Influences on Literature and Art from the Middle Ages to the Twentieth Century* (Cambridge: Cambridge University Press, 1988b), pp. 167–90

Hopkins, David, 'Dryden and the Two Editions of Sandys's Ovid', *Notes and Queries*, 23 (1976a), 552–4

Hopkins, David, 'Dryden's Cave of Sleep and Garth's *Dispensary*', *Notes and Queries*, 23 (1976b), 243–5

Horace, *Satires, Epistles, and Ars poetica*, ed. and trans. by H. Rushton Fairclough (Cambridge, Mass.: Harvard University Press, 1926)

Howatson, M. C., *The Oxford Companion to Classical Literature*, 2nd edn (Oxford: Oxford University Press, 1989)

Hulse, Clark, 'Wresting the Alphabet: Oratory and Action in *Titus Andronicus*', *Criticism* 21 (1979), 106–18

Iliffe, Robert, 'Author-Mongering: the "Editor" Between Producer and Consumer', in *The Consumption of Culture 1600–1800: Image, Object, Text*, ed. by Ann Bermingham and John Brewer (London: Routledge, 1995), pp. 166–92

Jackson, H. J., *Marginalia: Readers Writing in Books* (New Haven: Yale University Press, 2001)

Jackson, William A (ed.), *Records of the Court of the Stationers Company 1602–1640* (London: The Biographical Society, 1957)

Jacobus, Mary, 'The Difference of View', in *The Feminist Reader*, ed. by Catherine Belsey and Jane Moore (Basingstoke: Macmillan, 1989), pp. 49–62

Jakobson, Roman, *Language in Literature* (Massachusetts: Harvard University Press, 1987)

James, Heather, 'Shakespeare's learned heroines in Ovid's schoolroom', in *Shakespeare and the Classics*, ed. by Charles Martindale and A. B. Taylor (Cambridge: Cambridge University Press, 2004), pp. 33–48

James, Heather, 'Ovid and the Question of Politics in Early Modern England', *English Literary History*, 70 (2003), 343–73

Johnson, Alfred Forbes, *A Catalogue of Engraved and Etched Title-Pages* (Oxford: The Bibliographical Society, 1934)

Johnson, Andrew (ed.), *Pylemon and Baucis* (Cambridge: The Gabriel Press, 1999)

Johnson, Barbara, 'Women and Allegory', in *The Wake of Deconstruction* (Oxford: Blackwell, 1994), pp. 52–75

Johnson, James William, *The Formation of English Neo-Classical Thought* (Connecticut: Greenwood, 1967)

Johnson, Samuel, *Lives of the Poets*, ed. by Peter Cunningham, 3 vols (London: John Murray, 1854)

Jones, Ann Rosalind and Peter Stallybrass, *Renaissance Clothing and the Materiality of Memory* (Cambridge: Cambridge University Press, 2000)

Jones, Ann Rosalind and Peter Stallybrass, 'Fetishizing Gender: Constructing the Hermaphrodite in Renaissance Europe', in *Body Guards: The Cultural Politics of Gender Ambiguity*, ed. by Julia Epstein and Kristina Straub (London: Routledge, 1991), pp. 80–111

Jones, Richard Foster, *The Triumph of the English Language: A Survey of Opinions Concerning the Vernacular from the Introduction of Printing to the Restoration* (Stanford: Stanford University Press, 1953)

Jones, Vivien, *Women in the Eighteenth Century: Constructions of Femininity* (London: Routledge, 1990)

Jones, William Powell, *The Rhetoric of Science: A Study of Scientific Ideas and Imagery in Eighteenth-Century English Poetry* (London: Routledge and Kegan Paul, 1966)

Kairoff, Claudia Thomas, 'Classical and Biblical Models: the Female Poetic Tradition', in *Women and Poetry, 1660–1750*, ed. by David Shuttleton and Sarah Prescott (Basingstoke: Palgrave Macmillan, 2003), pp. 183–202

Keach, William, *Elizabethan Erotic Narratives* (London: Harvester Press, 1977)

Kendall, Gillian Murray, '"Lend me thy hand": Metaphor and Mayhem in *Titus Andronicus*', *Shakespeare Quarterly*, 40 (1989), 299–316

Kennedy, Kathleen K., 'Changes in Society and Language Acquisition: The French Language in England 1215–1480', *English Language Notes*, 35 (1998), 1–15

Kewes, Paulina (ed.), *Plagiarism in Early Modern England* (Basingstoke: Palgrave Macmillan, 2003)

Kewes, Paulina, *Authorship and Appropriation: Writing for the Stage in England, 1660–1710* (Oxford: Clarendon Press, 1998)

King, John N., *English Reformation Literature: The Tudor Origins of the Protestant Tradition* (Princeton: Princeton University Press, 1982)

King, Kathryn R., 'Elizabeth Singer Rowe's Tactical Use of Print and Manuscript', in *Women's Writing and the Circulation of Ideas: Manuscript Publication in England, 1550–1800*, ed. by George L. Justice and Nathan Tinker (Cambridge: Cambridge University Press, 2002), pp. 158–81

Kinghorn, A. M., *The Chorus of History: Literary-Historical Relations in Renaissance Britain 1485–1558* (London: Blandford, 1971)

Kinney, Clare, 'The Masks of Love: Desire and Metamorphoses in Sidney's *New Arcadia*', *Criticism*, 33 (1991), 461–90

Kinney, Daniel, ed., *Ovid Illustrated: The Renaissance Reception of Ovid in Image and Text*<http://etext.virginia.edu/latin/ovid/ovid1563.html5> accessed June 2004

Klein, Ernest, *A Comprehensive Etymological Dictionary of the English Language,* 2 vols (Amsterdam: Elsevier, 1967)

Klein, Lisa M., 'Your Humble Handmaid: Elizabethan Gifts of Needlework', *Renaissance Quarterly*, 50 (1997), 459–93

Klindienst, Patricia, 'The Voice of the Shuttle is Ours', *The Stanford Literature Review*, 1 (1984), 25–53

Koller, Katherine, 'Abraham Fraunce and Edmund Spenser', *English Literary History*, 7 (1940), 108–20

Kristeva, Julia, *Nations Without Nationalism*, trans. by Leon S. Roudiez (New York: Columbia University Press, 1993)

Kristeva, Julia, *Tales of Love*, trans. by Leon S. Roudiez (New York: Columbia University Press, 1987)

Kroll, Richard, *The Material Word: Literate Culture in the Restoration and Early Eighteenth Century* (Baltimore: John Hopkins University Press, 1991)

Krontiris, Tina, *Oppositional Voices: Women as Writers and Translators of Literature in the English Renaissance* (London: Routledge, 1992)

Kruger, Kathryn Sullivan, *Weaving the Word: The Metaphorics of Weaving and Female Textual Production* (Selinsgrove: Susquehanna University Press, 2001)

Kuskin, William, 'Caxton's Worthies Series: The Production of Literary Culture', *English Literary History*, 66 (1999), 511–51

Lacan, Jacques, *Écrits: A Selection*, trans. by Alan Sheridan (London: Routledge, 1977)

Lamb, Mary Ellen, *Gender and Authorship in the Sidney Circle* (Wisconsin: University of Wisconsin Press, 1990)

Lamb, Mary Ellen, 'The Countess of Pembroke's Patronage', *English Literary Renaissance*, 12 (1982), 162–79

Lambert, José, 'Literary Translation', in *The Routledge Encyclopedia of Translation Studies*, ed. by Mona Baker and Kirsten Malmkjæ (London: Routledge, 1998), pp. 130–33

Lanham, Richard, *The Motives of Eloquence: Literary Rhetoric in the Renaissance* (New Haven: Yale University Press, 1976)

Lefevere, André, *Translation/ History/ Culture* (London: Routledge, 1992a)

Lefevere, André, *Translation, Rewriting and the Manipulation of Literary Fame* (London: Routledge, 1992b)

Lenten, Francis, *The young gallants whirligigg; or Youths reakes Demonstrating the inordinate affections, absurd actions, and profuse expences, of unbridled and affectated youth* [...] (London: 1629)

Leupin, Alexandre, *Barbarolexis: Medieval Writing and Sexuality*, trans. by Kate M. Cooper (London: Harvard University Press, 1989)

Lever, Tresham, *The Herberts of Wilton* (London: John Murray, 1967)

Levey, Santina M., *Elizabethan Treasures: The Hardwick Hall Textiles* (London: National Trust, 1998)

Levin, Harry, *The Myth of the Golden Age in the Renaissance* (London: Faber, 1966)

Levine, Joseph M., *The Battle of the Books: History and Literature in the Augustan Age* (Ithaca: Cornell University Press, 1991)

Lewalski, Barbara Keifer, 'Into the Maze of the Self: The Protestant Transformation of the Image of the Labyrinth', *Journal of Medieval and Renaissance Studies*, 16 (1986), 281–301

Lim, Walter S., '"Let us Possess One World": John Donne, Rationalizing Theology, and the Discourse of Virginia', in *The Arts of Empire: The Poetics of Colonialism from Ralegh to Milton* (Newark: University of Delaware Press, 1998), pp. 31–63

Lindeman, Yehudi, 'Translation in the Renaissance: A Context and a Map', *Canadian Review of Comparative Literature*, 8 (1981), 204–16

Llewellyn, Nigel, 'Illustrating Ovid', in *Ovid Renewed: Ovidian Influences on Literature and Art from the Middle Ages to the Twentieth Century*, ed. by Charles Martindale (Cambridge: Cambridge University Press, 1988), pp. 151–66

Lonigan, Paul, R., *The Druids: Priests of the Ancient Celts* (Connecticut: Greenwood Press, 1996)

Lonsdale, Roger, ed., *Eighteenth–Century Women Poets* (Oxford: Oxford University Press, 1989)

Love, Harold, 'Some Restoration Treatments of Ovid', in *Poetry and Drama 1570–1700: Essays in Honour of Harold F. Brooks*, ed. by Antony Coleman and Antony Hammond (London: Methuen, 1981), pp. 136–55

Lovell, Mary, *Bess of Hardwick: First Lady of Chatsworth* (London: Little, Brown, 2005)

Lummis, Trevor and Jan Marsh, *The Woman's Domain: Women and the English Country House* (London: Penguin, 1990)

Lyly, John, *Gallathea. As it was playde before the Queenes Majestie at Greene-wiche, on Newyeeres day at Night. By the Chyldren of Paules* (London: 1592)

Lyne, Raphael, 'Ovid in English Translation', in *The Cambridge Companion to Ovid*, ed. by Philip Hardie (Cambridge: Cambridge University Press, 2002), pp. 249–63

Lyne, Raphael, *Ovid's Changing Worlds: English Metamorphoses 1567–1633* (Oxford: Oxford University Press, 2001)

Lyne, Raphael, 'Golding's Englished *Metamorphoses*', *Translation and Literature*, 5 (1996), 183–99

Lytel, Guy Fitch and Stephen Orgel (eds.), *Patronage in the Renaissance* (Princeton: Princeton University Press, 1981)

Macaulay, G. C., Analysis, in John Gower, *Confessio Amantis*, ed. by G. C. Macaulay (Oxford: Clarendon Press, 1901), pp. xxix–xcii

Mace, Nancy A., *Henry Fielding's Novels and the Classical Tradition* (London: Associated University Presses, 1996)

Madan, Falconer, *The Early Oxford Press: A Bibliography of Printing and Publishing at Oxford 1468–1640* (Oxford: Clarendon Press, 1895)

Mainzer, Conrad, 'John Gower's Use of the "Medieval Ovid" in the *Confessio Amantis*', *Medium Aevum*, 41 (1972), 215–29

Marshall, Madeleine Forell, *The Poetry of Elizabeth Singer Rowe* (Lewiston: The Edwin Mellen Press, 1989)

Martensen, Robert L., 'Garth, Sir Samuel (1660/61–1719)', *Oxford Dictionary of National Biography*, online edn (Oxford University Press, 2004), http: //www. oxforddnb.com/view/article/10414, accessed 4 June 2005

Martin, Christopher (ed.), *Ovid in English* (London: Penguin, 1998)

Martindale, Charles, 'Shakespeare's Ovid, Ovid's Shakespeare: A Methodological Postscript', in *Shakespeare's Ovid: The Metamorphoses in the Plays and the Poems*, ed. by A. B. Taylor (Cambridge: Cambridge University Press, 2000), pp. 198–215

Martindale, Charles, Introduction, in *Ovid Renewed: Ovidian Influences on Literature and Art from the Middle Ages to the Twentieth Century*, ed. by Charles Martindale (Cambridge: Cambridge University Press, 1988), pp. 1–20

Maslen, R. W., 'Myths Exploited: the Metamorphosis of Ovid in Early Elizabethan England', in *Shakespeare's Ovid*, ed. by A. B. Taylor (Cambridge: Cambridge University Press, 2000), pp. 15–30

Massey, Irving, *The Gaping Pig: Literature and Metamorphosis* (Berkeley: University of California Press, 1976)

Mater, N. I., 'Peter Sterry and the Puritan Defense of Ovid in Restoration England', *Studies in Philology*, 88 (1991), 110–21

Matthiessen, F. O., *Translation: An Elizabethan Art* (New York: Octagon, 1965)

Mauriès, Patrick, *Cabinets of Curiosities* (London: Thames and Hudson, 2002)

Mazzio, Carla, 'Staging the Vernacular: Language and Nation in Thomas Kyd's *The Spanish Tragedy*', *Studies in English Literature*, 38 (1998), 207–32

Mazzio, Carla, 'Sins of the Tongue', in *The Body in Parts: Fantasies of Corporeality in Early Modern Europe*, ed. by David Hillman and Carla Mazzio (London: Routledge, 1997), pp. 53–80

MacCulloch, Diarmaid, *Reformation: Europe's House Divided 1490-1700* (London: Penguin, 2004)

MacIntyre, William Myron, 'A Critical Study of Golding's Translation of Ovid's *Metamorphoses*' (unpublished doctoral thesis, University of California, 1965)

McKeown, Adam, '"Entreat Her Hear Me But A Word": Translation and Foreignness in *Titus Andronicus*', in *The Politics of Translation in the Middle Ages and the Renaissance*, ed. by Renate Blumenfeld-Kosinski, Luise von Flotow and Daniel Russell (Canada: University of Ottawa Press, 2001), pp. 203–18

McKerrow, R.B. (ed.), *A Dictionary of Printers and Booksellers in England, Scotland and Ireland and of Foreign Printers of English Books 1557–1640* (London:

McKinley, Kathryn L., *Reading the Ovidian Heroine: "Metamorphoses" Commentaries 1100–1618* (Leiden: Brill, 2001)
Biographical Society, 1910)

McKittrick, R, *Catalogue of the Pepys Library at Magdalene College, Cambridge* (Cambridge: Brewer, 1992)

Meres, Francis, '*Palladis Tamia: Wits Treasury*', in *Elizabethan Critical Essays*, ed. by G. Gregory Smith, 2 vols (Oxford: Oxford University Press, 1904), pp. 317–18.

Messenger, Ann, *Pastoral Tradition and the Female Talent: Studies in Augustan Poetry* (New York: AMS Press, 2001)

Metz, G. Harold, 'Stage History of *Titus Andronicus*', *Shakespeare Quarterly*, 28 (1977), 154–69

Miller, Nancy K., *Subject to Change: Reading Feminist Writing* (New York: Columbia University Press, 1988)

Mills, Rebecca M., 'Mary, Lady Chudleigh: *Poet, Protofeminist and Patron*', in *Women and Poetry 1660–1750*, ed. by Sarah Prescott and David Shuttleton (Basingstoke: Palgrave Macmillan, 2003), pp. 50–7

Minh-Ha, Trinh T., *Framer Framed* (London: Routledge, 1992)

Minnis, A. J., *Medieval Theory of Authorship*, 2nd edn (Aldershot: Wildwood, 1988)

Minnis, A. J., A. B. Scott and D. Wallace (eds.), *Medieval Literary Theory and Criticism: Criticism c. 1100–c. 1375: The Commentary Tradition* (Oxford: Clarendon Press, 1988)

Miola, Robert S., '*Titus Andronicus* and the Mythos of Shakespeare's Rome', *Shakespeare Studies*, 14 (1981), 85–98

Moi, Toril, *Sexual/Textual Politics* (London: Harvard University Press, 1988)

Montagu, Mary Wortley, *Essays and Poems and Simplicity, A Comedy*, ed. by Robert Halsband and Isobel Grundy (Oxford: Clarendon Press, 1977)

Montagu, Mary Wortley, *The Complete Letters of Lady Mary Wortley Montagu*, ed. by Robert Halsband and Isobel Grundy, 3 vols (Oxford: Clarendon Press, 1965)

Montagu, Mary Wortley (nee Pierrepont), 'Poems, Songs, etc.', Harrowby MS 250 (Stafford: Sandon Hall, c. 1701–5)

Montagu, Mary Wortley (nee Pierrepont), 'The Entire Works of Clarinda', Harrowby MS 251 (Stafford: Sandon Hall, c. 1701–5)

Moore-Smith, G. C., Preface, in *Victoria: A Latin Comedy* by Abraham Fraunce (Louvain: A Uystpryst, 1906), pp. ix–xl

Morris, Harry, 'Thomas Watson and Abraham Fraunce', *Publication of the Modern Language Association of America*, 76 (1961), 152–3

Moss, Ann, *Ovid in Renaissance France: A Survey of the Latin Editions of Ovid and Commentaries Printed in France before 1600* (London: Warburg Institute, 1982)

Munari, Franco, *Catalogue of the MSS of Ovid's 'Metamorphoses'* (London: University of London, 1957)

Munby, A. N. L. and Lawrence W. Towner, *The Flow of Books and Manuscripts* (Los Angeles: William Andrews Clark Memorial Library, 1969)

Murray, Murray, 'Twice Marginal and Twice Invisible: Lesbians in the Middle Ages', in *Handbook of Medieval Sexuality*, ed. by. Vern L. Bullough and James A. Brundage (New York: Garland, 1996), pp. 191–222

Myers, Sara K., *Ovid's Causes: Cosmogony and Aetiology in the 'Metamorphoses'* (Ann Arbor: University of Michigan Press, 1994)

Nashe, Thomas, *Pierce Penilesse. His Supplication to the Divell* (London: 1592)

Nashe, Thomas, Preface to *Syr P.S., His Astrophel and Stella* [...] (London: 1591)

Neill, Michael, 'The World Beyond: Shakespeare and the Tropes of Translation', in *Elizabethan Theatre Essays in Honour of S. Schoenbaum*, ed. by R. B. Parker and S. P. Zitner (Newark: University of Delaware Press, 1996), pp. 290–308

Neill, Michael, 'Broken English and Broken Irish: Nation, Language and the Optic of Power in Shakespeare's History Plays', *Shakespeare Quarterly*, 45 (1994), 1–32

Nida, Eugene, *Toward a Science of Translating* (Leiden: Brill, 1964)

Niranjana, Tejaswini, *Siting Translation: History, Post-Structuralism and the Colonial Context* (Berkeley: University of California Press, 1992)

Nussbaum, Felicity A., *The Brink of All We Hate: English Satires on Women 1660–1750* (Kentucky: University of Kentucky Press, 1984)

Nuttall, A. D., 'Ovid's Narcissus and Shakespeare's *Richard II*: The Reflected Self', in *Ovid Renewed: Ovidian Influences on Literature and Art from the Middle Ages to the Twentieth Century*, ed. by Charles Martindale (Cambridge: Cambridge University Press, 1988), pp. 137–50

Oakley-Brown, Liz, 'Translating the Subject: Ovid's *Metamorphoses* in England 1560–7', in *Translation and Nation: Towards a Cultural Politics of Englishness*, ed. by Roger Ellis and Liz Oakley-Brown (Clevedon: Multilingual Matters, 2001), pp. 48–84

Olive, Barbara, 'A Puritan Subject's Panegyrics to Queen Anne', *Studies in English Literature*, 42 (2002), 475–99

Olmsted, Wendy, 'On the Margins of Otherness: Metamorphosis and Identity in Homer, Ovid, Sidney, and Milton', *New Literary History*, 27 (1996), 167–87

Ong, Walter J., 'Latin Language Study as Renaissance Puberty Rite', in *Rhetoric, Romance and Technology* (Ithaca: Cornell, 1971), pp. 113–41

Osborne, Dorothy, *Letters to Sir William Temple*, ed. by Kenneth Parker (London: Penguin, 1987)

Ovid, *Metamorphoses: A New Verse Translation*, trans. David Raeburn (London: Penguin, 2004)

Ovid, *The Metamorphoses*, trans. by Frank Justus Miller, rev. by G. P. Goold, 2 vols (London: Heinemann, 1984)

Ovid, *The Metamorphoses*, trans. by Mary Innes (London: Penguin, 1955)

Ovid, *Ovide moralisé en Prose: Texte du Quinzieme Siecle*, ed. by C. de Boer (Holland: North Holland Publishing Company, 1954)

Ovid, *Fasti*, trans. by James George Frazer (London: Heinemann, 1931)

Ovid, *Tristia ex Ponto*, trans. by Arthur Leslie Wheeler, 2nd edn, rev. by G. P. Goold (London: Heinemann, 1924)

Ovid, *Ovide moralisé: Poème du Commencement du Quartorzième Siècle*, 5 tom, ed. by C. de Boer (Amsterdam: Johannes Müller, 1915–36)

Ovid, *Heroides,* trans. by Grant Showerman (London: Heinemann, 1914)

Palmer, D. J., 'The Unspeakable in Pursuit of the Uneatable: Language and Action in *Titus Andronicus*', *Critical Quarterly,* 14 (1972), pp. 320–39

Palmer, Patricia, *Language and Conquest in Early Modern Ireland* (Cambridge: Cambridge University Press, 2001)

Paré, Ambroise, *The workes of that famous chirurgion Ambrose Parey translated out of Latine and compared with the French. by Th[omas] Johnson* (London: 1634)

Parker, Blandford, *The Triumph of Augustan Poetics: English Literary Culture from Butler to Johnson* (Cambridge: Cambridge University Press, 1998)

Parker, Patricia, *Shakespeare From the Margins: Language, Culture, Context* (Chicago: University of Chicago Press, 1996a)

Parker, Patricia, 'Virile Stile', in *Premodern Sexualities*, ed. by Louise Fradenburg and Carla Freccero (London: Routledge, 1996b), pp. 199–222

Parker, Patricia, 'On the Tongue: Cross-Gendering, Effeminacy and the Art of Words', *Style*, 23 (1989), 445–65

Parker, Patricia, *Literary Fat Ladies: Rhetoric, Gender, Property* (London: Methuen, 1987)

Parnell, Thomas, *Collected Poems of Thomas Parnell*, ed. by Claude Rawson and F. P. Lock (Newark: University of Delaware Press, 1989)

Parry, Graham, 'A Troubled Arcadia', in *Literature and the English Civil War*, ed. by Thomas Healy and Jonathan Sawday (Cambridge: Cambridge University Press, 1990), pp. 38–58

Parry, Graham, *The Golden Age Restor'd: The Culture of the Stewart Court 1603–44* (Manchester: Manchester University Press, 1981)

Parry, Hugh, 'Ovid's *Metamorphoses*; Violence in a Pastoral Landscape', *Transactions and Proceedings of the American Philological Association*, 95 (1964), 268–82

Patterson, Annabel, *Fables of Power: Aesopian Writing and Political History* (Durham, N. C.,: Duke University Press, 1991)

Patterson, Annabel, *Pastoral and Ideology: Virgil to Valéry* (Oxford: Clarendon Press, 1987)

Patterson, Annabel, *Censorship and Interpretation: The Conditions of Writing and Reading in Early Modern England* (Wisconsin: University of Wisconsin Press, 1984)

Pearcy, Lee T., *The Mediated Muse: English Translations of Ovid, 1560–1700* (Connecticut: Archon, 1984)

Pearsall, Derek, 'The Gower Tradition', in *Gower's 'Confessio Amantis': Responses and Reassessments*, ed. by A. J. Minnis (Cambridge: Cambridge University Press, 1983), pp. 179–97

Peend, Thomas, *The Pleasant Fable of Hermaphroditus and Salmacis with a Morall in English Verse* (London: 1565)

Pepys, Samuel, *The Diary of Samuel Pepys*, ed. by Robert Latham and William Matthews, 11 vols (London: G. Bell, 1970)

Pigman, G. W., *Grief and English Renaissance Elegy* (Cambridge: Cambridge University Press, 1985)

Plutarch, *Moralia*, trans. by L. Pearson and F. H. Sandbach (London: Heinemann, 1927)

Pope, Alexander, *The Twickenham Edition of the Poems of Alexander Pope: Pastoral Poetry and an Essay on Criticism*, ed. by E. Audra and Aubrey Williams (London: Methuen, 1961)

Pope, Alexander, 'Sandys's Ghost' in *The Twickenham Edition of the Poems of Alexander Pope: Minor Poems*, ed. by Norman Ault and John Butt (London: Methuen, 1954), pp. 170–6

Porter, Roy (ed.), *Rewriting the Self: Histories from the Renaissance to the Present* (London: Routledge, 1997)

Powles, Marie A., 'Dramatic Significance of the "Figures" Prefacing Each Book of Sandys's Translation of Ovid's *Metamorphoses*', *University of Dayton Review*, 10 (1974), 39–45

Prescott, Sarah, *Women, Authorship and Literary Culture 1690–1740* (Basingstoke: Palgrave Macmillan, 2003)

Pugh, Syrithe, *Spenser and Ovid* (Aldershot: Ashgate, 2005)

Puttenham, George, *The Arte of English Poetry*, ed. by Gladys Doidge Willcock and Alice Walker (Cambridge: Cambridge University Press, 1936)

Pym, Antony, *Epistemological Problems in Translation and Its Teaching* (Spain: Edicions Caminade, 1993)

Quennell, Peter, *Caroline of England: An Augustan Portrait* (London: Collins, 1939)

Quilligan, Maureen, 'Elizabeth's Embroidery', *Shakespeare Studies*, 29 (2001), 208–15

Quintilian, *Institutio oratoria*, trans. by H. E. Butler, 4 vols (London: Heinemann, 1920–22)

Ravenscroft, Edward, *Titus Andronicus, or the Rape of Lavinia* (London: 1687)

Redwood, John, *Reason, Ridicule and Religion: The Age of Enlightenment England 1660–1750*, 2nd edn (London: Thames and Hudson, 1995)

Ricks, Christopher, 'Metamorphosis in Other Words', in *Gower's 'Confessio Amantis': Responses and Reassessments*, ed. by A. J. Minnis (Cambridge: Cambridge University Press, 1983), pp. 25–49

Roberts, Sasha, *Reading Shakespeare's Poems in Early Modern England* (Basingstoke: Palgrave Macmillan, 2003)

Robinson, Douglas, *Western Translation Theory from Herodotus to Nietzsche* (Manchester: St. Jerome, 1997)

Robinson, Douglas, *Translation and Taboo* (DeKalb: Northern Illinois University Press, 1996)

Robinson, Douglas, 'Theorizing Translation in a Woman's Voice: Subverting the Rhetoric of Patronage, Courtly Love and Morality', *The Translator*, 1 (1995), 153–75

Robinson, Douglas, *The Translator's Turn* (Baltimore: John Hopkins University Press, 1991)

Robyns, Clem, 'Translation and Discursive Identity', *Poetics Today*, 15 (1994), 405–28

Rosenberg, Eleanor, *Leicester, Patron of Letters* (New York: Columbia University Press, 1955)

Rothstein, Eric, *Restoration and Eighteenth-Century Poetry 1660–1780* (London: Routledge, 1981)

Rowe, Elizabeth Singer, *Poems on Several Occasions. Written by Philomela* (London: 1696)

Rowe, Katherine A., 'Dismembering and Forgetting in *Titus Andronicus*', *Shakespeare Quarterly*, 45 (1994), 279–303

Rubin, Deborah, 'Sandys, Ovid and Female Chastity: The Encyclopedic Mythographer as Moralist', in *The Mythographic Art: Classical Fable and the Rise of the Vernacular in Early France and England*, ed. by Jane Chance (Gainesville: University of Florida Press, 1990), pp. 257–80

Rubin, Deborah, *Ovid's 'Metamorphoses Englished': George Sandys as Translator and Mythographer* (New York: Garland, 1985)

Rudd, Niall, 'Daedalus and Icarus: From the Renaissance to the Present Day', in *Ovid Renewed: Ovidian Influences on Literature and Art from the Middle Ages to the Twentieth Century*, ed. by Charles Martindale (Cambridge: Cambridge University Press, 1988), pp. 37–53

Rudolph, Julia, 'Rape and Resistance: Women and Consent in Seventeenth-Century English Legal and Political Thought', *Journal of British Studies,* 39 (2000), 167–84

Rumbold, Valerie, *Women's Place in Pope's World* (Cambridge: Cambridge University Press, 1989)

Runsdorf, James H., 'Transforming Ovid in the 1560s: Thomas Peend's *Pleasaunt Fable*', *American Notes and Queries*, 5 (1992), 124–7

Salter, Thomas, *A Mirrhour mete for all Mothers, Matrones, and Maidens, intituled the Mirrhour of Modestie* (London: 1579)

Sambrook, James, *The Eighteenth Century: The Intellectual and Cultural Context of English Literature 1700–1789* (London: Longman, 1986)

Sanders, Eve Rachele, *Gender and Literacy on Stage in Early Modern England* (Cambridge: Cambridge University Press, 1998)

Sandys, George, *Ovids Metamorphosis Englished*, 8th edn (London: 1690)

Sandys, George, *Ovids Metamorphosis Englished*, 7th edn (London: 1678)

Sandys, George, *Ovids Metamorphosis Englished*, 3rd edn (London: 1638)

Sandys, George, *Ovids Metamorphosis Englished, Mythologized, and Represented in Figures* (Oxford: 1632)

Sawday, Jonathan, *The Body Emblazoned: Dissection and the Human Body in Renaissance Culture* (London: Routledge, 1995)

Sawday, Jonathan, 'Mysteriously Divided: Civil War, Madness and the Divided Self', in *Literature and the English Civil War*, ed. by Thomas Healy and Jonathan Sawday (Cambridge: Cambridge University Press, 1990), pp. 127–46

Schiesaro, Alessandro, 'Ovid and the Professional Discourses of Scholarship, Religion, Rhetoric', in *The Cambridge Companion to Ovid*, ed. by Philip Hardie (Cambridge: Cambridge University Press, 2002), pp. 62–78

Schleiner, Louise, *Tudor and Stuart Women Writers* (Bloomington: Indiana University Press, 1994)

Scott, Kathleen L., *The Caxton Master and His Patrons* (Cambridge: Cambridge Bibliographical Society, 1976)

Segal, Charles Paul, 'Myth and Philosophy in the *Metamorphoses*: Ovid's Augustanism and the Augustan Conclusion of Book 15', *American Journal of Philology*, 90 (1969), 257–92

Shaffer, E. S., 'Translation as Metamorphosis and Cultural Transmission', *Comparative Criticism: An Annual Journal* (Cambridge: Cambridge University Press, 1984), pp. xiii–xxvii

Shakespeare, William, *Titus Andronicus*, ed. by Jonathan Bate (London: Routledge, 1995)

Shakespeare, William, *Cymbeline*, ed. by J. M. Nosworthy (London: Routledge, 1988)

Shakespeare, William, *II Henry IV*, ed. by P. H. Davison (London: Penguin, 1977)

Shakespeare, William, *Titus Andronicus*, ed. by J. C. Maxwell (London: Routledge, 1953)

Shapin, Steven, 'Of Gods and Kings: Natural Philosophy and Politics in the Leibniz–Clarke Disputes', *Isis*, 72 (1981), 187–215

Sharpe, Kevin, *The Personal Rule of Charles I* (New Haven: Yale University Press, 1992)

Sharpe, Kevin, *Criticism and Compliment: The Politics of Literature in the England of Charles I*, (Cambridge: Cambridge University Press, 1987)

Sherburne, Edward, *Salmacis* (London: 1651)

Sidney, Mary, *The Tragedie of Antonie*, in *Renaissance Drama by Women: Texts and Documents*, ed. by S. P. Cerasano and Marion Wynne–Davis (London: Routledge), pp. 13–42

Sidney, Philip, *An Apology for Poetry*, ed. by J. A. Van Dorsten (Oxford: Oxford University Press, 1966)

Silberman, Lauren, 'Mythographic Transformations of Ovid's Hermaphrodite', *Sixteenth Century Journal*, 19 (1988), 643–52

Silverman, Kaja, *The Subject of Semiotics* (Oxford: Oxford University Press, 1983)

Simmons, J. L., 'The Tongue and Its Office in *The Revenger's Tragedy*', *Publication of the Modern Language Association*, 92 (1977), 56–68

Simon, Sherry, *Gender in Translation: Cultural Identity and the Politics of Transmission* (London: Routledge, 1996)

Skretkowicz, V., 'Abraham Fraunce and Abraham Darcie', *The Library*, 31 (1976), 239–42

Sloman, Judith, *Dryden: The Poetics of Translation* (Toronto: University of Toronto Press, 1985)

Smith, Eric, *A Dictionary of Classical Reference in English Poetry* (Cambridge: Brewer, 1984)

Smith, Hilda, 'Humanist Education and the Renaissance Concept of Woman', in *Women and Literature in Britain 1500–1700*, ed. by Helen Wilcox (Cambridge: Cambridge University Press, 1996), pp. 9–29

Solodow, Joseph B., *The World of Ovid's 'Metamorphoses'* (Chapel Hill: University of North Carolina Press, 1988)

Sotheby and Co., *Sale of Bibliotheca Phillippica: The Celebrated Collection of Manuscripts formed by Sir Thomas Phillipps*, new series, 2nd part (London: Sotheby's, 1966)

Sowerby, Robin, *The Classical Legacy in Renaissance Poetry* (London: Longman, 1994)

Spenser, Edmund, *The Faerie Queene*, ed. by A. C. Hamilton (London: Longman, 1977)

Spivak, Gayatri Chakravorty, Translator's Preface, in Jacques Derrida, *Of Grammatology*, trans. by Gayatri Chakravorty Spivak (Baltimore: John Hopkins, 1979), pp. ix–xxxviii

Springarn, Joel Elias, *A History of Literary Criticism in the Renaissance* (London: Macmillan, 1899)

Stafford, Barbara Maria, *Body Criticism: Imaging the Unseen in Enlightenment Art and Medicine* (London: M.I.T. Press, 1991)

Stallybrass, Peter, 'Patriarchal Territories: The Body Enclosed', in *Rewriting the Renaissance: The Discourses of Sexual Difference in Early Modern Europe*, ed. by Margaret W. Ferguson, Maureen Quilligan and Nancy J. Vickers (Chicago: University of Chicago Press, 1987), pp. 123–44

Stanley, Thomas, *Poems and Translations*, ed. by Galbraith Miller Crump (Oxford: Clarendon Press, 1962)

Stanyon, Temple, *The Grecian History* (London: 1707)

Staton, Walter F., Thomas Watson and Abraham Fraunce, *Publication of the Modern Language Association*, 76 (1961), 150–2

Stein, Gertrude, 'Poetry and Grammar', in *Look At Me Now And Here I Am*, ed. by Patricia Meyerowitz (London: Penguin, 1971), pp. 125–47

Steiner, George, *After Babel: Aspects of Language and Translation*, 2nd edn (Oxford: Oxford University Press, 1992)

Steiner, Grundy, 'Golding's Use of the Regius-Micyllus Commentary Upon Ovid', *The Journal of English and Germanic Philology*, 49 (1950), 317–23

Steiner, T. R., *English Translation Theory 1650–1800* (Amsterdam: Van Gorum, 1975)

Stevenson, Jane, 'Women Latin Poets in Britain in the Seventeenth and Eighteenth Centuries', *The Seventeenth Century*, 16 (2001), 1–36

Stewart, Alan, 'The Early Modern Closet Discovered', *Representations*, 50 (1995), 76–100

Sutherland, Kathryn, 'Editing for a New Century: Elizabeth Elstob's Anglo–Saxon Manifesto and Ælfric's St. Gregory Homily', in *The Editing of Old English*, ed. by D. G. Scragg and Paul E. Szarmach (Cambridge: Brewer, 1994), pp. 213–38

Taylor, A. B., 'Animals in "manly shape as too the outward showe": Moralizing and Metamorphosis in *Titus Andronicus*', in *Shakespeare's Ovid: The 'Metamorphoses' in the Plays and the Poems*, ed. by A. B. Taylor (Cambridge: Cambridge University Press, 2000), pp. 66–80

Taylor, A. B., 'George Sandys and Arthur Golding', *Notes and Queries*, 33 (1986a), 387–91

Taylor, A. B., 'Abraham Fraunce's Debts to Arthur Golding in *Amintas Dale*', *Notes and Queries,* 33 (1986b), 333–6

Thomas, Peter W., 'The Tragedy of Absolutism', in *The Courts of Europe*, ed. by A. G. Dickens (London: Thames and Hudson, 1977), pp. 191–212

Tissol, Garth, Introduction, in *Ovid: 'Metamorphoses', Translated by John Dryden and Others, Edited by Sir Samuel Garth* (Hertfordshire: Wordsworth, 1998), pp. xi–xxiv

Tomlinson, Charles, 'Why Dryden's Translation's Matter', *Translation and Literature*, 10 (2001), 3–20

Tomlinson, Charles, 'The Presence of Translation: A View of English Poetry', in *The Art of Translation: Voices from the Field*, ed. by Rosanna Warren (Boston: Northeastern University Press, 1989), pp. 258–76

Tooley, Brenda, '"Like a False Renegade": The Ends and Means of Feminist Apologetics in *A Dialogue Concerning Women* and *An Essay in Defence of the Female Sex*', *The Eighteenth Century*, 36 (1995), 157–77

Traub, Valerie, *The Renaissance of Lesbianism in Early Modern England* (Cambridge: Cambridge University Press, 2002)

Traub, Valerie, Afterword, in *Ovid and the Renaissance Body*, ed. by Goran V. Stanivukovic (Toronto: University of Toronto Press, 2001a), pp. 260–68

Traub, Valerie, 'The Psychomorphology of the Clitoris, or, The Reemergence of the *Tribade* in English Culture', in *Generation and Degeneration: Tropes of Reproduction in Literature and History from Antiquity to Early Modern Europe*, ed. by Valeria Finucci and Kevin Brownlee (Duke University Press: Durham, 2001b), pp. 153–186

Trickett, Rachel, 'The Heroides and the English Augustans', in *Ovid Renewed: Ovidian Influences on Literature and Art from the Middle Ages to the Twentieth Century*, ed. by Charles Martindale (Cambridge and New York: Cambridge University Press, 1988), pp. 191–204

Tudeau-Clayton, Margaret, 'Scenes of Translation in Jonson and Shakespeare: *Poetaster*, *Hamlet* and *A Midsummer Night's Dream*', *Translation and Literature*, 11 (2002), 1–23

Tuve, Rosemond, *Allegorical Imagery: Some Medieval Books and Their Posterity* (Princeton: Princeton University Press, 1966)

Tyler, Margaret, *A Mirrour of Princely Deeds and Knighthood*, ed. by Kathryn Coad (Aldershot: Scolar Press, 1996)

Tyler, Margaret, *The mirrour of princely deedes and knighthood wherein is shewed the worthinesse of the Knight of the Sunne, and his brother Rosicleer, sonnes to the great Emperour Trebetio: with the strange love of the beautifull and excellent princesse Briana, and the valiant actes of other noble princes and knightes. Now newly translated out of Spanish into our vulgar English tongue* [...] (London: 1578)

Tytler, Alexander Fraser, *Essay on the Principles of Translation* (London: Dent, 1907)

Vance, Eugene, *Mervelous Signals: Poetics and Sign Theory in the Middle Ages* (Lincoln: University of Nebraska Press, 1986)

Velz, John W., 'Topoi in Edward Ravenscroft's Indictment of Shakespeare's *Titus Andronicus*', *Modern Philology*, 83 (1985), 45–50

Venuti, Lawrence, *The Scandals of Translation* (London: Routledge, 1998)

Venuti, Lawrence, *The Translator's Invisibility* (London: Routledge, 1995a)

Venuti, Lawrence, 'Translation and the Formation of Cultural Identities', in *Cultural Functions of Translation*, ed. by Christina Schäffner and Helen Kelly–Holmes (Clevedon: Multilingual Matters, 1995b), pp. 9–25

Venuti, Lawrence, '*The Destruction of Troy*: Translation and Royalist Cultural Politics in the Interregnum', *Journal of Medieval and Renaissance Studies*, 23 (1993), 197–219

Venuti, Lawrence, Introduction, in *Rethinking Translation*, ed. by Lawrence Venuti (London: Routledge, 1992), pp. 1–17

Venuti, Lawrence, *Our Halcyon Dayes: English Prerevolutionary Texts and Postmodern Culture* (Wisconsin: University of Wisconsin Press, 1989)

Virgil, *Eclogues*, trans. by H. Rushton Fairclough, rev. edn (London: Heinemann, 1932)

Vitkus, Daniel, *Turning Turk: English Theatre and the Multicultural Mediterranean 1570–1630* (Basingstoke: Palgrave Macmillan, 2003)

Vitkus, Daniel, 'Turning Turk in *Othello*: the Conversion and Damnation of the Moor', *Shakespeare Quarterly*, 48 (1997), 145–76

Vives, Jean Luis, *A verie fruitfull and pleasant booke, called the instruction of a Christian woman. Made first in Latin, by the right famous Clearke M. Levves Vives, and translated out of Latin into English, by Richard Hyrde*, 2nd edn (London: 1592)

Voss, Paul J., 'Books for Sale: Advertising and Patronage in Late Elizabethan England', *Sixteenth Century Journal*, 29 (1998), 733–56

Vout, Caroline, 'The Myth of the Toga: Understanding the History of Roman Dress', *Greece and Rome*, 43 (1996), 204–20

Wall, Wendy, *The Imprint of Gender: Authorship and Publication in the English Renaissance* (Ithaca: Cornell University Press, 1993)

Warner, Marina, *Fantastic Metamorphoses, Other Worlds* (Oxford: Oxford University Press, 2002)

Warton, Joseph, *An Essay on the Genius and Writings of Pope*, 5th edn, 2 vols (London: W. J. and J. Richardson, 1806)

Watson, Thomas, *Amyntas* ed. by Walter F. and Franklin M. Dickey (Chicago: Chicago University Press, 1967)

Watt, Diane, *Amoral Gower: Language, Sex and Politics* (Minneapolis: University of Minnesota Press, 2003)

Weinbrot, Howard D., *Augustus Caesar in "Augustan" England* (Princeton: Princeton University Press, 1978)

Wheale, Nigel, *Writing and Society: Literacy, Print and Politics in Britain 1590–1660* (London: Routledge, 1999)

White, Harold Ogden, *Plagiarism and Imitation During the English Renaissance* (London: Frank Cass, 1965)

Wilkinson, L. P., *Ovid Recalled* (Cambridge: Cambridge University Press, 1955)

Williams, Gareth, 'Ovid's exile poetry: *Tristia*, *Epistulae ex Ponto* and *Ibis*', in *The Cambridge Companion to Ovid*, ed. by Philip Hardie (Cambridge: Cambridge University Press, 2002), pp. 233–45

Wilson, Penelope, 'Classical Poetry and the Eighteenth-Century Reader', in *Books and Their Readers in Eighteenth-Century England*, ed. by Isabel Rivers (Leicester: Leicester University Press, 1982), pp. 69–96

Wind, Edgar, *Pagan Mysteries in the Renaissance* (London: Faber, 1968)

Wiseman, Josette A., 'Christine de Pizan and Arachne's *Metamorphoses*', *Fifteenth-Century Studies*, 23 (1997), 138–51

Worden, Blair, *The Sound of Virtue: Philip Sidney's Arcadia and Elizabethan Politics* (New Haven: Yale University Press, 1996)

Wormald, Francis, 'Caxton's Ovid Re-United', *Times Literary Supplement*, 19 September, 1968, p. 1059

Index